Question and Answer:
Forms of Dialogic Understanding

Theory and History of Literature
Edited by Wlad Godzich and Jochen Schulte-Sasse

For other books in the series, see p. 284

Question and Answer

Forms of Dialogic

Understanding

Hans Robert Jauss

Edited, translated, and
with a foreword by Michael Hays

Theory and History of Literature, Volume 68

University of Minnesota Press, Minneapolis

Published by the University of Minnesota Press
2037 University Avenue Southeast, Minneapolis MN 55414.
Printed in the United States of America.

Library of Congress Catalog Card No. 89-40613

ISBN 0-8166-1746-5
ISBN 0-8166-1747-3 (pbk.)

Contents

Foreword
Michael Hays

Hans Robert Jauss's work no longer needs an introduction. Thanks to the two previous volumes of essays published by the University of Minnesota Press,[1] Jauss's literary theory and hermeneutic method have already entered the arena of Anglo-American critical discussion. The particular interest aroused by his work stems in large part from the fact that his project, along with that of the "Konstanz School" of critics of which he is a leading figure, involves a systematic effort to revise critical procedures in such a way as to overcome the separation between literary interpretation and cultural criticism, and, at the same time, suggest ways in which the aesthetic experience of the individual may be grounded in the intersubjective, that is, in the realm of shared human experience. The central term in this project is, of course, the "horizon of expectation," that necessary sociohistorical perspective that enables one to perceive, understand, and represent both the social world, and, as critic or reader, the world of the text.[2]

The present volume evinces Jauss's continued interest in developing and refining his critical methodology, but whereas the first two volumes in the Minnesota series embody an effort to define the new aesthetics of reception and show its usefulness in elaborating a coherent hermeneutic practice with regard to general problems of literary understanding, the current volume is far more concerned with allowing the reader to examine the practical results of extended applications of this method. Thus, the essays included here focus in large part on specific literary texts, or the questions raised by these texts, on the manner, that is, in which they have been read, understood, and, most important, put to use by contemporaries and by later readers.

This notion of the *uses* of the fictive is the point of departure for the first series of essays, "The Communicative Function of the Fictive," and serves as a basis for the work in the remainder of the book insofar as it allows us to understand the links between the reader's horizon of expectation and his or her active experience of the life-world. In these first essays, Jauss sketches a genealogy of the uses to which fiction and the idea of the fictive have been put, and in so doing, demonstrates the historicity of the fictive, its historical conflation with or divorce from that which in different epochs was construed to be reality. Jauss reminds us that the idea of the fictive first comes into play in criticism—as a means of distinguishing those texts that *fail* to represent life-world reality from those that do.

In the Middle Ages, for example, the aesthetic pleasure offered by the fictive was deemed a temptation, a means of turning one's back on reality. But, Jauss argues, the desire to seek release from the world also contains within it the possibility of imagining new worlds, or new interpretations of the world: reality is deessentialized. And although fictive worlds can still be interpreted ontologically, and serve to reveal transcendent orders of meaning, the very fact of interpretation also brings with it the possibility of calling such orders into question, of rethinking them as illusions, or, as Jauss refers to them, as a "Platonic residue." The need to interpret, then, opens up a horizon of fiction in which aesthetic experience, rather than ontologizing the text in order to figure a higher world, can, as indicated by Cervantes' *Don Quixote*, confront both the text and the here and now in all their contingency and ambiguity. Thus, as Jauss shows, fiction makes possible the construction *and* critique of life-world experience: the relation of the author and the reader to the text is, of necessity, *motivated*.

This demonstration of the uses of the fictive opens up the space for the next three sections of the book. Taken together, they form an extended consideration of the manner in which question and answer—questions about the individual and the world, the status of a mode of discourse, and the text itself—emerge in and then are responded to in the textual interplay that founds and enables (transformative) work on myth, theology, philosophy, poetry, and literature in general. In the first of these sections, Jauss suggests ways in which the aesthetic uses of question and answer are related to all others precisely because it is the aesthetic that activates the endless dialogue of meanings that is the core of textual play, and that makes possible the overcoming of one representational or discursive mode by another.

This possibility leads to detailed discussions of question and answer as means of elaborating and subverting the representation of the individual in a discourse with power, thus indicating the significance of question and answer within the "competitive spaces elaborated by real intellectual powers and social institutions." Using, among others, Diderot's *Neveu de Rameau*, Jauss examines the manner in which the field of play elaborated by the aesthetic mode counters the dominant monologic discourse produced by theology or ideology. Aesthetic fiction allows one to enter the realm of the taboo, testing truths or asking impudent questions, thereby replacing the old catechetic structures and forcing open the closed horizon in which priority was given to already formed, canonical answers.

This same problem is approached from a different angle in Jauss's extended reading of Rousseau's *Nouvelle Héloïse* and Goethe's *Werther*. The manner in which these texts problematize the relation between art and nature, and between the individual and society, allows Jauss to examine the readerly culture elaborated by the middle class in the eighteenth century, and in so doing elucidate the ways in which these texts functioned and were understood differently by readers whose literary and social horizons were the products of the French Enlightenment and German idealism.

In the closing section of the book, Jauss very generously provides a critical summary of the recent developments in literary hermeneutics, and uses the opportunity to critique his own contribution to this development. As he himself makes clear, although his work had led to a rethinking of the historical relations between the reader, the text, and society, it has not been immune to criticism of its procedures. Indeed, Paul de Man's introduction to the first volume of Jauss's essays in English (*Toward an Aesthetic of Reception*) sought to show that despite the merits of Jauss's analysis of canon formation and his exposure of the unstated assumptions that underlie canonical literary history, and, more important, despite his recognition of the endless interplay of question and answer in the interpretive process, his work failed to consider "the play of the signifier," and, thus, fell prey to the very practice from which he wished to free literary interpretation. De Man accused Jauss of reaestheticizing the text, of ontologizing that which a rhetorical analysis would reveal to be only grammatical and linguistic, and, thus, alien to the meaning structures that the reader might assign to it.[3]

If I mention de Man's critical assessment here, it is not in order to take up the debate on one side or the other. Rather, I have (all too briefly) summarized his argument so that Jauss's discussion of de Man's notion of the rhetorical, and his reworking of the theory of the horizon in the present volume, can be read in part as responses *avant la lettre* to de Man's critique.[4] They first appeared in print (in German) prior to de Man's introductory essay, but he makes no mention of them. Jauss also responded directly to de Man.[5] But given the recent discussion that has erupted around Paul de Man and his work, these early comments by Jauss, which emphasize the need to examine the historical context in which literary and critical languages are *put to use* have a particular poignancy. As Jauss suggests in his discussion of the dialogic nature of critical activity, if the process of understanding literary texts is not to give way to a free-floating production of differences, the process of apprehension arising from the examination of a literary work and its context must be anchored in a prior understanding of the "already said, misunderstood, and previously valid"—of the critic as well as the text and its author. The last word in this debate has certainly not been spoken, but by opening the critical context to scrutiny in this manner, Jauss has firmly reminded us that the questions that emerge in our critical practice, and the answers we discover in the works of others, usually do not arise because of any misunderstanding; they arise from a — largely unexamined — need to *understand differently*.

As will become evident to the reader, these essays move across an enormous expanse of literary-historical terrain. In order to maintain some of the adventure of this journey, I have left all citations from non-German works in their original languages. For readers not wishing to undertake the labors of such a voyage, and for those without a working knowledge of the languages involved, I have appended translations of Jauss's longer citations in the notes. In addition, since there are in some cases no adequate equivalents in English for Jauss's critical terminology, I have let certain words stand, either supplying brief explanations, or relying on the text itself to make the usage clear. Concerning such questions, I am especially grateful to Andreas Huyssen and Miriam Hansen for the valuable suggestions they made while I was at work on this translation. I have also tried to keep Walter Benjamin's admonitions to the translator in mind. How well I have succeeded in this effort is for others to judge.

Ithaca, New York

Notes

1. Hans Robert Jauss, *Toward an Aesthetic of Reception*, trans. Timothy Bahti, and *Aesthetic Experience and Literary Hermeneutics*, trans. Michael Shaw, both 1982.

2. For an extended discussion of Jauss's theory and its implications for literary reception and cultural criticism, see Wlad Godzich's introduction to *Aesthetic Experience and Literary Hermeneutics*.

3. See *Toward an Aesthetic of Reception*, pp. vii–xxv.

4. See "Mais où sont les neiges d'antan," pp. 83–94, and "Understanding and Interpretation as Means of Mediating between Horizons," pp. 199–206.

5. One version of this response can be found in the letter from Jauss to de Man recently published in *Reading de Man Reading*, eds. Lindsay Waters and Wlad Godzich (Minneapolis: University of Minnesota Press, 1989), pp. 202–8.

Question and Answer:
Forms of Dialogic Understanding

A. The Communicative Role of the Fictive

The recent revival of interest in the problem of aesthetic experience – its historical manifestations, and its functions in the praxis of life – also led to renewed interest in a classical problem of aesthetic theory, a problem that soon became the subject of much interdisciplinary discussion: the nature of the relationship between fiction and reality. This problem came to the fore because critics no longer assumed fiction to be the opposite of the real, no longer construed it as "another world," and instead inquired as to what the fictive, as reality's other, could bring to light concerning the latter – what it could convey of the subjective world of the other, and what aspect of the no-longer-real of history it could open to narration. In the *Act of Reading* (1976), Wolfgang Iser asserted that "the time has come . . . to replace ontological arguments with functional arguments. . . . If fiction and reality are to be linked, it must be in terms not of opposition but of communication." And in his critique of self-referential poetics, Karlheinz Stierle (1975) developed the thesis that fiction is no more a reflection of the world than it is a representation of something entirely other than the world. It is rather the "horizon of the world." Both of these notions arise from and are symptomatic of the "change in paradigms" that emerged in France – particularly in medieval studies – as a result of interest in the "imaginary," and in Germany in recent discussions about the "function of the fictive" (*Poetik und Hermeneutik X*).[1] The following three studies came into being as part of this context. They are included here in order to make clear what literary hermeneutics can contribute to our understanding of the historical origins of the fictive, the derivation of the imaginary

3

from the perfect, and the function of fiction as a mode of perceiving and representing historical experience.

1. On the origins of the differentiation between fiction and reality

However natural it may seem to us to define the fictive as the nonreal, to regard it as an autonomous construct, and conceive of it in contrast to the real world, this presumed ontological antithesis between fiction and reality is nonetheless a far cry from the understanding of the world maintained in earlier epochs.

A glance back into literary history shows that whereas the older literatures of the European tradition clearly reveal an initial nondistinction between fiction and reality, the modern era assumes a separation between the two that is played out on a number of levels. In classical literature and then again in the new literature of the medieval period, however, the division between fiction and reality that is so self-evident to us is neither an initial given nor even an early assumption. Rather, in both instances, evidence for such a separation is found only at a comparatively late date. For us, therefore, the nondistinction between fiction and reality in the earlier stages of literature is an aspect of their disturbing alterity. To the best of my knowledge, the point in time, the cause, and the social and psychological conditions for the genesis of the notion of fiction underlying our current understanding of fictional writing have not been examined in much detail.

Manfred Fuhrmann and Wolfhart Pannenberg have proposed the hypothesis that the idea of fiction first appeared in both the Greek and the biblical tradition as an instrument of criticism. If, in the Homeric age, history and mythos, nature and superhuman powers, remained undifferentiated, this sensual-spiritual totality collapsed after Xenophanes criticized the poets' representations of the gods as too human, that is, in our terms, interpreted them as fictions in the sense of projections. This same threshold is passed in the Old Testament when Isaiah 2 derides the cultic veneration of idols that are the mere creation of human hands. In both traditions, "that which has been seen through—seen as a fictive human construct—loses its divine dignity and truth."[2] The later elaboration of a genuine Christian literature was, meanwhile, not just caught in the tension between fiction and inspiration. It also had to come to grips with a new, third category, one announced theoretically in Aristotle's poetics and in aesthetic practice by the Hellenistic comedy and Heliodor's model for the novel: the probable. If there is a historical way in which literature and art have been able to compensate for the Pauline "Have as if you had not," and to resurrect and legitimize the here and now (which had been if not eschatologically destroyed at least negated from the Christian point of view) by means of the fictive,[3] it seems to me that this new consciousness of reality can most readily be traced in the history of the *verisimile*.

The concept of the *verisimile*, which, according to Hans Blumenberg, was really put in circulation by Cicero,[4] already presupposes a separation between fiction and reality. This is evident in the manner in which it mediates their difference through the metaphorical ambiguity of "resemblance to" (reflection) and "semblance" (illusion) of reality.[5] The positive sense of the concept, enhanced by a "Platonic residue," emerges out of the notion of *eikós* in Aristotle's definition of tragedy, and could—as the possible and general in contrast to the very real and particular—serve as a means of granting fictional writing precedence over factual historiography. The aforementioned Hellenistic literary genres, on the other hand, correspond to the negative sense of the fictive—the merely fabricated, that which arises from fantasy and, in the end, the wonderful as well, where inauthenticity is taken for granted. During the process of an ongoing worldly appropriation of aesthetic experience through the fictive mode, the probable separates (according to Fuhrmann) into two functions: clinging to and release from the world. A demarcation between these two functions of the probable can also be found in those paragraphs where Aristotle discusses exceptions to the rules he establishes in the *Poetics*. If, in Chapters 24/25, the impossible that is believable is given preference over the possible that is unbelievable, then the probable (insofar as it is held to be impossible) must also be justified by some general principle ("higher reality, or . . . received opinion"; 1461b). The example provided points once again to the "Platonic residue" in the Aristotelian notion of the probable (*pithanón*): "Again, it may be impossible that there should be men such as Zeuxis painted. 'Yes,' we say, 'but the impossible is the higher thing; for the ideal type must surpass the reality.' " Fuhrmann may have been a bit too negative in his assessment of the other function of the probable. He assigned it to the oldest repertory of "trivial" literature—that which aims only at entertaining by creating "ersatz worlds." We are in fact dealing with an aesthetic object that is able not only to outdo reality, thanks to the fantastic, but actually counter it with another, purely fictive world, and in so doing engender a different attitude in the public as well: the joy of conscious fiction, of accepted unbelievability, or—according to a well-known modern definition—a "willing suspension of disbelief." Whether this attitude, which should manifest itself in the distinction between the fabulous and the probable, is operative or can be assumed to exist in the literary reception of the Hellenistic period is a question that exceeds my competence.

As far as the literature of the Christian era is concerned, it is not surprising that it was obliged to begin as antifiction and almost at right angles to the aesthetics of the probable (the long-delayed reception of Aristotelian poetics may not be a simple accident of historical transmission). An art that wished to do justice to the transcendence of the Christian faith had to give the invisible or future and, consequently, unreal truth a degree of certainty in contrast to which all the probabilities of the visible, everyday world would pale into "as ifs," if not into delusions. Fuhrmann's interpretation of the legend of the Seven Sleepers of Ephesus demonstrates this in impressive fashion by showing the transformation of the everyday into the higher reality of a Lazarus miracle: the sign of God (*visio*) confirms the resurrection of the flesh, elevates the previously unbelievable (Malchus is accused of lying—*fingere*) to the highest degree of certainty and at the same time devalues the probable of the everyday world to mere appearance. This typical example of Christian hagiography obviously does not fit with the aesthetics of the *verisimile*, since the evidence of the resurrection miracle cannot be drawn from a (feasible) possibility, not to mention from the acceptance of a fiction. Neither can it be grasped by means of the earlier-mentioned Aristotelian paragraphs on exceptions, since the miraculous in the Christian sense does not have to be secured within the general—not to mention general opinion: here, the truth of transcendence prevails because of the pure unreality of everything probable, and transforms the real world into an intermittent "as if."

Thus, the new literature of the Christian era had begun by erasing the "Platonic residue" from the probable.[6] It regarded the fictive as an illusion, and, in opposition to the aesthetic (i.e., to the enchantment experienced because of the beautiful illusions in heathen literature), it developed not only the hagiographic canon of transcendence but also literary forms of antifiction such as the devotional, the sympathetic, and the exemplary.[7] The Platonic residue, along with the image field elaborated by *eikós*, *imago*, and *imaginatio*, progressively regained its stature as Christian literature and art went about revalorizing the previously negated world of the here and now as a manifestation of God's creation. The theological aesthetics found in the Platonism developed at Chartres is symptomatic of this change, and came into being during a period in which the literary process bifurcates in a remarkable manner, with Latin poetry and the cosmological epic taking, as Odo Marquard says, the road to ontologization, while popular literature and the Arthurian novel trod the path of fictionalization. Soon thereafter Johannes de Garlandia's *Poetria* appears, and, at the same time, though in another context, Aristotle's notion of the probable reemerges as part of a triad that is of significance for the medieval genesis of the fictive, since it witnesses to the intervening recognition or at least tolerance of the notion.[8]

It is important to remember this transformative period when dealing with the questions of when and how the divorce between fiction and reality might have announced itself in the literature of the Middle Ages. What preceded it was a sense of reality that, in contrast to the classical notion of a reality derived from the immediate evidence of human knowledge, might best be characterized as an indifference to the probable in comparison with the contrafactual truth of Christian religious conviction. The best-known and, for us, most surprising indications of this attitude are the countless forgeries that crop up in the cult of the saints and in documents from the period. They place before us a remarkable aporia: "The deep faith of the Middle Ages is beyond doubt, and yet, more was forged then than at any other time."[9] This nondistinction between true and false, real and fake can in part be explained by the judicial notion of *aequitas*, from the medieval principle that old law was per se good law, or on the basis of the selfless intentions of pious minds desiring to find "some aspect of the divine order of salvation in such activity as well."[10] Nonetheless, for us it remains strange to note the naturalness with which everything preserved in writing, handed down in precious manuscripts, was held to be true per se, and the manner in which, in view of such truth, the value of the source or the various intentions of religious, philosophical, or poetic texts remained unexamined.

In medieval historiography, as in the epic of the Middle Ages, historical fact and significant fiction are often intertwined in an unfathomable manner; in most of the *chansons de geste* (the sole representations of history available to the largely illiterate population), the historical events referred to are totally unrecognizable because they have been reshaped by the process of legend making. A distinction between historical and poetic truth is so foreign to this period that even the exempla in the *Divina commedia*, those figures that Dante selects as a means of taking moral stock of worldly history, could be drawn from three different epochs—from the Bible, the classical period, and the modern Christian era—without concern for their sacred, mythical, historical, or fictive origins. Tristan, a product of medieval fantasy, is to be found (V, 67) in Dante's exemplary series of "grand lovers" (an expression that avoids reference to the "lascivious"). But with him one finds historical and mythic characters such as Semiramis, Dido, Cleopatra, Helen, Achilles, and Paris on the one hand, and Paolo and Francesca, real lovers from the recent *chronique scandeleuse* on the other. Among the traitors in Caïa one finds Mordred, known in romantic fiction only because of his attempt on the life of his uncle, King Arthur, but with him are culprits drawn from the political reality of the thirteenth century. In the series of six good princes, those who in Jupiter's heaven combine to form the image of the eagle's eye, we find David, Trajan, Hezekiah, Constantine, William of Sicily, and Ripheus. Here Dante—reverently lending a hand to devine grace—elevates the Trojan Ripheus (a minor figure in the *Aeneid* whom Virgil mentions in only two lines) into Christian paradise.[11]

The nondistinction between historical truth and epic fiction in the *Divina commedia* (whose author certainly did not wish to construe it as pure fiction) first becomes clear when one realizes that it is precisely Dante's sources for figures such as Tristan and Mordred—the novels of the Arthurian cycle (the so-called *Matière de Bretagne*)—that produced a new consciousness of literary fiction in both authors and public in the middle of the twelfth century. On the other hand, it is in criticism that the nascent separation of literary fiction from historical-legendary reality first emerged. John of Salisbury warned his monks, who delighted in the stories of Arthur, Gawain, and Tristan, not to forget that only a passion for Christ's suffering would lead one to salvation, not, however, the tears one shed over the tribulations of the purely fictive heroes (*fabulosa quaedam referunt histriones*) who then enjoyed such great popularity.[12] In the same period, the Norman poet Wace, who was the first to mention King Arthur's imaginary Round Table, launched a critique of the fictions of the *Matière de Bretagne* in the form of a report: he had personally inspected the magic forest of Broceliande, but found nothing wonderful.[13] In this and other examples of the Church's criticism of the fictive (*fable*) in recently successful literature, it is not just its illusory nature (*monsonge*) that is mentioned; notions crop up that indicate a fascination with conscious fiction (willing suspension of disbelief): the wonderful (*merveille*) and the dreamlike (*songes*). The wonderful in the Arthurian novel stands in direct opposition to the wonderful of Christian legend: in the former, an event in the real world is not a sign of a transcendent, higher reality. Instead, whatever happens in the *aventure* unfolds according to the principle underlying the fairy tale, where the wonderful (borrowing Jodelle's well-known definition) no longer represents an exception but the rule according to which reality, which is sensed to be immoral, is transformed into a world of dreamlike wish fulfillment. The dreamlike quality of the Breton stories is described by some contemporaries as a temptation ("Whoever listens to them feels absolutely as if he has been asleep and dreaming"), a temptation that we today would refer to as daydreaming.[14] Thus, aesthetic pleasure arising from conscious fiction became a means of turning one's back on the fears and pains of everyday life and entering a world of naive justice and good fortune. Such stories are delightful because, as Denis Piramus, one of their critics, claims, they "relieve the mind of pain, hardship and tribulation, / leave anger and grief behind / And free the heart of brooding thoughts."[15]

The intention and reception of the *Matière de Bretagne* (which also distinguishes itself from the knightly epics in the *chansons de geste* by shaping the first romances of this era) confirm the medieval suspicion that release from the world can easily function in tandem with a new interpretation of the world. In his prologue to *Erec et Enide* (written between 1160 and 1170), the first and also greatest author of this tradition, Crétien de Troyes, lays claim to having extracted a *molt bele conjointure* from the existing *conte d'aventure*, in which (in a manner analogous to the antithesis *matière et sens* found in his *Lancelot*) he has hidden a *sensus moralis* that requires the reader to interpret the literal fable. In fact, the Arthurian novel satisfies not only the need for the imaginary, for the "other world" of the adventure story, it also serves the social function of initiating the reader into courtly life and love, an initiation that includes its own educational ideal. This liberation and elevation of the fictive to the level of the noble took place in a period during which the Latin poets of the Chartres school opened a new realm of play for the imagination.[16]

> O noua picture miracula! Transit ad esse
> Quod nichil esse potest picturaque simia veri,

Arte noua ludens, in res umbracula rerum
Vertit et in uerum mendacia singula mutat.
(I 122–25)[17]

This quotation from the *Anticlaudianus* (1182–83) of Alanus ab Insulis (Alain de Lille) must be understood in terms of its Neoplatonic background. A new *Poetria* had laid claim on the *vis imaginativa*, a claim that moved beyond that of theological and philosophical usage: the imagination was granted the status of a creative capacity belonging to the poet, who is able to illustrate ideas and archetypes (those with which Neoplatonic thought had populated the Christian cosmos) through his use of the figures and fictions of rhetoric and, finally, through the fictive discourse of a *fabula*. The transformation of the *mendacia singula* into the true becomes possible because the *imagines* are more than mere fiction; they are representations of the ideal reality belonging to eternal archetypes. Thus, the imagination can assume the higher responsibility of giving form, through elements of the sensible world, to the invisible world of divine reality. From this point on, allegorical verse, in its role as the poetry of the ideal, presupposed this new understanding of the imagination, an understanding that (as Douglas Kelly recently demonstrated) was introduced into the vernacular in the thirteenth century by the poets of courtly love. This understanding thereafter defined the poetic technique of authors from Guillaume de Loris to Charles d'Orléans. The rediscovery of poetic fiction then moved along two different paths during the remainder of the medieval era; one ontologized and the other fictionalized the world of sensual experience. The first justified itself in terms of the "Platonic residue," and the second through the moral claim of the *verisimile*.

The end of the Middle Ages is sealed by a work that takes the divorce between fiction and reality as its theme. Cervantes's *Don Quixote*, a founding text of the modern era, not only attests to the complete separation of fiction and reality, but also shows the medieval ontologizing solution to be a fiction – the delusion of a leftover hero. The fiction of a "last knight" is nothing other than the embodiment of the ideality of a world irrevocably lost, one peopled by heroes without reproach or fear, and by great lovers. Because Don Quixote wishes to oppose his own era by reviving and translating this prior ideality into action, he collides with the reality of the actual world, where things and events have become prosaic, that is, where they are no longer understood as signs of a higher order and can no longer be ontologized in the medieval fashion. Don Quixote (through whom the reader himself finally becomes the "hero") constantly but vainly tries to reinterpret reality according to the laws of fiction, and thereby embarks on the long road to disillusionment – without noticing that his negative experience also opens the way to new knowledge. Never before had the world of the here and now been thus presented in its contingency and ambiguity or opened to description as it was here within the horizon of fiction. Neither had the ideality of poetic fiction been so recognizably the result of human creativity as here when set against the horizon of the unideal world of the everyday.

Thus, the first antinovel, from which spring the endless riches found in the history of the modern novel, makes clear to us that literature, including the modern movement toward antifiction diagnosed by Marquard, cannot do without fiction. After all, the critique necessitated by the progressive fictionalization of the life-world would remain nothing more than a critique if it were not fed by that peculiarity of aesthetic experience that allows fiction to become the horizon of the world, and then again allows the world to become the horizon of fiction.[18] Only from this possibility of a reciprocal construction and thematization of horizons can the aesthetic emerge as the opportunity for new experience, experience that, through a release from the world, arrives at its interpretation.[19]

2. The perfect as the *fascinosum* of the imaginary

Wolfgang Iser recently enriched the discussion of the function of the fictive by suggesting that the dichotomy between the fictive and the real should be expanded into a triad including the imaginary.[20] In the model to be evaluated here the fictive is no longer characterized as merely contrafactual, but acquires an additional mediating function: as it negates a particular reality it at the same time lends conciseness and form to the imaginary. "Thus, the act of fabricating acquires its special nature by bringing about the reappearance of life-world reality in the text and, precisely through this repetition, gives form to the imaginary through which the reemergent reality becomes a sign of and the imaginary an effect of that which is described in the fiction" (p. 2). In other words, in the act of fabricating, a double transgression of boundaries takes place: "In the transformative re-presentation of life-world reality as a sign of something else, the transgression of boundaries manifests itself as a derealization; through its transformation into something diffuse within the certainty of purpose the imaginary becomes real" (p. 3).

The reversal, the process in which the derealization of a particular reality (through selection and combination of its elements) allows an immemorial imaginary to become real, can also be described as a relationship in which a figure or a theme brings the ground or the horizon of the imaginary to light. It is clear that this interplay between the real, the fictive, and the imaginary can better explain the *fascinosum* of aesthetic fiction—the impact of its peculiar oscillation between the real and the unreal—than can any dyadic theory.[21] Whereas in the latter aesthetic fiction is defined in the purely traditional sense of the mimetic (as the semblance or illusion of a real world), or in a free-floating manner (as the realization of an autonomous, other world), the mediating act of fabrication opens a dimension that, as something that itself can no longer be fabricated, instead hovers above all possible fictions as an immemorial imaginary that can only be evoked.

Iser did not pose questions about the origin and the internal definitions of the imaginary; instead he handed the discussion over to others as a project for future resolution. I would like to contribute to that effort by providing an anthropological explanation of the particular power of the imaginary—its *fascinosum*—in terms of the need for the perfect. Historically it can also be explained in relation to the process whereby the aesthetic is detached from religious experience.

I have given particular emphasis to the fact that Iser's triadic model presupposes a basic distinction between the fictive and the imaginary, between something fabricated or produced and something that cannot simply be made, only evoked. If knowledge of the condition of being fabricated, that is, a consciousness of the "as if," always accompanies us in our experience of aesthetic fiction, the imaginary can apparently also be experienced as something that does away with this "as if"—as something unreal that is of greater fascination and greater believability. Its greater believability must come from the appearance it awakens of not only not having been "invented," but of being something that, even in its new form, still seems old and familiar, something forgotten or repressed. Its greater fascination must also arise from the fact that it satisfies a need, one that aesthetic fiction satisfies most fully—the need for the complete and perfect [das Volkommene]. As an ontological category, we know that the need for the perfect is older than the beautiful. The experience of the perfect always includes a moment of the unreal; it sets the imagination in motion and is, therefore, akin to aesthetic experience. In the experience of the perfect, the imperfection of the real world can, despite the facts, be surpassed to such a degree that the unreal of the perfect appears to be the actual real next to which a more difficult reality pales. This might be explained by the fact that the perfect outstrips the merely probable thanks to its self-sufficiency, and because its believability remains untouched by doubt thanks to its ideality. The analogues to the function of the imaginary in Iser's model are obvious. Therefore, one might suspect that the perfect, as used in art, points back to mental structures and forms of the imaginary that come to art second-hand.

At first the need to experience the perfect as something that is denied us because of the insufficiency of the real world was apparently satisfied by religious or mystic experience. Perfection was, to begin with, a predicate that in the Judeo-Christian tradition belonged to God alone, one that was in like measure a happy privilege of the classical gods. Since, however, divine perfection cannot be conceived of and experienced without the use of the imagination, aesthetic experience found that the medium of the imaginary could serve as the starting point for a gradual usurping of the figures and the signifying structures of the perfect, and finally lay claim to the aura of divine perfection for art as the highest form of human accomplishment. One could object that this thesis tacitly assumes a specific concept of the perfect, one that Greek ontology, with its idea of a perfect cosmic order, implicitly passed on to aesthetic experience, and which, therefore, can do justice to artistic experience in the European tradition, but not to religious experience, for the latter is by no means fully consumed in the effort to satisfy the need for the perfect. On the contrary, it is defined first through its contact with the numinous, and most fully by the experience of the *tremendum*. I believe I can accommodate this objection by arguing that religious experience, when it emerges with fear and helpless trembling from a confrontation with the divine, has always and repeatedly overcome the *tremendum* of the absolute by replacing the total otherness of divine power with the predicates of its perfection. Whether this overcoming of religious anxiety (in which Hans Blumenberg sees the effect of myth already at work) must, from a rigorously theological point of view, already be suspected of aestheticizing the absolute is not a question I need to worry about here, no more so than whether Greek ontology and in particular the Platonic doctrine of the ideal, given its concept of the perfect, has had an aesthetic basis from the very start. In what follows, I am concerned only with demonstrating aesthetic experience's progressive appropriation of a perfect invested by religion or metaphysics, an appropriation to be substantiated by evidence found in representative examples from the occidental tradition. These examples also suggest that it might be worthwhile to investigate this process further in order to see whether it explains how the *tremendum* of the absolute, which was regularly revived by dogmatic shifts in religion and by the ideologizing of politics, could always be dismantled again by new thrusts from aesthetic experience.

The longing for the perfect, which itself embodies man's initial effort to transcend the limits of purely physical need, first sets the imagination at work searching beyond human existence for the ideal and the most desirable. These are then concretized in images of inaccessible divine perfection. In Greek myth the elevated human figure embodied in the Olympians is ageless, untouched by pain, cares, or death; their perfect existence remains absolutely separate from that of human beings. It is even a jealously guarded privilege, as the widespread myth of the gods' envy indicates: "Every earthly bit of luck, every great quality is, as it were, an attack on the privilege of fortune and perfection belonging to the gods, and usually brings the humans in question under the charge of having wished to 'spite' the gods."[22] The songs dedicated to the Old Testament God sing his praises as perfect in his ways (Psalms 18:30), in his laws (Psalms 19:8), in the "wonderous works of him which is perfect in knowledge" (Job 37:16). The distance from humankind is, however, less radical here, since God's perfection can include a demand imposed on humans, one that Jesus first formulated in Matthew 5:48: "Be ye therefore perfect even as your Father which is in heaven is perfect." In the history of Christian piety it is assumed that this demand can be met through eschatological hope; the saint, who tried to anticipate future perfection through an ascetic life, and in his desirelessness and sinlessness embodied a kind of negative ideal of perfection, was named *perfectus* in the Middle Ages. The idea of happiness based on some future salvation or messianic world was in competition with another one arising from the classical ideal of *theoria*, which, according to Hans Blumenberg, had an influence on the Christian expectation of the *visio beatifica*: "something akin to the projection of the classical sage as the final stage of the Christian blessed," which he mockingly referred to as "good fortune from theoreticians for theoreticians."[23] Behind this idea stands the Aristotelian figure of divine perfection, the unmoved mover: "In the scholastic system, it is this god who is wholly preoccupied with the theory of himself that gives qualitative definition to the goal of salvation for humankind as well—as the definitive, pure theory of the *visio beatifica*."[24] Corresponding to this was an understanding of art that made gradual participation in the perfect the criterion for the beautiful. This transformation of the ontological priority of the perfect into the beauty of appearances indicates the shift by which the incipient modern era emancipated aesthetics as an autonomous "science."

Bacon's *Advancement of Learning* marks one starting point for this shift: through a tripartite division in the capacity of the human mind, the imagination acquires the capacity to compensate for the insufficiency of the real world at that point where the experience of history is felt most sharply. "Because the acts or events of true history have not the magnitude which satisfieth the mind of man, poesy feigneth acts and events greater and more heroical; because true history propoundeth the successes and issues of actions not so agreeable to the merits of virtue and vice, therefore poesy feigns them more just in retribution, and more according to revealed providence."[25] Here the desire for a more perfect ("magnitude") and just world is recognized and legitimated as a fundamental human need that can be satisfied here and now through a capacity for poetic fiction. Certainly, this accomplishment of the poetic imagination is only defined *ex negativo* by Bacon, and subordinated to the capacity for reason that, through a growing understanding of nature, was to achieve the historical goal of reestablishing paradise. But with the progressive emancipation of aesthetic experience the transcendental authority of divine justice ("according to revealed providence") is replaced by the immanent authority of poetic justice, the compensatory function of the imagination is made an autonomous human activity, and the second, other nature embodied in poetic fiction is proclaimed the sole model for a more perfect world. At one of the high points of this development, Proust could claim that art was "the veritable last judgment,"[26] and Nietzsche could praise "idealizing" as the highest human activity and the only possibility for human completion. "Man in this condition transfigures things until they reflect his power—until they are stamped with his perfection. This compulsion to transfigure into the perfect is—Art. Everything—even that which he is not—is nevertheless to such a man a means of rejoicing over himself; in Art man rejoices over himself as perfection."[27]

The history of the concept of the perfect shows meanwhile that this development does not progress uninterruptedly into the later modern era, but instead moves as a dialectical process. On the one hand aesthetic activity, as a "transformation into the perfect," repeatedly assumes control of new contents,[28] while on the other hand, perfection as an aesthetic ideal is in contrary fashion called into question by being cast as a necessary illusion, lowered to the rank of a heuristic principle, and finally discarded from modern poetics and art theory as an illusion of classically educated recipients. If there is a common denominator for the modernity of the art of our epoch, then it probably lies in its pangeneric and constantly renewed resistance to "closed form" as the embodiment of perfection. But that the art of our modern era *needs* to oppose the aesthetic totality of the perfect is the best demonstration of the strength of its fascination, and speaks for the fact that the need for the perfect could not be extinguished despite all the intellectual development and critical reflection. I would prefer not to venture onto the terrain of a new solution to a problem that is well known in the modern philosphy of art. Nonetheless, I hope to provide another of the prerequisites for such a solution by verifying my hypothesis that the *fascinosum* of the imaginary can be derived genetically from the structures of signification associated with the perfect that are imparted to aesthetic fiction by the experience of the numinous. In this effort, I will draw primarily on examples from the older literary tradition.

The easiest way to begin an examination of the prestructuring of the perfect is by looking at the form of the imaginary found in the fairy tale. Historically speaking, the fairy tale is one of the earliest literary forms to take for granted a conscious fiction and, therefore, a full enjoyment of the imaginary.[29] It thematizes the absolute difference between the probable and everyday, historical reality by idealizing space, time, characters, and morality. In conjunction with the imaginary, this idealizing move constantly brings attributes of a perfect existence into play that are otherwise withheld from man. (a)The *space* of the fairy tale, which is constructed by the anarchistic dualism of the oppositions between inside and outside, near and far, friendly and hostile, is traversed by a hero who oversteps boundaries.[30] He thereby makes visible what is at first a latent and finally harmonious order in the world. In this more perfect order the hero's discovery of that which he seeks is guaranteed in advance. The fairy tale's gift has already furnished him with the answer, even before he arrives at the spot where the question will be asked. (b)The *time* of the fairy tale is the imaginary and indeterminant "once upon a time," which even in its painless movement remains apart from historical time. In the purer contingency of the former, whatever appears in the guise of accident is ruled by a secret and well-meaning providence. And when the time of testing is completed, the hero and his princess (in accord with the cheerful formula of positive resolution: "And if they have not passed away, they are living still") find a bit of the eternal in an earthly other world — an immortality granted by poetic form! (c)The *characters* in the fairy tale, though introduced in terms of the pure oppositions between good and bad, beautiful and ugly, young and old, do not need to engage in any tragic conflict: nature and status are demonstrated sufficiently by what happens to them. The prince is for the princess, the princess for the prince, an *ens perfectissimum*, each completely transparent to the other despite disguise, both unblemished from the beginning and precisely for that reason destined for each other. (d)The *morality* of the fairy tale fulfills our expectation that "what happens in the story takes place in accord with our sense of how the world ought to function."[31] This naive morality overrides all the demands with which religion and philosophy meet the seriousness of life: it moves away from hard reality into the dream state of fulfilled wish. Thus, it satisfies the deep need for a perfect world in which one can feel secure about good being rewarded and bad punished, since in the context it creates, it is not some far-off day of judgment that prevails, but an omnipresent poetic justice.

a) The structures of signification used by the imaginary, at least those revealed in the fairy tale, prove more difficult to locate in the higher reaches of literature because they are considered naive or trivial in the modern era and can be employed only under restricted conditions. This trivializing is generally explained as an effect of overuse and mechanization. However, it also indicates an erosion of trust in the world. The trivial "happy end" can serve as an example. It has so degraded the positive resolution that the latter's mythic substratum has been rendered almost unrecognizable. The positive resolution is the most diminished stage of one of the most effective basic models of the imaginary: the return to the place of origin. In his history of reception Blumenberg recently examined the movement from the *Odyssey* to *Ulysses*, and further, from *Narcissus* and *Oedipus* to Freud's death wish. He interprets the mythic function of the Odysseus figure as a proof of the restitution of meaning, one that "protects the tenor of order in the world and life from any appearance of fall or arbitrariness."[32] This paradigm also allows one to discover the mythic analogue in a few major variants present in the history of literary form. The journey through the world—the basic model for the beginning and the end of the novel and the autobiography—can elevate the end (which is already determined at the beginning), or the latent order that comes to light along the way, to the level of mythic significance. This final return to the point of origin stands in direct opposition to the model that provides a fully realized plenitude at the beginning: the earthly paradise that, lost and sought after, is the *fascinosum* par excellence in all those imaginary happy worlds that appear again and again in European literature, from the *Roman de la Rose* through pastoral poetry to *A la recherche du temps perdu*. The telos indicated in a beginning perfection can, however, fail to work out, so that the entire journey turns into a tale of doom once the first misstep is taken. This is the case in Rousseau's *Confessions*: after the first experience of injustice during the affair with the comb, which thrusts him out of paradise (*dès ce moment je cessai de jouir d'un bonheur pur*), whatever he might have been as an *homme naturel* and *bon citoyen* is forever lost to Jean-Jacques.[33] His life goes astray, and during the episodes in his sanctuary from society all attempts to recover his lost natural existence fail, leaving him the victim of a universal conspiracy.

The structure of signification embodied in the journey, which allows the resistant world as a whole to be deciphered as a system of signs referring to a more perfect, gradually visible order, is probably first represented in the type of novel written by Heliodor. Its most important form of reception, the heroic/gallant novel of the seventeenth century, renders the familiar world even more enigmatic, turning it into the impenetrable confusion of a reality in which a hostile *fatum* often withholds the anagnorisis and, thus, the desired union of the lovers — often for more than five thousand pages.[34] The *medias-in-res* technique of narration is taken to the extreme: if, in order to heighten the tension, the reader begins in the middle of the action in the *Oethiopica*, and if the meaning of this action is revealed step by step through the recovery of anterior events, the reader of *Astrée*, *Clélie*, or *Cléopâtre* on the other hand is drawn, to his growing distress, into a narrative labyrinth in which numerous (often up to thirty!) narrative paths run parallel to and across one another. He can only begin to decipher their enigmatic figural meanings to the degree that cleverly measured doses of light from anterior events illuminate the darkness of the beginning. What remains of progressive action after these regressive anterior events is little more than its conclusion — the final recognition of all the participants, consecrated by a monumental wedding ceremony marking the beginning of a pastoral *Age d'or* for all the couples (as many as thirty). This later era is not presented, however. If one interprets these heroic/gallant novels with the help of Iser's triad, narrative fiction on the one hand makes the real world unreal by rendering it enigmatic (historically speaking, it elevates the unreasonable reality of a period of religious wars — its temporally bound difference — to an impenetrable *fatum* of separation), while on the other hand it deciphers the imaginary, thus allowing a more perfect world to become real (by reuniting all the characters, the final recognition scene in these novels confirms the latent possibility of an endless happiness that is contrafactual to the helplessness of the present). Poetic fiction in which the progress of the narrative is actually a return to the beginning embodies a movement akin to the gradual opening of a curtain behind which one discovers the presence of an unchanging picture, one that had been there all the time. By bringing into view the true picture of a perfect harmony that was only latent in the illusory opening images of a problematic reality, poetic fiction behaves in a manner analogous to a theology that, confronted by an evil world, tries to justify the perfection of the divine world order by asserting that it is nonetheless present, though latent in its effects.

That poetic fiction has surreptitiously slipped into the space formerly occupied by theodicy is also evident in modern novels, except that here — in Proust's *A la recherche du temps perdu* — the schema of making and resolving a riddle is displaced by the transformative power of memory. For Proust, the day-to-day world in itself has become so opaque that its reality, which can no longer be plumbed, even by the most penetrating perception, becomes recognizable only through the unconscious work of memory. The narrative structure, embodying a reciprocal movement, corresponds to this condition: the passage through time, which submits Marcel to a contingency alien to the senses and leads him to doubt his identity (because he believes he has failed his *vocation* — the sufficient reason for his writing), until, in the end, he recognizes that the sign he had not understood, his *souvenir involontaire*, has opened the way to the reality of the past. This allows him to recover lost time and thereby discover the authentic object of his work. In this return from the end to the beginning, from the path of experience to that of memory, the senseless contingency of life acquires fullness and transforms the fragmented experience of time into the perfect image of its duration embodied in the work: the alienated reality of the world, presented as rediscovered time, again — as in the old theodicy — becomes object of an *adoration perpétuelle*. This formulation derives from a triadic division of the work, one that Proust finally abandoned, in which it stands for the third of the "three ages": *L 'âge des noms, L 'âge des mots, L 'âge des choses.*[35] The "Age of Names" is the world of the imagination, which, along with their names, grants things and persons their singularity, and which arrives at a higher truth because it arises from the *idée de perfection*. The "Age of Words" enters when the imaginary meets the real, when the desired meets its object and names are replaced by concepts whose generality makes all individuation disappear. A reality that has been thus rendered unrecognizable can once again become transparent in the "Age of Things" if things, and with them the former "I," are rediscovered in the depths of the state of forgetfulness — thanks to the work of memory, which, in a sort of catharsis of being, is able to separate the essence of things from the illusions of perception and once again grant the alienated world aesthetic justification.

b) The need to pass beyond the final horizon of experience into a more perfect time is satisfied in religious experience by the promise of resurrection, by immortality or other figures of the move into the timeless. Poetic fiction has probably taken most complete possession of this attribute, (a perfection originally reserved for the gods), either in the explicit immortalization of its heroes or in the implicit agelessness that is the rule for the heroic age and, later, for the shepherds of the idylls. Achilles strikes one as the epitome of the eternally young hero; Nestor is always the old man; Odysseus returns home as if his years of wandering have left no physical trace behind; and poetry has nothing to say about a Helen, a Penelope, or an Isolde grown gray with age. Not to have to grow old is a temporal wish structure whose imaginary fulfillment is characteristic of the naive idealism of all the early phases of European literature. In the epic poetry of the Middle Ages one can distinguish between Christian and pagan variants: the heroes of the *chansons de geste* achieve immortality through martyrdom, while the heroes of the Arthurian novel have already been granted eternal life in this world. Before the battle

Turpin reveals to the twelve paladins in the *Song of Roland* that they will die in order to "achieve their place in greater paradise as holy martyrs" (ll.1134/1539). King Arthur's Round Table, to which the elect are admitted at the end of thir adventures, thus concluding their quest for being, is as removed from time as Avalon, the isle of the blessed, where Arthur remains beyond death's reach until at last an author puts an equally perfect end to the imaginary immortality of the circle of heroes by letting them perish in toto in that eschatological event found in *La mort le roi Artu*. The *paradisus amoris*, conceived of as an atemporal place of perfect happiness for true lovers, figures as the innermost circle of the topographical contrafact of the Christian world in *De amore*, written by Andreas Capellanus, the theoretician of courtly love. In courtly poetry itself, the paradise of love usually appears only intermittently, as the unique high point of fulfilled love — as it does in the lovers' grotto in *Tristan and Isolde*, or as a daemonic place of happiness belonging to Venus, such as that found in *Tannhäuser*. Blessing and curse continue to intersect in the *fascinosum* of atemporality even in Thomas Mann's *Magic Mountain*. The novel's hero only escapes this *fascinosum* thanks to the thunderclap signaling the outbreak of a world war — he escapes, that is, from the omnipresent, ironized perfection of the number seven which encompasses everything from temperature taking to the seven-year duration of his stay.

Another temporal wish structure, one fulfilled primarily through the lyric, is that of the eternal's presence in a single moment. This embodiment of the imaginary, which here achieves the succinctness of poetic form, probably points back to an aspect of divine perfection, the *Nunc stans*, in which everything past or future is present for God. The prototype, "Tarry a while, you are so fair,"[36] Goethe's line conjuring up the counterpoise to Faust's striving, is so richly represented in the history of the lyric from Petrarch (e.g., "Benedetto sia 'l giorno e 'lmesse e l'anno")[37] to Rilke (e.g., "Again and again, even when we know the landscape of love")[38] and Celan (e.g., "Black milk of dawn, we drink it at dusk"),[39] that I can limit myself to a single, threshold case. Baudelaire's poem, "A une passante," transforms the imaginary's model of the beautiful — which eternalizes the instant of beauty's appearance — into its opposite, the *fugitive beauté* of a happiness that is lost forever at the very moment it is experienced. The appearance of the beautiful passerby, the self-recognition arising from an almost intoxicated glance, and her disappearance once more in the crowd, embody the *fascinosum* of a beautiful that is perfect because it appears in order to immediately disappear (a *nunc non stans* so to speak), so that the eternal, which it could not endure, can be experienced *ex negativo*:

> Un éclair . . . puis la nuit! — Fugitive beauté
> Dont le regard m'a fait soudainement renaître,
> Ne te verrai-je plus que dans l'éternité?

Ailleurs, bien loin d'ici! trop tard! jamais peut-être!
Car j'ignore où tu fuis, tu ne sais où je vais,
O toi que j'eusse aimée, ô toi qui le savais![40]

c) God as *ens perfectissimum*, as Being (in Anselm's formulation of his proof of God) more perfect than which no other can be conceived and, therefore, which must be conceived as existing, is appropriated by poetic fiction in two different signifying structures: the superlative norm, (self-experience) and the comparative norm (experience of the other). The transformation of religious into aesthetic experience was provoked by the unreality of a highest, divine perfection, one that necessarily set the imaginations of the faithful in motion.[41] The endless distance separating their imperfection from the perfection of their creator nonetheless allowed some participation in that latter condition. The most powerful *fascinosum* of the imaginary was evoked by this possibility as figured in the notion that human beings were made in God's image. It appears in the Christian poetry of the Middle Ages as the image of a perfect self (*divina psyche*) mirrored in the soul, a self that the observer experiences from the paradoxical distance of a *laetus horror*: joy in his participation in divine being and, at the same time, horror at the abyss separating him from God's perfection.[42] The final turn toward aesthetic emancipation of the individual can be seen in Montaigne's essay "De l'experience" (III, xiii) where the principle of divine autarchy is put to work in the process of human self-discovery: "C'est une absolue perfection, et comme divine, de scavoir jouyr loiallement de son estre.[43] Here, "rightfully" [*loiallement*] means in recognition and affirmation of the necessary imperfection of the *condition humaine*. This must be the case, since, in the same context, and with a rather graphic image, Montaigne ironizes about elevating oneself to a self-made perfection, something that had shocked him about Socrates: "Et au plus eslevé throne du monde si ne sommes assis que sur nostre cul."[44]

This self-limitation was silently dropped when Rousseau allowed *The Reveries of the Solitary Walker* to culminate in the fullness of the simple *sentiment de l'existence*, by drawing on the model of divine autarchy: "De quoi jouit-on dans une pareille situation? De rien d'extérieur à soi, de rien sinon de soi-même et de sa propre existence; tant que cet état dure, on se suffit à soi-même comme Dieu."[45] Later, Goethe's position was so transformed by this manner of asserting the autonomy of the human being that in the "grand confession" of his work the contingency of a fragmented life that had fallen away from natural existence (for which Rousseau blamed society in the moral tribunal of his *Confessions*) was aesthetically mastered, sublated in the educational ideal of the German classical period. "Everything perfect in its kind must pass out beyond, must become somthing other, something incomparable. In many of its tones the nightingale is only a bird; then it rises above its kind, and seems to want to show every feathered creature what singing really means":[46] by means of an aesthetic existence, humans move beyond their condition as generic beings and arrive at the perfection of an incomparable individuality. Whatever resists this elevation into the absolute must nevertheless serve the great individual, as does everything that Goethe felt was daemonic in the accidents along the path of his life. This is so because the oppositional and even that which is evil can be subjugated through aesthetic self-education (thereby evading moral reflection à la Rousseau) if, in its opposition, this evil adds to the perfection of the autonomous subject — as suggested in the "dreadful maxim" whose mysterious authority was recently discussed by Hans Blumenberg, who suggests that the maxim itself was probably fabricated by Goethe: "Nemo contra deum nisi deus ipse."[47]

The basic, altruistic model for the *ens perfectissimum* can be elucidated on the basis of an astounding transformation found in the reception history of the Narcissus myth. In the *Roman de la Rose*, the high point of courtly love allegory, the lover arrives at the "Fontaine d'amors" as he moves along the path of his initiation. His glance into the spring conjures up the myth, but only to transform its traditional meaning through a bold topical rendering. While the classical Narcissus — struck by unrequitable self-love after seeing the image of his own perfect beauty in the water — falls in love with his reflection and drowns in the attempt to embrace himself, his medieval counterpart finds not himself but two crystals in the "fountain of love." According to one interpretation these signify the eyes of his beloved, which are mirrors of her soul; according to another, they are the reflection of his own eyes, transformed by an inescapable longing for her.[48] The loved one as *ens perfectissimum* is the imaginary *fascinosum* that shaped the powerfully influential Ur-scene of the European courtly love lyric. As most perfect being, she combines the courtly virtue of the "Lady" with the divine attribute of unmoved mover, and becomes the sole authority able to grant mercy. The lover on the other hand submits himself to his chosen one as unconditionally as a Christian *perfectus* would to his divine ruler: he experiences his suffering in her absence as a happy condition, one that distinguishes his love from the less perfect love of ordinary mortals, and that, as the inexhaustible source of his singing, includes a cathartic "joy in song."

The wider tradition of love poetry shows how the postulate of perfection found in courtly and Petrarchan idealism was progressively dismantled, and the unreal attributes of the idolized lady transformed into the carnal figure and personal identity of a real loved one. The threshold of complete individualization is to be found at the point where the chosen other, despite imperfections, is recognized, loved, and praised for her or his own sake. This threshold, over which Montaigne's lines on friendship could be inscribed (*parce que c'était lui, parce que c'était moi*),[49] is crossed when concrete individuality rather than the *forme universelle de mon être* is proposed as the theme of personal experience worth sharing. Evidence for this change can be found in the epoch during which historicism emerged. This epoch develops a new interest in the individual aspects of historical events, one that can be best understood in terms of its opposition to the timeless and perfect. For Herder, every human perfection is "national, secular, and, when examined carefully, individual." Therefore, imitation of beauty in nature distances us from precisely that nature "in which individuals exist, but never the perfections of art, individuals in whom imperfection itself is both the definition and limit of beauty."[50] The imperfect, which at this point is still regarded as the frontier of beauty, will lose this limitation as well when German idealism's cult of genius begins to extol the imperfection of the individual — individual uniqueness itself — as perfection (as the "greatest fortune of earth's children"). The aura of the perfect is given new depth in the paradoxical perfection of that which is in itself imperfect. This is evidenced even more clearly in a modern text that insists on the experience of fascination in the incomplete and ugly in order to allow the perfect to shine forth all the stronger *ex contrario*. A passage in Walter Benjamin's *Einbahnstrasse* provides the finest example of this development:

> He who loves is attached not only to the "faults" of the beloved, not only to the tics and weaknesses of a woman. Wrinkles in the face, moles, shabby clothes, and a lopsided walk bind him more lastingly and relentlessly than any beauty. This has long been known. And why? If the theory stating that feeling is not located in the head is correct, that we feelingly experience a window, a cloud, a tree not in our brains but, rather, at the place where we see it, then we are equally outside ourselves when looking at our beloved. But in a torment of tension and rapture. Feeling, dazzled, flutters like a flock of birds in the woman's radiance. And as birds seek refuge in the leafy recesses of a tree, feelings escape into the shadowy wrinkles, the awkward movements and inconspicuous blemishes of the body one loves, where they can nestle in security. And no passer-by would guess that it is precisely here, in what is defective and blameworthy, that the swift stirrings of love reside.[51]

d) The conclusion of Goethe's *Werther* sets in play the last of the structures of meaning of the imaginary that is to be discussed here, one that was granted self-evident validity in classical and Christian poetry, but that was explicitly elevated to the level of poetic norm only during the Renaissance: poetic justice. Its gradual canonization can be seen in the definition of the tragic that emerges from the reception of Aristotle's poetics.[52] In Aristotle it comes into play in the discussion of types of action (Chapters 13/18). There, the need to choose "someone between these extremes," someone whose misfortune is due to an error (*hamartia*), is based on the idea that seeing a person without fault perish despite his innocence is repulsive and no more a source of fear than seeing a bad man end unhappily. These extremes eliminate the possibility of tragic effect because they are not "friendly to man" (*philánthropon*). In other words, they shake one's faith in a meaningful world order. Italian poetic theory brings this implicit norm to light. Robertello comments that "the demise of a perfect hero is intended to raise doubts about the justness of the divine order of the world, even to breed a religion of fear."[53] At this point, the martyr, the most perfect hero in Christian poetry, is, of necessity, excluded from tragedy. The incompatibility of a transcendental last judgment and a world-immanent justification of poetic justice was later masked by various compromises until the poetics of the Enlightenment raised the immanent principle to the highest priority of autonomous poetry. With this, the theodicy concept finally had to be abandoned too, as when Lessing, in his famous metaphor of the "mere outline of the whole of the eternal creator," tried again to establish poetic justice as the work of the poet (*Hamburg Dramaturgy*, no. 79). Lessing's critique reveals the threshold that was crossed when, in *The Sorrows of Young Werther*, Goethe satisfied the need for poetic justice in a manner that was, at the time, still unusual.

In the debate about *Werther*, it was Lessing who held that "a brief, cold closing comment" was necessary in order to have the reader avoid "simply mistaking poetic beauty for moral beauty and believing that the person who so powerfully engaged our sympathy must have been good."[54] This misunderstanding, which, according to Lessing, Goethe should have worked against, is based on more than the supposed naïveté of an unenlightened reader. That which is presented here as naive expectation was, prior to the turning point in German literature represented by Goethe's *Werther*, still an aesthetic norm of secular validity — the concept of perfection found in Platonic aesthetics, according to which moral truth unquestionably arises out of poetic beauty. From this point of view the perfect representation found in *The Sorrows of Young Werther* seemed to justify Werther's "sickness unto death" as self-evident, and called forth "admiration and love" for his character. Goethe's move toward aesthetic autonomy was initially, therefore, also a break with Platonism, and took place at a time when the neoclassical conflation of moral and aesthetic perfection was being called into question (in Diderot's *Neveu de Rameau*, for example). At this same time the *fascinosum* of evil was again being openly thematized and the criminal, to whom neoclassical tragedy granted only the role of antagonist, became interesting in his own right and was able to generate a literature of his own. But this new court of aesthetic judgment, which was to assess the justness or injustice of the sufferings of the bourgeois individual, came into being only slowly and hesitantly, and without being able to rely on the perfect evidence of the moral truth found in beauty.

Although it had not yet been established, such a tribunal was urgently called for in the works of Choderlos de Laclos and the Marquis de Sade, who further developed Rousseau's ideas and wanted to turn the emancipation of a formerly repressed nature against society, which was now judged culpable. Both authors nonetheless offset the *fascinosum* of the perfect with a traditional legitimation of right and wrong: as punishment, Madame de Merteuil is finally disfigured by smallpox, and in Sade's novel, perfect sin brings down virtue, apparently in order to call forth the greatest possible sympathy from the public.[55] The new court of aesthetic judgment is first established by the step Goethe takes in *The Sorrows of Young Werther*, when he refuses to rely on guilt and punishment as a means of establishing a more perfect justice in poetic fiction. Instead, he satisfies this need by enabling the reader (who functions as authoritative representative of the bourgeois public) to understand suicide. Any judgment about its morality is then left to the reader's discretion. The young Goethe thereby provided a new solution to the problem facing poetic fiction: how to construct a more just world in the face of an alienated reality. At the same time, Bodmer, one of his critics, could still counter with the neoclassical formula of poetic justice: "Goethe says that his *Sorrows of Werther* is both history and nature, and that the historian has no need to portray his characters as just. In fact, however, they are nothing but a fabrication. He is the *poietes*, the maker, of these sorrows. And a poetic creator should, in his world, that is, in his story, punish, since he cannot do so in the world to come as can the true Creator."[56]

Nonetheless, one can doubt whether Lessing's "brief, cold closing comment" or the warning that Goethe himself placed at the beginning of the second edition ("So, be a man and do not do what I have done") could satisfactorily disempower the *fascinosum* of this text. The history of its reception amply demonstrates that even enlightened readers, those who, in the absence of any moral guidelines, were able to see that Goethe's poetic fiction made it possible to understand and judge suicide differently than did the theological and juridical structures of the day,[57] were nonetheless unable to escape unshaken from the particular *fascinosum* generated by *Werther*. This *fascinosum*, evident in its tremendously widespread impact, and in the scandalous fashionability of Werther's style of clothing, is not entirely explicable in terms either of breaking taboos or of the success of sentimentality as the epoch's behavioral model. There was, in addition, what one might call the distressing manifestation of the perfect in successful aesthetic fiction or—in critical terms—fiction's gilding effect:[58] suicide, which Goethe's literary "pathography" neither defends nor attacks, is inevitably transfigured by Goethe's perfected poetic fiction, despite its newly won objectivity. Fictionalization of the real apparently leads of necessity to its idealization. However, from our present vantage point, we can say that, through this idealization, the imaginary acquires form and succinctness to the degree that the perfection of the representation summons up the perfection of the represented. In the "Story of Poor Werther," the central figure, whose letters provide an unmediated view of the new gospel of nature, takes on more and more of the characteristics of a martyr to sentimentality, if not, as one contemporary interpretation would have it, the features of a "crucified Prometheus."[59]

Nietzsche praised the transformation of things into the perfect as the highest accomplishment of art, but in so doing he also indicated the ambivalence of this

perfection (in the formulation "compulsion to transform" [*verwandeln-müssen*]).
The perfect is ambivalent as the *fascinosum* of the imaginary because fictionaliz-
ing things *inevitably* brings with it their idealization. Thus, the aesthetic object,
in its perfection, reflects both the power of the individual to enjoy himself in his
work and also human powerlessness to make perfect the imperfections of the
world in any other manner than through their idealization. The idealizing consciousness must constantly defend itself from the danger of unintentionally becoming the prisoner of its own, self-created world. It is often art alone that retains
the memory of the sufferings of humanity, presenting them as past events. But
that art always also transfigures these sufferings as it gives them expression is pro-
tested in commentaries from Rousseau's first *Discours* down to present-day critiques of ideology, when they accuse art of amorality and complicity with the
dominant power. Ever since, the tendency to work against the inherent idealization of the aesthetic object with the techniques of estrangement, destruction of illusion, fragmentation, and montage — in short, antifiction — has emerged in modern literature and art much more powerfully than before. Rousseau, who,
according to the foreword to his *Nouvelle Héloïse*, wished to enlist the work as
an antifiction aimed at a corrupt society — a society that could no longer see
through its own alienation, that is, its self-imposed illusions — is, as far as I can
see, also the eighteenth century's first advocate of the current sense of the perfect.
Since his second *Discours*, the concept of *perfection*, usurped by art, has found
itself in a relation of tension with *perfectibility*. Measured in terms of the human
capacity for self-perfection (whether for better or worse, since Rousseau's neolo-
gism has no teleological intent), perfection must lose its ontological primacy, and
must finally be given up once its illusory nature has been perceived: "Ne cher-
chons point la chimère de la perfection, mais le mieux possible selon la nature
de l'homme et la constitution de la société."[60]

The implication of this idea for modern aesthetics was probably first recognized by Valéry: "Un temps qui interroge tout, qui vit de tout essayer, de tout
regarder comme perfectible et donc provisoire . . . ne saurait être un temps de
repos pour les lettres ni pour les arts. La poursuite des perfectionnements exclut
la recherche de la perfection. Perfectionner s'oppose à parfaire."[61] For Valéry,
the result of this situation is that our modern art is no longer permitted to create
"products of the desire for perfection." The need for "perfection" is to be fulfilled
in the finality of nature, whose products appear to us as perfected forms despite
changes in their shapes. On the other hand, the work of art, always only a possible
solution standing before an endless task, has to be redefined.[62] Thus, along with
the aesthetic ideal, the neoclassical notion of the closed, formally perfect work
and its corollary, the receiver's passive contemplation, were abandoned. From
this point on the reader or viewer had to become the poïetic interpreter of a meaning always in need of reconstitution. He thereby becomes the cocreator of the no
longer perfectible aesthetic object.

I doubt whether this discrediting of the neoclassical aesthetics of perfection also entails the elimination of the need for the perfect. It is clear that even the most radical avant-garde art, when it problematizes its own aesthetic status by selecting the most arbitrary, aesthetically indifferent objects, still relies on the horizon of understanding engendered by the previous artistic canon. This is necessarily the case, since it is only such predication that can set in motion the observer's aesthetic reflection as to whether "this is still or also art." So it is that although perfection seems to lose its secular validity as an aesthetic norm, it survives by functioning heuristically. How else could modern art become understandable, enjoyable, and communicable despite its proclaimed resistance, if not through an "anticipation of perfection," which, according to Hans-Georg Gadamer, governs all understanding.[63] It is not my job to dispute this premise of philosophical hermeneutics. If it turns out that Gadamer has incorrectly judged other comprehension in terms of aesthetic comprehension, that would be a final plus for my thesis, since it would mean that even philosophy cannot effortlessly separate itself from the aesthetic *fascinosum* of the perfect.

3. The use of fiction in the perception and representation of history

a) The res fictae *as historiographic nuisance*

Reinhart Koselleck recently introduced two demands into the theoretical debate about historiography, demands that are also relevant for literary hermeneutics. According to Koselleck, modern historiography must ponder more seriously than before, "first, that despite his theoretical zeal and consciousness, today's historian is still faced with the epistemological challenge posed by the classical juxtaposition of *res fictae* and *res factae*; and second, that it is especially the modern discovery of a specifically historical time that has since forced the historian to adopt a perspectival fiction about reality if he wishes to render the past."[64] As a result, today's historian can no longer cling to the ideal of a naive historical realism, or believe that it is only necessary to free representation of the *res factae* from the fictional in order—as Ranke formulated it—"[to arrive] at a perception of what is objective about important facts."[65] Recognizing the role of the *res fictae* in constituting the meaning of all historical experience, the historian must, from now on, consciously begin to employ the agency of fiction, whose cognitive and representational achievements have been overlooked because of a prejudice that needs further examination: the objection to a so-called aestheticization of reality. This prejudice arises directly from the assumption that *res factae* and *res fictae* can be separated in the same way material and form, historical process and rhetorical trappings are—as if the historian can draw from his sources some higher or-

der of facts that is pure and objective, and that it is only a second act, the translation of reality into a narrative fiction, that brings aesthetic means into play—
means the historian usually tends to regard with a certain anxiety and bad conscience. This prejudice has been eliminated from hermeneutic reflection thanks
to the realization that the *res factae* is not something primary, but the result of
an effort to constitute meaningful facts on the basis of elementary patterns of con-
ceiving and representing historical experience. Historical and literary hermeneutics together should take up the task of elucidating the fictional status of these conceptual patterns.

It should be clear that "aestheticization" can no longer be dismissed as the supposed naïveté of the older rhetorical mode of writing history. Neither is it primarily the result of the application of epic or novelistic forms of fictional narrative
in historiography. *Aestheticization*, or, using a term here that is less open to misunderstanding, *fictionalization*, is always at work in historical experience. The
what of the event is always conditioned by the perspectival *when* of its being perceived or reconstructed. It is further conditioned by the *how* of its representation
and interpretation. Thus, its meaning is continually adjusted by additional deter-
mining factors. If we are able to confirm the working hypothesis that "every form
of representation is also grounded in a particular experience of historical reality,"
then, as Karlheinz Stierle suggests, a particular role played by the fictive might
be worth examining as the means of mediation between the primary modes of perceiving historical experience and secondary, representational modes: "Fiction
makes it possible actually to grasp the various modes of perceiving historical experience" and produces the reader's "first real awareness of his own capacity to
construct complex experiences."[66] This puts both historical and literary hermeneutics on notice as to their responsibility for producing more precise concretizations of those functions of the fictive that come into play, usually unnoticed,
in the prenarrative practices of exemplary history as well as in the now-classic
narrative modes of historiography, and, finally, also in the postnarrative descriptions of long-term processes of "social transformation." They must inevitably
come into play when historical writing claims to be more than a mere archiving
of knowledge about the past—when it is a question of opening up the experience
of the past and making it communicable for any given present through the functional use of the fictive.

Literary historians are familiar with the communicative accomplishments of
the fictive because of their knowledge of the genesis of the *verisimile* and the history of its functions. Its most recent phase began during the Enlightenment—at
the same time, that is, as the "discovery of a specifically historical time" that made
it necessary "to intermix fiction and factuality again"[67]—and can likewise be
characterized in literary practice as an interaction between fiction and reality,
while in poetological theory it appears as the assertion of a specific "truth of
fiction." The one-sided understanding of autonomous art that developed there-

after always left concealed or forgot that poetic fiction, once it became autonomous, claimed to express a "truth" about the historical world even as it turned its
back on and disputed the "reality" of history in order to produce an "other world"
or "second nature." The fictional literature of the bourgeois era is no less involved
in the discovery of the world as history than is the new discourse of historicism.
The invention of the historical novel by Walter Scott is only *one* phase in the process of a literary comprehension of the world, an undertaking that includes
Richardson's epistolary novel and Balzac's *Comédie humaine*, and that employs
the medium of fiction to explicate and judge history in terms of everyday reality
and social totality.

In this process the classical separation between *res fictae*, the realm of poetry,
and *res factae*, the object of history, is abolished. Poetic fiction becomes the horizon of reality, and historical reality becomes the horizon of poetry. The specific
"truth of fiction" is, at this point, none other than that probability through which
history, from Chladenius on, has been able to perceive "a historical form of reality that it could call its own."[68] It is clear that the probable, by its very nature,
draws on a truth that stands as a "general mean" between the universal, that is,
the always true, and the actual/individual. Aristotle's *Poetics* shows this most
clearly when, in dealing with the handling of fictional means, it discusses the bor-
derline case in which a literary work embodying something impossible (even invented) that is believable is to be preferred to one embodying something possible
(even historically factual) that is not believable. This distinction is also of interest
to a theory of historiography, since, according to Aristotle, that which is purely
fictive, but probable, becomes believable when it is supported by a general principle ("the intention to represent that which is better," or "received opinion"; Chapters 24/25, 1461b). The probable, by mediating the difference between fact and
fiction in this manner, also generates the cognitive and communicative functions
of the fictive. The poetics (after Diderot and Lessing) and the historiography of
the Enlightenment activated this notion of the probable once more, and it has constituted the common zone of literary and historical writing ever since.

The famous, even notorious question as to whether these two genres part company during their competition to represent the world as history can, at this point,
no longer be answered by saying that historical representation in literature opens
itself to fiction, while history, which conceives of itself as the expression of reality, excludes it. It makes no difference whether the modern novelist narrates what
might have happened, whereas the historian reports what in fact happened; they
are both dependent on fictive means as soon as they begin their narrations—when
the novelist decides to construct "a picture of the past" or the "life and customs
of his age," and when the historian, because of the distance in time, is forced to
construct an abbreviated account of some prior reality on the basis of a diffuse
mass of sources.[69] Literary and historical writing can better be distinguished on
the common ground of the probable, in terms of the different ways they employ

the means of fiction, and the different expectations they may arouse in their readers. The reader of Scott's *Quentin Durward* can enjoy the fiction of a prior world as fiction, without posing questions about actual truth and invention. On the other hand, the reader who wishes to learn from Ranke how French history really unfolded in the sixteenth and seventeenth centuries can assume that the *res fictae* only serves to bring the *res factae* into view. These different attitudes toward the fictive or the factual aspects of a story can, of course, be reversed: *Quentin Durward* can also be read as a bit of medieval history (when the fictional parts are removed, a picture of the past remains that is replete with authentic details). Ranke's *French History*, on the other hand, can easily be regarded as a "historical work of art" and thus be enjoyed in the same manner as a Scott novel. That this is not just an empty claim, but, rather, a quite common mode of reception among Ranke's readers is revealed by the satirical critique in Droysen's *Historik*: "We seem to have established artistic representation and the 'historical work of art' as the primary aims of our science, and we celebrate as the greatest historian of our era the man whose representations stand closest to those found in the novels of Walter Scott."[70]

In Droysen's *Historik* this critique of Ranke's work is supported by an analysis of the narrative means used in historiography such as Ranke's. Droysen focuses particularly on three things achieved by the "form of the narrative": the completion of a process, the closure of beginning and end, and the representation of a picture of the past. Typically enough, he deals with the use of these constitutive narrative devices under the negative rubric of fiction as *illusion*. "Even the manner in which narrative form is usually employed creates illusion, willfully so—as if we had before us a completed process, a series of interlocking events, motives, and goals" (p. 144). Typically enough, that is, since Droysen, for whom historiography can be neither a philosophy of history nor a "physics of the historical world," and "least of all a poetics for the writing of history" (*Grundriss*, §16), completely avoids the concept "fiction" in his *Historik*, replacing it with "illusion."[71] Droysen is obviously intent on depriving narration in general of its traditional primacy in historiography. In his four "forms of explanation," he juxtaposes the narrative to the investigative, the didactic, and the discussive (§§ 90–93), as if the latter do not rely on narrative form. But it turns out that the investigative (as the "mimesis of our searching and finding"; p. 274), the didactic (insofar as it explains the past as the process of creating our present; p. 306), and even the discussive (as the elucidating of an event in the present in terms of its coming into being; p. 276) must narrate in order to mediate between the past and the present, or to explain the "coming into being of this present."

The question "How do you handle narrative?" has since become the crucial question. Whether Droysen was able to resolve it *in praxi* after failing to answer it sufficiently in his *Historik*, and whether it ever occurred to Ranke, are questions that can be passed over here and left to the judgment of the professional historian.

In an earlier essay I showed that Ranke's historical writing is largely characterized by its use of the fictional (that is, artistic) tools of the narrative. He adopts them as a matter of course, not recognizing that they undermine his claims to objectivity.[72] At the same time I tried to answer the additional question as to which literary models have—often surreptitiously—codetermined the narrative form of academic historiography. They are, first, the history of stylistic periods shaped by Winckelmann, which is visible in the stages of development and the notion of self-contained epochs found in Ranke's work, and, second, the paradigm of the work of art that reveals its full significance in time—through the labor of interpretation. In this sense, conceived of as an unfolding event, the work of art is definitely analogous to Droysen's notion of continuity as *historical work*, which "creates something new and more with each new and individual appearance" (p. 91). It is the right of both historical and aesthetic observation to construe the facts or the work "in the light of the significance they have acquired due to its effects" (p. 91). If I mention my earlier essay again here it is in order to submit it to substantial revision. At the time I was satisfied with finding Ranke guilty of illegitimate use of fictional means (in the light of his claim to objectivity); now I am interested in legitimating the use of fiction in writing history by tracing the elementary conceptual forms from which are derived the fictional means employed by classical narrative history and—in contrast to it—exemplary historiography.[73] It is these forms that first make it possible to lift historical experience from the diffuse events of historical reality, present it in model terms, and pass it on from generation to generation. Thus, the use of fictional means serves historiography in ways other than simply mediating between the results of current academic research and its addressee, "the circle of readers on the other side."[74] Such usage also bridges the gap between present and past, and in so doing first makes the alterity of distant and alien worlds comprehensible and communicable—thanks to the revelatory power of fiction, or, borrowing Droysen's (less precise) formulation, through "analogies of historical experience" (p. 159).

b) The hermeneutic function of the "three illusions" of classical narrative history

Droysen's polemic against narration omits any recognition that even investigative, didactic, and discussive representations of history (if one understands them as he does, as "the mimesis of becoming") cannot do without the "story" form if they are to include and reflect upon "our conception of significant events from this standpoint, this point of view" (p. 285). But his polemic hits its mark—the "artistically" closed narrative form of the historical school—with hitherto unmatched precision. In so doing it brings three essential functions of the fictive to light *ex negativo*, as "illusions" that have not been subject to reflection. These three functions of the fictive are constitutive of narrative historiography.

The first of these fictions is the "illusion of the complete unfolding of a course of events." Although every historian should know that our historical knowledge remains forever incomplete, the prevailing form of narrative (thus runs the critique to be examined here) awakens "illusion that serves to engender a sense of having before us a complete unfolding of things historical, a self-enclosed chain of events, motives, and goals" (p. 144). Historical narrative makes itself useful insofar as readerly comprehension experiences no interruption, even when its fiction narrates a real course of events that, in itself, is markedly incomplete. Thus, one of the primary achievements of a fictionalization of that which is narrated is the construction of a fictive consistency that eliminates both gaps in the narrated series of events and surplus details. This allows a gradual integration of the originally disparate events into a homogeneous structure of meaning, and, finally, the production of a self-sufficient whole, "complete in itself" (p. 285). This is the aesthetic effect Droysen has in mind when he calls upon historians to leave such gaps visible and avoid "wanting to fill them in with fantasy." A historical presentation would otherwise inevitably "become a novel" (p. 285). But the fiction of a complete course of events, one that allows no interruption, cannot automatically be regarded here as aesthetic. Historiography must always rely on this initial fictionalization if the historian hopes to present historical experience in a coherent manner. If gaps are allowed, they nonetheless point to a meaning structure that reaches beyond the facts, one that can experience no fragmentation except when it finds itself at the threshold of the future, which inevitably sets limits on the historian's current point of view.

What is aesthetic in a real sense is the illusion of a "totality complete in itself" that transforms a segment of narrated history into an aesthetic object, into a "novel" that appears to be a self-sufficient work of art. In order to avoid this aesthetic effect, leaving gaps is not enough. What is required is a particular countercurrent that aims at a representation whose significance remains open. This sort of oppositional narrative structure is more intimately a part of the modern artistic prose that came into being in the eighteenth century than it is of historiography. One needs only to think of *Tristram Shandy* or of *Jacques le fataliste*, novels that not only regularly thematize the gaps in their narratives (gaps the reader must fill in by drawing on his own fantasy), but that also develop an extremely rich set of means for breaking through the "totality complete in itself" and thus prepare the way for the "open work" of our modern era.

The second fiction of classical narrative historiography is the "illusion of a clear origin and definite end." Here Droysen demonstrates a clear-sightedness unusual for his time by uncovering and rejecting the "false doctrine of the so-called organic development of history" (p. 152): "It is completely outside the realm of historical research to arrive at a point that could be, in a full and complete sense, the origin, the unmediated beginning" (p. 150). And it is equally invalid to assume "that an earlier moment has within it all the seeds of that which occurs later," or that historical matters end in the definite manner found in Ranke's presentation of the history of the Reformation period, since "that which has already come into being contains within itself all the elements of new unrest" (p. 298). It is precisely when historical narrative proceeds along genetic lines and tries to explain something of its origins that it once again falls prey to a law of fiction, namely, the Aristotelian requirement that a plot have a beginning, middle, and end— moreover, a beginning that does not itself necessarily arise from something else, and an end after which only some other matter can make its entrance.

Thus, beginning and end are always a more or less fictive arrangement tied to a historically grounded structure of meaning, even when they deal with factual events. They are the first and last segments of a sequence of occurrences that sets itself off from the uneventful sameness of the historically quotidian and acquires meaning through its eventful middle or transitional sections. This is quite evident in the well-known embarrassment historiography experiences at its inability to take a historical event of the magnitude of the Reformation or the French Revolution and extend it backward or forward, to its prehistory or to the history of its aftermath, starting from the middle of such a "transition from one epoch to another." Thus, the teleological principle embedded in the poetic plot line, the need for a beginning, middle, and end in order to achieve a higher truth than that found in the mere contingency of reported history, also emerges as a necessary "illusion" in scientific historical writing. It is necessary because the beginning and end are the hermeneutic agents that first reveal the meaning of an event; and also because the beginning, if set or evaluated in some other manner, could suggest a different meaning for the same events when considered in relation to the end result.

It is not the (meaning-productive) fictionalization of beginnings and ends that is unscientific, therefore, but rather, as Droysen showed with regard to mythic beginnings, their overvaluation or mythification: "The illusion becomes even more problematic if one wants to look for the beginning in this manner in hopes of discovering there the essence of things, the true seeds from which all developed" (p. 149). Nevertheless, it is worth thinking about this when examining the modes of experiencing history implicit in various representational forms. On its own, the classical/Aristotelian structural formula for the fictional narrative can thematize the meaning of historical experience in fundamentally different ways, depending on whether the historian gives precedence to the beginning, the end, or the difference between the two (e.g., a difference indicating a totally transformative epochal change) as a means of constituting the significance of his history. Herein lies the largely unexplored potential for a specific theory of historiographic genres. I will return to this question later.

The third fiction of classical, narrative historiography is the "illusion of an objective picture of the past." Whoever believes, as Ranke did, that the historian needs only to turn away from his self-interest and forget the present (p. 306) in order to arrive at the undistorted past can no more guarantee the validity of the longed-for "pictures of the past or images of that which has been" than can poets or novelists (p. 27). Even if the past could be captured "in the total expanse of its former presence" (p. 27), the "measure of weight and significance" (p. 283) would not reside in things past, but would result from reflection on a point of view from which their fullness and variety could be presented as a relative whole. "Only that which is without thought is objective," since "it only seems that [historiographic] 'facts' speak for themselves in a totally 'objective' manner. They would be mute without the narrator who allows them to speak" (§91).

The logical way to reverse this objectivist illusion would be to recognize the perspectival function of the fictive. Droysen was less clear on this point than Chladenius in his *Allgemeinen Geschichtswissenschaft* (1752): "It redounds to Chladenius's credit that he was able to show that the reality of the past cannot be recaptured through representation. Moreover, it can only be reconstucted by means of reductive statements. And the historian's awareness of historical perspective forces him to be all the more conscious of the agencies of fiction (Chladenius refers to rejuvenated scenes) if he wishes to give a meaningful account of history."[75] Distance in time does not simply force the historian to fabricate some prior reality; it also allows him to use fictive means to actually set this reality in perspective vis-à-vis the immense and growing wealth of things past. That is, it allows him to reduce and thereby rejuvenate, but also to fill in the detail and thereby accent, the significance of the reality he represents. Perspectival fictionalization is the narrative equivalent of the situation within which the historian is bound, just as, on the other hand, the probability achieved in the resulting narrative leads to the limited, testable, and repeatable and altogether historical form of the truth found in the historian's judgments: the conscious use of fiction turns that fiction into a source of knowledge.

The charges leveled against aestheticism should only be brought to bear on the sort of history written by Ranke when it submits to the ideal of scientific objectivity, and refuses to admit that the reality of the past cannot be reexperienced or represented without the use of fiction, or, more precisely, without the necessary fictions embodied in the consistency of the unfolding narrative, the structuring of beginning and end, and the perspectival ordering of factual events. A historian who uses fictive means without further thought is the one most likely to run the risk of turning history into an aesthetic object—into a *theatrum mundi* or a self-representing "play of the past."[76] Ranke, who stands for the principle that the historian must erase himself in order to let history more or less narrate itself, was not aware that the immanent aesthetic in his "objective representation" was finally no other than that found in the contemporary historical novel with which historiography was competing. The extraordinary success of the novelistic form developed by Walter Scott cannot be explained merely on the basis of its ability to reveal new material and give the past new poetic-anecdotal life—thus better satisfying the historical curiosity of a romantically inclined public than did traditional political historiography. Another reason that Scott's novels could challenge academic historiography in producing a singularizing representation of the past, one that history had previously been unable to create, is to be found in a formal principle.

What so impressed Augustin Thierry, Guillaume de Barante, and other historians of the epoch was not simply the suggestive power of the historical details and coloring of Scott's novel, nor the particular physiognomy of an earlier age that they bring forth; neither was it the perspective that made it possible to look at a historical event in terms of various groupings of individuals rather than the usual operations of the state. It was, before all else, the new form of "drama" as Scott proudly called it, an appellation that, for his contemporaries, implied a still unfamiliar form of dramatic narrative much more than it did a dramatic knotting of events: since the narrator in the historical novel was to remain in the background, history itself could be played out, and produce in the reader the illusion of being involved in the actions of the characters in the drama. This also puts the reader in a position to draw his own conclusions and make his own moral judgments, acts that, up to this point, had always been anticipated by the raisonneur-historian, a Hume or Robertson, for example.[77] These analogies between the poetics of the historical novel and the ideal of objectivity found in the historiography of the period speak for themselves.[78] In both cases we find the narrator playing a dubious role of avowed withdrawal while constantly serving as mediator or judge, a role that arose with the illusion of an unmediated representation of the past. Ranke's presence is revealed far more in his histories than is Scott's in his novels, mainly because Scott can delegate the function of narrator to one of his characters or adopt a perspective that masks it. Ranke constantly betrays himself by adopting ex post facto points of view and categories of aesthetic organization that could not have been employed by an eyewitness and/or judge of these historical events (such *post eventum* narrative assertions will be marked *n.a.* in what follows). His pointed severing of the links between epochs "as they really were" and "that which arose from them" is avenged in his historiography, though, especially at those points where a moment of judgment, of selection, of motivation, or of trying to unify events clearly presupposes the belated perspective of the historian. These moments create the impression that this perspective, which can only arise from historiographic reception and retrospective positioning, is already a part of the immanent order of prior things. In Ranke's histories, such inconsistencies are masked by the fictionalized narrative movement; indeed, they are masked in such a way that they remind one not so much of the developmental action in Scott's novels as of the historical movement in that art history that is conceived of in terms of stylistic periods.

c) An analysis of the use of fictional means in Ranke's historical writing

By analyzing the era of the English wars dealt with in Ranke's *Französischer Geschichte* (Chapter 1, Part 3), the following will expand on the thesis that Ranke's historical texts are defined by aesthetic categories best understood in terms of the latent paradigm embodied in a history of stylistic periods. The form Winckelmann gave this history is characterized by the transition-like emergence of each new period (a change of styles);[79] by the transparent diachrony of developmental gradations (for example, the four stages of Greek art: the old, the high, the fine style, the imitative style); and by the closure of its periods (styles have clear beginnings and definite ends, ends that are marked by the exhaustion of their particular lines of development).

In Ranke's presentation, the era of the English wars begins with a radical and manifold turn toward the new. After Louis IX, *the prototype for all religious monarchs*, and from the same Capetian lineage, *a character of another sort finally emerges*: Philip the Fair, representative of a specifically modern form of power politics (p. 78). He *was the first* monarch whose *reckless ambition* led him to *break through* the limits his forebears had imposed on the German empire's sphere of power. Here Ranke singularizes the beginnings of a political process as the deed of a "great man." Thus, he stages the new as a total break with the old. Philip, the "last" Capetian king, is the "first" to transgress the limits his ancestors had placed on power politics. This step is interpreted as a *hazardous* move into the uncertain, and, metaphorically, as a *breakthrough*; then comes a concluding reference to the *reckless pride* of one who is willing to act. The movement into the new is then thematized in terms of the conflict with Pope Boniface VIII, the collapse of the politics behind the Crusades, and the destruction of the Templars. In the last of these cases Ranke at first makes no effort to examine the truth of the charges leveled against the Templars. His justification is that "it is sufficient to note the change in ideas" (p. 79). The epoch-making significance of the dividing line between the old and the new can then be announced: "The era that had been invigorated by the idea of a general Christendom was finished (*n.a.*); the goods whose proceeds were to be used for the reconquest of Jerusalem were collected and put to use in the kingdom. . . . His (Philip's) whole being was already penetrated by the biting wind of the new history" (*n.a.*, p. 80)

Historical processes of such a general nature as those Ranke has chosen to examine here tend in reality not to meet at a dividing line between the old (" . . . was finished") and the new ("already penetrated . . . "). Instead, as structural history has shown us, multiple levels, crosscurrents, belatedness, and seduction bind them together. Ranke the narrator strides lightly across the heterogeneity of the contemporaneous, thanks to the use of perspective-granting and foreshortening fiction. He gives the moment of the new a function that one might call aesthetic. A "change in ideas" and the developemnt of a new period eventuate from an originary set of actions, and the way the world is viewed suddenly changes.

The idea of an originary moment (emphasized by the use of fiction) is only one aspect of Ranke's conception of the event. Events also transpire at ideal moments. From Ranke's narrative perspective, the struggle over the succession, in which the claim of Edward III of England to the French crown was denied on the basis of the Salic laws of succession, greatly enhanced the development of the modern state begun in France by Philip the Fair. It seems that the decision against the foreign pretender to the throne could not have taken place at a better time: "This reckless, isolated politics, which focused on France alone, had hardly been implemented when an event transpired that plunged the country into general confusion and threw it back entirely on itself" (*n.a.*, pp. 80–81).

Over this temporal stroke of fate, which leaves something to be desired in terms of dates ("had hardly been . . . "), Ranke covertly allows a teleology to reign, one that is visible in the linkage and gradation of the events that lead to the formulation of a final result: "The world was amazed not only to see the French flag fly in Normandy, but by the weakening of the centuries-old possession of Aquitaine by the English as well. England held only Calais. This was perhaps as great a piece of good fortune for the vanquished as it was for the victors, since the two nations had to separate so if each was to develop according to its inner drives" (*n.a.*, p. 95).

The narrative assertion, "since the two nations had to separate," embodies a naively applied *post hoc-propter hoc* argument. Ranke's narrative perspective ascribes an inner necessity to the contingent events that led to the early modern development of the nation-state, a necessity that was not visible to those who experienced the English wars, but which the narrator himself fully affirms—as his retrospective words of consolation to the vanquished reveal ("as great a piece of good fortune . . . "). One syntactic construct faces another here. The teleological (had to/was to) confronts the contingent (if/could have): "If the knights of France had done what those of Austria and Swabia did at Morgarten, a republicanization of northern France could have taken place" (p. 85). I found a syntactic construct thematizing contingency only once in our sample text, the historical "otherwise." Only a thorough reading could determine whether perspectival awareness of other, not yet realized possibilities remains this rare in Ranke's work as a whole. In the present text, the historical "otherwise" finally only serves once again to thematize a covert teleology. Historical significance manifests itself in that which had to happen in a certain way, not in that which could have happened, or that at which the active agents were unsuccessful. What Hegel referred to as the "cunning of historical reason" seems to prevail here, despite the fact that Ranke believed he had surmounted Hegel's "speculative philosophy of history."

Ranke assumes the history of the new epoch has its own telos, like that of a newly developing style, a telos that renders the individual or accidental event meaningful while making clear its place in the whole—as clear as the movements in those works that focus on a specific style, that involve themselves in each new turn of its development, and identify only those changes that are useful in describing it. This is most readily demonstrated in those places where Ranke's narrative art employs the fictions of temporal gradation and harmony in order to fit the heterogeneous into the general course of things. Heterogeneous events are introduced in stepwise fashion ("for centuries . . . , before long . . . , finally . . . "; p. 79) in order to enter the central action with the resounding "now" accorded a moment of great significance ("These important factions now came into play in the struggle over the succession"). Or the main plot can bring a previously hidden, heterogeneous event to the fore, marking its significance with a "fully," in order to include it in the general process. Thus, for example, the new power of the cities is first "organized in silence," then *supported by all deeper working elements*, and at last "fully" released by the English wars (p. 82). The temporal structure implicit in the word "fully," in the typical use of "now" (which often suggests "precisely now"), or in the combination "yes . . . but"; (p. 86) leaves out those chronological dates whose objective certification would be difficult, or which would disturb the harmonious course of things. It aligns the contingency of events in such a way that a pure diachrony of emphatically significant moments is produced.

The temporal continuum thus idealized follows the same steady upward and downward movement found in the process organized by a history of stylistic periods, but in this case the curve of events moves in the opposite direction, since Ranke's perspective illustrates the decline and reestablishment of monarchic power. The moment at which all heterogeneous activities are fully harmonized corresponds to the telos of a periodic history: "Meanwhile, the English wars broke out once more, and a moment arrived at which all these questions, however little they had to do with each other in the beginning, merged" (p. 88). The ideal nature of this moment is revealed when one notes that it is not synonymous with any of the events of this period (Agincourt, the Treaty of Troyes, Henry V's entry into Paris), and, moreover, that it symbolizes the deepest decline of the French crown. The upward movement begins with a hint of some higher necessity: "But his sword alone . . . could hardly have saved him [the dauphin]; he first had to separate himself from the . . . Armagnac faction . . . if he really wanted to be king of France" (p. 89). Once again, the "grand and saving moment," a moment upon which Ranke, as narrator, likes to dwell, fails to correspond to any concrete event. His description of the upward movement homogenizes the events and changes that serve to strengthen the monarchy, while the countercurrent of defeat is reserved for moments of decline. Thus, the idea, which was hidden within the events, and brought to light by the narrator as a moment of transition from one stage to another, can be fully realized, as mentioned previously, when the reader draws his conclusion about the history of the epoch: the idea of a new monarchic order, accompanied by the launching of a new concept of the nation—a nation that "develops in terms of its own inner necessities" (p. 95). However, the historian who seems to describe the closed historical individuality of this epoch so objectively also needs to explain the grounds for an interpretation and narrative perspective that betray a preference for the solid order of the monarchy (p. 94) and opposition to the suppressed idea of urban-popular and class movements.

It remains for me to discuss the perspective-producing fictionalizations that up to now have been looked at primarily in terms of foreshortening or enlarging presentations that permit general reflection or illustrative detail. It is striking that Ranke makes rather limited use of explicitly literary means that might awaken the reader's interest, such as apostrophe,[80] emphatic turns of phrase,[81] or picturesque details. On the other hand, his frequent narrative assertions and historical reflection have a much more powerful subliminal effect on the reader's point of view because of their ostensible objectivity. A simple detail, in itself expendable, can help one visualize a past event, as, for example, when Robert Lecoq lets the violence against the government take its course: "Finally two marshals, the dauphin's leading advisers, the king's representatives, were killed *before his eyes* by a rebellious crowd that burst into the palace under the leadership of the city's leading magistrate, Etienne Marcel" (p. 85). Such visualizing detail is also occasionally staged and rounded out as a tableau that speaks for itself. This is the case when Ranke deals with the history of the rupture between Orléans and Burgundy. This highly effective narrative (which brings a series of events to their conclusion) culminates in a macabre description: "For a while, the Armagnacs found themselves in power again, and exercised that power with great force; in 1418 the citizenry rose up and took terrible vengeance on them." The populace feasts its eyes on the amassed bodies "of those it had previously been obliged to obey" (p. 88).

A foreshortened perspective is provided, among others, by Ranke's narrative ex post facto assertions. They seem to provide an overview of a series of heterogeneous events and are frequently clothed in the trappings of historical reflection. The prototype for this can be found in Ranke's commentary on Philip's successful use of modern power politics: "He knew, or felt, that he was in accord with the nature of things" (p. 79). It is clear that a historian from our epoch (apart from Golo Mann) would avoid such statements, and leave to the novelist the task of saying what a "great man" thought or felt. From the point of view of narrative technique, the recourse to historical actions that are in accord with the "nature of things"—the imposition of a single perspective that forces everything that runs counter to it to submit to a finally victorious tendency—is the (hardly dispensable?) mode par excellence of fictional foreshortening. Ranke supported his boldest narrative assertion ("The biting wind of the new history blew through his entire being" [p. 80], an expression that has, not surprisingly, become a commonplace) with two additional historical concepts. One informs the first sentence of this chapter: "Two different conceptions of the highest degree of power can be distinguished among those who use such power self-consciously" (p. 78). This sort of distinction, which generates particular types of rulers (those whose actions are aimed at maintaining the given order of things, and those who seek to expand the power of their country), is certainly a usable "historical truth," that is, a statement whose validity lies in its capacity to produce generalizations, not universal truths. As such it can be used to elaborate on the gap between Philip and earlier French kings. But today it is unlikely that anyone would accept Ranke's next notion: "Generally speaking, what matters most with regard to actively effective men is the sum of their thoughts" (p. 80). This sentence obviously contains a *petitio principii* intended to salve the historian who takes the "sum of their thoughts" as a given when dealing with a great historical figure—after having already provided a foreshortened description of the total effect of these thoughts on an age.

Another type of foreshortening can be found in Ranke's representation of the urban-popular movement after 1357. Here he abbreviates a series of events that extend up to 1418 by introducing three exemplary happenings, which are, moreover, linked by (what seems to me to be cheap) reflection: "Sometimes changes in events also manifest themselves in subordinate personalities" (p. 88). Once Ranke even steps out of his role of knowing which group acts "in accord with the nature of things," and adds, "who would deny that the cities had justifiable complaints." But this move toward a presentation from the point of view of the opposition is immediately subverted by the addition of a moral judgment: "Their violent and dastardly behavior got in the way of their own desires and awakened in their opponents the feeling that they were defending a good cause" (p. 85).

On the other hand, some of Ranke's historical reflections achieve particular weight, effectively summarizing the insight gained from different events without relying on the teleology elsewhere sought after in secret. As an example one can look at Ranke's discussion of the results for France of the English wars—the firmer organization of the corporative state and the power of the crown: "The means of struggle became national institutions, just as in other grand epochs" (p. 91). In the context of this present discussion, it seems to me that it would be worthwhile to elaborate on the theoretical status of such judgments. In so doing one can discover a particular expectation embedded in their logic, one that may well be, as Hegel suggested, an enemy of the philosopher, but not so great an enemy of the historian. For Ranke, historical truth always carries within it the possibility that a single cause can produce opposing effects (as Odo Marquard says, a *bonum* from a *malum*), as the following thought demonstrates: "Although the danger arising from the inner divisions produced by the English wars was very great, the opposition to English domination also contributed to a reconciliation" (p. 90).

d) Approaches to an understanding of prenarrative modes of perceiving and representing history

The research program generated by a theory of historiographic genres, a program that should lead us from clear-cut representational forms to the operations of as yet unexplored modes of perception or analogues to historical experience, cannot limit itself to the classical, that is, to the form of historical narration corresponding to Aristotle's structural formulation. The poetics of fictional narration cannot be used to analyze the multiplicity of witnesses and texts that transmitted historical experience prior to the professional historiography of the nineteenth century. The norms for the literary function of the narrative are insufficient when it is a question of those preliterary forms of exemplary speech in which historical experience was shaped and handed down (as in the *historia docet*). Neither can it help us grasp the topical transposition of events into stories on the level of everyday linguistic communication. In addition, it is all too seldom noted that the grand forms of historiography, which arose when these stories were integrated into a single history, have in turn modified the classical structure of fictional narrative to such a degree that the same history can produce different meanings and transmit different experience depending on the various and thoroughly legitimate interests that provide the "emplotments" (Hayden White) that engender them.

In his analysis of narrative in everyday communicative processes, Wolf Dieter Stempel gives striking proof that, there, the transposition of the experienced into story does not follow, or only partially follows, the rules of literarily closed narrative fiction.[82] His experiment, which uses tape recordings to highlight the act of transposing experiences from everyday life, shows that when one returns to an event in the past the constitution of meaning does not necessarily depend on Aristotelian norms of plot: beginning and end do not have to be fixed absolutely in such stories. Neither must narrative connections be consistent. The selection of lived experiences and its interpretation can remain primarily subject oriented, and thus without need of referential support. The addressee does not measure believability primarily in terms of objective occurrence. Instead, believability stems from the exemplary aspects of the stories—those beyond truth or falsehood—that, as experiences, are both an experiencing of self and an experiencing of something other (in the realm of history before all else, the confirmation or correction of previous experience).[83]

The threshold to another stage in the articulation of life-world experience can be located at the point where experience of the self is depersonalized and its content elevated to a norm by enclosing it in exemplary speech acts. This level of meaning construction is familiar to the historian thanks to his experience with the secular tradition of the exempla. Even the representational form of the exempla does not at first require the fictional structure provided by classical narrative. This poses problems for the contemporary, hypertrophied 'narratology," which, following Greimas, claims to ground the deep semantic structure of all discourse in narrative.[84] Narrative should be looked at neither as the genetically primary or universal form of interpersonal communication, nor as the uniform matrix of all articulation of historical experience. Narrative, insofar as it is determined — literarily — by the unity of a plot's beginning, middle, and end, presupposes a whole gamut of preliterary forms of communication (i.e., forms that are not yet worklike, or have not yet been fixed as autonomous texts) that can be delimited by various *modi dicendi* (citing, attesting, announcing, persuading, demonstrating, etc.). I will not go into their life-world function as vehicles for thematizing the experience of daily life, since I can refer the reader to my attempt to revise André Jolles's morphology of *simple forms*. There I suggest that medieval variants of these forms embody a communication system based on the forms of exemplary speech.[85]

The claims of the exemplary are not simply surrendered at the moment one moves across the threshold and into the narrative representation of historical experience. Instead, these normative claims expand beyond the realm of individual actions to include the meaning of human action in the larger context of the world experienced as history. Even the literary forms of historiography do not produce primarily disinterested narratives. They do not answer the question of "how it really was." Neither do they serve to satisfy some free-floating historical curiosity. Their primary life-world function — to secure the past from forgetfulness — is guided by a practical interest in knowledge that (as Jörn Rüsen formulates it) constitutes historical experience "as a meaningful linkage of past human actions with things present and future."[86] Thus, in narrative historiography, be it religious or secular, meaning no longer simply arises from the lesson that can be drawn from an action regarded as a precedent for future acts. Instead, meaning, which must take the form of a narrative, stems from the way historical fact takes on the allure of an event. According to Karlheinz Stierle, this allure can be defined as the "conceptual difference" that arises because of the historical fact's dual dependency — on both the beginning and end of an occurrence. "The narrative structuring of history unites beginning and end both as a real course of events and as a conceptual configuration. Only then does a history come into being . . . that not only asserts a connection between beginning and end, but makes this connection 'relevant.' However, it is only relevant when it reveals the basis for its selection from the dichronic and synchronic orders of universal connection."[87]

Not the smallest advantage of this definition of the relationship between historical experience and narrative form is that it allows us better to grasp the status (as event) of that which is today often only described in an objectivist manner as a "structural transformation," and left unexplored from the hermeneutic point of view. I see here a resolution to the debate about the advantages and disadvantages of the "event" as a concept in historiography. A historical fact would not, in this case, become an event as soon as "human actions and plans are clearly and unexpectedly altered by the action of other human beings."[88] Historiography (and, for that matter, the history of any art) must include openness of meaning in its overall notion of the event: a historical nexus first becomes relevant in the experience of the retrospective observer; that is, it acquires meaning that the participants or those affected cannot recognize while in the midst of diffuse and not yet completed happenings. "The eventlike lies, here and everywhere, in the opening of a horizon of possibility by distancing and reassimilating that which remains closed to those who live the occurrence as a continuity."[89] Thus, a historical fact, understood as an event, is not a simple subjective schema of appropriation, since meaning—the meaning of something for someone—must arise in equal parts from the objective, closed occurrence and its subjective relevance for the position-bound observer. Thanks to narrative form, historical meaning, understood as the conceptual difference between beginning and end, can be thematized as an event whose relevance varies according to the different arrangements of beginning and end. A spectacular historical moment or a *commutatio rerum* of the type "See, everything has been made new," is unnecessary in this case.

I can provide an example of this from an essay by Arno Borst: "The French thought September 1792 so important that they began a new calander on the twenty-second of that month, not because of the cannonade of Vlamy, however, but because of the proclamation of the republic in Paris." For the German participants in the *campaign in France* on the other hand, September 20, 1792, and the cannonade of Vlamy (given another beginning and a different end) formed the center of an axis of relevance, an event that Baron von Messenbach would later (1809) use as a personal justification, apostrophizing it as "the most important day of the century" ("We lost more than a battle"). Still later (1820–21), Goethe wished to elevate and stylize this event, giving it general significance for world history ("Here, today, a new epoch in world history begins, and you can say that you were there"). But this evaluation has not withstood the criticism leveled by historical research. The results of this research do not grant the cannonade of Vlamy significance as an epoch-making event. It is presented as a historical fact that was overestimated because it had acquired subjective relevance for a well-known poet who saw it as a "turning point." This led to a falsification of the facts of the event and its results.[90]

Even the example Droysen uses to explain why the historian needs the "analogies of historical experience" fails to point out any single event (p. 159). At the beginning of the nineteenth century there were no longer any free peasant farmers in England, the so-called freeholders, of which there were still 160,000 in 1684. Conceptualizing this difference as the demise of the peasant class makes an event of a historical fact that can be comprehended only indirectly in terms of its end results. This happens despite the fact that the historian can provide a hypothetical reconstruction of this pragmatic nexus only if he calls to mind similar happenings

on the Continent (for example, the expropriation of peasant lands in Mecklen-
burg) that are already known and open to narration. From the hermeneutic point
of view, the change in the conditions of the English peasant class between 1684
and the beginning of the nineteenth century becomes historically comprehensible
by reconstructing the actual changes as an event "on the basis of other experience
and knowledge of analogous conditions." Thus, the event, which demands narrative form in order to make its relevance comprehensible to the retrospective observer, becomes a hermeneutic category not because of its singularity but, rather,
because of its capacity to open analogies of experience to historical knowledge,
or—if you will—because of its standardizability.[91] What is made available
through the notion of the event (conceived of as conceptual difference in the manner of Stierle) is a "historical truth" that, thanks to the use of analogy, allows the
experience of the past to be used as a means of understanding present or future
history. For Droysen, such analogies in historical experience were primarily a
matter of heuristics (see §26), not hermeneutics. He was content in his conviction
that "it is a question of human events that are comprehensible to us as such thanks
to our similarly constructed natures" (p. 146). As far as he was concerned, analogies between historical experiences were limited only by the "anomalous" ("the
individual, free will, responsibility, genius"; p. 427). The problem of establishing
norms of historical experience, and, along with it, the question of how the alterity
of past life can be recognized or slighted by using conscious or unconscious analogies, is certainly in need of further discussion. But this can only happen once the
repertoire of narrative models available to historiography and the types of events
that inform them are worked out.

Stierle's description of the characteristics of the event, based as it is on the conceptual difference between beginnings and ends, also allows us to distinguish
among transformations of historical experience within narrative structures—just
as different meanings can be granted to the pragmatic conditions of one and the
same historical occurrence depending on the conceptual configuration of its beginning and end. I would like to suggest that the simplest means of making such
distinctions is to ask whether the beginning or the end, or the transformation of
things between the beginning and end, of a narrative history has been overemphasized. If the beginning is overemphasized we have an originary narrative that follows the basic model found in the myth of the Fall: one event, placed or reconstructed at the beginning, becomes the origin and explanation of all later events.
Overemphasizing the end results in a teleological structure whose original model
can be found in Christian eschatology. If, on the other hand, the difference between the beginning and end is brought to the fore, the result is a thematization
of the contingent as a course of events that—formulated in modern terms—can
only be explained historically. This is known in medieval tradition as a narrative
type embodying the classical model of the *laudatio temporis acti* or the *fortuna*
schema.

The various means of inscribing historical experience in different narrative forms, each of which can legitimate a specific aspect of an occurrence, can be thought of as different and fundamental ways of mastering contingency: by absorbing that which stands in the way, by eliminating or preserving the singular, and by problematizing. When using the term "absorption," I have in mind the integration of pagan history in Christian redemptive history (as a prehistory or as topological or contrastive according to the schema of the two *civitates*). Alfred Ebenbauer has developed a new explanation of "elimination" using the hagiography that developed from classical biography. He suggests that it is a narrative type in which the redemptive events of the Incarnation and Parousia are significant only when they bear on the salvation of the individual. Everything else can be left out of this type of history.[92] The term "preservation," then, serves as a means of dealing with the annals or chronicle forms of historical representation that Gert Melville distinguishes from *historiographia*, which subordinates the temporal sequence of occurrences to the context of events in the *res gestae*. According to Melville, medieval annals and chronicles can be categorized as *chronographia* (*tempora rerum solum annotare*). The latter, because it is linearly unlimited and without factual closure, can only carry out, never bring to an end, the inscription of that which is worth preserving.[93] The word "problematizing" points to those modern forms of historical narrative that, according to Hermann Lübbe, try to deal with material that cannot be construed rationally as action or functionally as a system. Such material can be understood only historically, through the narration of a singular story. This is the source of the conceptual difference that, in Lübbe's examples, takes the form of a contradiction between the intention and the result of a historical action.[94] If the teleological principle of classical narrative history is undermined by this opposition, the experience of historical contingency itself tends to compensate for the disappointment produced by a desire for meaning: that one can give something a historical explanation, but still not comprehend it (an obvious example would be the witch hunt), must be accepted as the ultimate and, for us, only remaining sense of history. The historian who is unable to accept this possibility can problematize the implicit acceptance of the real by turning to a narrative form for which precedents can be found both in the older rhetorical modes of historiography and in the work of one of Ranke's contemporaries, a man who was of equal stature as a narrative historian.

e) J. P. Hebel's version of "the burning of Moscow" (rhetorical vs. scientific historiography)

The victorious campaign of the historical school not only reduced historical narrative to what seems to be a secondary function of historical research, it also discarded the idea of using rhetorical means to give presence to the past, since such gestures were simply "unscientific." On the other hand, Rüsen had good reasons for suggesting that contemporary historical theory ought to pay less attention to the (unnoticed) aesthetics of the historian and more to the rhetoric of the older historiography, especially when it is a question of discerning the site at which the process of constructing meaning employs facts from the past to produce something along the lines of a researchable history.[95] My example is not taken from the older tradition of exemplary history—the real site at which meaning is constructed from historical experience. Instead, it is chosen with an eye to that time in which a scientifically reoriented historiography devalued every sort of rhetorical history, leaving it to the naive didactics of the schoolbook, the diarist, and popular history. Johann Peter Hebel's reflections on the burning of Moscow (in the 1814 edition of the *Rheinischer Hausfreund* [The Rheinland Family Friend]) are more than a simple model of rhetorical historiography. From the the latter's repertory Hebel borrowed rhetorical and fictional devices he could use as elaborate means for transforming events from world history into case histories worth pondering. Indeed, it seems to me that it is just as worthwhile for modern historical theory to consider these cases as it was for his rather conservative readers in and around Baden. This is so because Hebel's seemingly naive version of the events proves to be more and more enigmatic and aporetic as one examines it. It problematizes the official historical explanations of this Napoleonic catastrophe and shows that "unscientific" rhetorical history can be more critical than a critical, scientific historiography that unknowingly objectifies its material aesthetically while believing that it is just providing historical explanation *sine ira et studio*.

When the war between France and Russia broke out in the year 1812, the situation in Europe was as follows: the House of Austria, with an expeditionary corps, all the princes of the Rhein alliance, Switzerland, the people of Italy, Illyria, Prussia, and Poland, almost all of Europe, was on the side of the emperor of France. On the Russian side were the English, and later, the winter as well. The Danes, the Swedes, and the Turks were neutral. — Spain and Portugal took separate stands.

After many heavy but victorious engagements the French emperor's dreadful army soon reached Moscow, the Russian capital. On the fourteenth of September the emperor entered the gates of the city as its conqueror. This might have been a time to speak of peace, had one so wished, but one did not. Better to have one's city burned to the ground and the enemy driven out.

Well, "Moscow was burned to the ground" is easily said. But gentle reader, a clear idea of this city might leave you speechless.

Moscow, arguably the largest city in the world, in fact consisted of four great, contiguous cities. The innermost was the Kremlin, which was fortified, and was destroyed by the French themselves. Surrounding the Kremlin was the town of Kitaigorod, and beyond it the town of Belgorod, the white city (as you know, your Family Friend speaks Russian), and around Belgorod was built Semlyanoigorod.

Four such cities, built together, would be big enough to burn. But Moscow had thirty suburbs as well, in all more than 20,000 houses and palaces, 1,000 churches and large chapels, close to 400 worthy inns, and who knows how many shops, factories, schools, and offices, a foundling hospital for 5,000 children, in a word, 400,000 inhabitants. It took twelve hours to cross. Anyone standing on an elevated site could see nothing but the sky and Moscow, no matter how far he looked. Later one saw nothing but the sky and flames. The French had hardly entered Moscow when the Russians themselves began to set fires everywhere. A persistent wind quickly carried the flames to every quarter. Within three days most of Moscow lay in ashes, and anyone passing through it afterward saw nothing but the sky and suffering.

Whoever considers the horror and suffering that result from a single house burning down, the terrible luminosity of the night and the redness of the distant sky, can imagine how it looks when, in a space it takes twelve hours to cross, 40,000 buildings are on fire or in danger of burning, when so many churches and castles burn at once, and when 400,000 human beings, men, women, children, the old, the infirm, the sickly, princes, beggars, must flee or burn, and nothing can be saved, no fire put out. All fire hoses had quickly been removed. The roads were filled with escapees to a distance of several days' journey, the healthy, the sick, the dying, women well advanced in pregnancy, nursing mothers, and there was no midday meal, no roof at night. Here lay a sick man, with no one to carry him further; there a dying man is blessed by his sons; elsewhere others buried members of their families, and then moved on. Farther along lay a woman suffering the pangs of childbirth, who had to bear her benoni, the child of her pain, unassisted; then she too moved on. A noble woman cooked a meager noontime meal for her children over a pile of twigs while sighing, "Oh, how unfortunate I am." Another woman with a poor little child looked at her and wept as if she wanted to say, "Oh, how fortunate you are that you have something to cook." Your Family Friend will not enumerate the number that perished.

Whoever set Moscow ablaze has a great deal to answer for. Is anyone else responsible for the withdrawal of the French emperor's victorious army, a withdrawal that took place in midwinter and in the freezing cold because of the absence of food and shelter, a withdrawal first from Russia, later from Poland, then from Prussia and from Germany up to the Elbe. The horses died from cold and deprivation. Artillery and baggage had to be left behind, surrendered to the Cossacks who swarmed in pursuit. Thousands of brave warriors died. Bayonets and marching to the attack are of little help against the winter; in such cases a warm fur and a leg of veal can accomplish much more than a chest swollen with courage.[96]

In terms of historical genres, this text can be defined as a literary arrangement of that "simple form" that Jolles named "memorabile." He regarded it as the modern equivalent of the classical *apomnemoneuma*.[97] The meaning produced by "something that has excerpted itself from history" is based on an experience of the factual, an experience that has concretized itself as an event looming above the everyday historical in such a way that it remains memorable. Unlike the example, which extracts a clearly formulated moral lesson from some earlier deed in order to guide future actions, the memorabile gives a meaning to historical experience that is complex, often paradoxical, and even unfathomable. This creates the formal possibility of using the narrative trope known as the "antithetical detail." In other literary genres the detail has a subordinate function. It helps in the gradual construction of a recognizable whole (e.g., a moral type in the example, an "active virtue" in the legend, a specific individuality in the anecdote), or, more generally, follows the dictates of an expectation of meaning that, in accord with the economy of the classical narrative, must be satisfied. The detail in the memorabile, however, has a coordinate function oppositive to that of a self-formulating expectation of meaning. It serves as a fact that is not part of the causal or fundamental context of the narrated incidents and thus produces an unexpected shift in the level of signification. Therefore, in Hebel's virtuoso performance, oppositive detail can both be a means of satisfying the reader's need for a concrete presentation of the major historical events of his day and, implicitly, serve the enlightened goal of making him "reflect on and think through, verify and correct, of leading him to exercise his critical faculties."[98]

Unlike Jolles, I want to give greater emphasis to the nonteleological function of the memorabile, despite the fact that it is clearly more difficult to show, since it requires a more sophisticated analysis of traditional rhetorical historiography. But even the trivial form of memorabile, in which coordinate detail validates a superordinate factuality, allowing what appears to be a higher truth to spring forth in the end, does not thereby produce an exemplary significance, that is, one that has relevance for later actions. What is thought-provoking about a memorabile such as that concerning the murder of the Prince of Orange or that on the burning of Moscow derives not from their ability to serve as guidelines for later action, but from their expression of the unavoidable contingency of historical existence. They can lead to insights that can be gleaned from both the older memorabilia and the more recent *faits divers* in the newspaper: "This is the way things are! In this single event, standing out from others as it does, the condition of the age manifests itself."[99]

Among the artistic means and structures of appeal Hebel is able to employ in this diarist's historiography, the oppositive detail takes the lead. In the text cited here, it first appears in the singular, positioned in an anticipatory manner in an enumeration of the warring parties, then intermittently in a description intended to literally bring the readers in Baden closer to Moscow, and finally in a whole series of concrete scenes that are set against the abbreviated statement of events embodied in the sentence "Moscow was burned to the ground," in order to make the historical reality of the war imaginable. Enumeration is the daily bread of the historian and is usually thought of as the boring aspect of historical narrative; but with Hebel one discovers again and again what rhetorical value it can have. In the middle of his enumeration of the opposing military forces, the reader bumps into a coordinate detail that projects two heterogeneous powers onto a plain of equality: "On the Russian side were the English, and later, the winter as well." The syntactical surprise of this equating of dissimilar things— England and winter—prepares the way for the catastrophic historical surprise of the arrival of winter as Russia's greatest ally. Later, the reader will think back to this forecast of the final situation, after the significance of having the full force of winter against you is made clear to him. First the "Family Friend" reports Napoleon's conquest of Moscow, adding a word of his own: "This might have been a time to speak of peace, had one so wished, but one did not. Better to have one's city burned to the ground and the enemy driven out." Who is this "one" to whom he refers? Whose side is Hebel on? Apparently on the side of the Russians, as becomes clear in the next sentence (a so-called interior monologue!). But this *parti pris* does not remain so clear in what follows, especially at the end, so the reader is constantly provoked into thinking things through for himself.

The very next sentence obliges him to feel dissatisfied with what the official historiographer has noted in his diary: "Well, 'Moscow was burned to the ground' is easily said." This perspectival foreshortening of the events as a completed historical fact is set against an increasingly expansive description of all that was encompassed by this fact—and generally left out of the heroic reports and descriptions provided by the parties involved. Then again, this apparently disorganized enumeration is so laid out that its ongoing summary sheds new light on an official figure such as the 400,000 inhabitants of the "largest city in the world" (finally the number itself is provided!), as do the oppositve details. Since the ironic comment, "big enough to burn . . . ," would still be ringing in his ears, the citizen of Baden, astounded by the multitude of suburbs, palaces, churches, and so forth, would be especially shocked by the "400 worthy [!] inns" and the "foundling hospital for 5,000 children," and by the terse climactic statement about the results: "[one] could see nothing but the sky and Moscow . . . but the sky and flames . . . but the sky and suffering." What such perspective-granting fictionalization can accomplish when used rhetorically can hardly be better demonstrated than with these passages from Hebel's historical narrative. In them he first employs factual details alone. Then, when he is finished with his description of the burning city, he introduces more and more fictive scenes into his report on the flight of the city's inhabitants. Here we need to make a theoretical distinction between a primary fictionalization that would be impossible without a fitting description of the historical facts, and a secondary fictionalization in which the invented details or statements are used to enhance the vividness of the portrayal. In practice the reader would not perceive any threshold between the real and the unreal as the narrator inserts first factual details ("All the fire hoses had quickly been removed") and then fictive ("Here lay a sick man . . . there a dying man is blessed by his sons . . . ") in his description of the fire and flight. The primary fictionalization that makes these two "facts" conceivable at the outset is able to absorb details of fictional origin unnoticed – as long as the narrator sticks, as he does here, strictly to that which is probable given this historical situation.

This example can also provide us with a more precise explanation of what "perspectival fictions of the real" (Koselleck) are – fictions without which the past, which has disappeared, could not be revivified. Fiction gives historical narrative more than an ordered beginning and end, and more than consistency in its development. It also provides a perspective from which to view the historical situation. Since all description is dependent on perspective if it wishes to generate meaning of some sort (from the hermeneutic point of view, this means a dependency on the "to what end" of a leading question), the historian must fabricate if he wants to set a historical fact in its context. Fabrication allows him to impose a perspectival and, thus, selective ordering on a multiplicity of factual details. Even the sequential order of the individual details in a narrative can thereby become the carrier of a meaning that is not available in a diffuse historical reality. This becomes clear in the following example: "One can imagine how it looks when . . . 400,000 human beings, men, women, children, the old, the infirm, the sickly, princes, beggars, must flee or burn." It is no doubt true that all the individual types mentioned here were present among those who escaped the fire. But it is only their fictional alignment – after the topical pairing of opposites, men and women, children and old people, comes the surprisingly asymmetrical and ironic insertion of princes between sick people and beggars – that inscribes the event in a concrete context that gives meaning to this confrontation with the history and society of the Napoleonic era.

When Hebel then rounds out his evocation of the historical situation by inventing a scene that contrasts the misery of a noble woman and her impoverished counterpart, his intention is first of all to awaken pity, then to open the reader's eyes to the inexcusable human suffering caused by war, and prepare for his later discussion of the problem of responsibility. But his narrative strategy also includes another function of the fictive, one that has not yet been mentioned: the situational reality of a catastrophic event cannot be revealed as fully through a reconstruction of the facts as it can through conversion into a fictitious narrative dealing with the fate of the historical subjects involved. Hebel's technique is none other than that which acquired renewed status thanks to the recent film entitled

Holocaust. It was not the rigorous and critically aware claim to documentary validity in depicting Hitler's extermination of the Jews, but the recourse to a fictional narrative concerning the fate of one of the afflicted families that broke through the reification of historical knowledge. This made it possible for the observer to reexperience events that had become sedimented historical facts.

"Whoever set Moscow ablaze has a great deal to answer for." If the question that follows in the text seems to blame Napoleon's Russian opponents for an act that appears totally irresponsible given the preceding report concerning the innumerable dead, the narrator's next thoughts seem to imply a counterquestion concerning Napoleon's responsibility for the lost campaign and the justness of his utter defeat, a defeat made visible during the retreat to the Elbe. Of course, the measured judgments implicit in these rhetorical questions and in the faint hint of doubt concerning Napoleon's desire for peace are also determined by the strict censorship regulations in the Grand Duchy of Baden as well as by concern for a readership that had little sympathy for French or allied politics. But, as Klaus Oettinger has shown in a recently published appreciation, it is precisely within this narrowly circumscribed political space that J. P. Hebel's diary-like historiography achieved its narrative greatness. His conclusion can serve very nicely to verify one final "antithetical detail" in our text: "Hebel kept his distance from all the belligerent parties. Rightly seen, his reports *about* the war are written *in opposition* to the war."[100] His memorabile about the burning of Moscow provides the historical beginning ("When the war between France and Russia broke out in the year 1812") with a fictional ending that insists on the conceptual difference between war and peace found in events of international scope. The provocative closing sentence of the narrative contrasts the idealizing tendency of grand historiography (which is attacked more and more during the unfolding of the narrative), and its irresponsible presentation of "great issues," with a final ironic justification of everyday needs and the peaceful nature of the unheroic citizen: "Bayonets and marching to the attack are of little help against the winter; in such cases a warm fur and a leg of veal can accomplish much more than a chest swollen with courage."

My interpretation ought to show why Hebel's memorabile not only was conceived for the reader in Baden, but should be of renewed interest for a modern theory of history as well. The text examined here demonstrates, in its clear refusal to reduce events to a single narrative statement ("In 1812 Moscow was burned to the ground"), how the horizon of experience of a historical fact can be reconstructed and made communicable through fictional means. This is certainly a problem that still faces today's historian (but in a different way). In Hebel's history the detail inserted as a countercurrent becomes the prime instrument with which to disturb the apparent or the hidden teleology of conventional historiography. It problematizes the unannounced idealistic assumption that everything that is, is also reasonable, and prompts the reader to find an answer to the renewed question about the meaning of events—an answer that must arise out of the reader's situation and out of his own reflection. Although today no one may feel free to narrate history in the manner of the Rhineland Family Friend, I would nevertheless like to have the historian ponder the question of whether the paradigm provided by J. P. Hebel's rhetorical historiography needs to be replaced by other procedures (and of course by other fictional means as well), in an effort to solve the problem of how to produce a nonteleological history—a problem that has lost none of its actuality since Hebel's era.

B. A Questioning Adam: On the History of the Functions of Question and Answer

1. Adam, where art thou?

As certain as it is that not all questions have been posed all the time, it is equally certain that this is not sufficient grounds for assuming that there must be a "history of the question and questioning"[1] that can be narrated as an independent history. The history of each individual question is the history of the answers that such questions have been given as the historical horizon of understanding changes. Question and answer lose the appearance of having a stable, continuing significance in this context. Whoever understands conceptual history as a history of problems must constantly deal with the fundamental question posed by historical hermeneutics: why is a particular question posed and answered at a certain time and answered in a certain way? (Why not earlier? Why the difference later? Why has such a question not been asked recently? Why not for a long time?) Although such histories cannot be reduced to a single history of the question without falling prey to a universalizing tendency, it is on the other hand possible and worthwhile to conceive of a history of the roles played by question and answer, a history that can illuminate the way in which question and answer are put to use in the various realms of signification found in the praxis of life. Question and answer and their anthropological, mythological, theological, philosophical, juridical, political, and aesthetic roles have, as a result, been investigated to some degree by the relevant disciplines (at least this is the case in my own). The unification of these beginning efforts into a comprehensive history of the functions of question and answer has not yet taken place, however. This could only result from a clarification of their relevance for practical life and theory building within the competitive spaces elaborated by real intellectual powers and social institutions, and an elucidation of their field of play in the realms of the irrelevant and the trivial. I hope what follows will prepare the way for such a project. The scope of this work is limited to literary hermeneutics, and its primary goal is to examine the use of question and answer in order to illuminate the proximity of aesthetic experience to other signifying realms in life's praxis. As an introduction to this problematic, it seems to me that no better evidence could be brought forward than that which is possibly the oldest, and which opens the field of play to question and answer in the occidental, Christian tradition.

"Adam, where art thou?" (Genesis 3:9). The first question in biblical history posed to a human being is a question leveled by God, the Lord and Creator, at Adam, his creation. It is a question that passes down from above, a question emanating from the highest authority and directed at its unequal image. It begins the interrogation concerning Adam and Eve's misdeed and results in their expulsion from Paradise for disobedience. In this pragmatic context it is natural that the Lord can ask, while his servant, Adam, can only answer. The right to pose questions is a prerogative belonging to the master; to be obliged to answer and speak only when asked is the lot of the underling. This authoritarian question-and-answer structure is in no way limited to the archaic world; it extends well into the social history of the modern era. It can be found in the ceremonial structures of feudal society,[2] and survives today in its end phase in the imperative ritual of the military "dialogue." Its mythic substratum is that of a divine authority that owes an answer to no one and therefore refuses to be questioned as well. This leads to the need for special efforts (oracles, casting of lots), or sacred acts (sacrifices) in order to discover the alien will of God. The mythic function of the narrative tale is correspondingly understood and interpreted as a "making unquestionable": "Myths do not answer questions; they make unquestionable."[3] Whether or not the mythic function of question and answer is thereby exhausted remains to be seen. It is all the more significant, however, that, in our opening citation, the Yahwistic narrator poses God's first question to mankind in an ironic form.

The question, "Adam, where art thou?" is, strictly speaking, a spurious question. God the Lord knows very well where and why Adam is hiding. And his creation, Adam, fully understands the underlying significance of this ironic speech. He does not answer the "where," but responds to the implicit "why," and thereby submits to the interrogation that has just begun. The reason for God's indirect question cannot be explained unambiguously. Does the ironic form of the question indicate the cynically played out superiority of an absolute authority, or the understanding that the biblical God evinces toward his partner, Adam, in a difficult situation? The ambiguity of the original context is increased when one remembers that Yahweh occasionally uses the ironic form in later questions—

therapeutically, it would seem, in the case of the insubordinate prophet Jonah. Or does the Old Testament God love the ironic, suggestive, or rhetorical question, one that has no real sense of question about it, because there can be no open question for an omniscient God? This might be the position taken by an enlightened follower of Voltaire in a later context. As my literary interpretation will show, the ambiguity of God's ironic statements arises from a function of the question-and-answer structure that is already aesthetic.[4]

The fact that the narrative in Genesis 3, although it borrows from the older myths of the first couple and their expulsion from Paradise, moves beyond the mythic explanation of being highlights the theological function of question and answer. According to Karl Barth, Christian theology, which holds narrative to be the first dialogic experience of the divine, can interpret the question "Adam, where art thou?" in the sense of the priority of God's answer (as revelation) in the face of all human questions. The fact that, in Adam, all human beings are called into question from the beginning is the ground for both a human being's questions about God and his questions about himself.[5] In Rudolf Bultmann's theology, on the other hand, experiential knowledge of God is preceded hermeneutically by questions about God, thereby creating a bridge to philosophical hermeneutics, which grounds the possibility of all experience in the openness of questioning.[6] The priority of question or of answer, which implies the precedence of dialogic or monologic discourse, produces a division of understanding, one that separates not only philosophical and theological hermeneutics, but other disciplines as well, for example, rhetoric and (since Baumgarten) aesthetics from logic, or the linguistics of *parole* from that of *langue*.

Still, the Adam who is called into question in Genesis 3 is not a querying Adam, nor, certainly, is he the *animal quaerens cur* that the philosophy of history likes to propose as a definition of the maturity toward which man is evolving. The Adam of the biblical creation story becomes an inquiring creature only if one treats the query "Adam, where art thou?" applicatively rather than reconstructively. The "where" then refers to the situation of human beings in general, so that the query and its implicit call for self-reflection implicate all of us equally. This is the step taken by Wolfhart Pannenberg when he interprets the question directed at Adam as the expulsion of all human beings into "[their] own historicity, into the independence of [their] freedom." "This question does not ask the individual for a preestablished catechistic answer; it is addressed to him directly, and it can only be answered with one's own life."[7] It must be remembered, however, that historicity does not mean the same thing for theological hermeneutics that emancipation means for philosophical hermeneutics. This explains why the theological interpretation of the Yahwistic story of Paradise makes the relationship to God the key to understanding the great question of meaning embodied in being.

The theological view of the manner in which Adam is led to pose his own questions is revised by philosophy in such a way that the function of the question becomes that of opening the road to emancipation. It is only by following this road that the Adam of the Creation story, who only answers, can become the questioning Adam embodied by Job. The latter defends himself against the greater might of his divine lord by asking counterquestions, thus rising above the problem of the "what" with which he had been reproached (inquiring about this was an ancient right of the accused in a judicial process) to probe the *why* of God's actions. If Adam broke the commandment not to eat from the Tree of Knowledge without wondering about its meaning, Job, contradicting the answers of his orthodox friends, lays out all future problems of theodicy (see "Three Case Studies in Aesthetic Application") as he ever more radically poses the question of why. If one assumes that the beginning of the Greek heritage of philosophical thought lies in astonishment—seen as the preliminary stage in raising questions—then one can justifiably assume that the beginning of the Christian philosophical heritage resides in Job's "why."

In the biblical story, the oldest question setting human beings on the path to their own questions is not, however, the earliest in anthropological function. The question with which the child reaches beyond itself and passes over the horizon of its personal existence is the question about the name of things: "What is that?"[8] In biblical history there is a philogenetic explanation for the ontogenetic phase of naming. After God had created the animals and birds, he brought them all to man "in order to see what he would call them: and whatsoever Adam called every living creature, that was the name thereof" (Genesis 2:19). The creation myth give Adamic man the power to name all the creatures created along with him, names that he will later have to ask about and learn once again—after his expulsion from Paradise into history. In what order does man learn to ask questions, and what makes it possible to recognize the nature and sequence of the questions in the process of his appropriation of the world? These questions are related to the anthropological role played by question and answer, and with them we can conclude this preliminary outline of the problem of historical function. The proximity and impact of the aesthetic on all the other modes of question and answer in life praxis can best be described in terms of that possibility of posing questions which Odo Marquard claims is characteristic of the aesthetic mode: "Can this text not be understood differently, and—in case that is not enough—still differently, and then differently once again?"[9] Insofar as literary hermeneutics pluralizes, and thus stands in opposition to singularizing hermeneutics, and insofar as it regularly activates the endlessness of dialogue as a means of countering a dominant monologic discourse, the aesthetic role played by question and answer can become an excellent means of opening the way to understanding the other in his otherness at the same time as it provides a means of understanding texts differently.

2. Thou shalt never ask me!

An awareness of the roles played by question and answer can open new perspectives with regard to the history of literature and art if (according to Hans Blumenberg) one no longer searches for the origin or initial form of a myth and instead begins by regarding the myth itself as a permanent overcoming of origins—an overcoming of fears of the Ur-period as well as of the anxieties aroused by a human history that has defied mastery. This move allows a more comprehensible notion of work on myth to replace the hypothesis about its Ur-form that has served to rationalize intellectual history's model of a one-way movement from myth to logos (while at the same time unconsciously Platonizing the structural model by giving it a formalist turn as part of the search for the generative system of an archaic logic). That "myth . . . has always merged in reception" and remained there does not mean its basic structure is indeterminable or that it should be regarded as an "empty slot" that can be arbitrarily filled or left unfilled.[10] Rather, work on myth proceeds in terms of demonstrable concretizations of something whose meaning is constantly expanded through formal variations and contentual reinterpretations (this corrects the theory of a progressive disappearance of mythic substance). The upshot is that it is not some professed originary superiority, but "that which remains visible in the end, that which can satisfy the needs of reception and expectation," that elevates a constantly told and retold myth to the status of a primary myth (p. 192). Literary hermeneutics can shed light on the work of retelling a myth—as my essays on *Faust* and *Amphitryon* show[11]—by dealing with it in terms of the process of reception. In this process new and differently formulated questions make it possible to understand authoritative answers in new and different ways, even in ways that contradict the oldest meanings. As this happens, these answers can be transposed into later historical horizons. But this also raises the question as to whether a genuinely mythic function in fact exists for question and answer, one that can be incorporated, used, and surpassed in literary work on myth.

According to Blumenberg, a secondary rationalization is necessary in order to present primary myths (myths that "are narrated in order to banish something, be it fear or merely time"; p. 40) as conclusive or insufficient answers to elementary and distressing questions. In raising this question he also casts a glance at the rivalry between polytheistic myth and monotheistic dogma. It was this dogma that first connected "the mythic complex to a canon of elementary questions" (p. 205). In contrast to this, André Jolles defines etiological myth as a "simple form" that creates the human world from question and answer. This is the case, for example, when, in the face of an event such as a mountain spewing fire, fear or amazement leads to the question of cause, a question that is so "conclusively" answered by the myth that the initial question is extinguished.[12] These theories stand in contradiction to each other only superficially. The etiological role of question and answer in the narrative form Jolles assigns to myth can be fully subsumed in Blumenberg's conception of the anthropological role played by myth. One does not have to turn the etiological mode into the (historically unprovable) prototype of all mythology simply because one wishes to attribute a historically obvious achievement of myth—the explanation *ab origine* of a natural phenomenon, or the legitimation of a cult or a still-existing institution—to the "work on myth." After all, given the results of Blumenberg's book, it might be naive to take the supposed originary nature of myth literally and assume that the form given over to stories of origins provides reports about real historical origins, but it is nonetheless also true that the temporal placement *in illo tempore* situates many myths in a mythic pre- or posthistory (the latter need not be dealt with here) that provides one of the basic classical models of mythic fiction. The transposition of a mythic tale into a distant and untamed earlier era implies a question about primal events, if not about the beginning of time as such, events that determine everything that comes after, events that can often have continuing albeit unrecognized effect in the present, and even give meaning to the future. The *fascinosum* of this basic etiological model stems from the belief in the perfection and higher worth of first things, and explains the particular usefulness of the mythic narrative form known as *ab urbe condita* for purposes of political or institutional legitimation. When legitimating an institutional order that stands in conflict with others that were themselves not present from the beginning, it is irrelevant whether the true or a fictive story about normative origins is told.[13] This is the case because the underlying mythic model engenders a certain believability. Even the axiom of historical experience that asserts something "can only be explained historically,"[14] can find itself thrust into the twilight of an absolutized genesis because the "only" eliminates all possibility of posing further questions.

An awareness of the etiological role played by question and answer can serve to supplement Blumenberg's theory in another way as well. Even if, anthropologically speaking, one assumes that the specific effect of myth is an elementary mastery of fear and uncertainty, relief from oppressive questions can obviously also be provided by an explanatory model that deactivates a threatening reality by means of a narrative that sublates the torment and malaise of the question in the conclusiveness of its answer. According to Blumenberg, when a primary myth "brings with it the suggestion that through and in it all is said" (p. 193), that which is so completely expressed may also provide an answer so radical that it excludes any further questions. This is precisely what Jolles has in mind when he asserts that "this answer is such that no more questions can be posed. Thus, at the very moment it is given, the original question is extinguished. The answer is final. It is conclusive."[15] Ultimately, both theories rely completely on the polar opposition between genesis and final effect as a means of explaining the role of question and answer in myth. Nevertheless, the difference between the mythic and the theoretical points of view does not disappear. As Vico had already noticed,[16] more pressing questions, questions that deal directly with the survival of mankind, tend to precede inquiry into the reasons behind matters of life praxis. According to Vico, myth answers the former because it embodies a genuine form of "natural curiosity." The latter type of inquiry, however, moves toward the threshold of theoretical curiosity, a threshold that man first crosses when he asks further questions instead of being satisfied with the definitve answer provided by myth.

Crossing this threshold, which leads from the difficulties of the *cura* to the space of free play offered by *curiositas*, is made easier by allowing question and answer to function aesthetically. Indeed, when theological or ideological dogma dominates, this may provide the only means of negotiating the passage. Once hidden away in aesthetic fiction, a cheeky question about its why and wherefore can dissolve fear of the primal era, and offend against the first commandment of mythic authority, "Thou shalt not question," with impunity. The mythic process, which renders things unavailable for questioning, is thus reversed through the poetic use of question and answer. The monologic discourse of myth, which is unquestionable in the beginning, is drawn into an endless dialogue between authors. As is demonstrated by the literary history of *Amphitryon*,[17] poetic work on myth makes it impossible for the latter to maintain its monologic dominance. Neither can myth be construed as the gradual revelation of an original purity and fullness of meaning such as a theologizing hermeneutics had proposed. Drawn into the dialogic structure of poetic discourse,[18] myth must open itself to inquiry, and reveal its history, that is, the progressive appropriation, from work to work, of the answer to some great question, one involving all mankind and the world, a question whose answer can acquire a different significance with each reformulation. The so-called dialogue of authors thus becomes a polylogue between later writers, their norm-giving predecessors, and that absent third party, the myth itself. Literary tradition is not a free-floating dialogue between texts and authors. This imaginary conversation survives and is activated only when a later author reopens it by recognizing an earlier author as his predecessor, and by finding those questions of his own that lead beyond the answers provided by this "source." The conversation is asymmetrical, since the author who is present must give presence to the voice of the earlier author; it can also bring that absent third party, the far-off myth itself, the source of all inquiry, into play, a myth that would remain mute were it not made to speak to us by having its alien thought reinterpreted as the answer to a contemporary question.

The poetic use of question and answer can, in its own way, accelerate "work on the deconstruction of the absolutism of reality" (p. 13). It can do so by contradicting the supposed finality of a myth, that is, by allowing a writer to impose a new ending in an "aesthetic demonstration of power" (p. 685). The inevitable result of such an event is that the author's solution challenges another, later author into trying out some other solution. This aesthetic event, which is repeated in the reception history of all the great myths, proves nothing more nor less than that the beautiful, as suggested by that famous line of Rilke's, is "nothing but the beginning of that awesome something" whose end cannot and will not be a myth that has supposedly been played out in full. One rather intricate question remains unanswered. Should the unending nature of the work on myth discussed here be regarded as a victory for the openness of the aesthetic over the closure of the mythic, or, on the contrary, as a final triumph of myth that, despite its interplay with an art, and art's refusal to lend it credence, remains historically indestructible? I leave the resolution of this question to the practitioners of philosophical hermeneutics.[19]

If, as Blumenberg claims, the primary and real achievement of myth is to subvert the "power of the undefined"—by scaling down its predominance, naming the nameless, distancing and eliminating anxieties of all kinds—then the simple literary form found in the fairy tale must belong to the earliest phase of mythic work, and one can assume that the narrative form employed by myth has always had an aesthetic orientation. This is certainly the case for the Aphrodite myth. Originally, she came into being from the froth produced by the dreadful emasculation of Uranus. Later, in Botticelli's painting and finally in Georg Simmel's interpretation, she arises "from the fleeting, drifting foam of the turbulent sea." The fairy tale accomplishes the same thing *mutatis mutandis*: "The frightening background is forgotten, and the process of aestheticizing completed" (p. 45). The fairy tale delights in conjuring up the uncanny, but only in order to make one forget it, and make the world comfortable once more by passing through separation, anxiety, danger, quest, and discovery. I would like to use an example from *Grimm's Fairy Tales* to support my thesis. As a starting point I will take Freud's essay on the *uncanny*, which clearly encountered some embarrassment concerning the question as to whether and how anxieties could be mastered by means of aesthetic experience, which in turn led Freud to relegate the question to the realm of aesthetic theory.

The assumption that something such as an aesthetic mastery of anxiety might exist is equally grave for psychoanalysis whether it is regarded as an exception, an irritation, or even a therapeutic opportunity. It contradicts Freud's thesis: "An uncanny experience occurs either when infantile complexes which have been *repressed* are once more revived by some impression, or when primitive beliefs which have been *surmounted* seem once more to be confirmed."[20] If the uncanny (*unheimlich*) (the most readily described prototype among the various manifestations of anxiety) is nothing other than the return of something once "secretly familiar (*heimlich-heimisch*), which has undergone repression,"[21] this recurrence not only does not produce any anxiety from the aesthetic point of view, it provides a peculiar pleasure. How can this surmounting of anxiety take place, given the Freudian dictum that "every affect belonging to an emotional impulse, whatever its kind, is transformed, if it is repressed, into anxiety"?[22]

The history of aesthetic theory has long had a classic answer to this question, an answer that in many ways anticipates Freud's "inoculation theory": Aristotle's theory of catharsis. The spectator at a tragedy can be so affected by the passions represented on stage that, through his own fear or trembling (*phobos*) and pity or emotion (*elos*), he identifies with the characters, gives free rein in his imagination to his own aroused affects, and feels relieved by their discharge—as if he had experienced a cure (*katharsis*). Poetry—this is how Aristotle corrects the rigid, mechanistic view of its effects that leads Plato to condemn art—"does not infect, it immunizes."[23] The necessary condition for the emergence of such joy from anxiety is, before all else, its mediation by the imagination.

On one hand, the relationship between fiction and a real or possible object grants the freedom of the spectator's role—that unruffled state, arising from an aesthetic orientation, that must be presupposed in both Freud's somewhat different description of regression in daydreams,[24] and in the sublimation involved in aesthetic pleasure, a sublimation understood as "self-enjoyment in one's enjoyment of the other."[25] The protective and relieving effects of aesthetic distance allow us to indulge in suppressed, unadmitted, or openly frowned upon types of identification without fear. In the end, even really unpleasant conditions such as fear and anxiety can be enjoyed. On the other hand, pleasure in one's own anxiety can be enhanced and sublimated by means of the imaginary, which facilitates the former's derealization. Since the imaginary anxiety produced by literature (with the exception of anxiety about death) is generally less mixed, more elevated, and less distorted than the real anxiety we must face in the random world of everyday existence, the emotions of the affected individual can also burn with greater purity, be consumed and experienced as a "purgation."[26] Cathartic pleasure can also open the way to a third and deeper experience, that which emerges from the play of anxiety in the flow of emotions between fear and hope. According to Freud, in the economy of the psyche, the *recurrence* of the repressed must inevitably be paid for with anxiety. But within the aesthetic framework such return can lead to a happy *rediscovery* of forgotten experience or "lost time." The cathartic pleasure derived from the anxiety triggered by an aesthetic shock of recognition can so transform the uncanny engendered by a recurrence of the repressed that behind its threatening features the homey signs of something that was originally familiar can be seen, thus allowing us to rediscover a more essential world that we thought was lost—a world likewise confirmed by the end of the fairy tale, which allowed an early, quite simple form of aesthetic experience.

Literary history does indeed seem to show that real anxiety, aided by its literary counterpart—by the pleasure in an anxiety produced and sublimated by narrative, that is—can be surmounted. Richard Alewyn's thesis is worth remembering here. "Literary anxiety" is supposed to permit a release of real human anxieties that, historically speaking, had already been overcome, by playing them out in forms of ritualized repetition.[27] Aesthetic experience is already at work in the emancipatory history of mankind when real anxiety such as fear of ghosts is named within the playing fields of fiction, freed of taboos, and dispersed through aesthetic sublimation or the catharsis of the comic — even if it has not yet been surmounted in the life-world. I would like to substantiate this point by examining the story "A Tale of a Boy Who Set Out to Learn Fear," which, unlike others, thematizes the dissolution of anxiety. This fairy tale represents a threshold case for the genre, not simply because of its openly enlightened intentions and hidden irony, but also because of the absence of an attribute indicating the elect status of the hero.[28] This attribute is often a gift granted him during his travels, one that he can use to withstand an as yet unknown danger. The gift, the purpose of which is not revealed in advance, assumes the role of an answer possessed by the fairy-tale hero even before the question is asked.[29] This reversal in the relationship between question and answer fulfills the expectation that the fairy tale will grant that which life generally denies. In the inscribed and generically restricted form provided by the Grimm brothers, the fairy tale transplants a naive circle of listeners into a world transformed, one in which things transpire as if our wishes — and at the same time a deeper, unfulfilled need for justice — could be satisfied. It is on this level that the uncanny of the fairy tale touches on the residue of a primitive, genetically surmounted, animistic view of the world. But while this residue of animistic psychic activity (such as animation of the dead, belief in the omnipotence of thoughts, granting magical powers) causes anxiety in real life and turns the anxious into the uncanny, such phenomena of the fictional uncanny are accepted without any anxiety. They are even understood to be and enjoyed as old, familiar tokens of a dreamlike world that refutes terrible reality.

This certainly did not escape Freud. He remarks that fairy tales "quite frankly adopt the animistic standpoint of the omnipotence of thoughts and wishes."[30] Prompt wish fulfillment, animating the dead, speechless things that speak, the return of the double, the reawakening of people thought to be dead, and other phenomena in the sign system of the uncanny, when experienced in quasi-real fashion as the anxiety-producing expressions of alien powers, allow the fairy tale to suggest that it is precisely in the alien and unreal that the most familiar of things reveal themselves. The aesthetic orientation called forth by the fairy tale solicits anxiety that normally accompanies the return of the repressed only in order to release it cathartically, and at the same time confirm the narcissistic animation of things to be the true and good reality hidden behind the evil, everyday world. And since both psychogenic anxieties (such as fear of castration) and exogenic, those stemming from a hostile, not yet civilized environment (such as fear of traveling through the woods, fear of the night, or wild animals), are encompassed in this cathartic course of events, the fairy tale, which at first seems so far from reality, assumes an apparently unappreciated importance in the social process of clearing away superstition and the so-called dehostilization of nature.

In the fairy tale anxiety is predominantly anxiety about the protagonists — an anxiety that the listener can give himself over to with pleasure, since a happy end is guaranteed him by the laws of the literary genre. The fairy-tale hero himself, who is not by definition heroic, since from the outset his providential gift makes him superior to the forces opposing him, experiences no fear, at most a moment of shock that he is soon helped over. Remember "Snow White":

> Now the poor child was all alone in the big forest and got so frightened that she even eyed all the leaves of the trees and didn't know what to do. She started running and ran over the sharp stones and through the thorn bushes, and the wild animals sprang past her but did her no harm.

Anxiety is overcome in three steps here. Snow White first looks at the leaves on the trees, but this animistic gesture does not help her. Then, however, the peaceful behavior of the wild animals gives an immediate indication of a turn to the good. And this sign is confirmed toward evening, when Snow White arrives at the little house belonging to the seven dwarfs. There she is rewarded in the nicest of ways for the anguish she has had to endure. The poetic justice embodied in the fairy tale dictates that only the bad suffer the final consequences of inescapable anxiety. At the close of the tale, Snow White's evil stepmother becomes "so very frightened that she [doesn't] know what to do." And although she really does not want to, and is under no obligation to do so, she attends the young queen's marriage. Once there, she is obliged to put on red-hot slippers and "dance until she drop[s] to the ground dead."

The fairy tale "The Boy Who Set Out to Learn Fear" gives the cathartic release of anxiety an ironic, educative turn. Whereas other fairy tales tend to present the younger brother as smarter and more competent than his elder sibling, this tale allows him to remain a dim-witted fool from beginning to end, but only while making the point that it is precisely to him that the role of savior will fall. The elder brother, who is "bright and clever," is afraid to walk through the church cemetery at night; the younger brother's stupidity manifests itself only in his inability to understand why others should be frightened. Thus, the fairy tale seems at first to corroborate the folk wisdom that regards the lack of fear as a possible sign of diminished intelligence. But the action of this fairy tale gives an ironic twist to such expectations. Whereas in everyday life learning how to master one's anxiety is important, this tale reverses the process and asks whether one can learn to be afraid. In response to the suggestion that he finally learn "something to earn [his] living by," our fairy-tale hero answers that he would like to learn how to feel fear, upon which he is laughed at because of his naïveté. The listener, who laughs as well, is given a corrective lesson by the rest of the action. It is precisely his supposed stupidity that proves to be the providential gift that protects the hero of this fairy tale from misfortune. And what is more, the tests that the "dunce" manages to withstand undisturbed are calculated to create anxiety in the reader at the mere hearing. They increase in intensity from the idle pretense of a ghost to corpses of hanged men warmed by a fire and a ribald collection of frights in a castle in order to arrive at a confrontation with death itself. With regard to this range of fears, which in no way belongs to the world of the fairy tale alone (in the life-world of the eighteenth century they were still under attack by the Enlightenment as actual manifestations of superstition), the listener cannot help but be amazed by the action of the fairy tale, especially since the fearless dolt shows sympathy for the ice-cold corpse of his cousin, and because he honestly earns the hand of the king's daughter by freeing the castle from its curse. The moral of the story is doubly pointed. It is precisely the person who set out to learn fear who, in all his naïveté, teaches the wise how, by refusing to grant its signs any hidden meaning, one can become master of the anxiety produced by the uncanny. The "bucket of cold water and minnows" his dear consort pours over him finally serves to teach the young king what it means to feel fear. It also completes the process of cathartic liberation from anxiety through an ironic purgation: fairy-tale wisdom allows the uncanny a domesticated role once it has surrendered the power it draws from superstition. Trembling at the experience of the physically unpleasant is permitted; that is, fear with a precise cause replaces the endless, uncertain anxieties of the world at large.

3. Inquiry as the source of understanding

Although one may find the dictum "Man is a questioning being" too emphatic, and the notion that, in contrast to animals, he is "self-questioning" a bit too poetic,[31] one can hardly deny that questions provide a beginning, though perhaps not the best, to the process of understanding. This is a presupposition held in common by philosophical and theological hermeneutics, one that Gadamer and Blumenthal work out in relation to Heidegger's analytic discussion of Being, and to which my approach to literary hermeneutics is also indebted. According to Gadamer, the priority hermeneutics gives to asking questions is grounded in the capacity to "open up and hold open possibilities." Without openness, the radical negativity of which is found in the knowledge of not knowing, experience of (in the sense of insight into) that which one does not know or had expected to be otherwise is impossible.[32] The priority hermeneutics gives to asking questions applies to interpersonal communication in direct dialogue, to the relationship between present and past, and to the understanding of human action that is not verbally articulated as well. Conversation allows question and answer to confirm for themselves whether the other has understood in the same way, has understood differently, or has misunderstood altogether. It also makes it possible to test and try out a point of view, including one's own preconceived views. It is this possibility before all others that makes a conversation dialectic.[33] Question and answer also provide access to the otherness of the past at those moments when the question is rediscovered to which the text, within its historical horizon, was the answer. This is true not only for the historical interpretation of a work of art, but for comprehension in the historian's work in general, insofar as each leftover bit of the past "first turns into a source because of our questions." Then all sources must in turn be interrogated concerning a network of events that is not visible on their surfaces, and whose significance and impact can be investigated only from the vantage point of a later period.[34]

Finally, the relationship between question and answer can also make nonverbal human behavior comprehensible. This is possible when an action is not regarded as purely mechanical—as a reaction to a stimulus—but instead as a stance taken with regard to something, a stance that is the response to an experiential situation. What the heuristic worth of the question-and-answer schema is once situation has replaced inquiry, and whether it is adequate when more complex actions by interference-producing subjects are to be explained (actions in which the behavior of one participant no longer befalls, or is no longer received by, the other in unmediated fashion as it is in play), are questions that can be left open here.[35] Gadamer's maxim "To understand means to understand something as an answer" is still of heuristic value at the point where it reveals the frontier beyond which the question-and-answer schema becomes metaphorical and other means of understanding come into play. It is no accident that, historically, the dialectic of question and answer developed along with the Platonic dialogue—as self-understanding enabled by an object. The equally original desire for knowledge of the alien "you" cannot be reduced to this dialectic, since it does not rely first of all on question and answer, and certainly does not require—as does the poetic text for its interpretation—a prior "anticipation of perfection" when it is a matter of understanding the other for its own sake, and understanding the self through the other.[36] To understand the other for his own sake does not mean to first of all regard him as an answer, but to understand him through his speech, as one does the poetic text that can reveal for me the different view of the world that comes through the eyes of another. This understanding does not occur in the initial act of aesthetic perception, that is, pleasurable understanding, but only in a secondary act of explicit aesthetic and historical analysis, where it emerges as the answer to the questions posed by an interpretation.[37]

The proximate situation of aesthetic understanding is of import for theological hermeneutics as well as philosophical, as will now be demonstrated by looking at Bultmann's work.

For Bultmann—and along with him all recent hermeneutics—the *Problem of Hermeneutics* really begins only when one steps beyond the objectivism of historical knowledge. Understanding is not a purely contemplative act in which the interpreter just has to extinguish his subjectivity and forget his historical situation in order to arrive at an objective awareness of a thing. Understanding is always a specific process of posing questions, is always oriented by a "whither the inquiry," and consequently guided by a prior understanding of the object that is grounded in the interests of the questioner. All interpretation that seeks to understand presupposes that "this interest stands in some kind of living relation to the text to be interpreted and is the stimulus for the communication between the text and its interpretant."[38] Although this common link seems to limit Bultmann's theory of understanding to texts and interpretations that arise from a common historical tradition, the "whither" he introduces later reaches beyond questions of particulars and establishes a hermeneutic bridge to the understanding of alien cultural expression: "What does the text, as the possibility of my own being, allow me to comprehend?" It is no accident that Bultmann's formulation of this general "whither" of all understanding, "human Being in all its potential as the potential of the understander himself," was developed with an eye to "genuinely literary works" (p. 221). Where theological or juridical texts are concerned, it would certainly be much more difficult to prove the capacity of understanding based on inquiry to mediate between experience of the alien and that of the self. Could this be because aesthetic texts enable not only a self-understanding with regard to the matter but also an understanding of form?

Several of Bultmann's attempts to define the specific interest aesthetics has in questions merit further thought. The range of initial suppositions that Bultmann lays out, which extends from the naive examination of a text to philosophical questions about truth, from an interest in the historical lessons or pleasure derived from a narrative to psychological, historical (reconstruction of the past), or formal interests, and, finally, to questions concerning the significance of God's actions, show aesthetic interest to be rather ambivalent. An "inward participation in the hero's fate, which the reader imagines to be his own," first serves as the hallmark of a naive reader, but later becomes the "appropriate means of understanding genuine works of literature," insofar as they reveal "human Being in all its potential [to be] the potential of the understander himself" (p. 221). In the end, philosophical, religious, and literary texts are equally relevant when it is a matter of "questions concerning human Being as one's own being" (p. 228). At this point in his argument Bultmann limits understanding primarily to the "whither" of the inquiry—as if the different constitutive modes of various texts played at most a secondary role, if any. The all-encompassing question about human Being as one's own can "in principle [be asked of] all texts—and history in general" (p. 228). But is it in fact only questions derived from this fundamental question that distinguish the hermeneutic approach to texts? Is not the whither of such questions also determined by the religious, juridicial, or aesthetic character of a text?

Bultmann's hermeneutics allows for only *one* theory of understanding, grounded anthropologically on the idea that man is a questioning being. This does not, however, mean that this premise, common to all regional hermeneutics, could not or should not be subordinated to a textual pragmatics, one that would have to be worked out by differentiating between the kinds of understanding allowed by the presuppositions of theological, juridical, or literary texts, and the various ends to which they have been interpreted and used. Bultmann's new position, which frees theological hermeneutics from the premise that obliges one to grant God's word its own discursive structure, will probably not please all theologians. Literary hermeneutics on the other hand can gladly and with impunity adopt the premise of Bultmann's theory of understanding, since it too is thereby freed from orthodox tradition. I am referring to the quasi-revelatory character granted to classical works, their supposed universal significance (which now would be incorporated into the process of interrogatory understanding), and its correlate, immanent aesthetic observation of the work of art. The formal analysis of an aesthetic text prepares the way, but in no way completes the "real understanding" of that text. Literary hermeneutics, too, must demand that the interpretant critique his understanding of the manner in which he comprehends a text, must put his understanding in jeopardy, or, stated differently, "allow the self to be cross-examined by the text while examining it, listen to the claims it makes" (p. 228).

To listen to the "claims made by a text" seems at first glance to be too much to expect of literary hermeneutics. After all, the metaphor of the claim is burdened by a specifically theological "hermeneutics of the word of God," according to which the claim of a text is constituted by its religious character as a "call" or "address" that can be heard only if the listener has faith. For Bultmann, on the other hand, hearing the claims of the text depends upon first having brought the otherwise mute text to the point of speech by asking questions: "Only one moved by questions about one's own existence can hear the claims made by a text" (pp. 230/233). The claims made by religious texts are no exception here. Indeed, Bultmann does not shy away from suggesting that even our understanding of reports about God's actions arises from questions about man. The boldest thesis in his theological hermeneutics is that "the individual can very well know who God is by the questions posed about him. If man's existence were not (consciously or unconsciously) animated by the question of God . . . , then he would be unable to recognize God as God in any of God's revelations" (p. 232). This thesis has been rejected on theological grounds. To understand a text as the *Verbum Dei* has its own premise: for the believer, the text takes on the "character of an address," and the I who understands this address is "always already an I who has been called" (Ernst Fuchs). The word of God, defined as "commitment," corresponds to man's definition in terms of his obligation to answer: "For his destiny is to exist as answer. He is asked about what he has to say" (Gerhard Ebeling).[39] But even if, on different theological grounds, one grants understanding God priority over understanding the self, and even if, following Wolfhart Pannenberg's lead, one chooses to construe the nature of the event embodied in the story of Jesus as the revealed meaning and beginning of all theological hermeneutics, understanding biblical texts as the "revelation of the historical God whose dominion is still to come"[40] indicates no recognizable hermeneutic preeminence that would render Bultmann's premise superfluous. Along with every theological hermeneutics that wants to invert the movement of question and answer when it is a matter of the *Verbum Dei*—so that the question the text poses to me (its theological "claim") has priority over my own question—an almost irrefutable objection reemerges. As Pannenberg said about Gadamer's notion of the classical text (and this undermines his own thesis about the priority of divine understanding as well), "Statements about the 'question' a text poses to us can only be metaphoric. The text becomes a question only for one who poses questions; it cannot be such in advance."[41]

If theological hermeneutics cannot surrender the priority it assigns to the "question the text poses to me," it may assume Bultmann's theory of understanding through questioning to be a hermeneutics with an unrecognized aesthetic foundation, whereas a literary hermeneutics that defines the classical in terms of the "superiority of origins and originary freedom" of "eminent texts" (texts that refer to themselves and serve to interpret themselves)[42] might be suspected of a rapprochement with the authoritative texts of theological hermeneutics. Given this divorce between a theological hermeneutics that grants an original superiority to the question posed to me by the text—that is, posed to one's understanding of oneself ("Adam, where art thou?")—and an aesthetic hermeneutics that gives priority to the interpreter's questions—through which the text's answer is constantly revised—the literary historian might be tempted to speak of a new phase in the *Querelle des anciens et des modernes*. Actually, this vantage point might offer some chance of a reconciliation, since theological hermeneutics could call on its literary neighbor in order to make a religious text or a work of religious art accessible again—any work that, in its *intentio recta*, once spoke of the religious convictions of the beholder, but that, as a sign of a distant world of faith, seems alien to us. In this case, an inquiring understanding, by tracing the *intentio obliqua* of its artistic features, might be able to construct a bridge back to such a work.[43] The relationship between man and God upon which theological hermeneutics is predicated does not necessarily build a bridge of understanding linking us to the otherness of a bygone world of faith. Religious texts dealing with the Christian persecution of heretics or the Inquisition can at best be explained historically; they cannot be "understood." But there are literary texts and works of art that a questioning understanding can open for us, revealing something about the conflicts of those who acted and suffered in the name of God. This is possible because of the mediating continuity of aesthetic experience, which serves to discover the horizons of distant life-worlds, to transcend and mediate between them and the contemporary life-world horizon. This is the special accomplishment of, and also the advantage of, literary hermeneutics.

4. First, ultimate, and impudent questions

Question and answer are closely related in their theoretical and aesthetic orientation, as is demonstrated by the history of aesthetic knowledge, which gradually acquired independence thanks to the "process of theoretical curiosity." Once art achieved autonomy, aesthetic knowledge entered into a competitive relationship with philosophical knowledge.[44] This relationship is already visible in the Ur-experience of wonder (*thaumazein*), the much-heralded "beginning of philosophy." According to this line of thought, questioning, which, unlike disputation, does not presume specific answers, and which therefore serves superbly in the construction of new experience, begins in wonder, or, more precisely, in the ability to be amazed about something that, without regard to its use "appears wonderful to anyone who has not investigated its cause" (Aristotle, *Metaphysics*, 983a). Plato used the rainbow — a *figura etymologica* — as an example of this (*Theaetetus*, 155d). To this cosmological example Aristotle added a technological (automated works of art) and a geometric (the irrationality of diagonals) (*Metaphysics*, 983a). Thus, in Greek tradition the primary act of amazement encompasses both a positive and a negative observational experience: amazement or estrangement. Aesthetic experience is obviously involved in this beginning of thought, too: amazement in the sense of wonder can be triggered by the beautiful; amazement in the sense of estrangement can be unleashed by the uncertainty of the cosmos. The later notion of the sublime combines wonder and estrangement.

The next experiential step, too, that taken when the ability to feel wonder is transmuted into a first question, is particularly well prepared for by an aesthetic orientation. Even simple sensory perception (*aesthesis*), as Aristotle notes, typically triggers pleasure in the observed "even apart from its usefulness" (*Metaphysics*, 980a). This is all the more the case with the figurative language of literature, which is able to so enhance perception that it awakens a wonder that leads to questions at the moment when "quite simple, even insignificant impressions . . . [open] cracks and crevices in ordinary, conventional perception." This is Ernst Bloch's description of the second step in human experience, which, in contradistinction to the idealist tradition, he claims is preceded by a first step: "Need teaches one to think." Interrogative wonder, which reaches out beyond the distress caused by need, and, thereby, beyond the body-oriented orbit of worries, can hardly turn at once to ultimate things, or to beings in general, as Bloch suggests in his first example: "Quite without affectation, children will ask the familiar question: why is there something and not nothing?"[45] Did Bloch mean to wax ironic about the metaphysical search for ultimate things by ascribing it to children? One of his later examples seems to come closer to that first question that emerges at the moment of naming ("What is that?"), and which has a tendency to extend over into the "Why is it that way?" posed by pretheoretical curiosity: "Problem enough this rusty wheel, but now it points to time — time that destroyed the wheel. And what is time?" For our purposes, these comments can help distinguish between first and ultimate, canonized and impudent questions. They show off to good advantage the competitive stance that literature takes vis-à-vis religion and philosophy when it too begins to employ question and answer.

If one defines philosophy in the Socratic tradition in a very general manner in terms of searching inquiry, then its developmental history shows that interrogative wonder, which had served as the origin of thought, was pushed into the background, if not fully submerged, by the growing acceptance of apophantic logic. Since the question does not assume the form of an assertion, since it cannot be true or false, and also remains independent of any judgment, it has no place in the logic of the Aristotelian tradition. Eric Weil offers this rather laconic description of the fate of the history of science: "The answers are scientific, at least insofar as they remain subject to rational criticism, the questions are not."[46] Nevertheless, it is assumed that progress in the history of science has been spurred by philosophy insofar as it has ranked the question above the answer. Out of the apparently naive questions posed by philosophy concerning human Being as a whole have supposedly come sciences that have lost their connection to such questions in proportion to their growing precision. Or these questions were left to philosophy after being dubbed "unscientific," thereby giving philosophy an enduring bad conscience, since science demanded that philosophy authorize only those questions that have implicit in them the possibility of an answer.[47] Weil saw in the rehabilitation of the question the one real chance for the human sciences, but the question had to be one whose validity was not immediately measured in terms of a demonstrable answer or some foreseeable solution. The question has since been given priority in hermeneutic reflection as well as in critico-theoretical reflection, and is espoused today by disciplines that originally gave priority to assertion or answer (logic), or to the "question the text poses to me" (theology). Along with this new awareness it also became clear that, as C. S. Lewis has pointed out, it is not necessarily new facts, but instead new answers to old questions, that shake canonical systems of response and alter our models of the world.[48] An example of this process is provided by drawing on a famous episode from Bede's history of the English church. The power this example has to convince obviously stems in great part from the new answer and the manner in which it has been expanded into a poetic image. It focuses on the argument by a heathen priest that led the Northumbrian court to convert to Christianity:

> This is how the present life of man on earth, King, appears to
> me. . . . You are sitting feasting with your caldormen and thanes in
> wintertime; the fire is burning . . . and all inside is warm . . . ; and
> a sparrow flies swiftly through the hall. It enters in at one door and
> quickly flies out through the other. For the few moments it is inside,
> the storm and wintry tempest cannot touch it, but after the briefest mo-
> ment of calm, it flits from your sight, out of the wintry storm and into

it again. So this life of man appears but for a moment; what follows and indeed what went before, we know not at all. If this new doctrine brings us more certain information, it seems right that we should accept it.

The preparation, assertion, and legitimation of the new has recently been of particular interest in the context of the problem of the history of the development of scientific theories. After the success of Thomas S. Kuhn's book, which marks the reemergence of historicism in scientific theory – a historicism that draws on Karl Popper's "logic of discovery" – the outsider can only wonder why the role of question and answer has not been more emphatically included in the explanation of "scientific revolutions."[49] Kuhn himself employs it only in the lesser form of the puzzle with an assured solution, which he claims is characteristic of the phase in which normal science unfolds. The scientist's activity is then primarily directed at creating greater precision within the framework of a paradigm that is no longer in question. This paradigm is the guarantor of the presence of a solution, and determines in advance which facts can provide useful insights, thus eliminating the risk of wasting time on insoluble problems.[50] Thus, for Kuhn, the new can only come from outside, introduced by the unexpected appearance of an anomaly, one that does not fit the dominant paradigm, that demands an explanation based on new premises and thereby leads to a change in paradigms. But how does one perceive of an anomaly in the first place? Surely it exists before it is noted for the first time. If it is the existing, dominant paradigm that leads one to find the expected while overlooking anomalies, how can an anomaly then suddenly become significant as the beginning of a new knowledge? The metaphor of the heaven-sent occasion seems to be in play here as a means of covering over the hermeneutically obvious content that is presumed even in the seemingly objective "whither" of an (already forgotten) prior question. One must change the direction of the question in order to see something else or in order to discover something new. An excellent example of this necessity, though one that may not be generalizable, is offered by the story of the discovery of the double helix, which implemented the transformation of the working model in molecular biology. "The key to [Pauling's] success was his reliance on the simple laws of structural chemistry. The [alpha]-helix had not been found by only staring at X-ray pictures; the essential trick, instead, was to ask which atoms like to sit next to each other."[51]

The hermeneutic logic embodied in question and answer was overlooked by Kuhn, but it had already been conceptualized by Hans Blumenberg, who explained it in terms of the reception of antique philosophy by patristic and medieval Christian theology.[52] In Blumenberg's interpretation, the morphological paradigms of the source, influence, and effect of an idea are historicized by a return to the level of the (often latent) problem; that is, they are absorbed in the functional paradigms of expectation and experience, reception and shift of horizon. From this standpoint, the new produced by an epoch can no longer in and of itself become a momentous event simply by replacing the old and formerly valid in a direct diachronic movement. It can only be accepted and develop in significance to the degree that it is able to solve, or promises to solve, a problem that is acutely felt in, or first intrudes on, the synchronic system of canonized questions and answers of a given life-world. The historical significance of an event such as the epochal transition into the Christian era can be measured by the gradual process whereby a new doctrine was accepted within the horizon of the time, in other words, on the "epochal threshold" of its reception. The paradigm of a history of problems replaces the old history of events, and, at the same time, deessentializes the so-called history of reception, making it possible to reconstruct the historical processes involved in terms of the relations between question and answer.

A new religion must make some connection with the old in order to plausibly refute it.[53] So Christianity "did everything it believed would enable it to represent itself as the *answer* to the *question* posed by the tradition. Everything new must appear to be an 'answer,' therefore; it must demonstrate that the prerequisite 'questions' belonging to the old are part of its content, and that it can make them relevant and pressing."[54] Old doctrine, such as that of gnosis, requires the new Christian teaching to provide its own, plausible answers to questions that, in the former, had long been thought to be resolved.[55] The new doctrine must take on the resulting burdens of the old, but it can do so only on condition that it occupy all the positions, and all the "empty spaces" in the former world model. It must also raise questions anew in cases where the answer seems so natural and irrefutable that the question to which it was once the answer has disappeared. The newly posed questions then make it possible to retain the answers, but to understand them differently or "better." From this perspective, the notion of epochs, and in particular the notion of a transition from one epoch to another ("See, everything has been transformed and made new") is given a temporal grounding; the event loses its mythic aura of uniqueness. The fullness of its meaning is manifest from the beginning – from the dawn of the new. It can only emerge from the historical work of reception – from the ongoing reorganization of the canon of question and answer that articulates the elementary knowledge that orients one's interpretation of self and the world and that transmits this orientation from generation to generation. Blumenberg's paradigm of a logic of historical knowledge presents the transition to the new as a "reorganization of functions" and thereby does away with a notion of the tradition that had been defined essentialistically, as a "transposition of contents."[56] With this gesture, it also sublates the supposedly transhistorical canon in a temporally determined dialectic within the history of ideas: not all questions can be asked at any given time; many are erased by a definitive answer, others are forgotten, renewed once more, or posed only at a comparatively late date. Belatedness itself becomes interesting here from a hermeneutic point of view, since it reveals the boundaries of experience established during the transformation of a horizon of world understanding. Blumenberg's theory bequeaths one task in particular to literary hermeneutics, that of examining the literary uses of question and answer, the uses through which literature manages to participate in the historical process of theoretical curiosity.

For an inquiring Adam who wants to withdraw from the system of answers given by a currently dominant worldview, literature provides two possibilities. Fictional actions can be used to test the religious truths or the ideas with which a theology or a philosophy answers ultimate questions, or, on the other hand, impudent questions can be asked. In either case, the license granted by aesthetic fiction allows one to enter the realm of the taboo. In that particular repertoire that signals the poetic use of question and answer one can also find the indirect answer, first inferred by analogy, that revivifies an extinct, repressed, or displaced question. Furthermore, one finds the indirect forms constituted by the "merely rhetorical," the "incorrectly posed" and even "dumb" questions that cannot be answered by the system and are therefore destined to interrupt an unquestioning view of the world.

We can thank Mikhail Bakhtin for showing us that since the classical period, and in the subversive wake of the Socratic dialogue, a literary genre dealing with "ultimate questions" has existed. This genre took over and carried forward the oppositional function of dialogically testing the idea and the person supportive of the monologic discourse and ready truths offered by theology and philosophy. It first appears in the form of the Menippean satire[57] and later as the polyphonic novel (with Rabelais and Dostoyevsky as its modern high points). The narrative format is that of the adventure, the sea voyage, the journey to the beyond — in a word, the passage through the world that allows a person, often a wise man or a rogue, to seek the truth or test an idea. The final propositions of the world are thus tested by the wise man's empirical knowledge or called into question by the rogue. Often a syncretic procedure also leads them into the aporia of an unresolvable pro and con. One only has to remember the cheerful question as to whether it is better to marry or not, a question that Rabelais's rogue, Panurge, poses to the world throughout the length of three books — making fun of modern public-opinion research before the fact; or the dead serious question as to whether this is the best of all possible worlds, which Voltaire tests against the fortunes of his philosopher, Candide, and which he in the end reduces to the absurd thanks to the now familiar *"mais il faut cultiver notre jardin."* I would also like to introduce a little-known series of examples drawn from the philosophical/theological epos in the tradition of Claudian, Boethius, Bernhardus Silvestris, Alain de Lille, and Brunetto Latini. Through its general question-and-answer structure as well as through its combination of emanatistic and viatoric narrative action this epic mode points back from afar to the Menippean satire.[58]

The works of the aforementioned authors are so permeated by a single "ulti-mate question" that they could be read as individual installments in a series, each of which provides a new answer to the problem of the ongoing existence of the world. More precisely, they wonder about the decadence of the world and its chances for renewal. In *De raptu Proserpinae* Claudian lets Natura answer the question. She complains to Zeus that since the golden age mankind has become sluggish, and recommends the establishment of farming as a means of providing a sensible goal for human activity. In *De consolatione philosophiae* blame for the way things have gone is laid at the feet of Fortuna, and Boethius, in prison, com-forts himself with Philosophia, which answers his complaints with a counterques-tion as to why he would want to seek his happiness in the world outside when it can only exist within him. In *De universitate mundi* Bernhardus Silvestris traces Nature's lament back to a first cause: the formless state of matter in the beginning. At the close of Natura's journey to heaven, Noys, a female emanation of the di-vine, answers by retelling the story of the creation of the world. She develops an idea of man in which his highest destiny is to be the microcosmic mirror of the macrocosm. In the *Planctus naturae*, which comes next in the series, Alain de Lille once again takes up the question as to why the world degenerates more and more, finding itself at present clothed in "iron's poverty." He does so by turn-ing to what was apparently a current question about sodomy, a practice that stood in the way of the regeneration of the human species. The anathema that Genius, serving as nature's priest, pronounces over all sinners is not, however, the final answer to the big question. Alain devoted a second work, the *Anticlaudianus*, specifically to it, responding to the question about the renewal of life by giving shape to a new *psychomachia* from which a *divinus homo* would emerge, one who would redeem all that had gone awry (an *iuvenis* that has surprisingly little con-nection with Christ the redeemer but a great deal with *Jove*, the epitome of perfec-tion in the lover according to the poetry of the contemporary troubadours!).

Finally, Brunetto Latini, in his *Tesoretto*, reposes Boethius's question as to how man can assert himself in the face of the catastrophic course of history. But he no longer answers the question resignedly in the manner of the Stoic sage or with the consoling arguments of Platonism. Instead, his response is rational and critical in the spirit of the awakening curiosity about the world that paved the way for the Renaissance and a laicistic educational ideal. What the wanderer now seeks and what unites everything observed during his allegorical journey is no longer some final wisdom but, rather, empirical knowledge, knowledge primarily defined by the ideal of *curiositas* and justified by a theoretical interest in things. The new manner of posing questions is most clearly demonstrated at the point where the wanderer, having entered the netherworld, asks Ovid the reason for Cupid's blindness. The laconic answer given by this highest authority of antiquity — "No one can know the power of love without having first experienced it" (ll.2374–2376) — reveals that Brunetto's question is purely theoretical, posed as if it did not concern him personally. But Ovid immediately gives him objective proof: the inquisitive wanderer suddenly realizes that he can go no further, since, quite against his will, he has been "taken in by Cupid" (this—possibly biographical—reference remains obscure). Another level of humor becomes clear at this point in the episode. Even in an early expression of theoretical and mytho-critical interest such as this, Ovid's ironic answer demonstrates *ad oculos* the superiority of practical experience over theory of any sort.

The questions posed in the course of everyday life are answered positively by exemplary literature and the fable, ironically by the proverb, casuistically by the novella and by the pointed humor of a comic tale. While collections of exempla, with their well-ordered presentations of historical precedent, have tried-and-true answers ready at hand for problems of practical behavior, the proverb teaches a lesson that is of no use to the concerned party, since it always comes too late to serve as a response to the situation. The ironic nature of the answer given by the proverb, the fact that the retrospective awareness of others ("That's the way the world goes") is of no use as a rule of action, makes it the simplest literary form able to shatter the certainty of a dying worldview. The *casus* has a more complicated form. It constructs answers only in order to have the reader himself decide which norm he wants to employ in evaluating the events at hand. "Which is the courtly lover's greatest pleasure, thinking of his beloved, or seeing her?" This and other more intricate questions were elaborated in the dilemma-based poems of debate (tenzone, partima) of the Middle Ages. Their popularity in fact continued into the seventeenth century, which regarded them as precious *questions amoureuses*. According to the well-known hypothesis proposed by André Jolles, they may have developed into the novella in which an "incredible event" resolves the *casus*.[59] This does not immediately resolve the moral problem, however, since the norms involved are themselves to be evaluated. Thus, the question-and-answer game continues and—as the narrative framework in Boccaccio's *Decameron* demonstrates—one decisive *casus* can immediately precipitate another.

For the Enlightenment thinkers, literary casuistics became a weapon against sanctioned religious and social morality as can be seen most effectively in the "true stories" inserted in *Jacques le fataliste* and in Diderot's narrative tales.[60] Kafka on the other hand seems to seek out the casuistic specifically for the sake of its insolubility. The parable of the doorkeeper perverts the parable form of the New Testament by allowing the vital question, "What shall I do to inherit eternal life" (Luke 10:25), to be the source of unavoidable damnation once the person desiring entry has set foot on the desired path. The insubordinate question to which the "man from the country" at last rouses himself in a final effort at the moment of death, "Everyone strives to attain the law . . . how does it come about, then, that in all these years no one has come seeking admittance but me?" refers back to the tradition of the redeeming question. One can neglect it, as does the elect in the novel of the Grail, but he is then summoned to make good that neglect by testing and proving himself during a long detour in his journey. For Kafka, however, the correctly posed question always comes too late; the resulting answer is slipped around the neck of the questioner like a noose. "No one but you could gain admittance through this door, since this door was intended for you." The parodoxical nature of this answer produces a hermeneutic trap. K., a questioning Adam, must involve himself in an interpretative problem that has no solution. He sinks deeper and deeper into the indecipherable implications of a sacrosanct scripture.[61]

If Kafka's parable, despite the aporia, confirms a maxim of philosophical hermeneutics, namely, that "it is more difficult to ask questions than to answer them,"[62] the repertoire of question and answers that literature has at its disposal also contains generic models in which a helpful mythic authority alleviates the need to pose questions and guarantees the right answer at the right time. First among these are the riddle and the fairy tale, which can be mustered against the superior strength of those all-too-large questions concerning guilt and innocence, the responsibility of men or gods, the meaning or absurdity of the world order—against the unanswerable "Why?" from which springs the shattering effect of tragedy.[63] While the riddle of life and even the so-called scientific riddle let one see the next, as yet unsolved problem lying behind every answer, every literary riddle has only one true answer, an answer that extinguishes all further questioning. A token of this is the Sphinx, which throws itself into the abyss as soon as someone solves its riddle. Oedipus, who succeeds in doing just this, is still very much like the chosen one of the fairy tale at this point in his story. The elect in fairy tales are able to answer one or even three questions with instinctive certainty although all their predecessors have failed to do so. I have already discussed the gift that grants the fairy-tale hero the answer while he is still on the way to the place where the question will be posed. The reversal of the usual order of question and answer satisfies the highest expectation of the fairy tale, which, according to Jolles, is not so much our inclination to the miraculous, which goes without saying here, as the need to have a "naive morality" satisfied—to see "what the world would be like if based on our feelings."[64] This is the way human beings in the end answer a question that was not foreseen in the Christian catechism or in its political surrogates—the question that longs for a world that would at the same time satisfy our subjective feelings about justice and individual desire for good fortune, and that would raise a fallen Adam to the level of a "lucky fellow."

5. Didactic questions, catechisms, and their consequences

Standing opposite the impudent question, which looks beyond the horizon of the known and the secure, is the didactic question, which aims for a solid answer and serves, in magistral dialogue, to transmit some doctrine or, then again, to undermine it. The span of the didactic question, which lacks openness, extends from maieutic instruction, which enables one to question while learning or to learn while questioning, to catechetical interrogation, which tests the student's knowledge of the faith by examining the correctness or insufficiency of his responses to a graduated arrangement of questions from the teacher. If the dialectic fulfills its Socratic mission in the art of extended questioning, the didactic works its way toward a fully developed canon, a canon that organizes a catalogue of necessary, and that often means authorized, questions in terms of a closed doctrinal system of answers. The history of the magistral dialogue is replete with instances of a process in which the openness generated by extensive questioning is arrested by a canonized mode of response. Then the priority of question over answer serves to privilege the authority of the teacher and the dialogic search for unknown truths ends in the monologic assertion of a single truth. The magistral dialogue, which grew primarily out of the Aristotelian commentaries of late antiquity, produced a rich literature of *Quaestiones et Responsiones* (*erotemata, zetemata, problemata*).[65] In so doing, the asymmetry of the magistral form could be legitimated through the priority of the answer, which guaranteed the soul's salvation – provided it was limited to "pious questions" concerning the Holy Scriptures – and, in the final instance, through the authority of Christ as teacher with respect to his pupils.

Even at the summit of the tradition of the *quaestiones*, in the theological summa of the Scholastics, the priority of the answer was maintained insofar as it stayed anchored in the unanalyzed revelatory truth of the Holy Scriptures. Nonetheless, the Scholastic theory of *quaestio* opened substantial room for play between the *interrogatio* and the *responsio*, and made it possible to exhaust both doubt and seeking.[66] This was so since the right to ask questions had always been granted when mutually contradictory *auctoritates* from the Bible or the literature of one's forebears could be cited when trying to solve a problem, or when grounds for and against a proposition could be established. In these cases, the distinguishing function of the question was to clear up the contradiction between the fundamental truths upon which each position was based and, by distinguishing between true and false, prepare the way for the correct answer.[67] As Erich Köhler has shown,[68] the courtly poetry of the period had quickly appropriated the Scholastic method of disputation propounded in the lessons of the *Artes liberales* and in theology, and had used the *sic et non* as a means of giving its own dilemma-borne representation of its highest values.[69] It also shaped the exchange of question and answer into independent forms of debate poetry (tenzone, jeu parti, partima). These lyric genres served above all to deal syncretically with conflicts between norms up to and including the Augustinian dualism of reason and will, and to sublimate the ideals of courtly love that had elevated the ritualistically admired *lady* to the highest seat of the true and the good.[70] The history of the partima provides an impressive example of how poetry again and again renews the principle

of open dialogue in opposition to the general tendency toward enclosure in monologue, and how it can go to extremes with unanswerable questions.[71] The Proven-
çal poets developed the partima in the form of a competition tied to a dilemmatic
question of the following sort: "Which is better, to love unrequitedly or to be
loved without loving in return?" The condition for such publicly held competi-
tions was that the person who posed the question had to give his opponent the freedom to choose either side of the dilemma. In contrast to Scholastic disputation,
which was meant to lead the pupils to clear insights by having them work out the
positive or negative grounds for their arguments, no *solutio* was expected of the
participants in a poetic disputation. Instead, an unresolved combat could, if
necessary, be referred to some authority standing outside the competition (but
even those few, mostly posterior, judgments that have come down to us fail to
provide a really definitive solution). In the partima, it would seem, the game was
not played for the sake of winning; the goal was not to respond to the dilemmatic
question, but to "playfully, not subversively, contemplate an unshakable ideal."[72]
As the principle of open-ended dialogue was revived, it came to embody, so to
speak, the unresolved state of suspense between longing and fulfillment that was
a feature of courtly love.[73] It also transformed the truth-seeking *sic et non* of the
theologians into a purposeless, and often self-ironic, game for poets.

In the *Divina commedia*, which can be regarded as the greatest "summa" of
the worldly poetry of the day, Dante used his aesthetic license to create his own
field of play for question and answer—this despite the fact that he unquestioningly
employs the doxological backdrop of the Scholastic theology that was part of his
own elite education,[74] and visualizes its worldview *in toto* in a hitherto unheard
of poetry of the invisible. After all, Dante was hardly willing to let his wanderer
journey through the three otherworldly realms engaging in magistral dialogue in
order to pose canonical as well as currently acute theological questions (such as
those related to the struggle over Averroism) just so his three authorities, his
guides, Virgil, Beatrice, and Bernard de Clairvaux, could answer them. An aesthetic boundary is crossed at the point where Dante has his wanderer question the
souls of the dead about their earthly fate, guilt, or contributions. In so doing, he
revives the freedom of human speech in the eternal realms of damnation, purga-
tory, and bliss. It is the thoroughly humane function of posing a question that allows the questioner to nourish himself both on all the affects of those individuals
singled out, whether friendly or unfriendly, and on disinterested *curiositas*. The
result is that this function constantly overflows or slips past the anagogic purpose
of the journey: instruction about the reign of divine justice. Such question posing
is a final and ultimate proof of human solidarity as far as those questioned are concerned, since "for the souls of the dead, Dante's journey represents their only
chance in all eternity to speak to one from among the living. This is an aspect
of the situation that impels many to express themselves with the utmost intensity
and which brings into the changelessness of their eternal fate a moment of dra-

matic historicity."[75] Thus, according to Auerbach's interpretation,[76] a *duplex sentia* springs from the questions of the living and the answers of the dead. This allows the *Divina commedia* both to be read allegorically and canonically—as an answer to the question about the latent justness of the divine world order—and to be understood literally and historically—as a mirror of the earthly world and its history, a mirror in which the ultimate fate of the dead allows their individual destinies to stand for hundreds of others.

At the point where the wanderer's sympathy runs up against the stiffest barrier of theological dogmatism—the expectation that the damned are to be denied all pity—Dante shifts from explicit questions to wordless interrogative gestures. The most famous example of this is at the close of the encounter with Francesca and Paolo. The wanderer's sympathy for those who have sinned out of passion has grown from question to question, and Dante's personal concern is betrayed at the mention of *Amor*. After hearing how the lovers recognized their feelings while reading *Lancelot*, his sympathetic gestures indicate extreme emotion, and he is overpowered by a deathlike swoon ("E caddi come corpo morto cade"; *Inferno*, V, 142).[77] It is only later that Virgil gives a meaningful answer to Dante's mute questions, including these gestures. When Dante breaks down in tears at the sight of the fortune-teller who has had his face twisted to the rear as punishment, Virgil's gruff reproach, "Qui vive la pietà quand' è ben morta" (*Inferno*, XX, 28),[78] embodies the dogmatic response that demands that one recognize the punishment as an act of divine justice. The contradiction between the measure of divine retribution (*contrapasso*) and that of human pity is hardly overcome with this comment; rather, the difference is provocatively brought to light, just as it is elsewhere when the incomprehensibility of divine justice is left uncomprehended instead of being accepted on the basis of faith.[79]

The field of play found in the Scholastic *quaestio*, which discovered truth by means of the contradiction between *pro* and *contra*, was absent from the catechetical examination in faith. But in the form of the catechism, to which Luther gave the most powerful expression, this method grew in importance not only for religious instruction but, little by little, as a model for the transmission of knowledge in the life-world. A profane counterpart also came into being in the form of a catalogue of literary questions. With its firmly established sequence of permissible questions and definitive answers, the catechism took the historically opposite pole from the Socratic question, since the latter was intended to cast doubt on the known and bring the person questioned to new insights through the use of the aporia. The Christian catechism has its roots both in the oral instruction given the (heathen) candidate for baptism, and in the questions posed (originally to the godparent) before the baptism.[80] A second, later, source was the confession, which, in the Middle Ages took the form of question and answer. During the Reformation, the confessional examination, which inquired about the hidden sins of the individual (a psychoanalysis *avant la lettre*), was replaced by the investigation of faith. According to Luther, it was not only to precede communion, but was also to be administered at home daily to children and servants—a demand that, along with the growing number of questions in the early catechism, might point the way to an instructional system governing life and behavior in general. The possibility of turning knowledge of the catechism into dogma, a threat that had existed from the very beginning, was soon realized: Luther, using the threat of punishment, had already made learning the catechism compulsory, and soon it was declared a requisite for salvation. Pietism sought to oppose this tendency by pressing for a "true understanding of the catechism" and by demanding its "constant application" to one's own life.[81] But this happened at a time when the Enlightenment was already usurping control of the didactically very effective catechetical technique.

During the Enlightenment, literature and philosophy shared equally in the dialogic process that supplied question and answer with a repertoire of didactic forms reaching from the letter writer's guide[82] to the encyclopedia. The object was to make theoretical knowledge available on a practical level, and thereby render it possible for the individual to take responsibility for the problems of everyday conduct. Philosophy in particular took up the catechetical questions in order to upset religious orthodoxy on its own ground, by laying claim to the right either to answer such questions on its own authority, or to examine their validity or, on the other hand, to raise questions that had previously been disallowed on theological grounds. Rousseau provides one of the most impressive examples of this change. His *Profession de foi du Vicaire savoyard* puts forward only four articles of faith for enlightened deism. In his apologia to the Archbishop of Paris, he rejected other questions from the catechism, such as those about the creation of the world, or the trinitarian unity of God on the grounds that they were otiose, since they were irrelevant for practical life.[83]

It would no doubt be worthwhile to interpret the victory of the Enlightenment as a historical process in which question and answer are recast to the greatest possible extent. But up to now there seems to have been no history of the catechism that has examined the catechetical question-and-answer technique both in terms of the history of dogma and religious pedagogy and the sociohistorical function of the technique. This move is necessary, however, if we are to understand the manner in which political literature, *belles lettres*, ethics, and the history of philosophy have replaced the religious paradigm as a means of explaining the world. In order to produce such a history one might want to pursue the following line of thought. The French Revolution was ushered in by a plethora of civil *Catéchismes*: an "anonymous" *Catéchisme du citoyen ou éléments du droit publique français par demandes et réponses* (by Joseph Saige) had already appeared in 1787. Its primary accomplishment was to translate Rousseau's *Contrat social* into easily remembered questions and answers. In August of 1789, Barnave proposed on several occasions that the *Déclaration des droits de l'homme* become the *catéchisme nationale.*[84] In the impressive list of such catechisms we even find an effort to produce a *Catéchisme du genre humain* (1792), in which the answers are attributed to a teacher while the questions (which are, naturally, only "suggestions") are ascribed to a student who is now assumed to be able to speak for himself.[85] The clearest demonstration of the effort to connect with the religious is manifest in the *Catéchisme du curé Meslier* (1790), which gives blasphemous answers such as the following to the questions posed in the Christian catechism: "What does 'a God became man' mean? It means that a man tried to claim he was God. / Is he really God and man and both in one? Stupid questions are not worth answering."[86]

In the poetry of German idealism one runs into catechetical questions at that high point of tragic entanglement when certainty of feeling and delusion about identity of the beloved other intertwine and, at the same time, depend on that other for clarification. In Kleist's *Amphitryon* Zeus repeatedly uses the confessional mode of questioning in an attempt to force from Alcmena the love she has refused him by getting her to acknowledge his divine authority ("Does he exist for you? / Do you perceive the world which is his handiwork?" ll. 1416–1417).[87] In contrast, Giradoux reestablishes the integrity of the human couple by reversing the direction of the questions; a critical Alcmena puts the catechizing creator of the world in the position of having to respond and with each answer forces him further back into his initial role as spectator.[88] The philosophy of history in particular made the major and "ultimate questions" of the Christian catechism its primary responsibility. Thus, Lessing answered the question as to the reasonableness of revealed religious content by suggesting that religious revelation serves to carry out the continuing education that has been bestowed on the human species throughout its history.[89] Likewise, Kant later answered the question as to the "Possible Origins of Human History" (1786) by interpreting each point in the story of the Fall as a step in the original development of freedom. And so too, Marx responded to the long-standing question about the goal of history by reinterpreting the idea of the advent of the kingdom of God—after the classless society has abolished alienation, it will not be the joy of leisure but rather work that will become the active manifestation of freedom.[90] That the new philosophy of history can be understood as a response to the old catechetical questions was amply demonstrated by the French moralist Théodore Jouffroy at the beginning of the nineteenth century when he commented that the schoolchild can find the answers to all the questions the philosophy of history is in the habit of posing by looking in his catechism.[91] Later, even lyric poetry entered the fray, as is demonstrated by the poems in Victor Hugo's volume *Les Contemplations* (1856), in which the religious pieces can be read as a sort of lay catechism.[92]

This series of examples should not come to an end without making some reference to the longest, most enigmatic, and most humorous catalogue of questions in modern literature: the Ithaca chapter in *Ulysses*. In it Joyce did not simply narrate an everyday event—Bloom and Stephen's nocturnal return to Bloom's house, and its mythic substratum, Odysseus's return home. Instead, he presents it in the form of an interrogative series of 249 questions, nine imperatives, and 303 answers. But who interrogates whom here? Why in this manner, and to what end? They are all didactic questions, since the answer is always already clear, but they also present a particularity that must have an unpleasant effect on the reader. In this interrogation, the excessive pedantry of the questions is constantly reiterated in the excessive precision of the answers; in fact, it is often surpassed. What is true for this type of question and answer is equally true for the pragmatic situation of the questioner and the answerer, and for the function of their "endless conversation": Joyce calls upon all the possible models in the tradition of the magistral dialogue, the catechetical examination, the now criminal, now confession-like interrogation, and questions that link hypothesis and verification in order to examine them *in extremis* as it were, and to drive them into a final aporia that invites a multiplicity of possible responses. In the context of our analysis, the phenomenological mode of interpretation that Eckhard Lobsien recently applied to the "everyday life of Ulysses" is most relevant.[93] According to this interpretation, the Ithaca chapter, by its use of question and answer as a type of game, confirms the thesis that *Ulysses* could only discover the whole phenomenon of the everyday by raising it to the level of an object of aesthetic reflection. The questions in the Ithaca chapter seem to correspond to the typical expectations of an everyday orientation, but the answers inundate whatever has been asked, either by an over-exactness in the description of actual causality, or by an overflow of imaginary possibilities. Thus, a view of everyday life is constituted specifically for the reader so that this constant overtaxing of his knowledge—and his desire for knowledge—can awaken him to the schematic manner in which he experiences the everyday, and reveal the irreducible complexity of the supposedly self-evident reality of life.

However convincingly presented this thesis may be, and however certain it is that the two types of answers it discusses provide us with a general understanding of the function of question and answer in the next to the last chapter of *Ulysses*, it also ends up reducing the reader's experience to the constitution and deconstruction of his view of everyday life. At the very least, this leaves us with a question as to what happens to such a fully elaborated repertoire of questions and answers when its traditional model is reemployed as a means of destabilizing the evidence of the everyday and opening up unforeseen horizons. To a degree that one might not expect elsewhere, the instrument of question and answer is both ironized and aporetically sublated here, beginning with the manner in which an originally asymmetrical and magistral dialogue is given an inflated symmetry, as if the traditional, ignorant schoolboy now had the chance to stand up majestically against the superiority of the interrogating teacher by providing excessive answers. The underdog is first of all the reader in this case, as long, that is, as he remains disappointed because his longing for a tension-filled series of events is not fulfilled by the seeming pedantry of the questions and answers and he fails to get involved in the unexpected, kaleidoscopically emerging changes unfolding in the background of his field of perception—as long, that is, as he fails to recognize and enjoy the fullness of physical, geographical, historical, and other as yet undefined horizons of knowledge embodied in this game of question and answer that is brought to the fore by the provocatively inconsequential details of a nocturnal return home.

I will take my example from the question-and-answer sequence that attends the second of the drawers opened by Bloom.[94] The first three questions are formulated in the manner of a police report: "What did the 2nd drawer contain? . . . Quote the textual terms of this notice. . . . What other objects relative to Rudolph Bloom (born Virag) were in the 2nd drawer?" But the very first answer overshoots the mark as far as its relevance to a criminal investigation is concerned. The life insurance policy is presented in full, the balance in the savings account book is given in figures and then again in words, and the rest of the inventory continues to provide details for which one could imagine no other interested party than a question answerer who had fallen prey to an insane desire for absolute completeness. The following three answers are directed at the inner reaction an envelope addressed "To my Dear Son Leopold" produces in Bloom: "What fractions of phrases did the lecture of those five whole words evoke? . . . What reminiscences of a human subject suffering from progressive melancholia did these objects evoke in Bloom? . . . Why did Bloom experience a sentiment of remorse?" This seems to involve some sort of conscience searching. But this cannot be a series of confessional questions, since they are posed and answered as if the conscience searching had already taken place. His father's progressive melancholia and suicide, as well as his own remorse seem merely to have been retrieved from Bloom's fragmentarily recorded memories. The question poser and the answerer have known all along what the all-knowing narrator gradually and carefully reveals to the reader. They draw the supposed narrative itself into their interrogation, and use questions and answers as a probe, a technique of hypothesis and verification, of theory and application, with which to isolate the already known ever more precisely and thereby place it in an unexpected light. In keeping with the diagnostic tenor of the questions, Bloom's "reminiscences of a human subject suffering from progressive melancholia" are rearranged as medical symptoms,[95] while his remorse is presented in a manner reminiscent of the conclusions drawn by an investigative report: "Because in immature impatience he had treated with disrespect certain beliefs and practices." The question "As?" further categorizes them in the context of a theory of possible disrespectfulness, but, ironically, this leads to a catalogue of answers that is so complete that the question becomes, *post festum*, rhetorical.

This example demonstrates a reversal in the didactic role of question and answer, a reversal that, it seems to me, is characteristic of this immense catalogue as a whole. If one assumes, as does Karlheinz Stierle, that narrative itself can emerge as the answer to a theory, and that it has in such cases always already gone beyond the question to which it responds,[96] then Joyce has revealed the premises of this narrative structure, and at the same time turned its didactic function upside down. The implicit preliminary questions, which are usually left unexpressed in a classical narrative, are explicitly posed in the Ithaca chapter. Simply stated, they are constrained within a theoretical form that is sometimes reportlike, sometimes hypothetical, and usually borrowed from the metalanguage of a specific field of knowledge. A corresponding, terminologically exact, often catalogue-like or systematic set of answers is then provided. When this happens, it is no longer an answering narrative that goes beyond the preliminary questions posed by theory, but instead the theoretical inquiry and the applicable answers that surpass what is as yet only presumed to be a narrative: thus interrogated, both the superficial and meaningless events of the everyday world and the enigmatic and highly significant events of the myth melt into a statement having no end, and the ordering principle embodied in question and answer itself succumbs to a final aporia. The reader, who is intent on finding out where the questions and answers of the Ithaca chapter's interrogation might lead, no longer finds any final answer. Instead, he is dismissed with a final question: "Where?" It is posed in reference to Sinbad the Sailor, who, on the mythological horizon of the text, suggests the final image of Odysseus after he has returned home, an image that, in the answer to the previous question about Bloom's fatigue, evokes the dream of far-off lands and the tribulations of endless travel: "He rests. He has traveled. – With? – Sinbad the Sailor and Tinbad the Tailor and Jinbad the Jailer," etc. (p. 737). The simplicity of the penultimate question, "Why?" is answered with a highly complex riddle that (despite its insolubility) uses the contrasting connotations of "dark" and "bright" to reveal at least that Bloom, the "Sailor," a Sinbad in a "dark bed," disavowing his bold dreams ("of Darkinbad the Brightdayler"), slumbers toward a new day: "Going to a dark bed there was a square round Sinbad the Sailor roc's auk's egg in the night of the bed of all the auks of the rocs of Darkinbad the Brightdayler."

From a typographical point of view, the final question, "Where?" is answered only by a period, but in terms of the overall composition, a response is provided by another, and final, chapter, one that sets a Penelope who rejects none of her suitors in opposition to the would-be Odysseus. Molly's inner monologue brings about the collapse of both the syntactic order of the narrative form and the division between "I" and "it." A monstrous "confession of life" erases the difference between confessor and penitent and thus builds an ironic counterpoint to the "catechetical interrogation" (p. 735) of the Ithaca chapter. In the latter, the deconstruction of the momentary evidence of the quotidian and the demythification of a recurrent, immemorial past were propelled by question and answer in such a way that the contoures of a new mythos—the polylogical mythos of theoretical science—took enigmatic shape in the kaleidoscopic alternation of citations from the horizons of all available knowledge. If, there, theoretical science's promise of a thorough explanation of the world ends up in a *regressus in infinitum* because of the impossibility of completing the game of question and answer, the aporia of comprehension through question and answer is sealed by the Molly chapter: the syntactic order of the narrative form and the logic of question and answer are totally disempowered.[97] The previously separate horizons of knowledge disappear in the absolute monologic stream of a single consciousness, a consciousness from which the insatiable libido emerges as the last remaining horizon, it too a *regressus in infinitum*, since Molly, despite the "sailor" Bloom and all the deconstruction, responds in the affirmative: "I said yes I will Yes" (p. 783).

6. Mais où sont les neiges d'antan?

Not too long ago, the rhetorical question, which had for some time been the stepchild of critical research,[98] was elevated to the position of a central problem, even a methodological problem in literary theory thanks to Paul de Man's *Allegories of Reading*.[99] If, traditionally, one had the habit of treating the rhetorical question as an interrogatory mode in which the question was always also the answer, so that it appeared naive to take the question literally and answer it directly, de Man, on the other hand, opposed the figural to the literal meaning in order to show that one and the same grammatical model of a rhetorical question could engender two different and even mutually exclusive meanings. In addition, he showed that it is impossible to determine through either grammatical or linguistic means which of the two meanings prevails.[100] The literal meaning of a rhetorical question of the type "Quousque tandem abutere, Catilina, patientia nostre?[101] is "deconstructed" as soon as the reader or hearer notices that an indirect, figurative meaning rather than a direct answer is intended in response to the "how much longer"—a figurative meaning that does away with the interrogative sense of the words. Thus, one mode of reading the question reveals the other to be an error. This is why the rhetorical question, when understood as "deconstructive" linguistic play,[102] can serve as a superb means of revealing the fundamental divergence between grammer and rhetoric, literal and figurative meaning, sign and referent. In the light of this divergence, de Man concludes that every text means something other than that which the author intended or the reader found. Thus, every reading must be (*aliud in verbis, aliud in sensu*) allegorical. According to de Man, the paradox of the rhetorical question—that grammar allows one to pose a question that rhetoric prevents one from taking as such—leaves in its wake another question, one that is itself rhetorical and unanswerable: "What is the use of asking, I ask, when we cannot even authoritatively decide whether a question asks or

doesn't ask?"[103] With this question de Man opens the way to a rhetorical interrogation of the literary text, an interrogation that inevitably uncovers the latter's
self-contradictory nature, and demonstrates the naïveté of all interpretations that
try to locate the meaning of a text in the concordance of signs and meanings (*signi-
fiant/signifié*). Plato was right, all poets lie, and de Man's theory provides a new
basis for understanding why they lie—of necessity and without wishing to do so.

This challenge to literary hermeneutics can best be met at the point where de
Man asks about the usefulness of the rhetorical question, first of all by remembering its function in the rhetorical tradition and then by suggesting a possible difference between the rhetorical and poetic uses of question and answer. De Man's
variation on Derrida's deconstructive philosophy contains two problematic
moves. It denies the polarity between the "rhetoric of tropes" and the "rhetoric
of persuasion," letting the former absorb the latter—this despite the fact that he
himself has shed new light on their oppositional status—and, without further ado,
it merges rhetoric with literature, never considering the corrective that poetry has
to offer, precisely in its use of question and answer as a means of avoiding the
"rhetorical fallacy." If one restores these differences, then a glance at the rhetorical tradition readily demonstrates what the rhetorical and what the literary uses
of a question might be when it posits no answer—thereby revealing the naïveté
of the person who takes a rhetorically intended question literally, answers it, and
perhaps, as in the case of Archie Bunker's wife in de Man's example, even provokes someone else's anger.

Especially since Quintilian the rhetorical function of the *interrogatio* has been
associated with an intensification of the latter's content. The goal of this intensification is to heighten whatever is to be said by means of affective clarification.
Because of the content and form of the question, this clarification is supposed to
put the addressee in a mood of indignation or wonder.[104] In the case of the classic
Ciceronian example, "Quousque tandem abutere, Catilina, patientia nostra?" the
speaker does not expect a direct answer to the question "How much longer?" (for
instance, "a month," "a week," or "a day"); on the contrary, he wants to bring his
public to the point of outrage suggested by the connotations that the rhetorical
question secretly proposes as emphatic answers: "You have abused our patience
long enough! The time has come to settle accounts with you! What are we waiting
for?" Of course the content of the rhetorical question would remain the same even
if it were transformed into an assertive statement; but the alliterations (first the
dark sequence *u/t/e*, then the bright sequence *a/t/i*, and finally the repetition in
the last word of the *o* from the first) and the emotive words in the interrogatory
sentence structure (the excessive length of the onomatopoeic conjunction, the re-
tardation of the threatening, as it were, detonating aspect of the subject pronoun,
"nostra") stir the emotions more than the direct form embodied in an *exclamatio*
could. This effect may also be enhanced by the fact that the addressee must contribute his own part even though the answer is already present in the rhetorical

question. This contribution is necessary in order to complete the transformation of the question into its implicit answer, a task that can be assigned the value of a *capatio benevolentiae*. So constituted, the "passionate character" of the rhetorical question (which *Peri Hypsous*, Chapter 17, gives special emphasis) renders its pragmatic function ambiguous right from the start. It can be used as a *pursuasio*, and to good ends, but can also be sophistically or ideologically misused as a *manipulation*. Political rhetoric offers notorious examples of the latter. Among them are the all-or-nothing schema of the tantalizing question, the classic example of which is the pamphlet *Qu'est-ce que le tiers état* with which the Abbé Sieyès rang in the revolution of 1789;[105] the simulated question of the type "Do you want total war?" which pretends that one still has the freedom to choose in order more easily to steer the already inflamed crowd toward an unconditional "Yes!";[106] and also the more subtle strategies of rhetorical manipulation that, today, despite the fact that we frown upon suggestive questions in criminal jurisprudence and are suspicious of them in public-opinion research, are able to emphasize the imperative element of the question at the expense of the Socratic.[107]

Hugo Friedrich has clearly demonstrated the difference between the rhetorical and poetic functions of the question, and suggests that "lyric question" be used as a designation for the latter. "This and the rhetorical question share only the capacity to intensify that which is said. But here it is another sort of intensification, namely, one that moves toward the indefinite and unlimited, even the mysterious. It has no implicit answer. Rather it is purely and simply without one. It steeps the known or the seen in premonition and in an eternal, usually painless, sometimes even joyful, noncomprehension that has no wish to encroach upon the incomprehensible."[108] To this I would like to add a more formal requisite: to understand a lyric question it is necessary to avoid the obvious answer or that nearest at hand, in order to operate a reversal of perspective. The poem opens the way to this reversal in superb fashion by posing questions, and to answer them directly would be "prosaic," since the process that has been initiated—that of searching further by asking more questions—and in which the aesthetic organization of a new meaning is brought to pass, would itself inevitably be reduced to a mere prosaic statement. Thus we can see that it is not the emphatic acceptance of an implicitly given answer, but the negation of the known (from which the change in the direction of the question arises) that is commensurate with the lyric question. It really begins only at the point where the rhetorical question has achieved its aims. The lyric question also dissolves the implicit answer suggested and affectively enhanced by its rhetorical counterpart, and in the state of suspense thus created, opens an unexpected horizon of possible meaning that the reader must then concretize through his inquiring aesthetic observations. This description of the aesthetic question has the hermeneutic advantage of being available for use with all grammatical and rhetorical models of the question, models that, in fact, are constantly employed by the lyric. The type of question described by Friedrich, one that is "purely and simply" without an answer, and that conveys a sense of unfathomability, marks the extreme point (or, if you will, the ideal instance) of the lyric question. Lyric poetry does not, however, have the answerless question among its presuppositions. It can also pose questions for which one has long known the answers, but poses them under poetic conditions that nudge the predetermined answer into the "indefinite and unlimited," that is, into the process of further modification for which the reader who knows how to ask questions is responsible.

One of the most familiar lines in all of French lyric poetry can serve as an example here: "Mais où sont les neiges d'antan?" ("But where are the snows of yesteryear?") In Villon's "Ballade des dames du temps jadis,"[109] this refrain serves as a response to the question that appears in every strophe: "Ubi sunt qui ante nos in mundo fuere?"[110] Villon gave this question (which in his time had already sunk to the level of a cliché about ephemerality) poetic shape in a triumphal procession of the most beautiful women of legend. By evoking them in this fashion, each new name comments on the old question, "What has happened to them?" and thereby increases its intensity. Formally speaking, this is a naively posed rhetorical question that, if taken literally, would only allow for a banal response. It becomes a lyric question when one suspends the world of the quotidian, inverts the direction of the question, and begins to look for its figurative meaning in a new question: why is it that that which is most beautiful must die, and has it passed forever? To name a possible place in answer to the question "Where?" would be prosaic; the answer prescribed by the Christian faith—that the souls of the dead await the resurrection of their bodies—must be rejected in order for the lyric question to come into play as part of the longing for new, as yet undefined, answers. Thus, whenever the lyric movement of a strophe seems on the verge of protesting or rising up against death, the refrain, instead of providing an answer, poses an open-ended question that has a calming influence, assuming the tone of a wise, fatherly authority: "Mais où sont les neiges d'antan?"[111]

Leo Spitzer has already said all that needs to be said about the poetic means employed in this line (the emotive "mais," the visual aspect of the plural "les neiges," the use of "antan" that has an archaically beautiful ring for us). He interprets the meaning of the refrain as a reference to a "useless question" behind which is hidden the insight that human life and death can be compared to the nature cycle; thus, it is as useless to rebel against the necessity of death as it is to rebel against the change of seasons.[112] On the other hand, the counterquestion posed by the refrain has the poetic function of a question that demands of the addressee that he suspend the answer that is most "logical" and readily available: "Last year's snow has melted." The counterquestion, "Mais où sont les neiges d'antan?" is itself already the answer insofar as it turns the direction of the question back toward the series of figures in the "ubi-sunt" strophes and invites one to comparisons such as "female beauty is like pure white snow," "the death of the beautiful is as gentle as the melting of snow in the spring." Melancholy, which endures, finds comfort in the thought that the beautiful in nature always reappears as it does in the shape of each of the women. After considering all that the counter-question may lead to on the horizon of possible answers, I would also like to inter-pret the prior, "ubi-sunt,' question differently than Spitzer, who gently complains that it is "not worth posing." Of course a definite, always already known, every-day answer would indeed be fairly useless. But since the traditional question em-bodied in the ubi-sunt is answered with a newfound counterquestion, the play of question and answer takes on the poetic function of opening the closed horizon of the known and unquestionable to the questionable situation of the human being poised between life and death. The final repetition of the refrain, in the so-called *Envoi*, supplies the useless, but for poetry legitimate, question with a final, and unexpected, answer:

> Prince, n'enquerez de sepmaine
> Où elles sont, ne de cet an,
> Que ce reffrain le vous remaine:
> Mais où sont les neiges d'antan?[113]

The deeper meaning of the ballad will become apparent to the receiver when he recognizes that the anxiety provoked by asking about the meaning of death cannot be overcome with the answers provided by life. It can, however, be overcome by its sublation in the encounter with poetry. Only the language of poetry is able to survive the natural round of life and death. In the unforgettable words of Leo Spitzer, "Le refrain doit 'rester,' le cortège doit disparaître sans laisser d'autre trace, le refrain seul est voué à l'immortalité."[114]

If one accepts my suggestion and defines the lyric question in terms of its im-pact on the direction of the question—thereby distinguishing it from the rhetorical question that is aimed at generating an accord with an affectively enhanced, al-ready prescribed answer—then it manifests its specific function. This function can be recognized in the fact that the lyric question is able to force open the closed horizon of questions that lead to a particular answer (while at the same time negat-ing it), or that leave the decision as to an answer with the questioner himself. The lyric question opens new horizons. Thus, it is possible to include all the imagin-able models of question and answer (the direct, the didactic, or the rhetorical question as well as the simple, the blunt, or even the implicit answer) among the terms available to the lyric as long as they satisfy the general demand that they bring about a change in the reader's horizons, one that leads from the known to the uncertain. This change of horizons can be understood as a realization of the poetic function in the sense that Roman Jakobson has suggested, for along with the shift in the direction of the question comes a shift in the reader's focus, from *what* to *how*, from statement to communication for its own sake. In this case, the unanswerable lyric question described by Friedrich would correspond to the ideal of a text without denotation, the condition that marks the absolute limit of the modern lyric descended from Mallarmé. But, needless to say, the historical multiplicity of lyric forms should not be relegated to the level of nonpoetry simply because it fails to comply with the norms of modern *poésie pure*. Paul Ricoeur's supplement to Jakobson's formulation is valid for the lyric tradition as a whole: the emphasis on communication for its own sake need not do away altogether with denotation; it can also double it.[115] As far as the poetic function of question and answer is concerned, this means that lyric interrogation need not end in the unanswerable. It can quite easily enhance the expression of a particular answer through the shift from *what* to *how*, thereby bringing it out into the open once more. To achieve this, lyric poetry does not just use the conventional models of question and answer, those that satisfy the logical expectation that questions be answerable. It also develops its own models, models that contradict this expectation, models that everyday speech treats as naive, senseless, or—to put it bluntly—stupid, or that alienate when directed at some imaginary interrogatory authority that is believed to have sole jurisdiction over the answer. As far as I know, the models for these lyric questions have not yet been inscribed in any poetics. The organization and interpretation that follow are meant, therefore, to serve as a beginning for such an enterprise.

We must start with the simplest form of direct or didactic question, one that, in the lyric, even if it stood fast by an answer, would be emphatically intensified or proudly enhanced, but that could also be undermined by its transposition into a riddle and its accompanying solution, or by the unexpected form of its answer. The simple linguistic act of naming becomes a solemn act of summoning when a lyric question delays the name and adds an *epitheton ornans* to the answer: "What is King Ringang's daughter's name? / Rohtraut, Fair Rohtraut" (Mörike, "Schön-Rohtraut").[116] The empty schema provided by the catechetical question, "Who created the heaven and the earth?" is filled out by the lyric question, "Who carries the heaven's countless stars? / who leads the sun from its tent," and provisioned with cosmic images that praise God: "The glory of God found in nature" (Gellert). The definitive ethical question, "What is self-mastery?" is heightened to the point of the superhuman, reworked as a riddle, as questions that have, metaphorically, already scaled the ideal heights of the norm, and given a paradoxical explanation of what the self-mastering individual is capable. Then, suddenly, a succinct answer provides a solution:

> Who slays the lion, who slays the ogre?
> Who conquers both the one and the other?
> It's done by one who has mastered himself.[117]

Finally, lyric use of everyday informative questions can lead to shockingly unexpected answers, and to a complete reversal of one's habitual perceptions of the world: "Wait. Where are you off to? Heaven lies within you . . . " (Angelus Silesius, *Der Cherubinische Wandersmann*).[118]

The horizon of prescribed answers is also exceeded by lyric questions in the narrower sense. Among such questions are the following, in ascending order of complexity: questions with provocative, open-ended answers; questions that, instead of leading to an answer, pose a counterquestion; questions that implicitly provide their own answers, and are therefore question and answer in one; ironic questions that imply the opposite of that which is asked; absurd questions that must be analyzed in order to draw some meaning from their self-contradictory elements. Baudelaire, for example, ends his poem "Les Aveugles" with a question that remains unanswered—"Que cherchent-ils au Ciel, tous ces Aveugles?"[119] Thus, he interprets the typical posture of the blind, who always seem to be looking up and off into the distance, instead of at the pavement, as a paradoxical gesture, a gesture that articulates both a final hope and an accusatory outrage. The counterquestion, which stands in lieu of an answer and calls the already known into question, is already familiar to us from Villon's work. Another example, this time from Heine's *Neue Gedichten*, sharpens the dilemma created by the counterquestion and, at the same time, can be used to elucidate the function of the lyric question:

> Emma, tell, and tell me truly,
> Was it love that made me silly?
> Or, because I was so silly,
> Did the love but follow duly?
>
> By my passion even, Emma
> By my lover's madness even
> I'm tormented less and troubled,
> Than I am by this dilemma.
> (*Emma*, IV)[120]

Here a cliché drawn from the mannered lover's lament is outdone by an unexpected, willfully displaced *exceedent*. It reveals an irony that shifts the unresolvable either-or question in the direction of the *excess* of reflection, and denies *ex post* the supposed seriousness with which the second strophe, in lieu of an answer, describes the tormenting dilemma faced by the lover.

A well-known morning song by Dietmar von Eist can serve as a focus in an exploration of the lyric question that already possesses an implicit answer. It also provides an example of the formal division of question and answer between two speakers that frequently occurs in this genre:

Schläfst du, Geliebter?
Ist süsser als mein Kuss dein Traum?
Hör nur, ein kleiner Vogel
Singt vor dem Fenster im Lindenbaum.
                    (translated by von Scholz)[121]

The initial question in the translation does not convey the immediate function
that it possesses in Middle High German, where it serves as a greeting upon
awakening that the translator has suspended by interposing a second question.[122]
He then delegates the task — and is once again true to the original — to the little bird
in the linden. It is obvious that one could provide philological grounds for doubting that the translator's intervention captures the simple tone of the medieval
morning song. But this makes the lyric function of his second question all the
clearer. It eliminates the almost unnoticeable contradiction embodied in the first
question (which the sleeper cannot answer in the positive or the negative as long
as he is asleep) by inserting a lyric question that is both an answer to the first and
ex negativo the confirmation of the couple's love: "Is your dream sweeter than my
kiss?" After all, if taken as an answer the question could be understood as follows:
"If you can sleep while I lie here awake feeling anxious about your departure and
our separation, then your dream must rival my kiss, but, even if it outdoes it, it
is still to be measured in terms of our love."

The absurd question can serve a polemic function, as it does in Hans Magnus
Enzensberger's "The wolves defended against the lambs," if its obvious contradiction paves the way to an insight that emerges in striking fashion because of an
unexpected analogy: "Should the vultures eat forget-me-nots?"[123] The absurd nature of a lyric question can also lead the reader into the *regressus in infinitum* of
a process that undermines all hypothetical meaning. Celan's poem "Mandorla" begins with a puzzling question: "In der Mandel — was steht in der Mandel?" If [in
German] something would normally be hidden or unseen (*stecken*) in an almond,
but would appear (*stehen/steht*) in a book, then we must wonder whether the contradiction embodied in the agrammatical union, "was steht in der Mandel" ["what
appears in the almond"], might be resolved by employing the metaphorical *ter-
tium* "book."[124] Should we assume someone is inquiring about what appears in
the almond (which is not a book), and that in this case the answer would be "nothing"? The answer in the poem comes close to this hypothesis and at the same time
calls it into question: "Das Nichts. / Es steht das Nichts in der Mandel. / Da steht
es und steht." ["Nothing. / Nothing appears in the almond. / It just appears and
appears there."] Even if the word "nothing" is elevated to the level of "Nothing-
ness," it still seems absurd to say that nothing "just appears and appears there."
So this answer simply involves the reader in another riddle, one that the next strophe takes up and gives a totally unexpected answer: "Im Nichts — wer steht da?
Der König." ["In nothing — who appears there? The King."] The obscurity of this

answer is lifted slightly when one remembers that "almond" can also signify an almond-shaped halo. If the nothing that appears in the almond is meant to indicate the king in his nimbus, then the direction of the question shifts, and a new interplay of question and answer can begin, one whose charm lies in great part in the fact that Celan's poem does not allow the reader to work out a final answer.

The lyric question gladly responds to the need to have answers to questions dealing with the ultimate meaning of life. It does so by bringing an imaginary authority into play: "Why did you give us such deep insights . . . why, fate, did you give us feelings?" (Goethe).[125] In this case, poetic license makes it possible to force an answer from a mythic authority that does not allow itself to be questioned. Such authority can also be called into question, as it is in Goethe's "Prometheus," where it is replaced by a new authority: "Who helped me / Against the Titan's insolence? / Who rescued me from certain death? / From slavery? / Dids't thou not do all this thyself, / My sacred glowing heart?"[126] The lyric question, which is basically monologic, fabricates a partner here, Zeus, who represents mythological authority, but is addressed familiarly. Then, at the high point of the hymn, it becomes dialogic, addressing the heart within. The dialogic principle that, according to Bakhtin, usually grants authority to some absent or sought-after third party is not constitutive of the lyric. Even if the poem is directed toward a "you," as when question and answer are split into two speaking roles, or when the poem fabricates a dialogue with itself, lyric speech remains predominantly monologic. The voice of the "you" toward whom the lyric question can turn does not emanate from some external other as it does in prose. It remains within the subjectively experienced world through which the lyric "I" and, by extension, the reader too is disclosed. Although the lyric poem is the preeminent medium of self-expression among monologic fictions, here an "I" seems to be speaking only to itself, as if it had no listeners. Because of this, it can still become dialogic on a second level insofar as it draws nearer to the reader through its questions and answers—through questions that it puts to the reader or uses to make insinuations about him, and through irritating answers that must be probed by the reader, since their meaning remains open and demands the reader's participation. I would like to conclude with an example of this process of understanding, a process that unfolds through a constant linking of question and answer. My example is drawn from Rilke's cycle of *Sonnets to Orpheus*.

This poem seems to me to have the richest possible orchestration of questions and answers, but that is not surprising considering Rilke's high opinion of questions and of legends that posed them.[127] The second sonnet, with its shift from monologic to dialogic discourse, brings the lyric question into play, and, in so doing, immediately raises the possibility that the "singing god" addressed in the poem may not answer, thus leaving the reader with the responsibility of seeking a possible response in the four questions posed by the poet, questions that are themselves the answer:

> From the joined happiness of song and lyre
> a girl, almost, was formed, came forth, glowed
> clearly through her April veils, and made
> a bed for herself inside my ear.
>
> And slept in me. And then her sleep was
> everything: trees I had wondered at, those
> vivid distances, the meadow I felt, every
> amazement that had ever been inside me.
>
> She slept the world. Singing god, how did
> you make her so whole she didn't first
> need to be awake? See, she rose up, still asleep.
>
> Where's her death? Do you have time to find
> that subject before your song burns up?
> Where does she drain out of me? . . . a girl, almost . . .[128]

Here, the classical division of the sonnet is so arranged that the two tercets (lines 9–14) transform into a string of questions all that the two preceding quartets had praised in apodictic and apparently unquestioning manner as the astonishing effect of "song and lyre." Apparently unquestioning, since the obscure connections of this irreal series of events may, despite its terse images, raise a whole series of questions for the reader. What does "a girl, almost" mean? Is the girl born of song merely a metaphor for the effect of music, or is she also an independent figure? Does the "bed . . . inside my ear" refer to the act of hearing? Is this possibility contradicted by "and slept in me"? How can "her sleep" be everything, when one's senses are closed off from the world by sleep? One can disregard these questions at first and try to bring a little consistency into the series of images by connecting the main clause beginning with "and" to an event of some sort. Then one could read "a girl" as the subject, arising out of the spirit of music, radiant as Botticelli's "Primavera," making her bed in order to sleep peacefully ("inside my ear"), and thereby experience the fullness of the world. "A girl, almost" and the awakening of spring acquire an interesting equivalency in this case. Together they stand in sharp contrast to the idea of the completion of experience ("sleep was everything") summarized in line nine: "She slept the world." How can that which has just begun already be complete? This question, which the reader poses implicitly, is aptly posed if we assume the following lines represent its reformulation: "Singing god, how did / you make her so whole she didn't first / need to be awake?" This is a rhetorical question with a poetic function, one in which the question already contains the answer. The reader only needs to change the "how" into a "thus" in order to see that the simultaneous creation of beginning and end is the work of a "singing god." But the poetic function of this rhetorical question comprehends more than the firm answer I have suggested is available to the questioner. The answer given by line eleven reinstates the full paradox of the girl's coeval origin and fulfillment and reopens the horizon of meaning: "See, she rose up, still asleep." Her fulfillment must have overcome her as she slept. Yet it is precisely this irritating answer that is directed at the reader by the "See."

In order to shed some light on this rather problematic response, the reader can try to associate it with other ideas it brings to mind. "She rose up, still asleep" corresponds *ex negativo* to Jesus' command to the cripple: "Arise and walk" (Matthew 9:5). In one case, the *restitutio in integrum* manifests itself in the act of standing up and going out into the world, in the other, in standing up and achieving a fulfillment that does not depend on any action. What is the significance of the sleep that engenders this pure condition? As a response, the reader might think of another of the *Sonnets to Orpheus* (II, v). It begins with "Flower-muscle, that unlocks, bit by bit, / the meadow-morning of the anemone," and ends with the following question:

> We violent ones last longer.
> But *when*, in which of all our lives,
> are we so open, such receivers?[129]

The implicit answer that this rhetorical question has to offer discloses itself when one sets aside the explicit answer to the "when" (Villon's "where" also functioned as a "shifter," inviting a change in the direction of the question). It is not the "when," some later moment, that is at stake, but the "now," the qualitative leap that is necessary in order to change life so that "we" can be "open" and "receivers." In this case, the girl's sleep can be understood as the purest possible state of reception, an undivided openness to the world that is normally suppressed by the force of action. But then sleep itself can no longer retain the significance ascribed to it by the secular tradition. It ceases to be one of poetry's most beautiful consolations — a metaphor for death, for the peaceful state of deliverance achieved by the departed. The complete release evoked by sleep, this "rest" so similar to that of the dead, can here be understood as the very essence of life in all its purity, of openness to an untroubled knowledge of the world.

But then the reader collides once again with the question a later line confirms: "Where is her death?" In this question (and unlike the "when" in the line just cited) the "where" cannot be set aside. It must be taken in its *intentio recta*. If the sleeping girl completely fulfills the possibilities of life, where is there space for actual death? Where can it come from? Who sends it? These questions can only be directed at an imaginary catechetical agency, a mythic authority — the same "singing god" to which this remarkable, future-oriented question is posed: "Do you have the time to find / that subject before your song burns up?" That death must be "found" indicates a rejection of the notion that there is some independent power that stands in the way of life. If death is tolerated only as the simple negation of life, it cannot enter the scene of its own accord; it needs a motive, one that must be called forth by the song itself, one that does not impose an external ending on the song. What began with the song can only end with the song. But this end does not simply arrive with the final word of the final line. The event itself, the sleeping girl's death, is left out. Only a "before" and an "after" point in that direction. The "before" corresponds to the forward-looking question posed to the "singing god," the "after" to the interrogation of the present found in the line: "Where does she drain out of me? . . . A girl, almost . . . " Instead of an answer to the final question the sonnet ends by naming "A girl, almost . . . " —a reprise of the beginning. The girl lauded in the poem, not her death, ends the song; her figure, in all its fulfillment, triumphs over death, and (like Villon's poem) by negating death's negation, offers poetry as that which endures.

C. Three Case Studies in Aesthetic Application

1. The myth of the Fall (Genesis 3) interpreted literarily

If one looks for possible explanations as to why there is still so much aesthetic interest in this text, the first place to turn is probably to its mythic form, a form that, for today's reader, offers the particular charm of the originary and, therefore, of that which is most distant in time. Its story, which was narrated to a circle of listeners whose archaic life-world has next to nothing to do with our own, nonetheless retains its claim to say something about all mankind, something that is supposed to be of concern to us, too. Looked at from the point of view of literary form, it is clear that Genesis 3 represents a myth, as long, that is, as we understand a myth to be not only a reference to a memorable historical event but also a narrative that seeks to immortalize an event *prior* to all history. This beginning event, which in its scope embraces the whole world, involves the relationship between man and god, or higher powers, and answers an elementary question in advance and for all time to come. It seems to me, however, that this text stands out within the expectation horizon of its genre because, upon closer examination, what at first appeared to be the succinct nature of an answer given by a simple myth acquires an enigmatic narrative complexity. The characters involved in the action correspond to an archetypal constellation, god/human being (both male and female)/animal; but the four archetypes embody more than elementary relationships, more than the nature and position of God, man, woman, and animal. They have additional features that individualize them and allow them to emerge in an almost "modern" manner from the behavior dictated by their roles.

Yahweh, the god, is not wholly involved in the role of provoked authority, authority that interrogates, punishes, and decides the future. He seems to delight in the use of irony from the very beginning. In verses nine through eleven, he poses the question "Ubi es?"[1] (as if he did not know), and later asks, "Quis enim indicavit tibi quod nudus esses?"[2] (as if someone must specifically have told Adam this); and finally, after they are clothed, verse 22 says, "Ecce Adam factus est quasi unus ex nobis" (which seems to border on—not quite godly?—mockery).[3] In the economy of narrative myth such irony appears to be an aesthetic supplement. This also seems to be the case for the rhetorical subtleties that the narrator employs in elaborating the motivation and speech of the other three characters. The serpent sets up his conversation rather cleverly by first provoking Eve herself into explaining the commandment; only then does the serpent claim that, although hierarchically the lowest, it knows a secret that God, the highest being, is withholding from mankind. Why the serpent takes the initiative in this manner remains unexplained, thus leaving a great deal of room for the play of fantasy. On the other hand, three reasons are given straight off for the woman's actions: "Quod bonum esset lignum ad vescendum et pulchrum oculis aspectuque delectabile" (v. 6).[4] It might be quite interesting to play with the various impressions one has of Eve's character depending on which of these reasons is given precedence in an evaluation of her actions (e.g., *delectabile* = "to be desired to make one wise"!). In contrast, the man seems almost simpleminded. He avoids the question as to why (verse 11) by unhesitatingly shoving responsibility off onto his wife (or does his response, "Quam dedisti sociam mihi"[5] [v. 12], represent a protest aimed at the being who holds ultimate responsibility?). God's response to Adam's shifting of the burden of guilt onto Eve and, through her, onto the serpent, is that of a consummate rhetorician. He reverses the sequence and, in so doing, brings Adam back into first position—almost as if he wished to restore some of the man's lost prestige in the very act of punishing him.

It is also of aesthetic interest to note how this relatively short, dramatically structured text is able to answer an astounding number of questions about beginnings quite succinctly, without ever slipping into didactic directness. The story of the first human beings' first transgression against a commandment, and the unforeseeable results of this action, seem mainly to be a response to the obvious question as to how and at what price mankind arrived at a knowledge of good and evil. Even if one assumes (based on verse 5 and its ironic repetition in verse 22) that it may have been this fundamental question that the text was meant to answer, one should certainly not overlook the fact that what is narrated immediately raises other, new questions, such as why the knowledge of good and evil thus achieved was the source of the shame caused by nakedness. The terse answer to the question regarding the origin of our knowledge of good and evil found in the myth of the Fall cannot erase all further questions. On the contrary, this same mythic narrative must now respond to a whole series of other questions, because the mythic event, in serving as an answer, constantly generates new questions. Such questions touch primarily on the "before" and the "after" of the mythological event, all that mankind must accept in the loss of paradisiacal perfection and the acquisition of knowledge: the pain of childbearing, the tribulations of toil, mortality, hostility between man and beast, the rule of man over woman! The big questions concerning the conditions of human existence beyond Paradise, each of which could use an explanatory narrative of its own, are all nonetheless authoritatively silenced by one and the same answer. The succinct answer provided by Genesis 3, that all of this is the result of the self-induced expulsion of the first human couple from the Garden of Eden, nonetheless leaves behind the strongest possible incentive to ask more questions—whether out of a legitimate need to know what meaning human activity can have under these conditions, or out of an illegitimate curiosity about questions that the mythic answer has suppressed. For example, why did God withold precisely the knowledge of good and evil? Did he simply permit the serpent its cunning, or did he wish, or perhaps even require, it?

A second reading of the text should separate the disturbing from the familiar, and thereby serve to contrast two different horizons: the familiar horizon of contemporary understanding and the alterity of the world as it was understood in the past. We are well acquainted with talking serpents thanks to our tradition of fables, but this tradition does not distinguish them from other animals on the basis of their cunning. Does this emphasis point to a hidden meaning? The disquieting special status granted the serpent is further emphasized by the fifth verse, which ascribes to the serpent knowledge that no one else seems to have. It alone can betray the significance of God's ban on eating of the Tree of Knowledge, thereby revealing what God wanted to withhold from mankind. The most immediately disturbing aspect of this situation is that God imposes this prohibition in lordly fashion, as a pure test of obedience, without explaining its actual intent or significance. Much more disquieting, however, is that God—assuming, that is, that the serpent is not lying (but verse 7 seems to speak against this possibility, "et aperti sunt oculi amborum")[6]—apparently used the prohibition to cover up his privileging of himself as the only one to know the meaning of good and evil. If that is the case, then nothing could seem more plausible to us than to reach out for the fruit that had been arbitrarily withheld. We would also have to forgo the rationale that justifies the Bible's intentional discrimination against Eve. If need be, a modern Eve could offer a provocative, antiauthoritarian addition to the pre-Platonic triad of reasons for her interest in the forbidden fruit (according to Luther's translation, it was *good* to eat, *delightful* to see, and *desirable* as a means of becoming wise): one desires it *because* it is forbidden. Further doubts about the motivation behind Genesis 3 are raised by the fact that, at the moment when Eve's action is condemned, not another word is said about the third, entirely honorable, and for us exculpating, reason for her behavior. One of the first major instances of alterity to issue from this bygone horizon of meaning occurs in the seventh verse of the narrative: "Et aperti sunt oculi amborum cumque cognovissent esse se nudos."[7] It is not the sudden recognition of one's nakedness, and the feeling of personal shame experienced by both genders (fig-leaf behavior!), that produces this sense of alterity. Even a modern reader can find this to be a "natural" reaction, one he can readily explain in terms of psychoanalysis, the history of social customs, or whatever. Rather, it is that the awaited knowledge of good and evil emerges at the same time as a shameful consciousness of one's body and one's sexuality that strikes one here. It is precisely this convergence that leaves an inexplicable and still mysterious stigma on the latter.

The second episode is rather well suited to deepening the mystery surrounding the nature of this stigma. The personal sense of shame felt when faced by an Other is transformed into fear upon the arrival of a third party. Adam is driven to the childish and helpless gesture of trying to hide from the all-knowing Lord of the Garden. Is it the remarkable fear of being seen naked by his Creator, although the latter has never seen him otherwise and his body remains the same, that leads to Adam's behavior, or is this fear only displaced anxiety about the punishment to be meted out for transgressing against a commandment? The ironic question posed at the beginning of Adam's interrogation ("Quis enim indicavit tibi quod nudus esses?" verse 11)[8] supports the second hypothesis (especially given the final clause in the sentence: "Nisi quod ex ligno . . . comedisti").[9] But beyond this point the text leaves us in the dark as to the connection between personal shame regarding one's body and sex and the knowledge of good and evil that was originally withheld and acquired only by transgressing against a commandment. Does this connection belong to the anthropology of an alien life-world, one that can only be reconstructed historically, or should one assume the presence of an esoteric (allegorically encoded) knowledge, or even a deliberate, and, consequently, "poetic" indeterminacy?

The interrogation as such presents no serious hermeneutic problems. With regard to literary form, one might mention in passing that the ironic introduction and the handing on of guilt from the highest to the lowest of the accused is a tried-and-true comedic technique. The elevated style appropriate to a venerable subject and worthy occasion seems not to be sought after in Genesis 3; perhaps biblical myth is not so far from the comic tales about the Greek gods after all. The first of the etiological motives provided by the judgment seems rather more curious than disturbing today. After all, that the serpent must henceforth go "upon [its] belly" readily leads to a rather impudent question as to how it had moved before (iconographic fantasy is provided with a splendid task here). But, if one tries to draw conclusions about the "before" on the basis of the "after" of the remaining etiological motives, the alterity of the original horizon of meaning reappears. Should we assume that the characteristics announced as belonging to the woman (the necessity of conception, the pain of childbearing, sexual desire for the man, and, at the same time, his dominion over her; v. 16) were first imposed on her *after* the Fall? If so, the extremely negative valuation of her sex role is disconcerting, given that it is soon afterward contradicted by the name she is given: *Hava*, "mother of all living" (v. 20). Furthermore, their implied existence before the Fall would be disturbing insofar as Eve, though she had the same rights, and was Adam's *socia* [companion, partner], rather than his dependent, would appear to have had no longing for sexual union (a possibility that is once again in conflict with the text: "Crescite et multiplicamini"; Genesis 1:28).[10] Conjecture about the desire experienced by the first human couple while in Paradise (a desire that should probably not be thought of in entirely abstract terms) is hardly something that begins with the modern reader—as is demonstrated by the rich exegetic and poetic tradition that, by way of compensation, has filled in the empty framework of this "marriage in Paradise" in the most delightful manner.

Adam seems to have come off a lot better at the moment of judgment. Given what God first accuses Adam of, "Quia audisti vocem uxoris tuae" (v. 17),[11] one might suspect that God felt a need to remind him of his manly superiority and at the same time organize a patriarchal society. Only after this does he blame Adam for transgressing against the commandment not to eat of the tree. But since theirs is a relationship *inter pares*, why should the male not listen to the voice of his wife? Oddly enough, the narrator seems to have overlooked the contradiction created by his formulation in verse 17. According to verse 6, Eve is supposed to have *silently* handed the fruit to Adam after taking a bite from it. Moreover, the text not only fails (one might say fortunately fails) to address the question of who is guiltier, it also leaves open the lesser, but nonetheless momentous, question as to why Adam bit into the fruit offered by Eve, thereby overstepping the commandment. The palette of possible motives begins with bewitchment or seduction; but Adam's bite from the apple can also be explained by the reasons given for Eve's, and beyond this one might speculate about the noble motive of expressing solidarity with someone who had already "fallen." The next statement in the text, "Maledicta terra in opere tuo,"[12] is much darker. It lacks the aesthetic charm and the moral casuistry involved in leaving Adam's motivation unexplained. As their functions are assigned—when Eve has imposed on her the sufferings of regeneration and Adam the toil of feeding the human race—the earth is cursed as well. Why is the earth, or nature, in all its innocence, brought into this human problem? Does God's secret plan envision the world as an embodiment of nature in general, or the earth as farmland, or, more particularly, work as the activity with which man appropriates nature as a means of sustaining himself? Then again, given the curse with which all human activity is now burdened, it seems disproportionate (a contamination of sources?) and hardly comforting that God personally tailors the clothes the departing couple will wear. This is especially true given the (once again ironic) first words of the Lord's closing comment, "Ecce Adam factus est quasi unus ex nobis . . . " (v. 22),[13] which come immediately after he "clothes" Adam and Eve—a combination of events that tempts the reader to ask a rather disrespectful question as to what "one of us" normally wore in the Garden.

Of even greater significance, however, is that hiding one's nakedness and the knowledge of good and evil are again linked in verses 21–22, just as they were in verses 5–7, although there has been no intermediate explanation of their connection. From the point of view of literary hermeneutics, there is no textual reason whatsoever to suppose that the (much later?) theological notion of "sin" fills in this gap. Instead, the aesthetic curiosity that this text awakens (because of its highly poetic structures of indeterminacy) is likely to induce further questions, since its initial query concerning the high price mankind has had to pay for the knowledge of good and evil cannot be satisfactorily answered simply in terms of the expulsion from Paradise. Aesthetic curiosity, and along with it theoretical curiosity, might even reverse the direction of the original question and suggest a counterreckoning, one that need not obviate the mythical answer. This new calculation could run as follows: was the price really so high that it was not worth it? Equipped with the knowledge of good and evil, it becomes possible to begin a mature and responsible existence, even if this existence is postparadisiacal. And if it is only after taking such a step that something like history can come into being, would this beginning of human labor not also have been a matter of importance to God—a beginning that allows him forthwith to unburden himself of *creatio perpetua*, and that likewise frees him from the task of explaining the presence of evil in the "good" world he has created? Having gotten to this point, one can finally pose the most impudent questions of all, those that the myth has suppressed. Did God only pretend to impose a test of obedience on Adam and Eve while secretly fixing the high price to be paid for their disobedience? Was the divine indiscretion that made this price so attractive deliberate? And was this price the means of setting the first human couple—guilty of an "original sin" of which their descendants no longer had to be ashamed—on the road to history?

Reversing the direction of the original question has led us to a modern interpretation, and to a level of reception that has achieved fame thanks to Hegel and, more recently, Bloch, who regard the biblical myth of the Fall as the initial event in the liberation of humanity from a self-imposed dependency. "The real original sin would then be the wish not to be like God."[14] I do not, however, intend to let this philosophical use of Genesis 3—which, as a hidden theodicy (in Odo Marquard's sense of the term), should be of interest to contemporary theology as well—serve as a conclusion instead of further pursuing the literary applications of the biblical text. In the face of a theological dogmatism that (according to Helmut Thielicke, for example) would save us from the question as to how evil came into the world by defining it as an "incorrectly posed question,"[15] and in the face of the philosophy of emancipation that today seems to be nervously eyeing the price to be paid for the idea of autonomy, literary hermeneutics may nonetheless have its own means of justifying a lost Paradise to its theological and philosophical detractors. Although the theologian can only assign the *hortus voluptatis* a value *ex negativo*, as a precondition for the *peccatum originale* meant to satisfy the requisites of the demiurge and eventually lead to the salvation of a fallen humanity, and although the philosopher of history is obliged to belittle the Garden of Eden as a "park" in which "only animals, not human beings, could live,"[16] aesthetic reception can open new horizons of meaning for an earthly paradise that has been brought low both by a historiography predicated on God's grace and by the forward movement of emancipation. The literature and art of both the Christian and the post-Christian eras have had a predilection for Paradise Lost, and in each succeeding epoch they have renewed the effort to reconstitute the paradisiacal experience of humanity's first couple as a way of understanding human happiness.

Had the reception history of this lost Christian paradise already been written, it would read like an unorthodox, if not heretical, commentary on Genesis 3. Its spotlight would illuminate, among others, the *paradisus amoris* found in medieval courtly love poetry and allegory; the bucolic, happy world of Renaissance pastoral poetry; Milton's *Paradise Lost*; Rousseau's *Etat de Nature*, the romantic nostalgia for the *vert paradis des amours enfantines*;[17] Proust's paradise of memory (*les vrais paradis sont les paradis qu'on a perdus*);[18] and Stendhal's conception of art as the *promesse du bonheur*, which, paradoxically enough, finds its most beautiful contemporary expression in the context of Adorno's puritanical aesthetics of negativity. Obviously, one cannot do justice to the aesthetic project of restoring biblical paradise if one simply assigns it to the realm of fairy-tale wish fulfillment, or reduces it to the illusory satisfaction of the need for an "ideal world." The hermeneutics implicit in the aesthetic reception of Genesis 3. has always approached and productively interpreted this basic model of religious experience as more than mere daydreams about the "world as we might wish it to be." The productive component of aesthetic experience might interpret Adamite man's obligation to participate in God's work of creation (*ut operaretur et custodiret*; Genesis 2:15) as a legitimation of *homo artifex* [man the artist or artificer], who understood his production (poiesis) more and more as a second creation, and thereby worked off the curse that, after Genesis 3:17, lay on all labor. For the receptive component of aesthetic experience, the necessity of interpreting the sensual perfection of the lost *paradisus voluptatis* in words or pictures brought with it the provocative task of making the fullness and refinement of the sensual experience of the Adamite human conceivable for his or her descendants— descendants who had lost this perfect aesthesis because of the Fall. I have already sketched the Christian aspects of the intellectual history of poiesis and aesthesis, so I will deal here only with the paradigmatic significance of Genesis 3 for the communicative component of aesthetic experience (catharsis).[19] Milton's *Paradise Lost* provides what must be the most magnificent evidence of this connection.

When read as a commentary on Genesis 3, Books IV and VIII of Milton's work fill in a gap in the biblical text that becomes visible as soon as one poses an impudent question as to what Adam and Eve actually did and how they related to one another before they forfeited their paradise by taking a bite out of the apple. This question is not as futile as it appears, as is demonstrated by the rich patristic tradition of exegesis that focuses on the "paradisiacal marriage."[20] Erotic curiosity is already evident there, and even more so in Milton's work, when the deeper question as to the definitive beginning of the relationship between man and woman is posed. In these instances, literary hermeneutics throws more and more light on the ideal *connubium* Adam and Eve experienced in the Garden as opposed to the alienating conditions of their life in common after the Fall. In so doing, it reconstitutes the community *inter pares* established by the first couple rather than the founding act of that paternalistic society to which Yahweh's pronouncement in Genesis 16 seems to have led historically. As if intent on disproving in advance Hegel's assertion that "only animals, not human beings, could live" in Paradise, Milton displays the radiant, godlike qualities of Adam and Eve to a jealous and amazed Satan (IV, 288ff.). Set above all living creatures as "lords of all," they tower over the animals primarily because of the characteristic worthiness they achieve through their daily work:

> . . . other Creatures all day long
> Rove idle, unemploid, and less need rest;
> Man hath his daily work of body or mind
> Appointed, which declares his Dignitie,
> And the regard of Heav'n on all his waies.
> (IV, 616–20)

As will be the case after the realization of the classless society predicted by Marx, Milton's "pleasant labor" and "rest' mark the poles of a by no means indolent paradisiacal being. The dignity of the work to which Adam and Eve are called as protectors and cocreators of the Garden corresponds to the dignity of the mutual repose they enjoy in the "Rites / Mysterious of connubial Love" (IV, 742–43). Milton's epithalamium to Adam and Eve openly celebrates the joys of the marriage bower, and proclaims that such harmony of loving and being loved is justified particularly because of its "puritie" and "innocence"—the grounds that false shame and hypocritical morality give for believing they must pass over in silence or scorn the consummation of the first human couple's love:

> Whatever Hypocrites austerely talk
> Of puritie and place and innocence,

Defaming as impure what God declares
Pure, and commands to som, leaves free to all.
Our Maker bids increase, who bids abstain
But our Destroyer, foe to God and Man?
(IV, 744–49)

This revision of the Christian tradition of despising or making sexual love taboo—a tradition supposedly based on Genesis 3:7—is not the only supplement with which Milton enriched the interpretation history of Genesis 3. Theological hermeneutics must find one of the first conversations between God and Adam (VIII, 357ff.) equally worthy of note, since it precedes the creation of Eve. This context allows Adam himself to take the initiative and ask God if he might provide him with a being similar to himself:

Thou hast provided all things; but with mee
I see not who partakes. In solitude
What happiness, who can enjoy alone,
Or all enjoying, what contentment find?
(VIII, 363–66)

The dispute that follows is a profound summit discussion between creator and creature, one in which Adam—as is seen later (VIII, 437)—has to withstand a sort of theological interrogation, and does so with éclat. He knows how to respond with an argument of wide-ranging significance when God counters with a question about how Adam could feel lonely, surrounded as he is by a variety of living creatures, and knowing their names and their ways as he does:

Among unequals what societie
Can sort, what harmonie or true delight?
Which must be mutual, in proportion due
Giv'n and receiv'd . . .
(VIII, 383–86)

If God's creature cannot be alone and happy, if happiness can be found only in consort with a similar being, in the mutual pleasure two such beings find in each other, this is a token of the imperfection of human nature and, at the same time, represents the claim to something the Creator, in his perfection, apparently does not need. The questions God poses next move further in this problematic direction: does Adam think God has no need of happiness in his eternal solitude, and does he believe the contact between the Creator and his creations lacks that equality that *social communication* alone makes possible (VIII, 399ff.)? Adam evades the question as to whether God can be happy in his solitude by reminding the Lord of his self-sufficient perfection and by admitting his own human deficiency: his social incapacity to be sufficient unto himself. But according to Milton's interpretation, it is precisely this imperfection in the being God created, this inability to be alone, that gives Adam the chance to achieve happiness, if not perfection itself, through love of an equal:

> Thou in thy self art perfect, and in thee
> Is no deficience found; not so is Man,
> But in degree, the cause of his desire
> By conversation with his like to keep
> Or solace his defects . . .
>
> (VIII, 415–19)

When read as a poetic commentary on Genesis 3, Milton's *Paradise Lost* establishes a new horizon of meaning for the words with which the Christian demiurge, in a sort of self-revision, ends the series of positive judgments he has made: "Non est bonum esse hominem solum: faciamus ei adiutorium simile sibi" (Genesis 2:18).[21] It is not as the likeness of God, whom he looks up to with reverence, but, rather, as a fellow human being that Adam finds himself. Only when "mirrored" in an Other, in a "you" whom he meets as an equal,[22] does the first human being discover the conditions under which he can become more complete and perfect and, thus, happier. A later scene [VIII, 460ff.] shows what this completion and perfection can mean when it arises between free and equal creatures. There, Eve is bestowed upon Adam by God as the final and most beautiful work of his creation. She first appears to Adam in a dream and then, dreamlike, comes to him in reality. Shortly afterward they enter the paradisiacal *connubium* together, while the earth, along with all its creatures, expresses its joyous support. This not only establishes the *fellowship* (VIII, 389) of the first human couple as a community *inter pares*, it also deconstructs the traditional superiority of the male, a superiority that even Milton had maintained in Book IV, citing it as a condition of the couple's sexually determined inequality.[23] Here, in Book VIII, the relationship even comes close to reversing itself. Adam begins to wonder whether too much substance may not have been removed from his side at the moment of Eve's creation, leaving him subject to her charm, and even to the superiority of her whole being ("so absolute she seems / And in her self compleat"; VIII, 547–48). Raphael has to warn him against such mistaken submission and redirects his passion toward the mutual self-respect of love. Thoroughly chastened, Adam is also abashed, but not so much so that he is in turn prevented from embarrassing heaven's envoy by asking an impudent question: "Love not the heav'nly Spirits, and how their Love / Express they, by looks only, or do they mix / Irradiance, virtual or immediate touch?" (VIII, 615–17). The answer Raphael gives as to how angels can experience sensual love and at the same time remain on a plain above the sensual offers no great solution to the problem, and that Milton has him blush ("with a smile that glow'd / Celestial rosy red, Love's proper hue"; VIII, 618–19) when answering lends sublimely ironic support to Milton's ongoing effort to free sensual love from shame.

Milton's poetic commentary also leaves an important theological question unanswered, although it may only have occurred to critics at a more recent point in the reception of Genesis 3, namely, the question as to whether the first great recognition that Milton attributes to Adam, and which occurred before the bite into the apple—that the lonely cannot be happy—holds true for God as well ("Seem I to thee sufficiently possest / Of happiness, or not? who am alone / From all Eternitie . . . "; VIII, 404–6). Milton's *Paradise Lost* identifies happiness as a compensation for human imperfection, one that apparently endures despite the Fall. That perfection that seems to require no social intercourse is left to God: "Thou in thy secresie although alone, / Best with thy self accompanied, seek'st not / Social communication" (VIII, 427–29). But if this is the case (Adam's assumption is not contradicted by his Lord and Creator) God's motive for crowning his worldly creation with mankind's first couple is left up in the air. Did God only need a gardener for his Garden of Eden, or did this final act of creation perhaps conceal *ad imaginem suam* a lonely being's need for "its own kind," and for "human happiness" as well? This seems inconsistent with the disappointed demiurge's later need for satisfaction. But such disappointment, especially when it is the result of a very clumsy test of obedience, is just as inappropriate to the idea of divine perfection as is the lonely desire for a "you." And should we assume that the Christian God would fulfill this desire for the creature made in his image only in order to deny it to himself?

Would theological hermeneutics allow such impudent questions to supplement its exegesis of Genesis 3? The thought fills literary hermeneutics with curiosity, a curiosity that is its secret vice, but perhaps its *ratio vivendi* as well.

2. Job's questions and answers from afar (Goethe, Nietzsche, Heidegger)

There is no text in which question and answer have a greater role than in the Book of Job.[24] In it, the mythic and theological functions of question and answer come into conflict in a way that marks the history of the text's reception. This conflict brought philosophy into the act, and literary hermeneutics has its word to say as well (though certainly not a final word), since the work is highly poetic and deals with a theological problem that has aesthetic implications. The form of the text that has been handed down to us shows the unmistakable signs of various stages of literary revision, each of which adds to the ambiguity of the work as a whole. The original folk narrative, which was in prose, embodied a legend of the type that portrays the "sufferings of a righteous man." To this, the later Satan scenes were added, so that a highly literary motif, the bet (later used by Goethe for the

"Prologue in Heaven" in *Faust*), provided a frame for Job's story. But with this addition, God seems to be assigned the fatal role of merely watching the wicked game that he has allowed Satan to play with Job. Between the phase of the story when the three friends participate silently for seven days and nights, and the later moment of the *restitutio in integrum* with Job's intercessory prayer, his twofold repayment, and the blessed end to his life, comes the great dialogue with these friends. Starting in Chapter 3, and continuing through Chapter 42, verse 6, this dialogue consists of three cycles of statement and counterstatement that are elevated to the level of poetry by their verse form, and culminate in an insoluble aporia. The highly dramatic tension of the dialogue arises in great part from the fact that Job begins to turn his personal lament into a profound question about the suffering and injustice in the world only because of this dispute with his orthodox friends. It is also here that he discovers the courage to demand his rights from a silent God. But even the growing assertiveness of Job's inquiry is repeatedly transmuted into a moving plea for a response at those moments of his deepest distress.[25] After a long, obstinate silence, Yahweh finally replies, not with an answer, but with a monstrous catalogue of more than seventy counterquestions, all of which serve to arrest Job's complaint with a crushing argument: "Are you the Creator, since you dare to question me in this way?" This most remarkable of all God's utterances, with its enigmatic descriptions, and its hymns to Behemoth and Leviathan, goes far beyond the needs of a rebuke, and behind Yahweh, the historical god and just lord of Israel, the unmistakable figure of a mythic, Baal-like god of nature appears. The closing section of the text, which frees Job from his suffering, remains enmeshed in a final, theologically controversial, but poetically all the more powerful, ambiguity. Although Job submits to his Lord and God with the formulaic reply, "Therefore have I uttered that I understood not," Yahweh seems to prefer Job's heterodox questions to his friends' orthodox answers. He reprimands the latter after honoring his *servant* Job by appearing before him.

The ambiguity of this conclusion raises the question as to whether the Book of Job can justifiably be considered one of the first theodicies. And this question points toward the problematic relationship between theodicy and theology, a problem that was discussed at the third colloquium on "Poetics and Hermeneutics," and that I would like to take up again here. Hans Blumenberg suggested that we could distinguish between theodicy and theology by examining the way question and answer function—do they canonize or decanonize? When confronted by the evil and the human suffering that exist in the world, theodicy tries to demonstrate God's higher justice by pointing to an enigmatic *Order* that is merely veiled by what appears to be a quite terrible reality. Theology, on the other hand, dismisses the idea of any human justification of God, rejects the canon of a just balance as anthropomorphic, and returns to the idea of the incomprehensibility of divine *Will*. In terms of the relationship between religion and literature, this means that "theodicy narrows the realm of aesthetic phenomena because it tends to canonize the already permissible, [whereas] theology liberates phenomena and licenses the expansion of the spheres of the representable and the relevant."[26] From this point of view, the Book of Job—which is usually treated as a theodicy insofar as it is a justification of God's works, and addresses the question of suffering and its meaning—would have to be classified as a "theology," given Job's questioning and protesting. It is a theology that grants itself the literary license to discuss reality in a way that dogma and the canon of the representable had prevented up to this point. On the other hand, Jakob Taubes supported the notion that "it is theodicy that opens up the canon of the permissible and the sphere of the representable. . . . It is not the theology of the Pentateuch but rather in the theodicy of the Book of Job that Satan appears. The conciliatory bracketing of its subject matter by a theodicy makes it possible to give greater expression within those brackets to the suffering and ugliness of the world than the theology in Genesis would allow. Genesis's theology gives answers before the questions are asked: a fundamental darkness is covered over by the order engendered by God the Creator."[27] In his reply, Blumenberg insisted that the Old Testament Job clearly should not carry the title of theodicy in the sense that Leibniz's work does, especially given its aesthetic motivation. "Surely this game the 'noble Lords' play with human nature is not justified by its results? I maintain that [the text] is a bit of dualism that has been transposed into the realm of the voluntaristic by allowing only those questions to be asked for which an answer is already at hand. . . . God as spectator for the *theatrum mundi* where, according to Luther, all creatures are 'masks and mummery'[. . .]—that is a provocation aimed at theodicy, not theodicy itself."[28]

It would be all too easy to settle this dispute between philosophical and theological hermeneutics by assuming that Taubes has quietly reshaped theodicy (by granting it the capacity to decanonize) so that in the end it means the same thing that theology does to Blumenberg. Blumenberg's definition does, of course, make it incumbent on theodicy to provide a historical follow-up on its aesthetic transpositions. When it does, one finds that theodicy progressively destabilizes the canon of the permissible and thereby relinquishes the need for theological legitimation. In the end, theodicy so radically exonerates divinity of the evil of the world—Goethe and Nietzsche mark the final steps in this development—that art itself takes over the functions of final judgment and redemption, and soon permits the vile world to appear only when justified as an aesthetic phenomenon.[29] On the other hand, one can object that Taubes's "conciliatory bracketing" would be hard to locate in Job.[30] It would require understanding Job 19:25 as Luther translated it ("But I know that my redeemer lives")—a hermeneutic inversion that had already surfaced in the Vulgate, quite in opposition to the Hebrew text's " . . . that my advocate lives."[31] In this move one can see an early exegetic attempt to turn the archaic theology of the Book of Job into a harmonious theodicy. And, finally, how or in what way the theophany could be a general answer to Job's questions remains unclear to me, given the way they manage to erase Yahweh's counterquestions. It is certainly not an answer that resolves all of Job's questions with regard to their content or that establishes a new theologically viable norm.

Given these conditions, a new interpretation of the Book of Job may be worthwhile — one that centers on the function of question and answer in the text. In accordance with the rights of the Lord, the first questions are posed by God to Satan: "Whence comest thou? . . . Hast thou considered my servant Job? For there is none like him in the earth . . . " (1:7–8). Yahweh himself provokes the bet with his second question. Interestingly enough, it is Satan's first counterques- tion that rouses God's desire to make the bet: "Doth Job fear God for naught? . . . But put forth thine hand now, and touch all that he hath, and he will renounce thee to thy face" (1:9, 11). Satan's counterquestion is composition- ally aimed at a result (aided literarily by a motif that will only later reemerge): it is precisely at the moment he sees God face to face that Job will finally submit to his Lord. In this dialogue with Yahweh, Satan's counterquestion announces the bet and, thus, the nature of the game being played, which is further confirmed by God's comment just prior to Job's second test: "He still holdeth fast his in- tegrity, although thou movedst me against him [!], to destroy him without cause [!]" (2:3). Even if one assumes that God is sure of his cause, this admission of having acted *nolens volens* clearly exposes a latent dualism. Is this why Satan is no longer mentioned at the end of the text — to make us forget this possibility?

The exchange of questions and answers between Job and his friends — a dia- logue in which God is a constantly present, if silent, third party — turns the game to bitter earnest. This is already evident in the external conversational frame- work, given the brusqueness of the opening speech (12:2: "No doubt but ye are the people / And wisdom shall die with you") and the manner in which the others' competence is constantly challenged (13:2: "What ye know, the same do I know also: / I am not inferior unto you"; 13:13, "Hold your peace, let me alone, that I may speak, / And let come on me what will"). Here it is not a question of seeking truth together in Socratic fashion. Instead, what matters is to defend oneself against the other as one would in a legal proceeding. The complaint made by Job in his suffering, once it has reached its peak in the question "Why died I not from the womb?" (3:11), suddenly becomes a problem of theodicy: "Wherefore is light given to him that is in misery?" (3:20). This in turn triggers a dogmatic reply that brings about a reversal. Whoever suffers must be guilty: "Remember I pray thee, who ever perished being innocent?" (4:7). The pious suggestion added later ("Be- hold, happy is the man whom God correcteth: / Therefore despise not thou the chastening of the Almighty"; 5:17) is an unacceptable bit of appeasement as far as Job is concerned, one to which he at first replies with accusations of insincerity and self-righteousness, since it has not yet been proved that he has done wrong (6:24–30). Then, in order to avoid the dreadful conclusion that his suffering results from a guilt he has not admitted to himself, he turns to images of monstrous natural powers that transcend human capacity for understanding: "Am I a sea, or a sea-monster, / That thou settest a watch over me?" (7:12); "What is man, that thou shouldest magnify him, / And that . . . thou shouldest visit him every morning, / And try him every moment?" (7:17–18). These same images reappear later – as a literarily calculated inversion – in God's counterquestions to Job: the sea in 38:8 ("[Declare if thou hast understanding] who shut up the sea with doors . . . "); the sea monster in the form of the Behemoth ("Behold now, Behemoth, which I made with thee"; 40:15), ironically referred to here as "the chief of the ways of God" (40:19), and Leviathan ("He maketh the deep to boil like a pot"; 41:31). If one realizes that Job had earlier mentioned the sea and the sea monster himself in order to demonstrate the insignificance of his case in comparison with the enormous proportions of nature as God created it, then it must strike one as a grotesque and even malicious turn when Yahweh suggests that Job ought to know the very things that he had already recognized as part of the divine arcanum. What earlier, in Job's mouth, had been an expression of doubt and a lament that nonetheless included the hope of release ("If I have sinned what do I unto thee, O thou preserver of men? / Why hast thou set me as a mark for thee?"; 7:20), finds a response *ex negativo* in Yahweh's words, which embody a cynical literality on the part of an insidious God. Thus, Blumenberg's thesis proves to be well founded. The Book of Job is not a theodicy but a provocation of theodicy in the double sense that the system of answers belonging to the theology then current is shaken just as severely by God's mockery of justice as it is by Job's insubordinate questions.

There is no room here to examine the degree to which the theodicies of later theologians and poets took up and responded to the original context or to the long-term effects of this double provocation unleashed by Job's questions and Yahweh's counterquestions. I would like to point out, however, that the initial answer Job gives his doubting wife ("What? shall we receive good at the hand of God, and shall we not receive evil?"; 2:10) reveals the limits of his willingness to pose questions. His response does not resolve the questions as to whether evil is only permitted or is actually willed by God, and whether it can in fact be willed at all. These later, quite famous questions of theodicy are not formulated by Job himself, although he is obliged to recognize that a human being cannot be right in the face of God, regardless of whether he is guilty or not (9:22), not even after he draws the bitterest of all conclusions from his awareness: "I shall be condemned, / Why then do I labour in vain?" (9:29). Job here confronts the absolute, unquestionable will of God, and when this happens, the problem of God's justness immediately loses all significance. A voluntaristic God can be deemed self-contradictory from a human point of view, but he cannot be questioned concerning the reasons for his actions. Nonetheless, Job takes the risk of asking a bold question: "Is it good unto thee that thou shouldest oppress, / That thou shouldest despise the work of thine hands, / And shine upon the counsel of the wicked?"

(10:3). This question also responds to a theological reproach aimed at Job earlier ("Shall mortal man be more just than God? / Shall a man be more pure than his Maker?"; 4:17) by inverting its conclusion and asking how God can reject that which *he himself* has created in his image.

But the boldest question, the question with which Job reaches the high point of a defense that sets him on equal footing with his divine adversary, is found in the verses in which the depths of distress sounded by his complaint are suddenly transformed into an appeal to God the Friend, Relative, and Avenger to protect him from God the Enemy and Merciless Persecutor. "Mine eye poureth out tears unto God: / That he would maintain the right of a man with God, / And of a son of man with his neighbor" (16:20–21). Here, an enigmatic and voluntaristic God is called into question in the name of the God who loves his creations. This very linguistic move is later echoed in the appeal Goethe's Iphigenia makes to the gods:

> Save me
> And rescue your image in my soul!
> (*Iphigenie auf Tauris*, IV/5, ll. 1716–17)

It seems to me that Gerhard von Rad's theological interpretation ("In the tremendous tension of his struggle [Job's] conception of God threatens to tear him apart"), which tries to read into this segmenting of God an early, comforting, and beneficial knowledge of "God the Redeemer,"[32] does not come any closer to the archaic power of the scene than does the literary interpretation authorized by the analogy with Goethe's Greek drama. It cannot be his image of God that threatens to destroy him; rather, Job the Imploring is the subject who calls for the support of God the Friend against God the Enemy — if not in the idealistic sense of the perfect image of God in the soul, then at least in the archaic sense of that terrible aphorism that was also supplied by Goethe: "Nemo contra deum nisi deus ipse."[33] What Job seeks in the primary context of these two passages (16:19ff.; 19:23ff.) are his rights from and, if necessary, against God, not an act of mercy, and certainly not redemption. The appeal he makes to God the Guarantor is an appeal to a higher authority who is summoned when God the Silent appears to be biased. This is why, at the end of the lines in which he demands that he be judged ("Let me be weighed in an even balance, / That God may know mine integrity' " 31:6), he remains in the unbowed stance of one who is certain of his innocence. Job proves this innocence with an extended series of questions about crimes of which he knows he is not guilty, then concludes and seals the document with his signature. What follows next is a final verbal gesture in which Job demands God's response to an indictment he has not seen, a move that employs a metaphorics of indestructible self-certainty that could hardly be more "Kleistlike" and which seeks its own kind in the field of images generated by question and answer: "Here is my signature, let the Almighty answer me; / And that I had the indictment that mine adversary hath written! / Surely I would carry it upon my shoulder; I would bind it unto me as a crown" (31:35–36).

The divine allocution with which Yahweh finally emerges from his silence in Chapter 38 ("Then the Lord answered Job out of the whirlwind, and said . . . ") is striking insofar as it rigorously refuses to answer (by responding with a counter-question) and, nonetheless, in the end has given one (by instead answering in terms of a theophany). This refusal of dialogic parity is made manifest in the opening lines by the absence of the vocative that Yahweh otherwise uses to designate the person to whom he is speaking: "Who is this that darkeneth counsel / By words without knowledge?" (38:2). Thus, the partner in this dialogue is reduced from a "thou" to an anonymous "who," and the absolute distance between God and man is maintained. The asymmetry of the dialogue is preserved even after Yahweh reintroduces the "thou" in an imperative: "Gird up thy loins now like a man; / For I will demand of thee, and declare thou unto me" (38:3). The eristic formulation used at the beginning can only be meant ironically given that the All-knowing will soon mock the unknowing by asking him about things only God the Creator could know, and about things that are not in question as far as this questioning Job is concerned: "Yahweh answers moral queries with questions about the physical world; all at once an immeasurable, darkly wise cosmos confronts a limited, subordinate consciousness."[34] Ernst Bloch has probably best captured the strangeness of this theophany in which the force and loftiness of an Ur-poetry unite in an unholy alliance with the power of a mythical catechesis. The Yahweh of the creation story and the exodus from Egypt has nothing in common with the "other God" that comes to light here. Bloch suggests that this figure is more the descendant of a daemonized Isis, a Nature-Baal, or a Krishna.[35] I do not find Bloch's interpretation of the final scene as a conformist effort at "covering up heresy" convincing, however.[36] The philosophical interpretation of the Book of Job that presents it as an "exodus from Yahweh himself" embodying the messianic hope of a new earth and a new heaven, surpasses the original context as much as does the theological interpretation that suggests that Job's reaction to the theophany should be understood in precisely the opposite manner, as it does when it assumes that Job adopts the question as "the form of life God expects of him as the creature of the creator."[37]

This latter interpretation, whose modernism is also revealed by its metaphorical short-circuit ("The question, which is anthropological for Job, is something he must endure by himself"),[38] mistakenly relies on a line in Job's final speech: "I will demand of thee, and declare thou unto me" (42:4). This is a verbatim quotation from God's opening statement (38:3), so it can hardly be Job's response to the theophany, especially since Job has no more questions for God at this point.

He simply ends his life in unquestioning happiness, blessed by God: he dies "old and full of days" (42:17). Job's response to the theophany completes the compositional figure of the dialogue with God insofar as Job takes up the beginning of God's speech and, after the main clause, "I know that thou canst do all things . . . " (42:2), first responds to Yahweh's initial question and then to his suggestion, "and declare thou unto me." After citing the question "Who is this that hideth counsel without knowledge?" Job confesses, "Therefore have I uttered that which I understood not" (42:3). After the quoted challenge, "I will demand of thee, and declare thou unto me," come no questions, only Job's avowal of what Yahweh has granted him in lieu of an answer to his questions, and despite the sarcastic rebuff of the counter question—a face-to-face meeting. "I have heard of thee by the hearing of the ear; / But now mine eye seeth thee, / Wherefore I abhor myself and repent / In dust and ashes" (42:5-6). This formulaic recantation refers only to the theophany. It emphatically separates itself from that which was merely heard secondhand, and less emphatically from that which Job heard directly from Yahweh in the latter's countercomments. Can we understand this to mean that Job submits himself to God because he has recognized his Lord in their face-to-face meeting and, therefore, is able to accept him, but not because God's countercomments have taught him the answer that would resolve all his questions? This hypothesis is supported by the unexpected rebuke Yahweh delivers to the three friends immediately afterward: "My wrath is kindled against thee, and against thy two friends: for ye have not spoken of me the thing that is right, as my servant Job hath" (42:7). If the orthodox answers of these friends are rejected by God (who represents absolute dialogic authority here), does it necessarily follow that Job's heterodox questions, those that had "spoken of me the thing that is right," are suddenly granted validity—that they endure, and call for answers even if Job no longer does?

Job's questions are of the sort that have had to be asked again and again, because they could never be answered definitively. They have, nonetheless, provoked philosophy and literature into efforts to justify the world as God's creation—even after Job's God was relieved of the obligation by the Enlightenment. The best proof I can muster for this is Ernst Bloch, who thought of Job's rebellion as the "exodus from Yahweh," and a step toward the self-liberation of humanity. Despite this, his history of atheism in Christianity leads up to the following question: "Must not materialist dialectics itself—that is, its need of such a lengthy and dreadful process—also be justified?"[39] The simplest means of annulling theodicy, that promised by the French Enlightenment imperative, "Que dieu n'existe pas,"[40] could not simply render Job's questions superfluous at the same time. Philosophy would henceforth take up some of the burden of these questions,[41] while literature tried to incorporate theodicy into its own regime and justify the world in its own way: as an aesthetic phenomenon.

Goethe's *Faust* and the *Faust* written by Valéry clearly reveal a crisis in the late phase of the poetic history of theodicy.[42] Goethe rejuvenated the Faust myth by returning to Job; and he brought theodicy back into play by transforming the Devil's pact into the bet that, in the "Prologue in Heaven," opens the way to the drama itself. The play, which has the whole human race as its subject, answers the question Mephistopheles poses once again here: was this world in any way established for the purposes of human happiness? Goethe develops a modern interpretation of Faust's destiny as his response: Faust serves "in a curious fashion" (l. 300), and only because of his endless striving can he find salvation.[43] As far as Valéry was concerned, questions about the meaning of evil had lost their metaphysical validity, because the modern world constantly outdoes itself in its knowledge and ability to accomplish things. *Mon Faust* brings an obsolete theodicy to its end by casting Mephisto in the comic role of a seducer who is left in the lurch, unable to do anything but cite his past mythological glory. In fact, Valéry turns back to the oldest Christian mythos, that of the apple in Genesis 3, in order to revise the myth of the Fall and answer the question that Goethe left up in the air: can one experience the immanent fulfillment of his being after all Faustian striving has been renounced, including the illusion of a technical mastery of the world, and in the absence of "salvation from above"? Valéry's answer, at least in my interpretation, arises first of all from an overcoming of that Cartesian idol, the *moi pur*, at the moment when poetry's promise of happiness, that is, the communication of I and you in a (mythically named) *communion* of body and soul, seems to be fulfilled in the clearly fragile ecstasy produced by the union of Faust and desire [*Lust*].

From a hermeneutic point of view, this double example is also an instance of question and answer functioning in a literary context. It shows how a question that was originally answered by myth can fade away historically while the myth lives on. This can happen when the structure of the myth is reactivated as the answer to a question that seems just now to have been asked for the first time, or, more precisely stated, when the myth can be understood differently thanks to its appropriation by poetry. The original question in Johann Spies's *Historia* of 1587 (why the desire for knowledge is sinful and leads to damnation when one dares use magic to go beyond the limits set on one's knowledge of nature) had become obsolete during the process of the Enlightenment thanks to the crowning of theoretical curiosity. Symptoms of this change can be found in those fragments in which Lessing suggests that Faust is to find salvation at the end of his travels. In other words, Goethe, if his new *Faust* was to deal with more than things from the past, had to find a new answer, one that would make it possible for his subject to appeal to contemporary interests. The question he chose concerned whether man, once having come of age, could—or was obliged to—discover life's happiness in an uninhibited search for knowledge, a question that one could no longer answer with a simple yes given the developments in the *Premier Discours*, where

Rousseau makes clear the necessary discrepancy between progressive knowledge and retrograde morality. The new question actually takes shape in Goethe's *Faust* only after the old scholar is cured of his "[sickness] for knowledge" (1. 1768) — the question as to whether the totality of nature and of human Being, which can no longer be fathomed with the methods offered by scholarship, can be rediscovered through joyful recognition. But this question could only be answered in the affirmative after a prior question had been answered, one that brings Mephisto's doubt into play:

> Believe the likes of us: the whole
> Is made but for a god's delight!
> (*Faust I*, ll. 1780–81)

The theodicy question posed in the prologue rings out here, not simply as an ironic conclusion drawn from the Book of Job by the Enlightenment, but as one that in fact subsumes all Job-like questions in a grand counterquestion of highly painful dimensions for God, a question that justifies Job *post festum* since he was not able to pose it himself. This is how, in his Faust figure, Goethe takes up Job's case once more, and, through the old Devil's pact, brings it into the bet. The bet itself, through Faust's destiny, could then be used to prove the possibility of human self-fulfillment and, thereby, the hidden ideality of the divinely created world. I have already dealt elsewhere with the problematic solution of this poetic theodicy tendered by German idealism, one that, to be sure, no longer retains the hope that "my redeemer lives," but that nonetheless has need of guilt (the Gretchen affair) and deliverance from on high.

A notable, but apparently as yet unrecognized, confirmation of the idea that the provocation of Job's questions lived on even after the answer provided by the theodicy faded away can be found in the section entitled "the madman" in Nietzsche's *Gay Science* (no. 125). Martin Heidegger used precisely this text to explain how Nietzsche's phrase "God is dead" is the event with which Western metaphysics got itself into its current state of affairs.[44] Heidegger's maxim — that a correct elucidation, though it "never understands the text better than the author understood it, . . . does surely understand it differently" — proves its worth when dealing with the modern parable embodied in Nietzsche's text.[45] The hermeneutics of question and answer also allows a different understanding in this instance:

> *The madman.* — Have you not heard of that madman who lit a lantern in the bright morning hours, ran to the market place, and cried incessantly: "I seek God! I Seek God!" — As many of those who did not believe in God were standing around just then, he provoked much laughter. Has he got lost? asked one. Did he lose his way like a child? asked

another. Or is he hiding? Is he afraid of us? Has he gone on a voyage? emigrated? – Thus they yelled and laughed.

The madman jumped into their midst and pierced them with his eyes. "Whither is God?" he cried; "I will tell you. *We have killed him* – you and I. All of us are his murderers. But how did we do this? How could we drink up the sea? Who gave us the sponge to wipe away the entire horizon? What were we doing when we unchained this earth from its sun? Whither is it moving now? Whither are we moving? Away from all suns? Are we not plunging continually? Backward, sideward, forward, in all directions? Is there still any up or down? Are we not straying as through an infinite nothing? Do we not feel the breath of empty space? Has it not become colder? Is not night continually closing in on us? Do we hear nothing as yet of the noise of the gravediggers who are burying God? Do we smell nothing yet of the divine decomposition? Gods, too, decompose. God is dead. God remains dead. And we have killed him.

"How shall we comfort ourselves, the murderers of all murderers? What was holiest and mightiest of all that the world has yet owned has bled to death under our knives: who will wipe this blood off us? What water is there for us to clean ourselves? What festivals of atonement, what sacred games shall we have to invent? Is not the greatness of this deed too great for us? Must we ourselves not become gods simply to appear worthy of it? There has never been a greater deed; and whoever is born after us – for the sake of this deed he will belong to a higher history than all history hitherto."

Here the madman fell silent and looked again at his listeners; and they, too, were silent and stared at him in astonishment. At last he threw his lantern on the ground, and it broke into pieces and went out. "I have come too early," he said then; "my time is not yet. This tremendous event is still on its way, still wandering; it has not yet reached the ears of men. Lightning and thunder require time; the light of the stars requires time; deeds, though done, still require time to be seen and heard. This deed is still more distant from them than the most distant stars – *and yet they have done it themselves*."

It has been related further that on the same day the madman forced his way into several churches and there struck up his *requiem aeternam deo*. Led out and called to account, he is said always to have replied nothing but: "What after all are these churches now if they are not the tombs and sepulchers of God?"[46]

The effect of this text is ignited by explicit questions with different rhetorical functions; but they all point back to an implicit question that the reader, in accord with the appellative structure of the parable, must uncover and understand to be a question concerning him personally. Within the constellation of characters – the fool who from time immemorial has brought the truth to light through inversion (lanterns in bright daylight), and the people in the marketplace who have fallen prey to the *idola fori*—a dialogue arises in which God is the absent third party. The great laughter the fool elicits with his cry, "God is dead," is soon transformed into a series of questions meant to deride the God seeker by taking what he has said literally. These mocking questions prove to be enigmatically ironic, however, and turn against the mockers themselves in the end. It is their own naïveté that brings the fool's game to light. Taken literally, to seek God could mean that he could be lost like any other lost item, or could be like a child who had run away; but since God can be neither the one nor the other, the one who seeks him has to be a fool as far as the people in the marketplace are concerned. For the reader, who is supposed to think further about this, the obvious absurdity of the situation reverses the direction of the questions. The series of mocking questions brings to light a series of counterquestions: How can one seek without seeking that which has necessitated the search? How can one lose what one has never possessed? Must there not be something like God if someone is still searching for him? Must he exist in some other way if he cannot be lost like some object or a person? Do the people in the marketplace not believe in God because they no longer seek him? And if one cannot lose God as one loses other things in daily life, how can he have disappeared?

It is precisely these implicit questions that the fool now articulates with his cry, "Whither is God?" and which he then answers with the provocative admission, "I will tell you. *We have killed him!*" This monstrous accusation is cast in the style of a mythical answer: it is apodictic, since it offers no explanation; logically consistent, since it cancels the preceding question; and nonreal as well, since to be killed by human beings contradicts the nature of God. Nonetheless, the fool's answer does not cut off further inquiry. It seems, rather, to have been provided as a means of eliciting the counterquestion, "But how did we do this?" and in order to elucidate what has been asked by means of a lengthy series of counterquestions. It is the latter that is of primary interest to me in this interpretation, since these counterquestions are not only entirely on the order of the catalogue of questions that Yahweh uses to rebuke Job, that is, unanswerable, they are also surprisingly analogous to the Old Testament text in terms of content. The first question, "How could we drink up the sea?" corresponds to Job 38:8: " . . . who shut up the sea with doors, / When it brake forth, as if it had issued out of the womb?" The second question, "Who gave us the sponge to wipe away the entire horizon?" is reminiscent of 38:12–13, "Hast thou commanded the morning since thy days began, / And caused the dayspring to know its place; / That it might take hold of the ends of the earth?" The third question, "What were we doing when we unchained this earth from its sun?" could be based on 38:33: "Knowest thou the ordinances of the heavens? / Canst thou establish the dominion thereof in the earth?"

Sea, horizon, sun, and earth form the center of the cosmic images in both cases. In both cases they are that which is asked about, and that which is used to show what man is unable to accomplish on his own. The different metaphorics found in the selection of images can easily be traced back to a poetics of world creation on the one hand and a poetics of world demise on the other. The unanswerable aspect of the counterquestions in the former proves the inability of human beings to understand the works of the divine *poietes*, and in the latter is meant to prove how impossible it is to imagine murdering God — impossible but, paradoxically, it still happened, a deed whose greatness is "too great for us." Embedded in this paradoxical statement, "God is dead," lies the last implicit question, the question that comprehends all further questions, speech acts, and actions of the "madman," the question that remains a provocation as do Job's questions, those that Yahweh (here one is tempted to say the "mad god"), through his theophany, and contrary to the wisdom of his answer, grants a validity, those that no later theophany could erase. In what way can the provocation to thought engendered by Nietzsche's statement "God is dead" be taken up by philosophy? How can the question "But how did we do this?" be answered? Would not such an attempt necessarily come close to being a theodicy in extremely straitened circumstances, since it would have to justify the world and the history of humanity without attempting to resolve Nietzsche's paradox by means of the Christian religion (the experience of the crucifixtion and the resurrection of Christ) or by means of Enlightenment atheism ("Que dieu n'existe pas")? The "greatest recent event — that 'God is dead' "[47] — implies of necessity that he could not have been dead before — a proof of God *ex contrario* that nudges Nietzsche's nihilism into a strange half-light!

By reconstructing the implicit questions that Nietzsche's text serves up, literary interpretation readily arrives at the horizon of questions found in Heidegger's philosophical interpretation. There, the counterquestions posed by the madman, which, in the primary context, circumscribe the unthinkable possibility that God has been murdered by mankind, emerge in the secondary context in relation to the history of the modern era. After the question "What were we doing when we unchained the earth from its sun?" one might think both of the Copernican revolution and of Plato's cave allegory (p. 106). In that case, the next questions, "Whither is it moving now? Whither are we moving? Away from all suns? Are we not plunging continually?" and so on, elucidate the *horror vacui*, and join with the cosmic images of sea, horizon, sun, and earth in the human revolt of subjectivity, of the *ego cogito* that does away with the supersensory world that *is* in itself, and transforms that which is into an object, makes nature a mere object of technology. As a way of resolving the paradox that God had to be killed, although he cannot be murdered or lost like anybody else, Heidegger begins by interpreting the deed of murdering God as an event carried out by human beings "even though today they still have heard nothing about it" (p. 105). According to Heidegger, the monstrous event out of which first arose modern history, with its self-made autonomy and its metaphysics of the will to power, dates back to the beginning of Western metaphysics: "The history of Being begins, and indeed necessarily, *with the forgetting of Being*" (p. 109).

At this point, philosophical interpretation slips unnoticed into allegoresis: Heidegger substitutes a *forgetting* of Being for the *murder* of God, and in so doing, brings the ambivalence of *genetivus subjectivus* and *objectivus* to bear on the "forgetting of Being," thus making it possible to resolve Nietzsche's paradox. Insofar as the sentence "We have killed God!" itself can be understood as a symptom of the forgetting of Being, the victim can also rise again in the service of a mode of thought ready to retrace its steps—can arise, that is, as a forgotten God in the destiny of Being, Being that can withdraw into its truth, that can, therefore, once again emerge in the light of its own essence. If, according to Heidegger, the Western history of metaphysics is an as yet unthought epoch in the history of Being itself, it is also, insofar as it is a history of self-forgetting, a theodicy. Understood as a late if not belated theodicy, Heidegger's interpretation responds both to the recent provocation of Nietzsche's phrase "God is dead" and to the distant provocation of the Book of Job. The counterquestions raised by Heidegger's response to Nietzsche are the responsibility of philosophy. As an answer to Job, it seems to me that Heidegger's theodicy leaves us wondering whether his ontological solution in any way touches on the moral problem embodied in the inquiry into the meaning of suffering. Do not the Being in Heidegger's philosophy, which "withdraws into its truth" (p. 110), and the God of the Old Testament, who refuses his truth to Job, still have one thing in common—that divine essence neither has need of mankind nor seems to respond to mankind's love with counterlove?

3. The dialogic and the dialectic *Neveu de Rameau*; or, The reciprocity between Diderot and Socrates, Hegel and Diderot

If epochs can be characterized according to whether the literature of each is dominated by the polyphony of discussion or the unison of discourse, then the Enlightenment in Europe clearly unfolds against the background of a growing dialogization of literary and philosophical communication. Diderot's work is perhaps the most symptomatic of this development. His literary prose seems to employ the narrative form primarily in order to progressively undermine the telos expected of that which is narrated. The latter is transformed into an endless dialogue that serves to reopen the horizon of the questionable and the unresolved instead of creating the order that narrative discourse promises to grant the contingent. Diderot accomplished much the same thing in his philosophical essays by exchanging the monologism of the philosophical treatise for the dialogic concept of truth that he had restored to its original "Socratic" intent. Seen in this light, Roland Galle's thesis, that Diderot's work as a whole is to be regarded as a progressive "dialogization of the Enlightenment," can be carried even further.[48] His interpretation can be used to show how, step by step, in the texts from the *Pensées philosophiques* to *Le neveu de Rameau*, Diderot transforms the asymmetrical form of the magistral dialogue. He dismantles the authority of the teacher, grants the countervoice equal status, and gives the conversational openness thus recovered a new sharpness by employing a casuistry of question and answer. He does all this in order to provoke the reader and then, finally, send him away with an unresolved aporia.

Renaissance humanism had revived the Platonic dialogue in opposition to the institutionalized discourse of Scholasticism and thereby opened up a new discussion, one in which the distant authority of the classical period was constantly present in the role of a third party possessing jurisdiction over the truth. The Enlightenment continued the discussion—but in the form of a dialogue against this now questionable authority—and carried out a critique of the normative validity of all that had been handed down. The desire to change the aims of humanity while at the same time criticizing the prior realization of these aims was a peculiarity of the eighteenth-century Enlightenment's emancipatory movement,[49] and the dialogue was the preferred didactic medium for this effort because of its open, Socratic form. The triumphal march of the dialogic form, which from this point on appeared everywhere, and even forced its way into the conventionally monologic genres of literature and rhetoric, resulted in the dialogization of all subject matter over which criticism could exercise its power. This progressive dialogization undertaken by the Enlightenment, since it called classical ontology's concept of truth into question, both renewed and surpassed the classical model embodied in the Platonic dialogue.

Throughout the history of its reception, the model of the Platonic dialectic has always given right-of-way to an openness of inquiry, and, in addition, has always renewed the question as to how open the openness of the Platonic dialogue really is. If, at least in the early dialogues, the circuitous movement of Socratic inquiry did not aim at a ready-made answer, it was nonetheless limited by the latent presence of a preconceived truth, one that the collectively undertaken search was certain to arrive at, given the ontological input of anamnesis. The Enlightenment philosopher, who was obliged to abandon this Platonic guarantee of the truth, then faced the problem of opening up a new, Socratic-style discussion that would allow him to clear up the contradictions in contemporary society, and resolve the opposition between two positions without relying on the authority of a third. Was it possible to arrive at a truth through the aporia of differing opinions, a truth that, instead of being already found, would arise from the discussion itself? My thesis is that Diderot's *Neveu de Rameau* is a response to the problem as to how one might take the openness of the Socratic dialogue at its word—how one might test everything held to be true, down to and including "innate ideas," through a knowing ignorance. In order to solve this problem formally, Diderot fell back on a literary genre that—or so it seems to me—was incorrectly understood as long as critics, misled by the subtitle, *Satire seconde*, regarded his text as a satire in the style of Horace. It is a Menippean satire.

The subversive tradition of the Menippean satire has most recently and clearly been brought to light by Mikhail Bakhtin. His aesthetic of the polyphonic word deals with fictional prose in terms of its capacity to become a medium for the reflected speech of the other. The polyphonic word, that is, the word that incorporates the other's speech into itself, presents itself as a dialogic principle that opposes both monologic poetry and the monologism of philosophical discourse. Bakhtin elucidated this principle historically in terms of the polyphonic novel (most impressively with Rabelais and Dostoyevsky), which can, in the last analysis, be traced back to the Socratic dialogue and a related genre, the Menippean satire, with its mixture of seriousness and humor.[50] The Platonic dialogue had gradually abandoned the Socratic assumption about the dialogic nature of truth—a truth that could be found only in a collective inquiry that traversed the resistance created by the opinions of the other—as Plato, in his late phase, began more and more to assert an already found, ready-made truth in one-sided, magestral dialogues. The Menippean satire, on the other hand, began to take on the function of a dialogic testing of ideas and individuals (Bakhtin 1984, pp. 114–15).

In *Le neveu de Rameau* one can do more than locate the classical model of the Socratic dialogue and trace its historical filiation, since we know that Diderot took with him a *petit Platon* when he was imprisoned at Vincennes, and that he translated Socrates' *Apology* from it.[51] This fact does not, however, completely solve the problem of reception. Indeed, it poses the problem for the first time. The questions as to what is still, once again, or no longer "Socratic" in Diderot's dialogue; who undertakes the Socratic role in *Le neveu de Rameau*; and to what ends, (which at first certainly cause the reader some consternation) can be answered only with great difficulty, and only after one has discovered the function of the Menippean model that Diderot employs. Included in this model are the exceptional situation embodied by a person "who stands on the threshold," eccentric freedom in the "invention of philosophical ideas," a scandalous examination of "ultimate truths," moral-psychological experimentation that can lead to a "split in personality," and, along with all this, a metamorphosis of the individual into a series of roles, a metamorphosis that is brought about by staging the discourse of others.[52]

It is evident that Diderot did not just retain a deep and life-long respect for Socrates. That he also defended Socrates against his skeptical friends and especially against Rousseau's critique, that he identified with Socrates morally, and even secretly felt himself to be playing the Socrates of the French Enlightenment, is now well known thanks to Jean Seznec's *Diderot et l'antiquité*.[53] The biographical evidence, the dramatic sketch entitled *La mort de Socrate*, and the article "Philosophie socratique" in the *Encyclopédie* provide beautiful documentation of this connection. But, as far as I can tell, although a substantial amount has been written about Socrates as a personal model, little has been said about the Socratic form of the dialogue received and represented in *Le neveu de Rameau*. Whoever deals with this text as a "satire in the style of Horace" obscures our view of its strange, and not immediately evident, dialogic structure, and thereby misses the dialectical significance of the relationship between *Moi* and *Lui*. As Herbert Dieckmann has shown in his response to E. R. Curtius, the "contrast between the fool enslaved by poverty, everyday needs, desires, and passion, and the undemanding, modest, and thus really free, wise man" in Horace's seventh satire "does not serve to impart meaning to *Le neveu de Rameau*."[54] The generic designation, "satire seconde," was added belatedly to the title, and points out the thematic similarity between Diderot's *Satire I* and *Satire II*, a similarity that reveals the modern application that Diderot found for the tonalities of the satirical style. It is his "interest in the utterances of *individualité naturelle*," his desire to grasp *mots de charactère* [characteristic expressions], and *cris de nature* [cries of instinct] that, in their immediacy, "free from convention, intention, or manipulation," that call for the open form found in the dialogue, and for staging the discourse of others (p. 149). Dieckmann refers here to the nephew's pantomimic accomplishments, and draws our attention to Lucian, to Terence, and especially to the similarity of Petronius's *Satyricon*, which he believes to be generically closest to Diderot's dialogue (p. 154). These names trace a path back to the Menippean satire, that is, to the "genre of ultimate questions,"[55] whose polyphonic form Diderot in fact put to use in his narrative prose as well as in his late philosophical dialogues. We must first look at the former, in order to see how Diderot sublated the metaphysics of ultimate questions dialogically, and thereby drew his reader into the discussion as well.

The (all too) grand questions, those ultimate questions raised at the very beginning of *Jacques le fataliste* are left unanswered in order to shake the gentle reader out of his expectations—those that the novel in general satisfies—and, thus, out of his customary view of the world.

> Comment s'étaient-ils rencontrés? Par hasard, comme tout le monde. Comment s'appelaient-ils? Que vous importe? D'où venaient-ils? Du lieu le plus prochain. Où allaient-ils? Est-ce que l'on sait où l'on va? Que disaient-ils? Le maître ne disait rien; et Jacques disait que son capitaine disait que tout ce qui nous arrive de bien et mal ici-bas était écrit là-haut.[56]

The five questions to the implied reader bring to light more than the fictional imperatives of the traditional novel, which normally satisfied the teleological needs of beginning, middle, and end. The negation of this most natural of expectations strikes indirectly at the explanatory model of the world offered by the Christian faith, at the teleology of the authoritative answer to the whence, the

whither, and the why of human existence, and ironizes about the antinomies between name-possessing individuality and nameless destiny, accident and
predetermination, master and servant. In the course of the narrative, the claims
of religion and metaphysics of holding the answers to these ultimate questions are
propelled into an aporia by the ironic interweaving of theory and practice: the
master, who offers a theoretical defense of free will, proves to be a will-less "au-
tomaton" in practice, while his servant, who adheres to the fatalism of his captain,
proves himself to be master of the situation every time their trip turns difficult.
The "testing of ideas" that takes place through the events that befall *Jacques . . . et son maître* arrives at a negative result. The (all too) grand questions
posed by metaphysics end in an aporia that cannot be resolved by any ultimate
answer. Instead, the reader is asked to master through practical reason that which
theoretical reason cannot resolve.

Instead of maintaining the generic distinction between narrative and dialogue,
Diderot constantly plays off the open form of the dialogue against the closed form
of the narrative. One could even say that Diderot's prose becomes the site of an
ongoing clash between the dialogic principal and monologic discourse. The constant transformation of narrative into dialogue prevents the order-producing
potential of the monologic narrative from being fulfilled. The travel fable no more
arrives at an ultimate conclusion, one that resolves everything, than the past histories of *Jacques . . . et son maître* produce an originary beginning that sheds
light on everything that is unclear; whenever the ongoing action seems to reach
a point of stasis, the narrative falls into conflicting judgmental positions whose
reunification is left to the reader. The dominant relationship between question and
answer is, therefore, not one of dialectical development (a movement from contradiction through explanation and conceptual elaboration to the unified production of understanding), but of casuistic repetition. Questions are so posed that an
immediate answer cannot be hoped for. The reader is confronted with "the act
of weighing or evaluating, but not with the results of that act."[57] He is obliged
to question the validity of the moral norms according to which any given case
might be decided, and this evaluative effort itself drives him to ask further questions. He is, thus, drawn ever deeper into the problematic of the compatibility
of an individual case with the general norm. It is with this goal in mind that
Diderot allows his protagonists' endless dialogue to revert again to "lifelike stories" that thereafter juxtapose the reality of life, which has itself once more become a problematic *casus*, to novelistic fiction.[58] Whatever the reader then sees
brought up for discussion, whether from the perspective of the master or the servant, shifts the direction of the inquiry from the aporias of the metaphysical system to the problems of the everyday world. Antifiction is offered in contrast to
the escapist world of fiction; the most obvious of questions, those asked regularly
in daily life ("Est-il bon? Est-il méchant?"),[59] are raised in the face of the insoluble, ultimate questions about the meaning of the world. This shift in questions,

which brings them closer, in no way makes them easier to answer. The moral juncture once again involves the reader in a casuistry from which he can escape only by making a personal decision.

Diderot's narrative "Ceci n'est pas un conte" is a wonderful example of this process. The opening section justifies its use of the dialogic principle on the basis of the fact that, as in everyday narration, the speaker is constantly interrupted by the listener, and that a good narrative must be able to unleash a debate pro and con in all social circles of the city, one that will last for weeks. In this instance, the *casus* arises from the juxtaposition of two different stories, each configured as the inverted image of the other. First it is a man, *le bon Tanié*, who ruins himself because of his passion for a woman, proceeds to make a fortune in far-off lands, and finally dies after having been deceived by her in the most despicable fashion; then it is a woman, the unfortunate Mlle. de la Chaux, who experiences something similar. She sacrifices her fortune, her family, her ability to work, and her health only to be rejected by her unworthy lover at the moment of his greatest success. His excuse: "Je ne vous aime plus." Both stories could be worth telling in and of themselves, as uplifting/moral exempla of blind passion and base ingratitude. But it is only their contrary classification of characters that brings the *casus* to light and involves the reader in an evaluation of norms, a process that first calls into question social morality (can one judge the character of another human being on the basis of a single action?), then human nature (can one be forced to love after passion has died?) and divine justice (is providence unable to bring human beings together for the sake of happiness?). At the close of the narrative, these questions turn into a *regressus in infinitum* that is finally interrupted by a question aimed at the opponents (and at the implicit reader) that cuts straight through it: "Mais mettez la main sur la conscience, et dites-moi, vous, monsieur l'apologiste des trompeurs et des infidèles, si vous prendriez le docteur de Toulouse pour votre ami? . . . Vous hésitéz? Tout est dit."[60] The *casus*, which seems to be more and more insoluble from the point of view of moral philosophy, can still be resolved in terms of practical morality—thanks to a question *ad personam* that grants the individual conscience normative judicial authority.

The search for a resolution to this fictional dialogue, that is, the attempt to resolve the conflict between the authority of moral convention and that of amoral, human nature through a direct appeal to a third party, the reader, does not succeed here. The crux of the problem, as is demonstrated by the history of the text's interpretation, lies in the fact that Diderot's *Neveu de Rameau* is his philosophical dialogue par excellence. For the purposes of my own interpretation, the simplest way to review this history will be to focus on the instances of dialogic speech.[61] As long as the primary interpretive problem was assumed to be the question as to which character represented Diderot's point of view, one could resolve the antithesis between *Moi* and *Lui*, between the Philosopher and the Musician, in terms of one of the two discursive positions mentioned earlier. If one assumed that *Moi* represented Diderot, the philosophical spokesman for the *Encyclopédistes*, then *Lui* was seen as the embodiment of their enemies, and the purpose of the dialogue was to refute the nephew's extreme amorality. But even though a topical polemic against Diderot's enemies is clearly evident in the text, this conflation of Diderot and *Moi* is no longer accepted today (except, perhaps, by Paul Meyer or Roland Desné). Daniel Mornet's work has enabled us to see the subliminal dialogue the author carries out with himself in *Le neveu de Rameau*. It has, in turn, been interpreted as a dialogue in which the mature philosopher overcomes his earlier materialism; a confrontation between ego and id that introduces the specific traits of the internal monologue typical of modern man (Lionel Trilling); or as an act of self-liberation, one in which the genius frees himself from the constraints of his own deterministic philosophy by creating a "moral monster" (Jean Fabre).

In contrast to these positions, James Doolittle has suggested that the dialogue between *Moi* and *Lui* is best approached through the eyes of the former, and that the stronger discursive position taken by the nephew, which is much closer to Diderot's own, should be taken at its word. Understood in this manner, *Le neveu de Rameau* becomes a dialogic process in which the initially asserted superiority of the first model of discursive authority over the second (which is grammatically distanced by the use of the third-person "he") is gradually reversed: the dogmatic philosopher and ostensible representative of virtue is backed so far into an aporia by the genial musician and representative of social amorality that, by the end of the narrative, his only means of escape is in Diogenes' barrel.[62] Doolitle's interpretation might be compared with Jean Starobinski's essay. The latter claims there is a dialectical equilibrium between the two voices, and regards their "metacomedy" as a revised form of satire.[63] *Lui*, who is at first, but does not remain, the object of this satire, speaks out as a *persona inaequalis* who openly defends his sins and his *ridiculum*, and who grants himself the freedom of a mode of reflection that turns the satire's laughter against society by inverting the hierarchy of its values. *Moi*, who as narrator is the subject of the satire and serves as mediator for the discussion, responds to this provocation with laughter and indignation—the affects that are stirred up by satire—and then reestablishes the now jeopardized equilibrium of moral order by asking, "Qu'avez vous fait?"[64] This question, which posits a practical reason, throws reflexive freedom into embarrassment, since the latter spends itself in mere imitation.

A different interpretive tradition tries to eliminate the minor scandal of this unresolved aporia in Diderot's philosophical dialogue. It tries to bridge the gap between the incompatible opposites, *Moi* and *Lui*, by introducing a third point of view. In this case, Diderot stands above his two characters as their author, and *Le neveu de Rameau* is read as a satire in which various moral positions undergo the test of reality. Instead of being represented by one of his characters, Diderot is figured in opposition to *Moi* and *Lui*. Throughout the text, then, there is a growing ironic distance between Diderot as detached third party or narrator and the subjects of his moral experiment (Lester Crocker). By proposing the author as the implicit third party in the discussion, this hypothesis also covertly grants him the authority of truth, and makes it possible to program an implicit role for the reader as well. Passing over the incompatible positions of the moral philosopher and the amoral musician, it sublates the either-or of communicationless isolation and parasitic assimilation in Diderot's serene irony — at least insofar as the reader is able to detect a tripartite movement in the dialogue: "La bonne conscience du philosophe dialoguant détruite par la conscience déchirée du neveu, puis dépassée à son tour par la conscience supérieure du philosophe-écrivain."[65] Read in this way, as Roger Laufer suggests, the text would align Diderot's intention with the commentary in Hegel's *Phenomenology of Spirit!*[66]

All that is left to discover now is what point of view the superior consciousness of "Diderot the Philosopher" actually adopts, since it is expressed nowhere in the text. It can hardly be identical with Hegel's. We have to keep in mind that a threshold of reception separates the antithesis between *Moi* and *Lui* in *Le neveu de Rameau* from the dialectical surmounting of the *spirit alienated from itself* that Hegel elucidated with quotations from Goethe's translation of Diderot. The threshold is once again that between dialogue and discourse — between the dialogic antithesis that emerged during the later phases of the Enlightenment and the monologic dialectics that marked its end: when Hegel raises Diderot's antagonistic characters to the level of figures in the general dialectic of history, dialogue is transformed into the narrative discourse of the *Phenomenology* and the antithesis of their points of view is sublated in the stepwise movement of the spirit toward itself. It is this sublation of the dialogic relationship between *Moi* and *Lui* that turns the first of Diderot's characters into a naive, or honest, consciousness and the second into a consciousness that is disrupted, but *self-aware*, and heightens the nephew's tragedy (his failure to be a genius) by transforming it into the suffering produced by a society that has not yet become aware of its own self-contradictory nature.

The hermeneutic consequences of these historical facts are, first, a need to redefine the peculiar aporetic form *Le neveu de Rameau* acquired in its reworking of the Socratic dialogue, and then, a need to interpret the difference between the antithetical standpoints found in that text and their sublation in Hegel's reception of it.[67] Since Diderot did not have available to him the new, third stage of authority found in Hegel's dialectic, it may not be appropriate to grant him this superior point of view, but it might be possible to locate the third position of this renewed Socratic dialogue in the old metaphysics of the true, the good, and the beautiful, which *Moi*, as philosopher, supports and *Lui*, as amoral subject, challenges. The author's irony would then derive from the cryptic manner in which Platonic dialogue is restored to its open, Socratic form in order to turn it against philosophical dogmatism and, in particular, against the Platonic unity represented by the good and the beautiful. And, in this case, the Socratic role goes not to the moral philosopher but to his amoral adversary.

His article "Philosophie socratique" gives some indication of how Diderot himself regarded the Socratic dialogue. In it, the classical model is obviously, but not explicitly, presented as analogous to the Enlightenment insofar as Socrates opposed a dominant philosophy that concerned itself primarily with the world system and natural phenomena by holding aloft the study of morality and the question of true happiness in life. Socrates' contribution is to have brought philosophy from the chimeric heights of speculation ("Il ramena sur la terre la philosophie égarée dans les régions du soleil")[68] back to the firm ground of life practice and the polis ("Sa philosophie n'était pas une affaire d'ostentation et de parade, mais de courage et de pratique").[69] The Socratic mode of enlightenment unfolds in discussions with every sort of person. Its preferred means are irony and induction: "Un usage étonnant de l'ironie . . . qui dévoilait sans efforts le ridicule des opinions; de l'induction, qui de questions éloignées en questions éloignées, vous conduisait imperceptiblement à l'aveu de la chose même qu'on niait."[70] Socratic irony leaves no prejudice undisturbed, protects no social authority, and uncovers folly—as does Rameau's nephew in his "pantomimes of humankind" (p. 82)—in all walks of society. Diderot first introduces Socratic induction in the guise of the circuitous, elenctic inquiry, then deals with it in terms of a remarkable metaphor using light as a figure for the recognition of a truth whose beginning and end are lost in darkness:

> (Socrate) s'était aisément apperçu que la vérité est comme un fil qui part d'une extrémité des ténèbres et se perd de l'autre dans les ténèbres; et que dans toute question, la lumière s'accroît par degrés jusqu'à un certain terme placé sur la longueur du fil délié, au-delà duquel elle s'affaiblit peu à peu et s'éteint. Le philosophe est celui qui fait s'arrêter juste; le sophiste imprudent marche toujours, et s'égare lui-même et les autres: toute sa dialectique se résout en incertitudes. (*Encyclopédie* XV, p. 263)[71]

This commentary on the openness of the Socratic dialogue seems to me to be remarkable in several respects. The antisystematic function of the dialogue, which had already been apparent in the circuitous movement of the inquiry, is heightened by this double openness—of beginning and end. The truth emerges midway along the thread of the discussion. It is not grounded in an originary event; neither does it find realization in anything ultimate. To expect the truth to come from some ultimate answer is a delusion of sophistic dialectics. Truth, that truth generated by discussion, is bound to a context and, therefore, cannot be anchored in some original, innate knowledge. Beyond the darkness in which the thread of the discussion loses itself there is no longer a Platonic world of ideas that can be sought out and illuminated by memory. The new Socratic dialogue imagined by Diderot is no longer guaranteed by the metaphysical back reference offered by anamnesis. Finally, Diderot also gives up the anti-eristic element in the Socratic dialogue. It is no accident that his commentary omits the premise of a discussion among friends, since this type of discussion is most successful when the question-and-answer game is begun with assurances of a common set of preconceptions, or when the equivalent is arrived at by admitting to a common lack of knowledge. The Socratic dialogue produced by the French Enlightenment does not assume that adversaries hold presuppositions in common; it is once more a debate—one that can destroy the opinions of the other—rather than a discussion among friends concerned primarily with the other's lack of knowledge.

My contention, that *Le neveu de Rameau* grants the Socratic voice to the anti-philosopher, *Lui*, rather than to the Philosopher, *Moi*, to the amoral subject rather than to the moral idealist, may seem surprising at first, especially since it is first and foremost *Moi* who attempts to assert the superiority embodied in the act of posing questions. But even the manner in which the nephew is introduced, the description of his external appearance, his personal traits and their effect, constantly reminds the reader of things Socratic, things that are confirmed later in the actual dialogue as the arrogant Philosopher is slowly driven deeper into an aporia by his unworthy adversary. The place and the accidental nature of their meeting (on the bench in the Palais Royal and then at the Café de la Régence, where the Philosopher stops while out for a walk) lay out a quasi-peripatetic framework for the discussion the nephew accidentally unleashes upon his arrival. And he does so—again in Socratic fashion—by turning to the subject closest at hand for people watching chess players. It is almost as if he has taken the Philosopher literally, given the manner in which the latter toys with his thoughts in the opening narrative: "I let my mind rove wantonly, give it free rein to follow any idea, wise or mad. . . . My ideas are my trollops" (p. 8). This is a lovely metaphor for the kind of open dialogue that first serves the Philosopher in his conversations with himself, and then makes possible a surprising inversion of the conversational roles. It is *Lui* who follows his thoughts, then lets go of them like "trollops." *Moi* constantly returns to and dogmatically defends his preconceived ideas. This "oddest of characters," the nephew, is also assigned three traditional aspects of Socrates' appearance right at the very start: a beard, a stomach like Silenus's, and an ugly face (p. 12). His character astonishes the Philosopher first of all because of its unusual "compound of elevation and abjectness, of good sense and lunacy, . . . of decency and depravity," and then by its Socratic/provocative uprightness, "for he shows without ostentation the good qualities that nature has bestowed upon him, just as he does the bad ones without shame" (pp. 8–9).

The nephew comes closest to the Socratic model when *Moi* admits *nolens volens* why, though he has no great esteem for "such eccentrics," they are nonetheless useful in a society that has become ossified through education and social convention:

> If such a character makes his appearance in some circle, he is like a grain of yeast that ferments and restores to each of us a part of his native individuality. He shakes and stirs us up, makes us praise or blame, smokes out the truth, discloses the worthy and unmasks the rascals. It is then that the sensible man keeps his ears open and sorts out his company. (p. 10)

Here, the classical metaphor of the stingray — to which Menon compared the Socratic art of setting others in confusion and bringing them to the point where they admit their ignorance — is beautifully translated into a modern equivalent through the yeast image! Rameau's nephew is, thus, explicitly associated with the Socratic role of maieutic discussion leader. And, like Socrates, he will constantly claim that he knows nothing[72] while exercising the role of de facto midwife in the discussion.[73] But in contrast to the Socratic model, it will be intricate responses to often simple questions that upset the prejudices of the other. Diderot himself brings up the Socratic midwife, using it at an important juncture in his dialogue. In response to the final question the Philosopher directs at him, "But, given your large choice of means, why didn't you try fashioning a work of art?" (p. 77), Rameau's nephew answers with a demonstration — the pantomime of failed midwifery:

> He was aping a man who grows angry, indignant, who softens, commands, and implores. He improvised speeches full of anger, compassion, hatred, and love, sketching every passionate character with astonishing accuracy and subtlety. Then he went on: "Isn't that about right? It's coming, I should say. It only shows the value of having a midwife who knows how to prod and bring on the labor pains so as to bring out the child. When I take my pen by myself, intending to write, I bite my nails and belabor ny brow but — no soap, the god is absent. Though I had convinced myself that I had genius, at the end of the first line I am informed that I'm a fool, a fool, a fool. But how in the name of sense can one feel, think, rise to heights, and speak with vigor while frequenting people such as those I must frequent to live?" (p. 78)

The two famous Socratic associations, the stingray (alias a grain of yeast) and the midwife, certainly do not frame the discussion in Le neveu by accident. If one takes the whole of it more seriously than has been the case,[74] one must also rephrase the question as to the meaning of Diderot's adaptation of the Socratic dialogue.

If indeed the Socratic discursive role played by the nephew is so evidently begun and ended with an evocation of the loci classici of maieutics, then the dialectical content of his statements and his personal investment, the tragic side of his role, should no doubt also be understood against the horizon of the classical model. From this point of view, Doolittle's interpretation takes on more weight. He suggests that the early interplay of superiority between *Moi* and *Lui* is so transformed during the course of the discussion that one is less and less inclined to identify *Moi* with Diderot's thought and more and more prone to do so for *Lui*. The Philosopher, who at first — and in accord with his trade — lays claim to the traditional prerogative of asking questions, forfeits more and more of the truly Socratic (i.e., the maieutic) discursive role to his adversary. And although the latter usually only answers, he is nonetheless able to lead *Moi* into the aporetic. The antiphilosopher proves more and more to be the Socratic figure in the dialogue, the one, that is, to whom is given the responsibility of "forcing the truth out," unsettling the philosophical dogmatism to which his partner in the discussion clings — in a very un-Socratic manner — and enacting a virtuoso exposé of the masquerades of society as a whole.

What is actually Socratic about this Socrates *redivivus* of the French Enlightenment is only the function, not the technique, of maieutic inquiry. The nephew triumphs not so much through the interplay of question and answer as through the genius of pantomime. He is able to subtract himself from his own individuality and project himself into an unlimited multiplicity of "alien voices." Thus, the "beggar's pantomime" at the close of Diderot's dialogue becomes the means of revealing "what makes the world go round" (p. 83). It is the perfect instrument for representing one's fellow humans in their otherness, and, at the same time, exposing their roles in the social masquerade. With its fourfold repetition and ever richer staging of these "pantomimes of humankind" (p. 82), Diderot's *Neveu de Rameau* outstrips the form of a renewed Socratic dialogue and enters the polyphonic realm of the Menippean satire. This modern epitome of the genre functions as a means of "restor[ing] to each of us part of his native individuality" (p. 10), thereby revealing the social order to be an interplay of various roles of unadmitted dependency. That these possibilities are perceived by the amoral subject rather than by the philosophical moralist to whom this task should supposedly belong is another example of the ironic inversion of Platonic metaphysics that forms a central theme of the dialogue.

However distant Diderot's *Neveu* might be from the classical Socrates, this genius of pantomime stands in close proximity to him in one respect: like Socrates, who could not himself give birth to the truth, only help someone else find it in himself ("God insists on my serving as midwife, but he will not allow me to give birth"; *Theaetetus*, 150c), the nephew lacks the ability to create, or bring forth his own work. He can only make the work of others transparent through his perfect imitations. But where the classical Socrates takes this restriction to midwifery for granted (a subordination of poiesis to the episteme?), his modern counterpart suffers because he is not a creative "genius" — like his uncle — but instead only a "character." It was none other than Herbert Dieckmann who, during a colloquium at the Szondi Institute, suggested that the nephew's suffering — "that he can only play what he would like to be" — is part of his tragedy, the other part being his "inability to become a complete individual."[75] The nephew's suffering is not, therefore — or at least not yet — a suffering grounded in the social condition. After all, he himself exploits society; he is a parasite, and there is cynical validity to his comment that society wants him just as he is. His suffering stems primarily from his awareness that he is a failed genius, from the dissatisfaction of not-being-able-to, of always-having-to-play-at, whether in the aesthetic or the moral realm. The nephew is able neither to create like the "great Rameau," whom he hates for this reason, nor to become a great scoundrel, such as those he mimes so perfectly.

The tragic element in the nephew lies in the recognition of the threshold that he must cross but cannot — a threshold that, in the aesthetic realm, lies between the classical principle of imitation and the modern principle of creativity, one that, in the moral realm, is marked by the question as to what justification there is for postulating right action if one does not have recourse to the innate ideas of the true, the good, and the beautiful. One cannot expect the dialogue that *Moi* and *Lui* carry out at this threshold (and it must be kept in mind that *Le neveu de Rameau* also fits into the tradition of the Menippean satire in terms of its being a threshold dialogue) to formulate questions as they would be formulated on the other side of this threshold, that is, from the standpoint of German idealism. For *Moi*, the question that arises from the discomforting reality of *Lui*'s existence runs as follows: "How is it that with such fineness of feeling, so much sensibility where musical beauty is concerned, you are so blind to the beauties of morality, so insensible to the charm of virtue?" (p. 71).

This question reappears in various forms in the *décousu de la conversation*,[76] in the midst, that is, of an unexpected sequence of events that includes themes taken up, dropped, and recalled, but never brought to an end, their accompanying digressions, and a sprinkling of pantomimic scenes. It can be regarded as the central question in *Le neveu de Rameau*, the one posed in order to deny the reader an answer, and thereby draw him into the aporia that engulfs everything the dialogue touches on: society and justice, art and morality, education and good fortune in life, human nature and theodicy. It represents the contradiction that erupted between the aesthetic and the moral in the modern era — the shattered, aporetic premise of Platonic metaphysics that supposes that everything beautiful is so through its relation to the good, that all desire for the beautiful that does not have improvement of the soul as its aim is to be rejected, and that injustice is suffered by the unjust. I have drawn this formulation from the *Gorgias* (474d/e, 503a, 482b), because it is arrived at through the defeat of Callicles, who, as an immoralist, is a classical figure close to Diderot's *Neveu*.[77] One could in fact interpret Diderot's text as a continuation of the Platonic dialogue without its idealistic premises. The philosopher in this dialogue can no longer refute the modern immoralist, who, when asked about the reason for his insensitivity to the charms of virtue, can reply curtly: "It must be that virtue requires a special sense that I lack" (p. 71). But the nephew's materialism is equally unable to conquer his moral idealism. This materialism only *seems* to be a modern reprise of Callicles' proclamation of the law of nature—the rights of the stronger and better over the laws and customs that are instituted to protect the weaker (*Gorgias*, 483). After all, Callicles' move to equate the stronger with the better and nobler is not simply scorned sarcastically by the parasite; it is also exposed as an illusion manufactured by the wealthy, just as all positions in the social hierarchy are exposed in good Socratic fashion in the final amoral pantomime. Diderot, who revived the open form of the Platonic dialogue in order to use it against Plato's closed triadic system of the true, the good, and the beautiful, thus reveals the final, insoluble aporia embodied in the opposition between the idealist and the materialist points of view. This is most evident in the thematic presentation of a revised understanding of the interference between the aesthetic and the moral. It is this theme that I will deal with in what follows. By lifting it out of the confusing patterns of the text, I intend to show how it serves as a constant leitmotiv in the work.

The theme of the "man of genius," which is broached during the opening conversation about chess, moves from the level of the personal to the general when *Moi* asks *Lui* about his uncle: "Doesn't he do anything for you?"—"If he has ever done anything for anybody, it must be without knowing it" (p. 12). Although the nephew had earlier wished to grant only genius the right to exist in chess, in poetry, rhetoric, and music, and at the expense of mediocrity, he now denies genius this right in the name of "the true wisdom for [our] peace of mind"—the ideal of an average, moderate bourgeois existence:

> That's what I envy especially in men of genius. They are good for only
> one thing—apart from that, zero. They don't know what it is to be
> citizens, fathers, mothers, cousins, friends. Between you and me, one
> should try to be like them in every way, but without multiplying the
> breed. The world needs men, but men of genius, no; I say no! No need
> of them. (p. 12)

Genius, which is aesthetically irreplaceable, is morally—and, paradoxically enough, this thesis is put forward by the immoralist—unjustifiable. The Philosopher at first parries with a question *ad personam* ("So you developed . . . an undying hatred of genius?") that, both here and later, serves to cover his embarrassment at being unable to respond. Then *Moi* attempts to justify genius in a manner that leads him step by step into an unexpected philosophy of history. The man of genius, who is decried because of general misunderstanding, should be evaluated from the vantage point of a later time: "Which of the two, Socrates or the judge who made him drink hemlock, is today the dishonored man?" (p. 13). But *Lui* is able to respond to this with an even more intricate question: "A great comfort to Socrates! Was he any the less convicted? Any the less put to death? Was he less of an agitator? In violating a bad law, did he not encourage fools to despise good ones?" The long-term effect of that truth for which genius opens the way is a poor consolation, and hardly adequate compensation, for injustice that has been experienced personally. The nephew looks at the present and makes himself the advocate of peace and order, even at the expense of the truth; the Philosopher looks to the future and tries to sublate the difference between genius and society in the name of human progress. The contradiction is intensified by a casuistic question: "Well, which would you prefer—that [Racine] should have been a good soul . . . and nothing more; or that he should have been deceitful, disloyal, ambitious, envious, and mean, but also the creator of *Andromaque* (etc.)?" (p. 14). This case, which brings the norms of the beautiful and the good into conflict, is raised to the level of theodicy without ever being resolved. Once again, *Lui*, in contrast to his position on music, is inclined to give up the beautiful in art for the good of a fully enjoyed life. On the other hand, *Moi*, in weighing the case of genius purchased at the price of evil, is led to assert that there is a hidden plan in nature, an idea that points forward to the theory of nature's cunning proposed by Kant and Hegel: "Think of the welfare of the species and, supposing that we ourselves are not generous enough, let us thank nature for knowing her business better than we" (p. 16). For *Lui*, this philosophical postulate, which measures the individual's claim to happiness against the "welfare of the species" and future of the species, only pushes the problem off on nature: "But if nature is as powerful as she is wise, why not make them as good as they are great?" (p. 16). The Philosopher's answer falls back into abstract idealism: "If everything here below were excellent, nothing would be excellent." This provokes *Lui* into his most vigorous argument against metaphysics: "The best order, for me, is that in which I had to exist—and a fig for the most perfect world if I am not of it." Thus ends the first round of dialogue—in an open contradiction between the idealist and the materialist point of view. The nephew, who understands nothing of philosophy, has shown himself the equal of the moral philosopher by his defense of the concrete interests of the individual, while the latter has has gotten stuck in his effort to justify the discrepancy between art and morality, genius and society. The dialectical resolution of this discrepancy was not available to Diderot; it came later, with the philosophy of history produced by German idealism, when Kant, Hegel, and Fichte took up the challenge put forth by the French Enlightenment.

The initial superiority of the discursive position taken by *Moi* is severely shaken during the next round of dialogue. His arrogant question, "Do you ever feel such a thing as self-contempt?" (p. 21), strikes something in *Lui* that *Moi* had not expected: a sense of self that can be wounded and that sets about defending itself. The nephew turns the humiliating experience he has had in the Bertin home against himself and, at the same time, against society. His self-contradictory situation emerges formally as a monologue within the larger discussion when he aims ironic questions about the amorality of social success at himself: "Can't you lick boots like the rest? Haven't you learned to lie, swear, forswear, promise, perform, or cheat like anyone else?" (see p. 22). He often comes into contradiction with himself in these instances, as when he first claims the right to act like everyone else, and then insists on being unique and irreplaceable for the guests at the Bertins', who, in throwing him out, simply treat him like anyone else (p. 21). He narrates his disaster in the most amusing manner possible, through the comic refraction produced by that very Rameau who, as a parasite, bases all his behavior on opportunism, and wants to make the useful his sole moral criterion, when he denies this principle at the dinner table by abandoning it for the sake of a risky bon mot.[78] That he later glosses over this "mistake" by saying he lost everything because once in his life he showed "a little wit" makes his "failure" all the more a demonstration of the unruliness of the aesthetic, which seems to take vengeance on the useful by creating an irresistible movement toward the bon mot. Finally, the nephew falls into a contradiction that he himself notes. After he has rejected the Philosopher's suggestion that he prostrate himself, he says that the Bertin incident has awakened in him the feeling that "a certain dignity attaches to the nature of man," although there are other days when he "could be as vile as required without its costing [him] anything" (p. 21). The pantomime of the seduction of a very young bourgeois innocent, through which he presents the vile Rameau and his unexploited gift for flattery, upsets the Philosopher, since he now finds himself in a contradictory position too:

> I listened to him, and while he was acting the procurer and the girl being seduced, his soul divided between opposite motives, I hardly knew whether to burst with laughter or with indignation. I was in pain. . . . I was overcome by so much cunning and baseness, by notions so exact and at the same time so false, by so complete a perversion of feeling, by such turpitude and such frankness, both equally uncommon. (p. 23)

The contradictory feelings that lead him to burst out laughing and then become angry at having done so are elements in the conflict between aesthetic effect and moral indignation: the anger reveals an unadmitted admiration. This aporia, which, in contrast to the Socratic aporia, is brought about by purely affective means, leads the philosopher to no final, liberating insight. All he can do is suggest a change in the subject of the conversation: "He: But what do you advise me to do? Myself: To talk of something else. Unhappy man, to have been born or fallen so low" (p. 23). At another high point in the dialogue, the demonstration of sublime evil in the case of the Renegade from Avignon, the same thing happens as here, when the rhetoric of a cunning seducer is put on display. The subject is dropped and a sudden silence (in these two instances only) shows the impossibility of reaching any accord in the moral realm. Their communication, which is threatened with total collapse, is then rescued by a return to the aesthetic: "I was beginning to find almost unbearable the presence of a man who could discuss a dreadful deed, an abominable crime, in a way a connoisseur in poetry or painting discusses the fine points of a work of art" (p. 62). In both cases, after a brief interruption caused by *Moi*'s inability to respond with reasoned arguments, the discussion swings from the extreme immorality admitted by *Lui* to the contrasting theme of sublimely beautiful music. The extreme in this direction is reached with the demonstration of the triumph of the new Italian opera over the French style embodied in the music of the "divine Lully" and "the dear uncle" (p. 64).

The prophecy of the inevitable fall of this music allows the nephew to reach the highest possible metaphoric level—his famous symbiosis of the Platonic triad and the Christian Trinity. For *Lui*, "nature," which, like an alien god, takes its place next to the native idol in order to overthrow it without bloodshed, is also "the realm of [his] trinity," the realm where "the True, which is the Father, engenders the Good, which is the Son, whence comes the Beautiful, which is the Holy Ghost." *Lui* reclaims for the aesthetic realm that which he had earlier denied to the moral! "The true, the good, and the beautiful will prevail." Hegel will later correct this irritating relapse into Platonic metaphysics in a most interesting manner. After the theoretical legitimation of this new music as an *imitation des accents de la passion ou des phénomènes de la nature*, Diderot adds a practical elaboration, the display of an entire opera. What the nephew manages to accomplish at this high point of his pantomimic art so enthralls *Moi* that he once again finds himself confronting an emotional aporia: "[He] gripp[ed] our souls and [kept] them suspended in the most singular state of being that I have ever experienced. Did I admire? Yes, I did admire. Was I moved to pity? I was moved. But a streak of derision was interwoven with these feelings and denatured them" (p. 67). When the Philosopher's amazement is no longer obstructed by moral indignation, pity mixes with a grain of derision. The unspoken ground is the reflexive suffering of the mime, which, in the last round of the discussion, is juxtaposed to the philosopher's self-sufficiency.

How open is the dialogic execution in Diderot's revised version of the Socratic discussion? By the end of *Le neveu de Rameau* we can see that there is no irreversible movement in the course of the argument. There is a volatile movement from isolated themes to others that are repeated, interrupted, varied. This movement itself reveals an unmistakable desire not to sublate oppositional standpoints in some higher knowledge by means of a goal-oriented interplay of question and answer. Oppositions are always pushed to aporetic extremes. The antithesis between the participants in the discussion does not evolve in the same way, however: they are more and more fixed in a performative relationship (after the elimination of the magesterial superiority of the question poser) that allows them to reveal more personal traits than would the mere representation of an ideological position. The nephew, who at first appears to be a modern Proteus ("He has no greater opposite than himself," p. 9), develops a certain consistency through the self-contradictoriness that he freely reveals once he has been moved to it by the Philosopher's questions ("Master Philosopher, isn't it true that I am ever the same?" p. 87). The Philosopher, who, as a moralist true to his principles, wants to be consistent in his point of view, is frequently driven to bold speculation by his unruly adversary. The most surprising instances of this emerge along with the questions about the historical usefulness of genius (pp. 13–14), and the pantomimes to which one is compelled by society (pp. 82–83). The final controversy ignites over a question of theodicy:

> Myself: Whatever a man tries, Nature destined him for that.
> He: Then she makes some very odd blunders. I can't for myself see
> from those heights where everything comes to the same thing. . . . I
> find that it is no part of good order to be sometimes without
> food. . . . The worst of it is the constrained posture in which need
> holds you. The needy man doesn't walk like the rest, he skips, twists,
> cringes, crawls. He spends his life choosing and performing positions.
> (p. 82)

Once again the opinions held by *Moi* and *Lui* cross in surprising fashion through the antithesis of their discursive roles. The antiphilosopher, who does not want to look at things from a superior point of view, arrives nonetheless at a thoroughly philosophical critique of the natural order: it has distributed its wealth unevenly, and brought the needy man to the point where he must constantly assume "postures" and perform his mime as if he were on stage. The critical potential of these thoughts, and *Lui*'s pantomimic display, registers with *Moi* this time, despite his advocacy of the existing order. He restates the idea as a general proposition: "Whoever stands in need of another is needy and takes a position." From this he concludes that contemporary society as a whole functions as a system of unrecognized dependencies from which not even the sovereign can escape: "The King takes a position before his mistress and before God: he dances his pantomime steps. . . . Really, what you call the beggar's pantomime is what makes the world go round. Every man has his Bertin and his little Hus" (p. 83). When *Lui* then remarks, "It's very consoling to me," it seems that they might still arrive at a single point of view, one that moves beyond the aporia of the dialogue to some sort of conclusion. But *Moi* immediately recants his bold overture by calling on Diogenes, who "made fun of his wants," thus trying to free himself from the universal pantomime by reasserting his role as philosopher. After this, *Lui* drives him further and further into a corner by gradually casting doubt on the absence of want in this Diogenes *redivivus*, until at last they arrive at a fatal dilemma:

He: What if the courtesan was busy and the cynic in haste?
Myself: He went back to his tub and did without.
He: Do you advise me to do the same?
Myself: I'll stake my life it is better than to crawl, eat dirt and prosti-
tute yourself.
He: But I want a good bed, good food, warm clothes in winter, cool in
summer, plenty of rest, money, and other things that I would rather
owe to kindness than earn by toil. (p. 85)

The moral idealist, who must propose self-gratification in a barrel as his *ultima ratio*, has clearly been driven to an extreme position at the end of the dialogue, one that seems no less grotesque than the *ultima ratio* proposed by the immoralist, who would avoid work at all costs. The latter goes so far as to say he would prosti-tute his wife in order to satisfy his material needs, and in the same breath begins to cry about her premature death. This is how Diderot's Socratic dialogue ends — in an open contradiction between the counterpoles of a classical moral philoso-phy, revived and replayed in Menippean fashion, as a revelatory pantomime. One can also look at this final antithesis between *Moi* and *Lui* as a grotesque sublation of the ethical ideal of *sibi constare*, which forms a leitmotiv in the dialogue and is even reflected in the nephew's final sentence, a sentence that sets an ironic seal on the openness of the conclusion: "He laughs best who laughs last."

It is unlikely that any reconstruction of a reading of a famous text by an equally famous reader could offer more interesting hermeneutic perspectives than does Hegel's reception of *Le neveu de Rameau*. The unusual fascination that this posthumously published text had on readers such as Schiller and Goethe (and later, Marx and Freud to name only two) is attested to in Hegel's case by the fact that he immediately incorporated his reading of it into his just completed *Phenomenology of Spirit*. One can use the term "incorporated" almost literally here, as is demonstrated not only by three striking quotations from Goethe's trans-lation (cited verbatim in part, in part as a montage, and emphasized by the use of quotation marks, but without naming Diderot, though he is the only person granted the honor of being quoted in the *Phenomenology*!), but especially by the promotion of *Moi* and *Lui* to the status of modes of consciousness in the general dialectic of the spirit and history. Whoever simply criticizes this procedure as too limited or arbitrary, or downplays it as a "misunderstanding" of Diderot's inten-tion, overlooks Hegel's philosophical interest in something that Diderot did not and could not intend: a philological interpretation whose aim is to reconstruct the meaning that might have been attached to the text in its original historical context. On the other hand, it can be shown that, despite the striking partiality evident in the selection of these three quotations, Hegel interprets Diderot's text as a whole. It is also clear that his understanding derives less from the historical context of French thought prior to 1774 than from the later historical context embodied in the German idealism of the period around 1805. The supposed misunderstanding thus proves to be an exemplary case of productive and also norm-building reception (I prefer this formulation to "fruitful misunderstanding" because the latter still involves an aesthetic of identity).

The meaning of *Le neveu de Rameau* in Hegel's reading can be extrapolated from the selections he included in the *Phenomenology*: there one finds (in the chapter entitled "Self-alienated Spirit, Culture") *Moi* and *Lui*, who serve as representations of "honest" and "disrupted consciousness"; the supper at the Bertins', which reveals the degeneracy that "wealth . . . shares . . . with [its] recipient";[79] the music pantomime, which is understood as the "language of . . . disrupted consciousness," a language able to expose "the perverted action of the whole of the real world" (p. 319);[80] the nephew's "self-alienated spirit," which is the "Spirit . . . of culture," and superior to that of the philosopher (pp. 317–18); and, finally, the fall of the gods, which represents the uncontested victory of "pure insight" over superstition (p. 331). As Jean Hyppolite has shown, these borrowings are to be seen dialectically in the *Phenomenology*, both as moments in the return of the self-alienated spirit to itself, and as (fully concretizable) moments of historical reality — the culmination of the French Enlightenment in the Revolution of 1789.[81] They also allow us to interpret Diderot's dialogue from another point of view, one that emerges only with the later position. Hegel's reading interprets his predecessor's text in a manner that is succinct in its brevity, but rejuvenating at the same time. It opens up a meaning for *Le neveu de Rameau* that Diderot could not have imagined. Nonetheless, this meaning does not correspond to some merely subjective, arbitrary process whereby Hegel took possession of Diderot's work for his later text. It is the objective concretization of a significance that the earlier work achieved, and could only achieve, through Hegel's norm-setting interpretation, an interpretation without which Diderot's text can no longer be imagined because, to use Walter Benjamin's expression, it reveals "the critical constellation in which precisely this fragment of the past finds itself in precisely this present."[82]

The meaning of a text for a later period can, when measured against its meaning for the period of its origin, profitably increase our understanding in both directions, though certain things are lost along the way. In our case, the question arises during a reconstruction of Hegel's reading as to whether the dialectical solution that the *Phenomenology* supplies as a means of resolving the opposition between *Moi* and *Lui* can maintain the individualized interplay and open dialogic relationship that is characteristic of *Moi* and *Lui* in Diderot's text, or whether it is obliged to make that relationship one-sided. In other words, the reception problem is both hermeneutically and historically interesting here. It draws attention to a case in which the dialogic principle is sublated in a new, monologically narrative, philosophical discourse, a discourse that assumes itself to be a revival of the dialectic and that can, therefore, also claim to have maintained the polyphony of the Socratic dialogue in a scientific investigation of the experience that consciousness has of itself.

The first Diderot quotation serves Hegel as a means of elucidating the notion "culture" [*Bildung*] in terms of a necessary "alienation . . . from . . . natural being" (p. 298). The individual accedes to culture in a "transcending [of] the natural self," not in the "determinateness of its nature" for which Hegel first employs the German word for "kind" or "type" [*Art*] and then the French word *espèce*:

> The *particularity* of a nature which becomes purpose and content is something powerless and unreal; it is a "kind" of being which vainly and ridiculously strains every nerve to get going. . . . this presumed individuality really only exists in someone's mind, an *imaginary* existence which has no abiding place in this world, where only that which externalizes itself, and, therefore, only the universal, obtains an actual existence. That is why such an imagined existence is esteemed for what it is, for a *kind* of existence. "Kind" is not quite the same as *espèce*, "the most horrid of all nicknames; for it denotes mediocrity and expresses the highest degree of contempt." (p. 298)

Hegel turns to the meaning found in the French term *espèce* (used since 1740 in the derogatory sense of *une pauvre espèce d'homme*)[83] because the German word adds "an air of honesty" to this meaning. His intent, on the other hand, is to use this pejorative term as a means of belittling the natural self as uncultured. The cryptic significance of this quotation becomes clear only when one realizes that, in the conversations in *Le neveu*, the contemptible mediocrity of an *espèce* is contrasted with an ideal of perfection—the perfect depravity of the immoralist—that is hardly imaginable in terms of Hegel's notions of the individual and culture. After the lines cited by Hegel, Diderot's text continues as follows: "A great scoundrel is a great scoundrel; he isn't a 'type' [*espèce*]. If my son went askew because of his education, he would waste his best years before the paternal fiber could set him straight, and bring him to the state of perfect abjectness that I have reached" (p. 72).[84] Of course this cynically asserted lack of morality is not interpreted by Hegel as the necessary condition for the production of the individual; but in retrospect the citation nonetheless reveals that even in the original context Diderot's amoral subject would hardly have represented a "natural self." One must not overlook that the nephew's comments are ironic, first as part of an attack on the ideal of a natural education, then with respect to the fact that he himself is not perfectly abject, but, instead, perfect as a mime of others' abjectness. In reality he suffers because of his mediocrity, and is constantly torn between two poles—between the beautiful and the useful, between the musically sublime and the burden of his material needs. He has already suffered that from which he wants to spare his son: "He would be pulled by two contrary forces that would make him go askew down the path of life" (p. 72). Diderot's description of an *espèce*, which Hegel's citation reduces to the level of the "most horrid of all nick-names," already points toward definitions of the "ignoble" and the "disrupted consciousness," so it is easy to see the attraction the nephew exercised for him, and why he gave it such an important place in his dialectical presentation of the figures that unfold the history of the self-alienated spirit.

The place at which *Le neveu* enters the scene staged by the *Phenomenology* is the moment when the opposition between "noble" and "ignoble" consciousness is sublated by bringing universal power under the sway of "being-for-itself"; that is, "state power that is reflected into itself" (the absolute monarchy of Louis XIV) is sacrificed and exists henceforth as "wealth" (p. 312). But at this point, when self-consciousness finds itself estranged as wealth, as a thing and no longer as another person or a spiritual power, the deepest alienation begins, an alienation in which "pure 'I' beholds itself outside of itself and rent asunder" (p. 314). In the consciousness bound up with this absolute disruption, the distinction "of being noble, as opposed to ignoble falls away and both are the same." Hegel obviously turns to the dinner at the Bertins' as a means of elaborating on this dialectical transformation:

> Wealth thus shares its dejection with the recipient; but in place of rebellion appears arrogance. For in one respect it knows as well as the recipient that *being-for-itself* is a contingent Thing; but it is itself this contingency in the power of which personality stands. In this arrogance which fancies it has, by the gift of a meal, acquired the self of another's 'I' and thereby gained for itself the submission of that other's inmost being, it overlooks the inner rebellion of the other. (p. 315)

In the Hegelian context, the résumé of the dinner at the Bertins' acquires the added significance of being the site where the deepest humiliation of the parasite first reveals his superiority and then, finally, the possibility of the return of the self to itself. The revolt of a self-consciousness that repudiates its own repudiation finds a language of its own—the "language of disruption." In the nephew's mouth, the ignoble "language of flattery" is inverted into the noble "language of disrupted consciousness." It is the perfect form of speech because it is able to express the "absolute and universal inversion and alienation of the actual world and thought, their entire estrangement from one another" (p. 316). The new figure in the process of the construction of consciousness, that which resolves the antagonism between magnanimous and spiteful consciousness emerges—at the "true middle" between the extremes of state power and wealth—out of the spirit of language! The nephew, whose being consisted of "universal talk and destructive judgement" (p. 317) in Diderot's dialogue, emerges later, in the *Phenomenology*, as the "repudiated consciousness [that] changes round into the nobility which characterizes the most highly developed freedom of self-consciousness" (p. 317). If one takes this interpretation at its word, it is at first disturbing to realize that Hegel, who takes Diderot's "moral monster" to be the true spirit of culture and the future, seems to ignore his displays of moral depravity, or merely contrasts them with the moral reasoning of an "honest individual" in order to prove the latter to be "uneducated thoughtlessness" (p. 317). The move to identify the amoral musician with the "confused state [of mind]" in contrast to the "simple consciousness of the true and the good" (p. 318) embodied by the Philosopher is legitimated in the original context by a motive whose deeper significance again becomes visible only in the retrospective light of a quotation.

This second quotation from Diderot, through which Hegel represents the nephew's speech as the perfect language of disruption, proves on closer examination to be a montage of lines borrowed from at least three different places. The selection and the forced nature of their union reveal the direction of Hegel's inquiry into Diderot's text. The nephew interests Hegel as a representative of "disrupted consciousness," one that he defines more closely as the consciousness of the inversion of all conceptions and realities: "The universal deception of itself and others; and the shamelessness which gives utterance to this deception is just for that reason the greatest truth" (p. 317). The nephew's language is, therefore, referred to as "witty," but is not then interpreted on the basis of his remarks about the rich and the poor, tyrants and slaves, ideals and needs, but instead in terms of the "madness of the musician 'who heaped up and mixed together thirty arias' " (see pp. 317–18)—in other words, through a quotation from the great music pantomime. Hegel probably did not have in mind the effect of the Italian opera when he made this choice. He must have been thinking of the talent of the musician whose pantomime could expose the system of unadmitted dependencies behind the polyphony of roles played out in society. The remarkable reaction that he then ascribes to *Moi* is apparently Hegel's own supplement: "To the tranquil consciousness which, in its honest way, takes the melody of the Good and True to consist in evenness of the notes, i.e. in unison, this talk appears as a 'rigmarole of wisdom and folly' " (p. 318). In fact, in Diderot's text this speech produces a contrary reaction, one of wonder, tenderness, and sympathy (p. 67); the Philosopher is full of esteem for the musician, who provokes the moral indignation of the former only when he lays claim to being a "moralist." The supplement, with which Hegel shows sovereign disregard for all the rules governing the use of quotations, seems to me to correspond most closely to the desire to offer the polyphonic language of the disrupted consciousness as an alternative to the monologism of the ready truths produced by the Philosopher. This hypothesis seems to be corroborated by the next citation, which is drawn precisely from the section—probably the only section—in Diderot's dialogue where *Moi* recognizes that *Lui*, despite all his contradictions, stands out from his peers because of his uncommon frankness (p. 23):

To the tranquil consciousness . . . this talk appears as a "rigmarole of wisdom and folly, as a medley of as much skill as baseness, of as many correct as false ideas, a mixture compounded of a complete perversion of sentiment, of absolute shamefulness, and of perfect frankness and truth." (Hegel, p. 318)

In Diderot's dialogue this section concerns the Philosopher's moral indignation regarding the scene in which the perfect seduction of a naive young girl is depicted. Hegel's quotation assumes that *Moi* has this same reaction to the music pantomime, so that the contrast between *Moi* and *Lui* includes the moral and the aesthetic: the Philosopher thus becomes a Platonist who wishes to sustain the monotone of the old music against the polyphony of the new, and at the same time maintain the supposed unity of the true, the good, and the beautiful against the "frank and self-conscious eloquence of the educated mind" (p. 318). The decisive aspect of Hegel's intervention and "correction" (which remain covert) seems to me to be the manner in which he gives weight to *Lui*'s frankness. The moment of "perfect frankness and truth," which in Hegel's text is so powerfully emphasized by its displacement into a new context, remains a secondary aspect of the nephew's character in Diderot's work. It is mentioned only in passing, as yet another element in his contradictory being. The hermeneutic difference between the meaning of frankness in the original and the later context makes it possible to reconstruct both an unexpressed assumption of Diderot's about the relationship between *Moi* and *Lui*, and the new question, posed by Hegel, for which the "speech of this mind which is fully aware of its confused state" is the answer.

In Diderot's text, it was the frequency and variety of the contradictions between *Lui*'s aesthetic virtuosity and his moral degeneracy that, on the surface at least, fascinated *Moi*. These same contradictions led to the Philosopher's casuistic entanglements, and his inability to resolve them honestly without giving up his fundamental idealistic premise concerning the unity of the beautiful and the good. On a deeper level, however, the confusion *Moi* experiences is also provoked by the fact that it is precisely the immoralist, the person who mocks all the ethical norms of sociability and seems only to bow to the principle of *amour propre*, who is able to express himself with a *franchise si peu commune* (such uncommon frankness)—a frankness that ought to have shamed his contemporaries.[85] For Hegel, this frankness is more an expression of the truth of the self-alienated spirit as it is embodied in a consciousness of the conditions from which contemporary society suffers—without any awareness of the origin of these conditions in its own universal self-betrayal. For Diderot, however, the nephew's frankness is more a private, though surprisingly constant, aspect of his character than the provocative basis for a public suffering that protests its own social origins.

Rameau's nephew is obviously no Alceste. The latter can be laughed at in Molière's comedy because he takes himself to be the only upright person in a corrupt society. On the other hand, Diderot's *neveu* cannot be considered a tragic figure representative of the individual in the modern era either. He is not forced to shoulder the internal contradictions of society in romantic isolation. Diderot did not motivate the nephew's self-contradictory nature in terms of Rousseau's insights into the correlation between progress in science and art and the collapse of morality and social customs. The nephew is far from thinking that his contemporary society, which alienates life and makes it impossible for the individual to achieve happiness, has been generated by mankind itself rather than by nature. He assumes his vices are *natural*, acquired without effort, and entirely in keeping with the habits of his nation (p. 38): "I was bidden to be ridiculous and I made myself so. As to vice, nature alone took care of that; though when I say vicious I am merely using your language. For if we really thrashed things out, we might find ourselves each calling virtue what the other calls vice and t'other way round" (pp. 50–51). Thus, the honorary title of "unhappy consciousness" does not take on full resonance for the nephew of the original text. The contradiction between individual and society is not the basis of his suffering. His unhappiness becomes apparent to him only when his musical and pantomimic talents bump up against the barrier of creativity, and he confronts the difference between art and morality as a contradiction in his being.

The historical threshold that separates Diderot and Hegel can, therefore, be defined in terms of the manner in which the nephew's *franchise si peu commune* is reassessed. Sincerity, which in Diderot's dialogue is the only positive value or moral residue that remains as far as *Moi* is concerned, and which surprises him when he finds it in *Lui*,[86] becomes a negative category in the *Phenomenology*. There, frankness is a sign of disrupted consciousness; it also enables that consciousness to grasp the perversion of the real world in terms of its own contradictory nature. The final segment of the second quotation from Diderot draws once again on the music pantomime (though at first in the form of a free paraphrase), in order to comment on its effect in such a way that, in the end, even the ridicule that cuts across the Philosopher's admiration in Diderot's text can be erased by the frankness of this "mind which is fully aware of its confused state":

> It will be unable to refrain from entering into all these tones and running up and down the entire scale of feelings from the profoundest contempt and dejection to the highest pitch of admiration and emotion; but blended with the latter will be a tinge of ridicule which spoils them. The former, however, will find in their very candour a strain of atoning reconcilement, will find in their very frankness a strain of reconciliation, will find in their subversive depths the all-powerful note which restores Spirit to itself. (p. 318)

What is new in Hegel's interpretation arises at that place in Diderot's dialogue where the frankness of the disrupted consciousness would by itself have been enough to distinguish between *Lui* and *Moi*. In that case, the Musician's language is already superior to the Philosopher's because the former, despite its distraction, remains "fully aware" of itself, while the latter, though it seems to be ordered, can provide no new or different order, and is unable to call itself into question. The fact that Hegel refers to the Philosopher's speech as monosyllabic indicates that it is a monologic discourse, one opposed by the Musician's polyphonic principle of "frank and self-conscious eloquence." Here, the nephew's language becomes the "spirit of culture," in contrast to the moral idealism of the Philosopher, which, as the language of the "simple consciousness of the true and the good," must remain monosyllabic: "For it can say nothing that the [former] does not already know and say" (p. 318). The figures of the simple and disrupted consciousnesses in the *Phenomenology*—this much is clear so far—are not just superordinate to or independent of the antithesis between *Moi* and *Lui* in Diderot's dialogue, and, thus, merely useful as a means of interpreting the latter. They presuppose Diderot's text and obviously grow out of Hegel's reading of *Le neveu de Rameau* to become dialectical figures in his interpretation. That they have their genetic *fundamentum in re* in the prior Socratic dialogue of the French Enlightenment can, finally, also be demonstrated by the fact that Hegel's interpretation not only cites the conflict between *Moi* and *Lui* but also incorporates it critically—from the debate about Racine to that about Diogenes, which open and close Diderot's dialogue—and points the way to its dialectical resolution.

The next step in my interpretation will involve trying to answer the question as to whether the additional meaning acquired by *Le neveu de Rameau* through this dialectical resolution must be paid for at the price of some loss. With the sublation of the dialectical form in the narrative discourse of the dialectic one loses not only the equilibrium between the opposing voices but also the openness of seeking and finding. Although Diderot, in his reprise of the Socratic dialogue, turned against tradition and gave the maieutic discursive role more and more to the Musician rather than to the Philosopher, the dialogic relation between *Moi* and *Lui* nonetheless remained open and symmetrical because both individuals were driven to extreme positions by the contingencies of the discussion, and, thus, developed their characters more fully than might have been expected. But seen through Hegel's eyes, disrupted consciousness is from the very beginning superior (i.e., "the all-powerful note which restores Spirit to itself"; p. 318) to the simple consciousness (i.e., the uneducated thoughtlessness of not knowing that it is equally doing the reverse; p. 317). In the course of the argument an inescapable consequence arises as well, and for its sake Hegel will use a third quotation from Diderot to abruptly invert the structure of the Platonic triad and incorporate it into the victory of pure insight.

In Diderot's text, the case for the genius—who is not to be measured by the standards of morality—is made by the Philosopher, who claims that "the good and the noble . . . does not lose its value because it may be associated with or mixed with the 'bad,' " since "in this fact lies the wisdom of nature" (p. 318). In Hegel's interpretation, this assertion is derided as a trivial repetition of the language of disrupted consciousness, a repetition "thoughtlessly" intoned by simple consciousness. In the last analysis, the latter is only saying that "what is called noble and good is in its essence the reverse of itself, or that, conversely, the 'bad' is the excellent" (p. 319). Although the argument presented by Diderot's philosopher anticipates both Kant's thesis concerning the unnoticed purposes of nature—those that can be actualized only within the history of the human species—and Hegel's own "cunning reason," Hegel rejects the justification of evil propounded by the philosophy of history. Instead, he grounds Diderot's case [the case for the genius] in the insight that disrupted consciousness has about the perverted action of the entire real world. Should one conclude from the preceding discussion that, at this point in the movement of the spirit toward itself, its alienation may not be alleviated by a theory, or a hidden, modern theodicy, but instead calls for some sort of action?

The possibility is suggested by Hegel's inclusion of the Diogenes anecdote, which Diderot's philosopher believes he can use to prove his independence from the system of social dependencies. Hegel first attributes to him the radical demand for the "dissolution of this whole world of perversion," but only in order to refute his claim more completely later on. Such a demand would not appeal to the individual here represented by Diogenes in his barrel because his withdrawal from the world would be precisely that which "is reckoned to be bad, viz. to care for *himself qua* individual" (p. 319). Not wishing to stop there, Hegel extends his critique to Rousseauism, which labors under the illusion that reason "should give up the spiritually developed consciousness it had acquired, should submerge the widespread wealth of its moments again in the simplicity of the natural heart." But if reason fell back into the innocence of nature, it would leave this entire sphere of perversion as it now stands; the demand for its dissolution can, therefore, be addresssed only to the "Spirit of culture" itself, and can only mean "in order that it return out of its confusion to itself as *Spirit*, and win for itself a still higher consciousness" (p. 319).

Through Hegel's interpretation, Diderot's dialogue, which ends in the aporia of an unresolved opposition between moral dogmatism and cynical libertinage, acquires a superordinate perspective, one that must not be confused with the viewpoint of an impersonal author who has hovered over and served as a third party to this discussion from the very beginning. From Hegel's standpoint the antithesis between *Moi* and *Lui* can experience immanent sublation, as a negation of negation, only in a "higher consciousness" that must emerge from the second voice in the discussion: from the utterances of the disrupted consciousness. This consciousness alone is able to express the perversion of the contemporary world—it "derides existence and the universal confusion, and derides its own self as well" (p. 319). We can speak of a third voice in the discussion only insofar as one is present in terms of the authority of Platonic metaphysics and, as such, called into question in Diderot's dialogue, and insofar as its sublation by the sequence of figures in the *Phenomenology* allows the spirit of culture to become the third voice, that of a truth *in statu nascendi*. Although Hegel was thus able to bestow the highest accolade on the amoral subject in Diderot's dialogue, although he was able to invert the discursive roles of *Moi* and *Lui*, thereby countering tradition, and able to provide an irritating and not easily erased paradigm for future interpretation, the representation of the nephew in the dialectical process of the *Phenomenology* is not simply allowed to enact the return of alienated spirit to itself. Another step needs to be taken before this can happen. When announcing the vanity of all things, disrupted consciousness must be aware of "its own vanity" in order to lift itself from the level of mere witty phrases to that of "pure insight." This move resolves individual insight into universal insight and "manifests its own peculiar activity in so far as it opposes itself to faith" (p. 329).

Pure insight and belief are the new binary figure into which consciousness must now dissociate itself in order that the sublation of their contradiction — historically explicated as the struggle between enlightenment and superstition — allow the return of alienated spirit to itself. The final citation from Diderot is found in this chapter, and once again at an important point in the text — the point at which pure insight calmly ("comparable to a silent expansion or to the *diffusion*, say, of a perfume in the unresisting atmosphere") arrives at the Enlightenment's goal:

> . . . an invisible and imperceptible Spirit, it infiltrates the noble parts through and through and soon has taken complete possession of all the vitals and members of the unconscious idol; then "one fine morning it gives its comrade a shove with the elbow, and bang! crash! the idol lies on the floor." (p. 332)

In Diderot's text, the nephew spins this image out at somewhat greater length as a means of prognosticating the inevitable triumph of true music. Its victory over a still dominant false taste is seen as inevitable, and at the same time as gradual as the coming of the "kingdom of nature," which the Musician refers to as the "kingdom of my trinity," and explicates ironically with the help of the Platonic triad. But what is the target of this sentence, which was already quoted earlier: "The True, which is the Father, engenders the Good, which is the Son, whence comes the Beautiful, which is the Holy Ghost" (p. 66)? One could argue about whether this formulation, which transforms the Christian Trinity into a generative schema for the Platonic triad, is parodistic, and whether it has religious or aesthetic authority as its target. It seems to me that in the eighteenth century the nephew's speculation about the Trinity could have been a parody of the declining tradition of allegoresis, and would not have upset either orthodoxy very much. The annoying thing about it is not the rather ingenious formulation as such, but the use to which the nephew puts it: that the true, the good, and the beautiful in both the Platonic and the Christian sense should overcome the power of prejudice strikes one as both surprising and unbelievable coming from an immoralist. And it would only mean imposing one layer of parodied allegoresis on another if one tried to interpret these lines as proof that Diderot hoped to find in the realm of the beautiful that which political reality denied him, thereby anticipating the ideal of aesthetic education found in German classicism.[87]

Hegel's citation corrects the nephew's Platonizing impulse by relegating speculation about the Trinity to a footnote, and by transferring the motif of the fall of the idol from the aesthetic realm to those of the moral and political. In the context of the *Phenomenology*, the nephew's cheeky metaphorics offer a twofold interpretation of the importance of 1789 for world history—as a nonviolent realization of pure insight, which brings the rule of error to an end, and, with regard to the political revolution, as "a violent struggle with its antithesis." The violent event, the revolution, could succeed only after the nonviolent effect of pure insight had undermined the ground of domination. It is especially this subversive fulfillment of the Enlightenment that seems to have fascinated Hegel. He cannot find enough poetic and medical images ("the *diffusion*, say, of a perfume"; "if the infection has penetrated to every organ") with which to picture what Diderot laid out anecdotally through reference to the political methods of the Jesuit missionaries in China. Apparently Hegel saw in this interpretation the answer to his question as to how the Enlightenment could have hoped to manage against the ruling powers ("the will of the deceiving priesthood and of the oppressive despot"). Most significantly, it engages with the weakest of the three sides of its enemy: the "false insight" of the will-less masses. The isolated "spirit of culture," which is represented in the *Phenomenology* by the now dialectic *Neveu de Rameau*, finds in the insight of the masses, which "is devoid of will [and] which has no separable individuality of its own," the consciousness of its "true relation to the other extreme" (p. 330), out of which the new form of the spirit emerges.

This is the point at which the reception of Diderot's dialogue in Hegel's text comes to an end. It is not, however, the end of the history of the formation of consciousness in the *Phenomenology*. The victory of the Enlightenment is by no means the concluding moment of history for Hegel. It is not the event after which humanity falls prey to the ennui of "posthistory" (a term that has recently become fashionable once more). After the collapse of the rule of error, a new form of spirit rears its head, one that cannot keep its fateful lineage hidden from the initiate ("the new serpent of wisdom raised on high for adoration"; p. 332). In other words, at the very moment of its realization, pure insight is transmuted into its own negative, into the delusion of having to do battle with something Other, just as, later, the achievement of absolute freedom is transformed into the Terror by the abstract rule of virtue. The dialectic of enlightenment remains without conclusion here because the course of history since 1789 has shown that it cannot be brought to a close. And if, today, this unconcluded dialectic disquiets us more than the end of Hegel's *Phenomenology* (absolute knowledge and its putative consequences, the "end of art," so often discussed in the recent past, "the end of the philosophy of history," and all those other things that may have come to an end) literary hermeneutics feels itself obliged to direct one more question at philosophical hermeneutics—which is certainly more competent in this realm. Diderot's *Neveu de Rameau* has shown how open the openness of the Socratic dialogue can be, or could again become. Hegel's *Phenemonology of Spirit*, which was able to resolve the antagonism between the Philosopher and the Musician, has bequeathed a question that may have bothered others besides myself: How closed is the closure of the dialectic; that is, is it monologic of necessity? Must the philosophical dialectic always already know its resolution if, like Hegel, it wishes to look back and narrate the way to science in terms of the knowledge consciousness has had of itself? Is this why question and answer disappeared in the discourse of the *Phenomenology*? Does this mean that in the step from the dialogic to the dialectic, truth ceases to be open to the struggle of interpretations from which it de facto first arose, from the dialogue between eras, that is? Could the dialectical movement complete itself more dialogically than it does in Hegel's work—and allow new truth to arise from a polyphony of voices without garnering for the voice of the other the unhappy fate that awaits Diderot's philosopher in Hegel's interpretation?

D. Rousseau's *Nouvelle Héloïse* and Goethe's *Werther* within the Shift of Horizons from the French Enlightenment to German Idealism

to Jean Starobinski

However great the provocative power of a literary work may have been, this power inevitably disappears as time passes. The original provocation through which the autonomous work negates the normativity of the actual and, along with it, the authority of the past, finally falls prey to the cunning of the tradition; its original, situation-bound, and inherent negativity is lifted out of the movement of time and given the canonical force of the classical. In these circumstances, a historical reconstruction of the literary and social horizons within which the work appeared is first necessary if we wish to set eyes once more on the initial gap between received expectations and depicted experience. This is especially true in the case of *La nouvelle Héloïse*.[1]

A reader from our own era who regards Rousseau's notorious foreword as a – still very effective – defamation of the public will be disappointed as soon as he begins to read the work itself. It will be hard for him to understand what it was about this text that could have inspired or shocked Rousseau's contemporaries. The provocation announced so vociferously in the foreword, which at the time insulted readers of every imaginable sort while warning them against reading on, is hardly visible today in terms of the novel's execution. A reader from our own era will probably find the idea of following the story of the two lovers through six volumes of letters a bit much, since any such obligation soon overtaxes our less energetic reading habits. The effort of having to read through a series of more than 160 letters is rewarded neither by the pleasures of tension-filled action nor by a variety of perspectives. The reader will hardly be pleased to discover that the lovers and the small circle of people that surrounds them never tire of expressing their feelings and thoughts in writing. In this torrent of overflowing interiority, external events are insular outcroppings, and the supposedly quotidian nature of the action is anything but "natural." Rather, it at first seems pathetically overarticulated. This "tale of sentimental hearts" is also strained by moralizing or purely didactic digressions that unavoidably subvert the fiction of an exchange of letters. The epistolary fiction seems not to be maintained even in those places where one might expect that, as a medium of direct self-expression, it would allow the individuality of the letter writers to emerge polyphonically. It seems, instead, that there is finally only one, monologic tone to be heard in all their ejaculations, that of Rousseau hiding behind the role of the book's editor. If it really was a new language of sentimentality that Rousseau and his *Nouvelle Héloïse* helped to achieve an unexpectedly wide impact—an impact that was incomprehensible to the official organs of criticism—then, paradoxically enough, it must be the proclaimed immediacy of this very language that has created the barrier to comprehension that later generations have run up against.

If today's reader can still—or once again—have immediate access to the sentimental language in Goethe's *Werther* now that Plenzdorf's *Neue Leiden des jungen W.* has helped that classic text achieve unexpected relevance, it is all the more incomprehensible that the style of *La nouvelle Héloïse*, which strikes the reader as being highly pathetic, was once felt to be the "simple language of the heart." One wept while reading Saint-Preux's subtle rhetoric of seduction and the endless tirades of virtue that come from his *belle prêcheuse*. Their style became the practical ideal of the *homme sensible*, and normative to a degree that had never before been experienced in the history of reading. The best-known evidence concerning the initial reception of the book, that which has been gathered together as the Neuchâtel collection of the numerous letters Rousseau received from readers, and the documents concerning the continuing effect of *La nouvelle Héloïse* (in 1761 it had already gone through twenty printings, and had numerous translations; by the end of the eighteenth century it had had over seventy printings in French alone) have been discussed enough already. Symptomatic of the book's reception are: the case of the high-born lady who began to read the new novel while dressing for a ball, let the coach she had ordered stand waiting hour after hour, and then at four in the morning sent it away so that she could spend the remainder of the night reading (*OC* I, p. 547); the crowds around the the book lenders, who exploited the feverishness of their readers' desire, and could ask as much as twelve sous for handing over one of the six volumes for an hour; the flood of replies from naive readers who themselves took pen in hand and continued the *Lettres de deux amants* through missives to the author. These letters attest to an astounding degree of concern. Just imagine, some readers waited three days before daring to read the final letter from Wolmar to Saint-Preux (ML, p. 184), and then shed a flood of tears after learning of Julie's death (DM, p. 249); people could not bring themselves to reread the novel because they could not bear to reexperience the terrible emotional shock the first reading had produced (AA, p. 228); but then again, extensive reading turned into intensive reading, the cathartic effect of which had previously been experienced only with the Bible or devotional books;[2] and thanks to having read the book one could finally manage to turn away from a life of moral depravity, or, because of the fate that met Julie, Saint-Preux, and Wolmar, one found the means to renew the love and virture of one's own marriage.

However excessive the enthusiasm of a broad new segment of readers was in France, the criticism leveled by the Enlightenment philosophers and by the orthodox church was just as much so. With the exception of Duclos and an enthusiastic commentary in the *Journal encyclopédique*, the statements made by the *hommes de lettres* show a striking degree of misunderstanding when seen from our current vantage point. It was not just Voltaire who vented his feelings in a vicious polemic. Misunderstanding is the appropriate term, since this rejection of *La nouvelle Héloïse* by the recognized critical authorities of the day does not clarify why the novel, written by an author who had achieved rapid fame because of his two *Discours*, was thought to represent a break with both aesthetic and moral norms—a break that upset the *Philosophes* as much as their orthodox opponents. In contrast, the German reception of Rousseau's novel was incomparably more positive: it was not just the young generation of *Sturm und Drang* authors who celebrated the novel as the Gospel of Nature and as a signal for the rebellion against class barriers, or who frequently imitated, and openly or covertly responded to it. In Germany *La nouvelle Héloïse* also received a lively reply from the philosophers, and a more apt understanding, one that the rationalist Enlightenment thinkers put to use in the cause of practical reason, and their opponents for the benefit of the religion of feeling. Goethe's *Sorrows of Young Werther*, in which his contemporaries found a "second Rousseau" and a new, more intense Saint-Preux,[3] is the most significant German response to *La nouvelle Héloïse* and, in terms of its public effect, equally powerful. Goethe, however, does not refer to this grand competitive model in his own text, and furthermore mentions having read the book only in passing, although he had already read and been very impressed by it when he was in Strassburg. This will have to serve as an outline of the historical situation for the present. Clearly it is a situation that offers literary hermeneutics a particularly complex problem of reception.

A quite rich collection of material relevant to the reception of Rousseau's and Goethe's work has already been gathered and published, but this material has only begun to be interpreted from the standpoint of its continuity within the change of horizons between the French Enlightenment and later German idealism. Therefore, it seems to me that this well-known instance is especially suitable as the site of an effort to provide a practical as well as methodological elucidation of the problem of highlighting a horizon hermeneutically. The investigation is so laid out that my interpretation will follow from a series of questions that can be dealt with only briefly within the framework of this book. From what horizon of literary or social expectation can the provocation created by *La nouvelle Héloïse* and the unusual split in the public at its initial reception be explained? How did Goethe and his German contemporaries read the novel, given that Rousseau had been much admired and discussed as the author of the *Discours sur les sciences et les arts* (1750) and the *Discours sur l'inégalité parmi les hommes* (1755)? In what ways does Rousseau's text serve as a model in the *Sorrows of Young Werther* (1774)? What is the social situation to which the books are a response? In both France and Germany they were thought of as "Catechism[s] of Sentimentality" and were immediate successes as social indexes. To what degree can Goethe's *Werther* be considered a continuation of *La nouvelle Héloïse*, and thus a response to questions left unanswered by the contradictory resolution of the competing model embodied in Rousseau's "Idyll in Clarens"? How did Goethe himself later solve the problems of the separation of nature and society, autonomous self and heteronomous morality that he offered as the sources of Werther's downfall?

1. The gap between expectation and experience in Rousseau's *Nouvelle Héloïse*

The work of reconstructing the horizon of expectation that a text has sketched out for its original addressees—contemporary readers—is complicated from the beginning by the problem of selection. A six-volume novel sets practical limits to the ideal of a written record of reception, especially a record that moves from the title of a work to its conclusion, incorporating all explicit and implicit references to other texts, and all additional signals, so as to follow the process of continual construction and transformation of horizons and thereby reconstitute the implied reading for a reader in 1761. A consciously carried out selection of materials is, therefore, the first requisite for a hermeneutically sound interpretation. The procedure I follow here is one of selectively expanding the context. The preface, the vehicle for the reader's basic orientation, will be analyzed in full, syntactically and syntagmatically, that is, in terms of the sequence of meaning-constitutive moments (signals, appellative structures, and implied meanings), in order to come to grips with the horizon of expectation with which a reading of the text would begin. The early expectations traced in this manner will then be enlarged upon using corresponding instances in the text. In this manner, the literary horizon the work evoked for the reader of 1761 can be constructed in terms of the overall movement of the novel's action. This will make it possible to double-check the text-immanent starting point of this first analysis historically: through documents from the initial reception first of all (those that can provide evidence, either favorable or unfavorable, about how the work was experienced within the social horizon of the age) and then through the *Seconde Préface*, which was published later. There, Rousseau employs a fictive dialogue with a critic to justify his own intentions, which—he thought—had, of necessity, been misunderstood.

The title of Rousseau's novel, *La nouvelle Héloïse*, makes reference to a distant and, at the same time, a very current model. It promises to renew the original, in other words, to surpass it. The "true story" of Abelard and Héloïse, after surviving underground, had reappeared on the literary scene in 1697 in a translation by Bussy-Rabutin; and, contaminated by the *Lettres d'une religieuse portugaise*, and revised more than twenty-five times, it had proved more fascinating to the reader of the eighteenth century than conventional love stories (*OC* II, p. 1338). Rousseau, who first wanted to give his novel the title *Julie*, nevertheless finally drew on this literary myth, and thereby lent his *Nouvelle Héloïse* the fateful aura of these "grand lovers"—but not without discrediting their ominous example on moral grounds. Saint-Preux declares to his beloved that he can only feel sorry for Héloïse, because Abelard knew no more of love than he did of virtue and was, therefore, not worthy of her (*OC* II, pp. 85/363). The "modern" Héloïse was to be a "new" Héloïse (this final title correction was made by Rousseau himself), one who not only confronts her readers as their equal in freedom,[4] but—and this is why she became the title figure—always takes the lead in the realization of her love. The new claim—to have united passion and virtue, to be the first to have allowed the rights of the sentimental heart to prevail over all convention, and to allow it nonetheless to triumph in the end thanks to a self-achieved virtue and marriage to a third party—not only provoked Voltaire's biting ridicule,[5] but was also the first and only real point of contention for the admirers of the new Héloïse (AA, p. 256). According to the documents bearing on the novel's reception, it was seldom fully accepted. It also explains why the sympathy of many readers was limited to the first book of *La nouvelle Héloïse* and the novel's "sad conclusion."

Rousseau's subtitle, *Letters of Two Lovers, Inhabitants of a Small Town at the Foot of the Alps*, initiates the fiction of posthumously discovered letters, and thereby makes possible the use of a literary form that had recently helped Richardson to great popularity. The announcement surprises all the same because of the unusual locale in which the scene is set—a sublime landscape that was first assigned literary value and popularized as a destination for travelers by Rousseau. Haller's poem "The Alps" had preceded Rousseau's work (it was translated into French in 1749), but what people began to appreciate after its appearance was—as Marmontel's "Shepherdess of the Alps" (1759) shows—merely an eclogue displaced into the mountains (DM, p. 74). Rousseau was the first to make the sublime and wild beauty of the mountains, a beauty that surpassed any proposed by the canon of classical aesthetics, available to aesthetic understanding. He placed his lovers in a real scene, the Valais, and let their exemplary fate emerge from the "noble simplicity and quiet grandeur" of this landscape. Thus, Rousseau's subtitle stands in clear contrast with the setting of the epistolary novel, which, after

Richardson's turn toward everyday reality, always depended on the refined life of urban civilization; but the reference to a "small town at the foot of the Alps" also evoked for Rousseau's readers the added literary horizon of the pastoral poem and novel in order to dispel it later, that is, in order to transform it into a new ideal of the "natural," rural life.

The prescription for the reception of the bucolic embodied in the pastoral novel is not only demonstrable in terms of literary history, it is supremely evident in Rousseau's memories of the all-important reading he did when he was young. These novels were regularly read as escapist literature (SB, pp. 88ff.) despite Voltaire's criticism (1727). The bucolic leaves clear traces in the novel as well (the "inoculation of love" in Part III, letter xiv is, for example, an echo of *Astrée*). The genesis of *La nouvelle Héloïse*, which is described in Book 10 of the *Confessions*, begins, as Jean Starobinski has shown, with the novelization of a nostalgic daydream filled with pastoral figures and sentimental feelings that had haunted Jean-Jacques's imagination since his earlier reading of *Astrée*. He hoped to lift it out of the unreal and bring it to life — bring it into the reality of a landscape in which he was steeped, but which had not yet been discovered by others, and, at the same time, into the reality of a new self-esteem, a sense of self that Rousseau soon felt had been confirmed by his meeting Sophie d'Houdetot and being understood by a woman he loved (JS, pp. 403 ff.). Rousseau's novel led the contemporary reader into a real landscape at the foot of the Alps, not into the imaginary realm of Lignon. Neither did he rediscover arcadian shepherds or heroic lovers in the novel. If Saint-Preux reminded the reader of Céladon, Edouard of Don Quixote, Julie and Claire of Astrée,[6] these figures are only evoked in order to be dismissed once and for all. The new "Arcadia" in *La nouvelle Héloïse* is no realm of escape located far from reality. It is — just as Clarens embodies the degree zero of the idyll — the outline of a new form of society, one in which lonely shepherds no longer sing their love songs, but instead "beautiful souls" try to realize the transparency of a *société intime* in their everyday dealings. Although the language of their sensibility, which speaks so enthusiastically in the *décousu* of the new epistolary style, may appear to the reader to be no less artificial than that of heroic/gallant lovers, he is nonetheless expected to measure the fiction in these letters not by the degree of their probability but against the norms of the corrupt life led in society, a society that, while dreaming its arcadian pipe dreams, forgot what human beings, by their very nature, actually need in order to be happy.

The motto "Non la conobbe il mondo, mentre l'ebbe: / Conobbill'io ch'a pianger qui rimasi"[7] opens yet another horizon of expectation in *La nouvelle Héloïse*, that of another literary tradition, one meant to give poetic consecration to the fate meted out to the two lovers, and effect a subterranean, mythic legitimation. The reference is to Petrarch's *Canzoniere* and thus to one of the founding myths of the European love lyric. Rousseau conjures up this myth in the motto and maintains its presence with no less than eight further quotations spread throughout the text. The lines cited in the motto, which deal with sorrow about one's beloved, were themselves Petrarch's secularized version of John's reference to the light that was "in the world . . . and the world knew him not" (John 1:10). They place Julie in a typological relation with Laura, and enable one to read the story of the encounter between Saint-Preux and Julie and its entire arc of tensions from fulfilled passion to renunciation and sublimated love as a new "bourgeoisified *Canzoniere* in prose" (Denis de Rougement, *Love in the Western World*). On this level, important moments from the Petrarchian myth reappear as part of Saint-Preux's story: climbing Mont Ventoux becomes a walking trip through the mountains of the Valais; the return to Provence is transformed into the return to Lake Geneva; Laura's reappearance in a dream after her death becomes the frightening dream in Villeneuve (*OC* II, ix). And those involved can always make their feelings known to each other through references to Petrarch. When Saint-Preux complains about Julie's not looking at him (I, ii), praises the ascent to the mountain summit in terms of spiritual elevation (I, xxiii), imagines the idyllic joys of love to be found at the site of their agreed upon rendezvous (I, xxxviii), recommends that his beloved learn to sing in the Italian musical style (I, xlviii); when Julie exhorts her lover to comport himself in manly fashion after sending him away (II, xi), or sees his absence offset by the happiness of memories (II, xv); when Claire announces to her friend [Julie] the imminent return of the unhappy man for whom she has wept (IV, ii), and when he complains in the end that the course of his life has been cut off at midpoint (VI, vii)—when these references to Petrarch (which are also echoed in a number of quotations of similar mood: Tasso, four times; Marini, twice; and Metastasio, ten times) surface in Italian in the French context, the Italian acquires the aura and purity of perfect poetry. It emerges as a "unique phenomenon of distance" in the midst of the rhetorical prose of the letters.[8] The information conveyed by this prose is elevated to the level of mythical significance by the poetry of the lines cited in Italian, *le chant qui se sent dans l'âme*:[9] the Petrarchian mythos, according to which Laura bore the mortal remains of her triumph over Amor into the temple of chastity (*Trionfo de Castità*, l. 138), is revived in Julie's idealized being insofar as she is able to sublimate the passion of her love and, through the example of her self-mastery, create the foundations for a new, intimate social intercourse—a *Petit monde différent du notre* (*OC* II, p. 17)[10]—for the elect who love her.

If, after Rousseau resurrected it for his *Nouvelle Héloïse*, a canon of earlier works including Petrarch and the poetry of the Italians he preferred achieved the rank of a distant, even mythic authority, it was also and repeatedly juxtaposed to a classical model. In the works read by Saint-Preux and Julie, Plutarch apparently takes first place as their uncontested moral authority. Together they cite him twelve times. His authority can always be relied upon, as is demonstrated above all in the letters about the duel (I, lviii) and suicide (III, xxi); he can be put to use as *ton bon Plutarche* when it is a question of the clever student urging her teacher to a moderate consumption of wine (I, lii), or to reject as unnatural her far-off lover's rhetoric of untamed passion and sensual imagination (II, xv), or to ground her decision to cut off even epistolary communication after marrying Wolmar (III, xx). And just as Petrarch's presence was given greater force by the voices of the other Italian poets, so too Plutarch is evoked more powerfully through reference to other, primarily Roman, poets—after Epictetus come Cicero, Tacitus, Suetonius, and (as their modern counterpart) Montaigne.[11] These are mainly exempla drawn from historiography or moral philosophy. In other words, classical models, often manifesting the stoic virtue of standing up to a test, are again and again held up before Saint-Preux, who is prey to constant temptation. They are also the heroic contraparty to the lyric tonality shaped by the Laura-Julie relation.

In contrast, the canon of earlier texts meant to legitimate the new Héloïse pointedly excludes the classical French authors. It is almost as if they failed to pass the test to which Julie wants to submit all books: are they suitable for instilling goodness in the reader (II, xviii)? None of them is turned to as an authority, and they are named only in order to subject them to a merciless critique—Corneille, whose Pompeius and Sertorius no longer have anything to offer the people of Paris (II, xvii); the tragedies of Racine, who is not even named, are reproached because "On étouffe de grandes passions; rarement on les épure" (VI, vi);[12] La Rochefoucauld, whom Julie could hardly have read, because "jamais son triste livre ne sera goûté des bonnes gens" (III, xx);[13] La Bruyère, who is unable to explain why he is bored by opera (II, xxiii); La Fontaine, whose fables Julie's children will not be allowed to read because a veil of fiction hides their truth (V, iii).[14] The scolding Saint-Preux gives the contemporary Parisian stage (II, xvii) is equally apt for Racine and Corneille; only Molière, who is given a going over in the *Lettre à d'Alembert*, gets off lightly. But when Julie sees herself called upon to defend the honor of the French nation from Saint-Preux, who has behaved like a child rebelling against its teacher in his harsh critique of the corrupt taste of Parisian society, she offers rather moving evidence as to her literary education. In her eyes, "good books" have shrunk to Catinat (Marshal of France under Louis XIV, whom his soldiers referred to as *le père de la pensée*) and Fénelon, *les deux plus vertueux des moderns* (II, xviii). But, as a retrospective glance at his *Confessions* shows, Rousseau managed quietly to save one work from this *auto-da-fé* of French classicism (surely the most complete of its kind in the eighteenth century): *La Princesse de Clèves* by Madame de La Fayette, which he would place beside the fourth book of *La nouvelle Héloïse (OC* I, p. 546). This latter is the book that deals with Saint-Preux's return, his joining the *ménage à trois*, his responsibility as the educator of Julie and Wolmar's children, and the "unfortunate temptation" on Lake Geneva. Thus, Rousseau's contemporaries are invited to contemplate the quietistic resignation of the Princesse de Clèves and the active virtue of a self-mastering Julie as the classical and modern solutions to the problem of how to turn away from love.[15]

"Il faut des spectacles dans les grandes villes, et des romans corrompus. J'ai vu les moeurs de mon temps, et j'ai publié ces lettres. Que n'ai-je vécu dans un siècle où je dusse les jeter au feu!"[16] These are the lines with which the real provocation of the *Préface* begins, a provocation that Rousseau's contemporaries, whether friend or foe, were almost unanimous in regarding as an affront—thus reading it as the author wished, whether they wanted to or not. At the time, the offense lay not so much in the pretension of having written a work that ran counter to the novel as it had existed earlier, or in juxtaposing an ostensibly real exchange of letters to literary fiction. Certainly by the time Richardson's *Clarissa* appeared (1748), contemporary readers had abandoned the tradition of fictional adventures involving grand destinies. And *Pamela* had taught them to cherish the epistolary novel as a new medium, one that allowed them to see their own sense of self represented or attacked directly through the feelings of another "I" as they emerged minute by minute in the exchange of letters. Thus, the rejection of the traditional novel had already occurred before the appearance of *La nouvelle Héloïse*. The final move in this direction was embodied in the epistolary novel, which offered itself as an antifiction in contradistinction to the illusionary world inscribed in the earlier novel. It opened everyday life and the private interiority of the bourgeois world to literary presentation and discussion. This process of rejection was already the common stock of criticism at the time Richardson's novels were published and can justifiably be understood as the shift in horizons that led to their widespread reception. By way of proof I need only point to Albrecht v. Haller's *Beurtheilung der berühmten Geschichte der Clarissa*: "French novels . . . generally present grand individuals performing grand deeds; they totally ignore ordinary life and only offer heroes that possess neither our needs, nor our lifestyle, our virtues, or our vices."[17] That this shift in literary horizons goes hand in hand with the constitution of the bourgeois view of the world and life, and that in particular the broad success of the epistolary novel is symptomatic of the political process in which bourgeois "private space" is emancipated and opened to the public, is well known since the publication of the research by Reinhart Koselleck, Jürgen Habermas, and Wilhelm Vosskamp.[18] Rousseau's epistolary novel must, therefore, presuppose the horizon of expectations opened up by *Pamela* and *Clarissa*. This is also the case in the early reception of the novel, where comparisons between Rousseau and Richardson already seem to have become an almost obligatory critical move. This is one more reason for Rousseau to have later turned the provocative element of his *Préface* against his famous predecessor. In the novel this attack was marginal and hidden; in retrospect it came into the open.

The competitive model supplied by Richardson's work was especially apparent to contemporary readers in terms of the figures he presents, and the move beyond his novels was regarded as an abandonment of his perfectly finished characters. Julie was thought of as a "less developed Clarissa," Claire a second, but less "humorous" Miss Howe; Saint-Preux was compared to Lovelace, the basically kind villain, and judged to be a "more talkative and sentimental young man," "*raisonnant de l'amour comme un platonicien, et la pratiquant en épicurien*," according to the "Parallèle" written by J. B. Suard.[19] Light and shadow seemed to balance out in this case: one could equally reproach the English moralist with having drawn a *débauché aimable* and the Geneva philosopher with presenting in Wolmar an *athée vertueux*. The break with the norm of perfected characters was praised, but understood only insofar as the weaknesses of the two lovers made the moral ideal seem more attainable than did perfect virtue. What was not understood was the provocation aimed at religious morality that lay in the fact that Julie, after having "fallen," reestablished her "virtue" on her own, through an act of self-liberation that grants her moral autonomy. It is this "reformation" that allows her to found the community of love in Clarens to which the "beautiful souls" belong—a "*réforme des moeurs domestiques*" as Rousseau formulated it (*OC* II, p. 24), which was meant to prove that the individual, given the fundamental purity of his nature (which was first corrupted by society and its institutionalization of inequality), can reestablish himself on his own ("À qui vantez-vous la pureté qu'on n'a pas souillée? Eh! parlez-nous de celle qu'on peut recouvrer"; *OC*,I, p. 26).[20] This is why Rousseau, in the closing footnote, proudly asserts that his novel does not need the fascination of evil in order to create interest; and he takes aim at Richardson when he says he finds it incomprehensible that a "*lecteur de bon naturel*" (well-disposed reader) could find satisfaction in the character of a "scoundrel" rather than suffering because of the words and deeds of such a villain.[21] For Rousseau, the break with the norm of perfected character implies a new norm of completeness: the *simplicité* of a story. Its aim is to maintain interest in the spiritual histories of three sensitive human beings, an interest created solely by the exposition of feeling through the conversations between these sentimental hearts. In other words, there would be no adventure or intrigue, "no baseness of action or character" (*OC* II, p. 18). By setting forth this new expectation, which, in retrospect, he proclaimed to be the point at which he surpassed Richardson (*Confessions*, *OC* I, p. 546), Rousseau removes from his own purview the self-contradiction embodied in the fact that the author of the *Lettre à d'Alembert* is the same as the one who wrote *La nouvelle Héloïse*. The leap into the unknown embodied in the latter emerges as the most provocative point in the *Préface*: regardless of the expectations of its readers, the fiction embodied in this exchange of letters is meant to be an antifiction, one that will pave the way to a new reality.

Naturally, the critique launched by the *Philosophes* did not hesitate to use Rousseau's own weapons against him. They point out that this vehement critic of the imaginary world of the stage and the novel is the first to contradict his own moral rigor, since he himself, understandably enough, would not put his novel in the hands of a chaste young woman (AA, pp. 233, 236–37). The *Philosophes* had reason enough for their indignation. The "beautiful preacher of virtue" and her self-styled *Philosophe* do a thorough job of pulling to pieces the "empty sophism of a reason that is supported by nothing beyond itself" (III, xviii). Although the text contains numerous covert attacks on Voltaire and Diderot, Helvétius and Spinoza, their names are excluded from the canon of *La nouvelle Héloïse*, and they finally sink under the weight of the judgment that "the century of philosophy ought not come to a close without producing at least one true philosopher." Much to Rousseau's satisfaction, the unorthodox theology of a resident of Geneva, Firmin Abauzit—who is all but unknown today—came closest to the creed laid down by the *Vicaire savoyard* (V, i).

Although Rousseau secretly felt himself to be the one true philosopher of the century, it was only in the *Seconde Préface* that he responded as such to the critique launched by the *Philosophes*—a critique that Marmontel reduced to this simple formula: "Je le crois d'autant plus immoral que tout a l'aire d'y être honnête" (AA, p. 248).[22] According to the preface, Rousseau remained unmoved by accusations of being self-contradictory and insincere, since they were merely a repetition of something he had already fully disproved in his *Préface de Narcisse* in 1753. There, the accusation that the declared enemy of science and art had himself begun to write pieces for the theater and the opera was indeed a bitter satire—not of himself but of his century (*OC* II, p. 974). The century of philosophy had, up to that point, labored under an illusion, one he himself had long been unable to escape—the illusion that there was a correspondence between the customs and morals of contemporary society and the high level of its enlightened knowledge. His discovery that public progress in science and art came at the price of a latent decline in morals, a decline that was masked by the refined life-style of urban civilization, obliged the true philosopher to criticize the *simulacre publique* (this formulation of Rousseau's anticipates the "false consciousness" analyzed in modern critiques of ideology!) and necessitates uncovering the social vices that, clad in the guise of virtue, uphold the mere appearance of order so as to hide real ills (*OC* II, p. 972). This, Rousseau claims, is the deeper intention of his novel and the bitterly serious basis for his paradoxical wish: "Oh! que ne suis-je né dans un siècle où je dusse jeter ce recueil au feu!"[23] As long as his important insight and its call for change are misunderstood, he has only one therapy available to him, to cure "like with like" and lead a corrupt society to self-knowledge by using the form of art or literature that fits it, even if that form is morally questionable.

But included in this admission is also the belief that his novel, though it is meant to attract the current reader by using a form appropriate to the times, demands a new attitude as well, one that will open the reader to the new, forward-looking content of Rousseau's book. It is here that there will be a parting of intellectual ways. "Le style rebutera les gens de goût; la matière alarmera les gens sévères; tous les sentiments seront hors de nature pour ceux qui ne croient pas à la vertu" (*OC* II, p. 5).[24] It is the paradox of this hitherto unheard of insult to the public that contains the real provocation to be found in the *Préface*. It snubs philosophical criticism by turning it against itself: whoever is offended by *La nouvelle Héloïse* is himself to blame, thereby proving that he is blind to the truth of nature and sentiment, the very things that the new reader postulated by Rousseau will be able to recognize in the letters written by the lovers. If the book is destined to antagonize the old reader—the pious as well as the free spirited, philosophers, fashionable ladies, and more conventional housewives—and the reader's prognosis is as expected, then he (Rousseau) is ready to accept the possibility that he will, at first, be the only new reader pleased by the novel ("A qui plaira-t-il donc? Peut-être à moi seul").[25]

This much-maligned paradox reveals a historical shift within the history of middle-class reading—the new expectation that the truth of a book manage to prevail over currently dominant tastes and "establish a sphere of criticism aimed at public power,"[26] thus allowing it to generate a new public whose latent needs it would express. Understood in this manner, the reader who initially stands alone can be regarded as the first member of a new community of readers, since the building of such a community is the unexpressed desire that motivates handing this "book written from the heart" over to the public literary sphere. That this offer of a *Contrat littéraire*, which could be compared to his political outline for a *Contrat sociale*, was misjudged during the books initial reception,[27] that it was grasped only intuitively by ordinary readers, and either dismissed or ridiculed by the enlightened elite, is not surprising given the aggressive rhetoric of the *Préface*. There, the imminent shift in horizons from old to new reader is proclaimed in such a way that a line is drawn between previous expectations and future experience. Rousseau unquestioningly assumes himself to be in possession of true understanding, and, especially in the final section of the *Préface*, disqualifies on moral grounds any reader who, after reading his entire book, still maintains his original position, that is, persists in maintaining his prejudices.

The literary and social horizon embodied in the experiences of the *homme sensible*, the horizon that Rousseau wants to institute for the public of his day by means of *La nouvelle Héloïse*, can at this point be given a definition *ex negativo*—as the inverse image of the paradoxical propositions found in the prefaces.[28] A transformation in moral attitude is set in motion by the transformation of the traditional relation between fiction and reality:[29] "Ai-je fait le tout, et la correspondance entière est-elle une fiction? Gens du monde, que vous importe? C'est sûrement une fiction pour vous" (*OC* II, p. 5).[30] Rousseau claims that whoever is offended by the fact that Julie follows the dictates of her heart and, in consummating her love for Saint-Preux, fails her obligation to parental authority has not seen the real source of this "disorder"—the absolute rule of *inégalité* in the existing social order, which chokes all "natural feelings." In reality, it is the "despotism of the father" that produces the weaknesses and the misfortunes of the children: "La nature les fît, vos institutions les gâtent" (*OC* II, p. 24, 27).[31] Thus, Rousseau suggests, whoever chooses to reprimand the author for not following the rules of probability, and for using his "beautiful souls" to create imaginary beings in another world, unintentionally demonstrates that the truth of nature and true sense of self have sunk to the level of mere fictions for the *gens du monde* of his day. Rousseau's novel is both a fiction and an antifiction. It is a poetic fiction insofar as it is meant to put in place the horizon of a new type of experience, one that promises the rediscovery, in an autonomous sense of self, of a naturalness that has been lost, and that is meant to serve as an example of virtue in a new, middle-class mode of life. It is a socially critical antifiction insofar as, through the counterimage it offers, it reveals the illusory nature of the dominant order, and exposes the fictions through which contemporary society masks its denatured condition.

The initial reception given *La nouvelle Héloïse* by the defenders of the Enlightenment in their official criticism shows a total misunderstanding of this double, utopian and critical, function. On the other hand, it was emphatically accepted by his supporters, although they were hardly aware of the scope of its significance. Nonetheless, if we look back at the reception history of the novel, this double function may provide the best means of explaining why this work produced such a hitherto unheard of spate of identification with literary figures among its new readers. The new Héloïse, her dearest friend and confidant, and her sentimental lover were, despite their fictive nature, drawn into life and discussed with the author as if they were real people. They were wept over during pilgrimages to Vevey and Clarens, and in every way held to be so authentic that one can say that here, if anywhere, the reality of fiction caused the unpleasant reality of life to pale and seem unreal.

2. A reconstruction of the question to which *La nouvelle Héloïse* and *The Sorrows of Young Werther* were the answer

If, after reading *La nouvelle Héloïse*, the young people of France had the desire to be "lovers" like Saint-Preux instead of drinkers and roughnecks,[32] the youth of Germany opted for the Werther costume when it fell prey to "Werther fever." Such literary influences, which in a single generation can change the ideal of life espoused by a broad stratum of society,[33] are obviously possible only after the massive spread of the novel within the readerly culture established by the bourgeoisie. Research in the sociology of literature has supplied impressive figures demonstrating that the novels produced by the sentimental upsurge were at the forefront in this flood of reading, and that Werther fever aided in the trivialization of the novel and its reduction to the level of a sentimental love story.[34] This "triumph of sentimentality" is most beautifully attested to when one of its two spiritual fathers looks back self-critically, and allegorically sketches its unavoidable and well-deserved demise. Such is the case in Goethe's *Dramatische Grille* (written in 1777, revised in a second version 1786). It deals with the cure for a sentimental illness: after an obscure oracle that announces the disspiriting of a "palpable ghost" (sentimentality) is fulfilled, the lovesick Queen Mandandane is able to renew her bond with the humorous King Andrasen. Prince Ornaro, a figure meant to make fun of the sentimental, lugs with him the theatrical decors of a nature that is merely painted, and a doll that stands in for his beloved. He is ultimately left to his "lying, fatuous nourishment." In the linen sack that serves as her inmost being, the doll has a few sentimental books, a lot of straw and, as the broth in which all this is steeped, *La nouvelle Héloïse* and *The Sorrows of Young Werther* (*SW* 6, p. 541).

Although it is the only evidence we have to this effect, it is nonetheless important that, here, Goethe lumped the two works together and thought of them as the French and German "Ur-texts' for the wave of sentimentality that had, in the meantime, run its course. This ironic *auto-da-fé* of 1777 raises the question as to what Goethe actually hit upon and what, on the other hand, he may have covered up in his "comic opera." Debunking the cult of nature by having a character drag along a theatrical setting, or portraying his equally sentimental lover as a mechanical doll, exposes an empty "sentimentalizing," one caught up in itself, but it does not implicate the "true sentimentality" (*wahre Empfindsamkeit*) that Goethe (who, like Rousseau, discarded the tradition of the sentimental novel) proclaimed to be the new, epoch-making norm in both the moral and the aesthetic realm.[35] The earliest references to the German word, which had been in use since 1757, suggest that it is a translation of the French terms *un coeur sensible* and *sensibilité*. The French word, on the other hand, was not coined by a newly awakened middle-class self-consciousness. It was borrowed from courtly-aristocratic culture, and, more precisely, from the sentimental novel, which, emulating *La Princesse de Clèves*, tested the casuistics of "soul analysis" on a newly discovered theme, the renunciation of love, a theme that the heroic/gallant had not previously employed. This thematic presentation of the self-analyzed feelings of a sentimental woman (and the personal satisfaction she derives from them), and her concomitant superiority over her male counterpart are the literary indicators of deeper, psychogenetic developments, but they are not yet the sentimentality Rousseau brings to light as the sympathetic experience of "beautiful souls."[36] Madame de La Fayette's heroine experiences passion "as danger, not as an intensification of the self," only with Julie is there a full-fledged "*Sacrificium Voluptatis*, since the Princesse de Clèves avoids this sort of sacrifice by never becoming acquainted with sensual pleasure."[37] Stoic mastery of affect, the conflict between reason and passion and their final reconciliation—both fall under the rubric of *sensibilité*, which, however, as Rousseau himself notes, underwent a historical transformation between the high point of French classicism and the "sentimental, late Enlightenment." Its locus of signification shifted from the purely passive and psychological to the active and moral.[38]

In a central section of his second *Discours*, Rousseau provides an anthropological justification for the new meaning of *sensibilité* – "the ability to attach our affections to beings who are strangers to us." Commiseration is, after self-preservation (*conservation de nous-mêmes*), the second of two basic capacities that belong to human beings, even prior to reason. It arises from a natural aversion to seeing a "sensitive being" suffer or perish (*OC* I, p. 154). The range of meaning first opened for *sensible/sensibilité* in *La nouvelle Héloïse* presupposes the anthropological definition provided by the second *Discours*, but it responds to a different question, one that had never been resolved and that Rousseau's critique of civilization poses with a new sense of urgency, the question of defining human purpose and happiness. Given the fissure in his existence as *homme civil*, how can the human being in the modern world rediscover the lost wholeness of the *homme naturel* and thereby recapture the possibility of happiness? In looking for an answer, Rousseau so finalized his anthropological definition of man – the *être sensible*, who unites self-preservation (*amour de soi*) with commiseration (*OC* I, p. 126) – that sentimentality not only enables the original affective relation to the other, but also founds the enduring, ever present desire for the happiness of self-fulfillment: "Il faut être heureux, cher Emile; c'est la fin de tout être sensible; c'est le premier désir que nous imprima la nature, et le seul qui ne nous quitte jamais" (*OC* IV, p. 814).[39] In what way does *La nouvelle Héloïse*, a novel about the *homme sensible*, respond to this newly posed question as to the possibility of human happiness in a natual existence that remains to be rediscovered? This problem necessitates a resituating of our reconstruction of the horizon of expectation within that series of Rousseau's own works to which his contemporaries could turn as they took up the challenge of *La nouvelle Héloïse*.

The sensation that the first *Discours* provoked in France, and well beyond, immediately after its publication in the *Republique des Lettres* can best be documented here by citing a letter from the biography of the young Goethe. In 1767 he wrote to his sister Cornelia from Leipzig: "Don't laugh at the seeming foolishness of this philosophy. The terms that seem so paradoxical are the most splendid truths, and the depravity of today's world lies soley in the fact that no one pays attention to them. They are based on this admirable truth: Plus que les moeurs se raffinent, plus les hommes se dépravent."[40] Rousseau's response to the competitive question posed by the Dijon acadamy offered the biggest affront that could have been handed the philosophy of the Enlightenment, and, in fact, it drove a wedge into the latter's historical view of the world.[41] He asserted with high pathetic seriousness that the peak of human culture – which the enlightenment philosophers had seen climbed during this *siècle des lumières*, and which they would soon represent in their encyclopedia as the proud sum of *Sciences, Arts et Mètiers* – was nothing but an illusion as far as the customs and morals of life in society were concerned, an illusion that led one to underestimate the high and fatal price of the civilizing process. Rousseau's initial description of the fatal circle of human history, where knowledge and art progress to the degree that the forms of communal life degenerate, names this high and long since forgotten price by offering in contrast idyllic pictures of a lost natural existence. If human nature was not better in the "simplicity of earlier times," nonetheless, mankind had made its life secure when it discovered the *facilité de se pénétrer mutuellement* [the capacity for mutual comprehension] (*OC* III, p. 8) — part of a "natural equality" that fell victim to the constantly growing desire to dominate, to the struggle for property, and (already mentioned in this text) to the progressive division of labor: "Nous avons des physiciens, des géomètres, des chimistes, des astronomes, des poètes, des musiciens, des peintres; nous n'avons plus de citoyens" (*OC* III, p. 26).[42] Rousseau's counterimage to the ills of civilization distinguishes natural human existence by using the predicates "wholeness," "equality," "transparency," and the virtues of the citizens of Sparta and Rome. But this submerged nature, which in the first *Discours* rose up behind the illusion of contemporary society, could itself be rediscovered only at substantial cost: in the initial act of recognition, the true nature of the human being already appears as an inevitably lost nature.[43]

After the critique of the present offered by the first *Discours*, the second (1755) followed with a reconstruction of the *état de nature* in an effort to explain the previously diagnosed ills of civilization on the basis of their presumed origins. Given that he is by nature good, how could man, as a social being, become evil? The basic premise of Rousseau's new answer rejects the Christian dogma of Original Sin; in a single stroke it frees human nature and makes society itself responsible for current ills. The *homme de la nature* provides the measure for what the *homme de l'homme* (man produced by man) became as a result of the institutions he established *after* moving from nature into history. The first source of inequality was ambition; the wish to compare oneself with others, to stand out from others, was the real, social source of the Fall. It was the first step into "comparative existence."[44]

The *faculté de se perfectionner* [the ability to perfect himself] was the the dubious advantage man had over animals, according to Rousseau, but this led to the possibility that individual reason could be perfected while at the same time the human race took a turn for the worse (*rendre un être méchant en le rendant sociable*; *OC* III, p. 162). Thus, the heuristic fiction of a natural condition *prior* to history and society, in positing an original *indeterminateness* of human nature, can aid in measuring the manner in which a second, social, nature was organized during the course of human history, a history that, according to Rousseau, can no longer be interpreted teleologically. Thus, the *homme sauvage* does not describe a real or ideal point of departure for history. His hypothetical nature is intended rather to show *via negationis* what the historicity of man, in conjunction with the social process, has engendered: language (in lieu of the simple *cri de la nature*); labor (instead of the spontaneous satisfaction of needs and idleness); domination (beginning with the first boundary post meant to safeguard property); division of labor (following the discovery of iron and wheat); tradition (when experience began to be passed on from one person to another, i.e., became institutionalized). This description refutes a then dominant image of history: what man was by nature according to Hobbes is, according to Rousseau, what he became because of his history. The social state described as *bellum omnium contra omnes* (the war of all against all) is not produced by nature but, rather, is man's own work. And if man experiences this work that is specifically his own—human history, which can no longer be foisted off on God the Creator—as something alien, thereby mistaking his true nature, this illusion is the ultimate reason for his unhappiness, or—using a notion unavailable to Rousseau—the real blindness of his "alienation."

The new gospel of nature, for which Rousseau's *Nouvelle Héloïse* opened the way, was, from its very beginning (in the two *Discours*), sentimental but not nostalgic. It called for the liberation of an oppressed nature, a nature that had become alien because of the constraints of social development; it did not, however, espouse a return to some untouched nature that might be found in the naive existence of a child or in the *bon sauvage*. It was the backward-looking ideal of the *homme naturel*, later concretized in terms of the romantic spirit, and not Rousseau's notion of the *sentimental friend of nature* to which Schiller addressed this familiar warning: "That nature which you envy in those who do not possess reason is worthy of no respect, not worth longing for. It lies behind you, it must eternally lie behind you."[45] The sentimental reader who extracted a double longing for nature from Rousseau's works— a longing *for the happiness* and *for the perfection* found in nature—was actually following Schiller's advice before the fact: "But after you have been consoled about the loss of natural happiness, let nature's perfection serve as your heart's model." The double longing precipitated an effort to transpose the ideal of the "new Héloïse" from the realm of the idyll into life. The contemporary reader could find an answer in Rousseau's texts to the question as to "how that which is natural, which lies in man's past, can still or once again become possible."[46] The question itself could be formulated because of an understanding of the self-alienation in contemporary society that had been awakened by the two *Discours* and had become available to the general public. In the same period, Rousseau had sought his own answer to this fundamental question. In the *Contrat social* (1762) and in *Emile* (1762) this answer emerges in terms of a number of different possibilities.

In the introduction to *Emile* the question is raised to the point of antinomy: "Forcé de combattre la nature ou les institutions sociales, il faut opter entre faire un homme ou un citoyen: car on ne peut faire à la fois l'un et l'autre" (*OC* IV, p. 248).[47] The three works mentioned here can be regarded as different "experiments" made in an effort to resolve the antinomy here and now, in the existing social conditions (*OC* III, p. 123). The lost wholeness and self-sufficiency of the *homme naturel* is to be restored in opposition to the divided existence of the *homme civil*—the citizen, "whose existence is split into a business and a private life, whose private life is split into keeping up his public image and intimacy, whose intimacy is split into the surly partnership of marriage and the bitter comfort of being alone, at odds with himself and everybody else."[48] This work of restoration at one point focuses on the individual removed from society (the project for a "natural education" found in *Emile*); at another on the subject, who merges with the community (the projected constitution for a state without government in the *Contrat social*); and at a third on a small circle of "sentimental" individuals (the community of love that forms around a new originary couple in *La nouvelle Héloïse*). The third way promises a solution between the two extremes—between the solitary education of the individual outside existing society, and the total demand on the individual made by a newly refounded state. But all three ways lead back into contradictions, contradictions that the reception of Rousseau's works has bequeathed to us. They quickly become apparent in the concrete situations found in *La nouvelle Héloïse*, which, in Germany, was often responded to in conjunction with *Emile*.

The experiment embodied in *Emile* eliminates the danger of a comparative existence and the influence of parental authority by isolating the pupil from society. It opens the way to learning through personal experience. This experience is, however, silently guided by a tutor who is responsible for maintaining a balance between needs and ability (GB, 25ff.), and who, in his dealings with his pupil, must indirectly provide well-measured doses of sociability to compensate for that which the pupil lacks. Rousseau himself noted the unresolved problem in his experiment in natural education: "Mais que deviendra pour les autres un homme uniquement élévé pour lui?" (*OC* IV, p. 251).[49] The *Contrat social* tries to solve this remaining problem—how the solitary individual, when removed from his undivided existence and given the duties of a citizen, can be led to renounce his *amour de soi* and accept the morality of actions free of self-interest—in the reverse manner. There, the individual must freely and totally relinquish his natural freedom in order to regain it as civic freedom through a sort of "civil baptism" in the practical reason produced by the general will. Thus, the individual can rediscover his lost identity in the quasi-mystical wholeness of the undivided, infallible, and nonrepresentable *volonté générale*. The new notion of freedom as obedience to (self-prescribed) law resolves the antinomy between private and public interest (insofar as, according to Rousseau, no one can act against his own well-perceived interests). But this solution comes at the price of ambiguity. Those who do not understand themselves must have freedom forced on them by the law. And here, the *Contrat social* bequeaths the crux of an unavoidable "educational dictatorship": "Slaves must be *free for* their liberation before they can become free,"[50] if their liberation is not of necessity to come from outside and above—from an authority that must, paradoxically, force people to be free.

My thesis that, in contrast to *Emile* and the *Contrat social*, *La nouvelle Héloïse* offers a third option for healing a denatured society is initially supported by the fact that the difficulties confronting both the educational tract and the political blueprint for a social contract can be held in abeyance in the medium offered by novelistic fiction. In a novel about the *homme sensible* the subject does not first have to be educated in solitude, nor does one have to postulate an ideal consensus through which social dependency can be transformed into democratic freedom before beginning an experiment aimed at recovering a natural, undivided existence. In this novel the subjects of the action, by declaring their love, have, from the beginning, already discovered the "secret accord of their feelings," an accord untroubled by any social prejudice ("Avant que d'avoir pris les uniformes préjugés du monde, nous avons des manières uniforms de sentir et de voir"; *OC* II, p. 32).[51] This is not simply an assertion that the natural equality between man and woman is established at the moment they begin a new course in life; the passions of love are also inseperable from virtue ("Nous sommes jeunes tous deux, il est vrai; nous aimons pour la première et l'unique fois de la vie, et n'avons nulle expérience des passions: mais l'honneur qui nous conduit est-il un guide trompeur?" *OC* II, p. 42).[52] Thus, in what follows, the passion of love is not doomed to fall prey to the natural power of the affect. It can itself become the motor for a moral purification of the senses—can, through a third person, lead the self-centeredness of the couple into a more elevated community of love, a family, and there unite duty and inclination in a new mode of life. But to achieve this, *one* moral principle is still necessary—the transparency of unconditional honesty: "Ne fais ne ni dis jamais rien que tu ne veuilles que tout le monde voie et entende" (*OC* II, p. 424).[53] This astonishing maxim, which Wolmar applies immediately by grasping Julie's and Saint-Preux's hands in a bond of friendship, adding, "Embrassez votre soeur et votre amie; traitez-la toujours comme telle; plus vous serez familier avec elle, mieux je penserai de vous,"[54] is—although thoroughly un-Kantian—the "categorical imperative" of the new sentimentality!

If the new pact, the *ménage à trois*, forms the high point of sentimentality, Saint-Preux's and Julie's practical experiences in the course of the novel reevoke the anthropological definition of the *être sensible* in order to see if it is possible to rediscover the lost wholeness of natural existence in the transparency of requited love, and to reground it in the autonomy of self-esteem. This effort is certainly not without conflict. It brings the lovers up against the conventions and prejudices of existing society, and they learn "que c'est un fatal présent du ciel qu'une âme sensible" (*OC* II, p. 212).[55] Saint-Preux must learn that, as someone in service as a private tutor, he cannot assert the "honor that is solely his own" against the dominant conventions as long as his principle—"a sentimental heart is able to derive its laws only from itself" (*OC* II, p. 212)—is not generally recognized; Julie must learn that the truth of her conviction that a sentimental heart is unable to divide its love even for a moment (*OC* II, p. 72) has no effect on the snobbishness of the "best of all fathers." Rousseau's lovers are not revolutionaries. Denied it by society, they seek an accord of the inner and the outer in nature first, in a landscape that has been left undisturbed by men, and which they discover. Its wild beauty, which could "appeal only to sentimental hearts, while others loathe it" (*OC* II, p. 519), offers a sanctuary for the solitary lovers: its grandeur lays everything painful to rest in a view of the whole (*OC* I, p. xxiii). And when the lovers finally transform their passion into friendship, and found their own community, they follow the gentle law of "beautiful souls," which for Julie means the possibility of fulfilling her duties as wife and mother out of pure inclination, without effort and without thinking of "virtue" (*OC* II, p. 498). It means this for her, but in truth only seems to! For when Julie, at the very end, confesses, in the letter she leaves behind, that it is a blessing from heaven that she is dying, since she sees that she had lived long in an "illusion," believing as she did that she had smothered her *premier sentiment*, that from which she in fact had lived and nourished herself—when, that is, with her last words, "On m'a fait boire jusqu'à la lie la coupe amère et douce de la sensibilité" (*OC* II, p. 733),[56] she names the unspoken, ultimate price that had to be paid for her "reform," the close of the novel lets this reform fade into the twilight of a necessary illusion.

Thus, the third way, which was to have led through the passions of an *amour partagé* to social virtue, also ends with an extorted reconciliation between reason and feelings. Julie's ultimate hope, that she and her one true love will be forever united before the heavenly father ("La vertu qui nous sépara sur la terre nous réunira dans le séjour éternel"; *OC* II, p. 743),[57] can hardly supply the answer demanded by Rousseau's new question as to how the division of natural and social existences can be overcome, and how a lost wholeness can be reclaimed in the unfolding of subjectivity within sociability without either dissolving the individual in the state or removing him from it. The latent contradiction in this novel of the *homme sensible*, which Julie's final confession at last brings to light, is the problem inherited by the German reception of the novel. Although it is not seen with any great clarity, it is the real stimulus for Goethe's attempt to provide a new answer in *The Sorrows of Young Werther*. This answer, offered by a youthful Goethe, was not, however, an answer to Rousseau's initial question; instead—as Werther's suicide shows—it further develops the tragic aporia of the *homme sensible*.

A resolution for this aporia was not available to the *Sturm und Drang* generation. The dialectical resolution of the contradiction between reason and feeling, nature and civilization, would first be proposed by German idealism after Kant "had thought Rousseau's thoughts through to the end."[58] Sentimentality, the categorical imperative that Rousseau wanted to make the norm for an undivided, natural existence, leaves the unfolding of subjectivity entirely dependent on the transparency of "seeing and feeling." But this alone is not a sufficient ground for morality when the latter is understood as man's obligation to oppose himself. Kant's resolution of the contradiction between natural and social existences presupposes a third step. After man's cultivation and his civilization comes his moralization,[59] which should show that "morality [is] a matter of art, not nature," that "perfect art [can] once again become nature."[60] And since, according to Kant, "proper behavior" can arise from a "taste for beauty,"[61] German idealism provided a genuine "third way" of resolving the conflict between man's two tendencies — aesthetic education, education in freedom and for freedom, makes the lost oneness of natural man the actional and developmental goal of man in the bourgeois world.[62] How the new path of aesthetic education led to the solution of problems that Rousseau's model of natural education left unresolved will be discussed at a later point, as part of an examination of Goethe's *Wilhelm Meister*. Here I want to return to the horizon of Rousseau's contemporaries that, in the above, was surpassed of necessity since the implicit question to which Rousseau's *Nouvelle Héloïse* was the — or a possible — answer could be reconstructed only from the whole of his work and its explicit concretizations, and, consequently, by distinguishing between earlier and current horizons of understanding.

3. Goethe's *Werther* within the horizon of expectation defining the German reception of Rousseau

The following investigation will likewise evolve in terms of a progressive expansion of the context. First the horizon of expectation within which contemporary readers of Goethe's *Werther* operated will be constructed intraliterarily — from the prescription for its reception found in the opening section of the novel, and through the overt references to other texts. The next step will be to examine the state of German literature in the year *Werther* was published (1774), especially with regard to the series of literary works Goethe finished prior to this date. At the same time, I will take up the question of how Goethe and his German contemporaries received Rousseau's novel, a work that was, as will be demonstrated, the secret pattern followed by the young Goethe. Next, the latent model derived from *La nouvelle Héloïse* will be sought out in *Werther*, and examined in terms of whether Goethe used — and renewed — it as part of a productive reception in which received expectations were corrected within the horizon of new experience, and whether, in his own way, Goethe resolved the contradictions and problems that had been left behind by his predecessors. Finally, my intraliterary reconstruction of expectation and experience will be supplemented by a historical interpretation that — based on contemporary evidence about the reception — will ask how Goethe's response to Rousseau, using an epistolary form that had become monologic and aesthetically autonomous, evidenced or anticipated a change in social experience. For a reader of Rousseau's novel, Goethe's *Werther*, through its critique of bourgeois institutions (class, family, religion, and work), immediately reveals an altered consciousness regarding the solitary individual, his moral autonomy, and also the danger he runs by drawing on Rousseau's *homme naturel*.

The title, *The Sorrows of Young Werther*, borrows from a secular tradition of Christian devotional works, and, if one includes the prefatory statement, with its references to "comfort" and "friend," can hardly be understood as anything but a provocative secularization. After all, the sufferings of "poor Werther," from which the sentimental reader ("you, noble soul who feels the same longing he felt")[63] can draw comfort, represent the thoroughly profane martyrdom of an unfulfilled, utterly sensual love that ends in suicide! Where Rousseau's new Héloïse evoked the distant, Petrarchian myth of a pure love fulfilled on a suprasensual level, Goethe's new Abelard was patterned after the model provided by earlier devotional and sentimental works, works that pious souls could not refuse their "admiration and love" any more than their "tears." The title, along with the explicit call for an intense, empathic reading (which for the literature of the 1770s was something new; see GS, p. 166), takes full advantage of the emotional need to feel moved and edified. The result is that *nolens volens* this Ur-text of German sentimentality disposes one to respond to it as if it were "a catechism," and to the "dear young man's suffering and death [as if it were] the life of a saint."[64] Whereas Rousseau called for a new reader by provocatively asserting that, if need be, he would serve as the first genuine reader of his novel, Goethe recommended his comforting little book as a constant "friend" ("when, because of destiny or some fault of your own, you cannot find a nearer and dearer one of your own"). He thereby brought into being a new bond of friendship, a bond whose fulfillment a lonely person could experience in sentimental reading, a bond that compensated for the suffering caused by an unfeeling world.

In order to grant Werther's destiny poetic consecration, the little volume goes on to invoke a new canon of texts, one that corresponds fully to the point of view recommended in Goethe's prefatory comments. As might a pious reader for whom extensive perusal of the Bible is enough to edify the spirit, Werther is almost curt in his rejection of Wilhelm's offer to send him his books. At the same time, he professes his faith in the book that for him is all: "What I need are cradle-songs, and I have found plenty of these in my Homer" (p. 7). Homer, who is presented as the mythic voice of the original, epic order of the world, is cited on two other significant occasions, and thereby lifted out of the distant past and returned to visible presence. Then, after Werther's social setback at the envoy's dinner table, Homer is invoked as a counterweight to the snobbery of the modern world. Even prior to the first mention of Homer, in the scene at the town fountain, the Homeric world seems to be immediately present for Werther, though conflated with the patriarchal customs of the Old Testament ("As I sit there, the patriarchal idea comes to life again for me"; p. 7). Following the scene in which several young girls carry out that simplest of tasks, fetching water—as once "even . . . the daughters of kings" did—come still others embodying similarly rediscovered originary situations: the young servant girl whom Werther helps to lift a pitcher to her head (pp. 7–8); the four-year-old boy holding a small child, whose "brotherly pose" so amuses Werther that he forgoes the idyllic context of his reading in the little square beneath the lindens ("there [I] drink my coffee and read my Homer") in order to sketch this lived idyll (pp. 13–14); the young woman who arrives shortly thereafter, who envelops the brotherly idyll with "motherly love," and whose "serene cheerfulness" gives Werther the feeling that he has found relief from the "tumult" of his emotions (pp. 16–17); the simple farm lad who tells the story of his love to Werther, who is ashamed of never before having seen, thought, or even dreamed of such "urgent and passionate desire combined with such purity of heart" (p. 19). Step by step, these scenes of "noble simplicity and quiet grandeur" prepare for the arrival of the longed-for beloved who appears shortly thereafter, completely fulfilling the expectations aroused by the living idyll that surrounds Werther. The manner of her appearance will become archetypally sentimental: Lotte emerges surrounded by a swarm of brothers and sisters, giving them bread, she is at once girl and mother. Homer alone replaces all other books for this lonely man; the "patriarchal idea" rediscovered in country life looked at through Homer's eyes, and a sense of the original nature of man, render poetry unnecessary, since this "loveliest idyll in the world" could not be captured, even if "truthfully written down" (p. 18). And so, *Werther* at first offers no express critique of the literature that, up to that time, had been in favor—the countercanon to sentimentality: Enlightenment aesthetic theory "from Batteux to Wood, from De Piles to Winckelmann . . . Sulzer," and "Heyne." It is dismissed wholesale in the form of the "young V . . . ," whose entire store of knowledge comes from the academies ("I let that pass"; p. 10). Later, Lotte will put novelistic literature to the test, just as Julie had, a test that leads to an equally rigid *auto-da-fé*. On the other hand, she praises *The Vicar of Wakefield*, which—as is Klopstock later—is deemed a worthy friend for the sentimental reader.

Lotte's acid test, which she uses to bid farewell to earlier romantic literature, is somewhat milder in its principles than Julie's: "Et j'imagine à peine quelle sort de bonté peut avoir un livre qui ne porte pas ses lecteurs au bien" (*OC* II, p. 261).[65] The new formulation introduced by the basic text of German sentimentality no longer proposes a moral standard, but instead the simple expectation of rediscovering and confirming the private world of one's own heart and home life in another's self-revelations: "And the author whom I like most of all is the one who takes me into my own world, where everything happens as it does around me" (p. 25). And still another moment at which the change in horizons between Rousseau and Goethe appears in the letter of June 16: sentimental harmony presents itself as a natural outgrowth of the experience of reading! What begins while discussing Goldsmith ("I was struck by the show of character in everything she said; every word revealed fresh attractions, and her flashes of intelligence showed in her face . . . when she felt that I understood her"; p. 24) is completed while watching a thunderstorm reminiscent of something Lotte had read earlier—an ode "which she had in mind," as Werther spontaneously realizes: "She looked up at the sky and then at me. I saw her eyes fill with tears; she laid her hand in mine and said: 'Klopstock'!"

This famous scene, which is equally distant from Rousseau (who would have had no patience with the idea of a book as the source of mutual, empathic comprehension), and from today's reader (who might well find the unexpected reference to Klopstock unintentionally comic), corresponds to the end of Goethe's little book where reference is made to a second source for the sentimental ideal of life. This second source is Ossian. Shortly after reading about Odysseus being entertained by his faithful swineherd (a passage Werther reads as a means of consoling himself for the subordinate treatment given him by the count; p. 90), Ossian "[takes] the place of Homer in [his] heart" (p. 110). Once again it is the perusal of a book that has become a holy text that discloses the horizon of a sentimental experience. Ossian accompanies Werther on his journey to an ever darker passion, a journey in which a sequence of scenes depicting the destruction of nature mirrors his internal collapse—the felling of the walnut trees (pp. 107–8); the transformation of the landscape outside his window into a "lacquered painting" (p. 114); the rocks among which the mad scrivener searches in vain for flowers (p. 120); the flooding of his "dear valley" (p. 133)—and which ends in his suicide. For the penultimate station of Werther's suffering, Goethe—whether with conscious reference to the *Divina commedia* or not—evokes the Ur-scene of sympathetic reading found in the fifth canto of Dante's *Inferno*: as were Paolo and Francesca when they read *Lancelot* together, Werther and Lotte are overcome by the feelings stirred in them while reading aloud from a translation of Ossian: "They felt their own misery in the fate of the Gaels, felt it together and their tears mingled." They are swept up in the forbidden kisses after which only a "farewell forever" could follow (p. 155). Then comes a reference to one final text, one that falls outside the canon of the sentimental.[66] Lessing's *Emilia Galotti* is found open on Werther's desk in the midst of the scene of horror, a provocative reference incommensurate with the outcome of Werther's suffering. After all, when "poor Werther" imagines Lotte has handed him the cup of death in giving him the pistol, and that, with it, he can release himself from his private conflict, he can hardly lay claim to the moral notion of freedom of will that Emilia and Odoardo assert in their conflict with the absolute power of a corrupt court.

The situation in German literature in 1774, the year *Werther* appeared, was described in retrospect by Goethe himself in *Dichtung und Wahrheit*. It was "that German literary revolution" with which his generation made its public debut.[67] Here it can only be looked at briefly in terms of one of its two new models— Rousseau and Shakespeare. If one uses Rousseau to examine the emergence of the *Sturm und Drang* movement (which came into being in Strassburg in 1770–71) and the literary events of 1774, one finds his powerful effect everywhere. In Germany, the philosophical conflict with Rousseau moved into a phase of productive literary reception at about this time. Goethe himself witnesses to this ("Rousseau really spoke to us"; *SW* 10, p. 533), and mentions a "quiet community" that "spread far and wide . . . in his name" (*SW* 10, p. 611) and a group that thought of itself as disciples of his "gospel of nature" (*SW* 10, p. 660). Rousseau's German admirers shared in his attack on the Encyclopedists (with the exception of Diderot), on Holbach's *Système de la nature*, and also on an aging Voltaire—insofar as he represented the ideal of a "polished nation" (HW, p. 210), and thus that "French quality" that seemed contrary to the "German love of nature and truth" (*SW* 10, pp. 531, 539). Herder, the *spiritus rector* of this movement, incorporated Rousseau's critique of the philosophical spirit of the "enlightened century," the "mechanical, cold world" of the Encyclopedists, and the "separation of head and heart" in his 1774 work *Auch eine Philosophie der Geschichte zur Bildung der Menschheit* (HW, p. 194).

But even here a shift in point of view arising from a historical mode of thought is already evident: Herder sublates the antinomy between the state of nature and social civilization in a new picture of history, one that contrasts the patriarchal or organic community of earlier cultures with the "policed state" created by absolutism (HW, p. 208). But at the same time, and in accordance with the principle of individual differences, he would let every nation and epoch have its own law. The integral human figure that Herder postulated concerning the individuality of peoples and cultures, and that Lavater postulated with regard to individual personality in his *Physiognomischen Fragmenten*, can be regarded, along with the incipient cult of genius and the "self-help plays" of the *Sturm und Drang* movement, as the earliest German answer to the rupture between natural and civil existence diagnosed by Rousseau. The Rousseauesque ideal of a lost human wholeness reappears in Herder's Shakespeare essays (1773) as the "simplicity" and near indivisibility of the plot in Greek drama. It also emerges in the call for tragedies with autonomous, individual characters found in Lenz's anti-Aristotelian *Anmerkungen übers Theater* (1774), which built on Mercier's programmatic *Du théâtre, ou nouvel essai sur l'art dramatique* (translated by Wagner in 1773). In it, "unity of interest," the precondition for spectator empathy, is played off against the three "Aristotelian" unities. But more than any other, it is the "figure of a rough, well-meaning self-helper from a savage, archaic period" (*SW* 10, p. 453) that points back to Rousseau, a figure that Goethe, drawing on Shakespeare, introduced in *Götz von Berlichingen* and with whom he hoped to reveal the "secret spot that no philosopher as yet had seen or defined," the spot "where that which is most characteristic of our 'I,' our supposed freedom of will, collides with the necessary movement of the whole" (*SW* 4, p. 124).

Something else that Rousseau could not have seen or defined is—one suspects—the possibility of rediscovering the lost wholeness of the *homme naturel* in the "nature" of the grand individual, a wholeness idealized as the self-realization of such an individual, but open only to tragic expression in the struggle against contemporary conditions, a struggle that pits autonomous freedom against heteronomous power. It was through this conception of the unity of nature and the individual—a transformation of Rousseau's retrospective ideal into the figure of the "self-helper," and, thus, into a norm for historical action—that Goethe paved the way for the historical drama of the *Sturm und Drang* movement. It was a drama that soon began drawing its material from contemporary society, as Mercier had proposed (HW, p. 220). Goethe's next play, *Clavigo*, clearly manifests this turn toward the present. The degree to which the historical world was seen through Rousseau's eyes in the *Sturm und Drang* history plays, and the degree to which his critique of the alienation in contemporary society had crept, unnoticed, into a newly awakened interest in the individual, is evident in Lenz's review of *Götz* (1774). There, from the outset, the social conditions that existed in the past, aside from those of the "anarchic period" during the Peasant Wars, incorporated in a metaphoric that transformed our civilized world into a "big machine." Lenz traces the biography of the grand individual back to the situation in which he "turns in one spot for a while like other wheels" until, in the end, he has to make way for another wheel, at which point he comes resignedly to this conclusion: "What else is man now but a superbly artificial little machine that fits more or less well in the big machine that we call the world, world conditions, or the way of the world" (HW, pp. 221–47). The Rousseauism in such criticism of civilization marks the historical plays that appeared at the same time as or in the wake of *Götz*: *Das leidende Weib* and *Sturm und Drang* by Klinger, *Julius von Tarent* by Leisewitz, *Der Hofmeister* and *Der neue Mendoza* by Lenz, and many others up to and including Schiller's *Die Räuber* (1782), which presents the "sublime criminal" who fails not only because of the social and natural order, but because of himself as well (HW, pp. 221–47).

But while these authors longed to rediscover the vanished wholeness of the *homme naturel* in the self-realization of the individual, Goethe himself had already bid farewell to the expectation "that action, action (is) the soul of the world, not pleasure, not feelings, not subtle arguments."[68] Over and against this doctrine, which Lenz had extracted from *Götz*, *The Sorrows of Young Werther* sets a new expectation—that the "soul of the world," given the "limitations imposed on the active and inquiring powers of the individual," should no longer seek itself in an action turned outward, and always doomed to failure, but instead in a return of the individual to himself: "All this, Wilhelm, leaves me speechless. I withdraw into my inner self and there discover a world" (p. 12). If the nature of the event embodied by a text ever lets itself be captured *in nunce*, then it is this line from the beginning of *Werther*. It introduces a change of horizons (in comparison with horizon of expectations operative in 1774) that shows the socially critical Rousseauism of the *Sturm und Drang* movement the way back to the interiority of a sense of self from which a new community of sentimental souls could be formed. This move also makes the model found in *La nouvelle Héloïose* significant from a formal point of view: Goethe's *Werther* raises the epistolary novel to the level of a genuine medium for the sentimental, but, at the same time, reshapes it as a new, one-sided correspondence that, in taking the step from the dialogic to the radically monologic, clearly reveals its break with the dramatic medium espoused by the *Sturm und Drang* movement, and with the sympathetic communication that Rousseau's *Lettres de deux amants* embodied.

La nouvelle Héloïse had already been translated by Gellius in 1761, and had been, in part, enthusiastically taken up by the elite (Herder, Wieland, Möser, Jacobi, Hamann), in part given a thorough critique (Mendelssohn, Lessing, Nicolai, Albrecht von Haller), and made the *Sturm und Drang* credo by Klinger and Lenz. It served as a model for plays like *Das leidende Weib*, and *Der Hofmeister* (1774) – the "new Abelard" – but also for a bucolic novel such as *Fräulein von Sternheim* (1771) by Sophie von La Roche. Even "love's threesome," which had offended almost everyone in France, played an exemplary role in Germany, as is apparent above all in 1775, in Goethe's *Stella* (according to H.-D. Weber) and, in 1779, in Jacobi's *Woldemar*. Jacques Voisine, in sketching out this phase of Rousseau's reception, notes a distinction between the German reception and that in France: whereas Rousseau's reception in France was split between the applause of the wider public and rejection by the official channels of criticism, his German reception was divided in terms of judgments made concerning the first and second parts of the novel (JV, pp. 124, 126). Some – like Klinger and Lenz – saw in Rousseau's work tidings of autonomous feelings, the gospel of nature, the rebellion against paternal arbitrariness and class tyranny; others – such as Mendelssohn or Albrecht von Haller – held fast to the idyll in Clarens, and extolled Wolmar's reform, country life, and the refounded family as Rousseau's real, exemplary discoveries.[69] The possibility of coming to grips with the contradiction in this partial understanding, and of resolving it in his own response to *La nouvelle Héloïse*, must have provided Goethe with more than a little incentive to write *Werther*.

Goethe's reading of Rousseau had already begun before his stay in Strassburg, as is demonstrated by his enthusiasm for the tidings announced by the "citizen of Geneva," an enthusiasm he shared with the supporters of the *Sturm und Drang* movement. It seems that he also excerpted material from Rousseau's philosophical texts as well (there are traces of the *Contrat social* in his dissertation for the *Lizenz*, of the *Lettre à Mr. de Beaumont* in the *Ephemerides*, of *Emile* in the "Letter from the Pastor of . . . to the New Pastor of . . . ").[70] His having read *La nouvelle Héloïse* is first evident in a letter to Behrisch (November 10, 1767) where the words "So it will be, tomorrow, the day after tomorrow, and always" appear. This paraphrase of a sentence from the seventh letter of Book V must have become something of a standard line for Goethe, since it reappears frequently: in a letter to Charlotte Buff (September 11, 1772), and to Kestner (April 14, 1773); in his reminiscence about the "German idyll" in Wetzler (*SW* 10, p. 595); in the *Venezianischen Epigrammen* (no. 92). If one adds the formulation in the closing of a letter to Charlotte von Stein (March 25, 1776), "Mais—ce n'est plus Julie—Adieu" (reminiscent of IV, vi), one has all the direct evidence as to how the young Goethe may have received Rousseau's novel, although these references hide more than they reveal. It is also known that, during his trip through Switzerland, he shed tears at the site of the novel's action—just as so many other readers had. This is surprisingly little, given the debate about *La nouvelle Héloïse* that had inflamed the German literary scene, and the thoroughness with which Goethe generally read Rousseau!

Nonetheless, these marginal references to the hidden model reveal something of the fascination that led Goethe to turn one quote into a nostalgic formula for happiness. The context from which it is taken is the letter about the grape harvest in Clarens (V, vii). In Rousseau's description, this work is transformed into a festival: "Tout vit dans la plus grand familiarité; tout le monde est égal, et personne ne s'oublie" (*OC* II, p. 607).[71] Saint-Preux, too, participates in this *douce égalité* that seems to restore the natural order, but not without a touch of melancholy: the old folk songs everyone sings during the evening reopen the wounds caused by his first love, wounds from which he has never fully recovered. Furthermore, this distracted houseguest is so inept at carding hemp that he is always last in the competition. Finally he tries a little underhandedness to help improve his chances, but he is caught and has to face Julie's reprimand. Thus, the events, which end with a round of toasts to the winner, are hardly glorious as far as Saint-Preux is concerned—they represent the collective ecstasy of a domestic community to which Julie's former lover remains an outsider: "Ensuite on offre à boire à toute l'assemblée: chacun boit à la santé du vainqueur, et va se coucher, content d'une journée passée dans le travail, la gaité, l'innocence, et qu'on ne serait pas fâché de recommencer le lendemain, le surlendemain, et toute sa vie" (pp. 610–11).[72] What Goethe later extracted from this scene conveys an almost contrary sense in the context of *Dichtung und Wahrheit*. There, a description of the lovely harmony between the young couple and their guest comes first, a harmony established after he has completely overcome the "dark spiritual forces" that had earlier inhabited him (*SW* 10, p. 592). He soon becomes "Lotte's" inseparable companion. She mediates between him and the "everyday world" in the garden and in the fields, and he passes a glorious summer in undisturbed harmony, even as part of the threesome formed when her fiancé's business allows him to join them: "Thus they passed a glorious summer, a true German idyll, for which the fruitful land provided the prose, and a pure affection the poetry. . . . And thus one ordinary day followed another, and all seemed to be holidays. . . . Whoever remembers what was prophesied about the new Héloïse's happy-unhappy friend will understand me: And sitting at the feet of his beloved, he will card hemp, and wish to card hemp today, tomorrow, and the day after, indeed for his whole life" (*SW* 10, p. 595). Here we have a striking instance of reversal of significance, one that the quotation undergoes because of its new context: Julie's friend did not sit at the feet of his beloved, and he did not go on carding hemp; nothing had been prophesied about him, and it was not his private wish that everything remain forever as it was. This change in significance reveals a change of interest and comprehension: what for Rousseau came from the desire to perpetuate the community that had come into being at the end of the day's work (the *douce égalité* actualizes a *Contrat social* in miniature!), for Goethe fulfills the promise of lasting happiness in a pure, but private, affection. Promise or delusion? After all, the new Héloïse's friend is referred to as "happy-unhappy," and immediately thereafter begins the section containing the story of Jerusalem, the young man in the Werther costume, whose passion for a friend's wife leads to his destruction.

The implications of this quotation should certainly not be overestimated. Neither should it be explained away simply in terms of Goethe's having reprivatized the social aspects of the idyll in Clarens. Here it is just a matter of uncovering an early indication of the hidden model that Goethe was more open about only later. "My biography does not show clearly enough," he said to Eckermann on January 3, 1830, "what sort of influence these men had on my youth, and what pains it cost me to defend myself against them, and to maintain my own ground in a true relation to nature." He means Voltaire and his great contemporaries, including Rousseau, who, according to this retrospective confession, offered the sort of challenge to the young Goethe that Harold Bloom has described as the "anxiety of influence."[73] The overpowering prototype, which remains unmentioned in *Werther*, makes itself felt in the reminiscences in *Dichtung und Wahrheit*. A close reading of the latter would show that Goethe's description of how *Werther* came into being as a symbiosis of literature and life is constructed along the same lines as the account of the development of *La nouvelle Héloïse* found in Rousseau's *Confessions*.[74] In these reminiscences Goethe mentions two sources for his "truly German idyll," namely, the etchings by Gessner, and Goldsmith's *Deserted Village*. Within the horizon of expectations operative in 1774, they mark the threshold between the old (classicist) and new (sentimental) idyll.

In the former, the arcadian world remains separate from social reality, a reality against which it is set as an ideal. In the latter, the ideal relations embodied in the idyll are themselves absorbed into the literary representation of the existing social conditions. It is no accident that the pastoral novel meets its historical demise somewhere between the fall of the *ancien régime* and the establishment of bourgeois society.[75] The need for the fiction of an unimpaired existence did not disappear; henceforth, however, it would be satisfied in one of two ways: by the sentimental—through the discovery of nature in the form of a lost naïveté and wholeness—and by the literary discovery of a concrete rural life. The demise of the bucolic novel, which is so to speak given its send-off by *La nouvelle Héloïse*, and the concurrent demise of the idyll as a literary genre (a genre from which the idyllic—as a general literary mode in Schiller's sense—was liberated and even survived as the degree zero of the nineteenth-century realistic novel)[76] can be traced back to the newly awakened interest in the *état de nature*. The fiction of an unsocial *homme naturel* who is supposed to find fulfillment in the satisfaction of his physical needs and in a simple *sentiment de l'existence*, while establishing a critique of civilization and culture, also reveals a latent contradiction in bucolic literature: its ideal of the simple life has no real connection to nature, and in fact actually reveals the overrefined tastes of an idle society. In the sentimental idyll embodied in *The Deserted Village*, bucolic fiction withdraws into remembrance of an "earlier, vanished mode of being." This way of being is contrasted with a contemporary, urbanized society that is separated from nature, a society that Goldsmith, like Rousseau, criticizes because of the way in which it urbanizes being while impoverishing those who are left behind. Goethe's *Werther* participates in this change of horizons—not, perhaps, in the tendency to incorporate the exploitation and misery of the peasant in the idyll, and to call for some remedy (as J. H. Voss did in 1775 in *Die Leibeigenen* and *Die Freigelassenen*), but certainly in the sentimental attitude that had developed since Rousseau. This was a given for those who read *Werther*, even if the patriarchal idea derived from Homeric and biblical prehistory, to which Goethe's "true German idyll" gives presence appears in the undeveloped form of a naive, rural existence. The horizon of expectations bequeathed by Rousseau's *Nouvelle Héloïse* is nonetheless surpassed here through a change in relations, one that is assumed in Klopstock's *Odes* and Young's *Night Thoughts*: "Whether he admires God's omnipotence while looking at the smallest of His creations or, on the other hand, sees the Lord in a thunderstorm, Werther's sense of nature (is) Klopstockian, and his feelings about life are likewise linked to religion in the intimate manner found in Klopstock" (ES, p. 220). Between *La nouvelle Héloïse* and *Werther* lies the line of demarcation between Rousseau's deism and the young Goethe's pantheism. This pantheism emerges in 1774 in "Ganymede," which invokes a nature "embracing and embraced," along with an "all-loving Father," while turning away from the rebellion against the gods proclaimed in "Prometheus" (1773/75). Werther's sense of nature has its disadvantageous side as well, however, and it is this side that dominates the second half of the book, which, in accordance with the tastes of the epoch, adopts the melancholy tone of *Night Thoughts* and *Ossian* while seeming to reject Rousseau's belief in the goodness of nature. My reconstruction of the horizon of expectations operative in 1774 concerning the "old and new Abelard"[77] can stop here. The question as to what it cost Goethe to "stand on [his] own feet in a truer rapport with nature" will be taken up in the ensuing interpretation.

4. *The Sorrows of Young Werther* as Goethe's initial response to Rousseau

That Rousseau's *Nouvelle Héloïse* was the hidden prototype for *Werther* is evident in the manner in which Goethe followed his predecessor's basic model step by step and, in his response to Rousseau, took advantage of the expectations thus evoked in order to point the German reader of 1774 toward a new sort of experience — the tragic experience of an autonomous sense of self. This change in horizons comes to light insofar as one discerns the act of productive reception involved in emulating the original, and sees that the self-sufficient form of the work is an aspect of its function as a response. Emulation and continuation, remembrance and revision of the basic model are not mutually exclusive here as they often are when the "anxiety of influence" weighs heavily. Goethe redeployed the plot of *La nouvelle Héloïse* in order to develop it further, and bring it to an unexpected conclusion. If, in Rousseau's text, it began *medias in res*, with admissions of love on the part of the teacher and the pupil, in order to allow Julie's story, the story of the new Héloïse, to culminate in a surmounting of love through love, for Werther, the new Abelard, it begins with the constellation created in Clarens, that is, with his love for a woman he cannot have, in order to see what the upshot of Saint-Preux's passion might have been, a question Rousseau's novel does not address. The first time Lotte appears before Werther she is surrounded by children, whereas Saint-Preux first sees Julie in the midst of her children after they have been separated for some time. Furthermore, in this "most charming scene," the girl in the white dress with pale red stripes plays the role of deputy mother, which leads one to wonder what difference there might have been in Goethe's view of the bourgeois institution of the family. In Goethe's triadic constellation of characters, Albert, the duty-conscious and industrious husband-to-be, takes Wolmar's role, that of a rationalistic and pedagogically dominant father of the family, who brings to life the ideal of an autarkic economy. But Werther has harsh words for the work ethic behind this middle-class industriousness, and one might ask whether Rousseau's observations on the division between natural and social existence was understood and reformulated by Goethe as the suffering produced by a reality built on the division of labor.

The basic model provided by *La nouvelle Héloïse* is divested not only of the old, authoritarian family structure (in place of the unbending Baron d'Etanges, there is only the widowed civil servant who — symbolically — is retired), but of Claire, the female counterpole to Julie, and Lord Edouard, the outsider who lends his assistance, as well. Their places are taken by Wilhelm, Werther's friend and correspondent, and — *mutatis mutandis* — the envoy. The latter represents the "outer world," a figure of authority in the class structure, who serves to show Werther in an additional conflict, a conflict with his middle-class background that he does not experience in the "inner world" of the idyll in Wahlheim. But while the enlightened nobleman (Lord Edouard) treats Saint-Preux as a friend, offers the lovers a far-off sanctuary, and saves Saint-Preux from suicide after he is rejected, the unenlightened Count of C . . . is the external impetus for Werther's throwing off the "yoke" of subaltern activity (*SW* 4, p. 326), and for his following the lonely path of self-realization to its bitter end. No friend can accompany him along this path. Instead, Wilhelm's place is taken more and more by God the Father, with whom Werther disputes, and from whom – through a series of images and similes that, for the orthodox, bordered on blasphemy – he claims the unmediated rapport of a lost son. The immediatizing of this relationship to God the Father belongs to the basic model found in *La nouvelle Héloïse*, but there is no provocative secularization of Christian beliefs in that text. Thus, another shift in horizons is made manifest.

That Wilhelm, Werther's earliest confidant, remains silent as far as the reader is concerned, as do Lotte and Albert, is the most significant change in the Rousseauesque model. This move from a dialogue of sympathetic communication to a monologue produced by an individual who is open only to the authority of his own conscience has already been discussed. Goethe's German revision of the original provisioned the ideal of the *homme sensible* with a new content and a new carrier – a passive hero in lieu of Julie, who was both active and always superior to Saint-Preux. At the same time, however, this change brought certain dangers with it. The new content operative in sentimental knowledge of the self is already evident in the linguistic history of the new notion of individual wholeness. In Rousseau's text, the French correlates lack the emphatic sense that focuses attention on the "indivisible whole"; therefore, *caractère* or *génie* must fill in for what "nature has instilled in man."[78] If at first a line already cited from the opening section of *Werther* ("I withdraw into myself and discover a world"; p. 12) seems to promise that the individual need only turn his back on society in order to rediscover a world in himself ("How happy I am to have gotten away"), the end of Werther's sorrows shows that the fullness of his sense of self was an illusion, one that encompassed the risk that in losing social being and its surrogate – the other who has been made absolute, who is loved and is at the same time unavailable – the certainty of self could be lost (GS, p. 167; PM, 1976, p. 20). The productive reception found in Goethe's reconstruction of the basic model generated by *La nouvelle Héloïse* could now easily be expanded through detailed prescriptive elements that reappear in *Werther*, that are recast, or given a different sense in the new context. There is no space for that here, however,[79] so I will turn directly to the question of how Goethe's response to Rousseau announces a change in the horizon of literary and social experience, a change that is of equal importance for the institutions of the middle-class society that is in the process of forming and for its relation to nature and art.

"Probably the most important thing that one could reproach the author of *The Sorrows of Werther* for," wrote Christian Garve in 1775, is that a writer is obliged "to reveal false conclusions to be false conclusions, incorrect notions to be incorrect, false grounds to be false, and the actions that spring from them to be truly reprehensible" (PM, p. 153). In the end, the criticism leveled by German Enlightenment thinkers, from Lessing through Campe, Bodmer, and Sulzer to Lichtenberg and, finally, Nicolai — who exploited it in his critical pamphlet — boiled down to reproaching Goethe for not having done so. Whoever rereads this criticism today must find Garve's reproach just as strange as the praise that most of those just named bestowed on the *Friends of the Young Werther*, a text that now seems a mere curiosity. For us, the contrary view has long seemed evident. As Blankenberg formulated it, a "writer [is] not always obliged to provide us with a moral ideal" (PM, p. 186), and a work like Goethe's, precisely because it is a "product of beauty," though devoid of moral teaching, can and must, according to Lenz (PM, p. 188), have a moral effect on the "public's feelings" because of its implicit "morality." What is strange about the early reception of *Werther* is that it was precisely the Enlightenment thinkers who thought the public so immature that it could not understand the morality of a work without a "brief, cold closing comment," and that, contrariwise, the book's apologists claimed, that "we always come away from reading the Sorrows of young W. more morally improved than we do from any of those inquiries as to whether W. acted properly" (PM, p. 189) — but the scandalous emergence of "Werther fever" contradicted the assertion "that sentimentality is prudence's noblest gift" (PM, p. 188). This situation, which is paradoxical for both camps, marks the moment at which the aesthetic autonomy claimed for *Werther* came into being, that autonomy through which Goethe in his own way actualized Rousseau's postulate that it is the task of literature, as antifiction, to shed light on the illusions produced by the dominant society, and to pave the way for an authentic experiencing and self-realization of human nature.

It was in *Werther* that the reversal of the traditional relationship between fiction and reality announced by Rousseau first actually took place. The enhanced immediacy of "writing to the moment," the epistolary form that had reverted to monologue, the rejection of any moral commentary, and the generally subliminal social criticism required a reader who is already mature, one who is able to involve himself in an empathic reading and nevertheless form his own aesthetic and moral judgments. Goethe was the first to release the "language of the heart" from its exorbitant pathos and rhetorical delivery. He did away with the steady development of emotion ("Le sentiment y est; il se communique au coeur par degrés"; *OC* II, p. 18)[80] and the contrasting moral discourse in Rousseau's novel employing a newly developed style of self-expression that seemed to catch the subject in all the spontaneity of his feelings, and these feelings in the evanescent moment of their occurrence. From this fiction of immediacy, an immediacy that had not previously been achieved, and that seemed to admit of "no distinction between the literary and the real" (*SW* 10, p. 641), sprang the *fascinosum* of an

authenticity that, for the naive reader, embraced the objective world—the stage
on which Werther's story unfolded, and which actually became visible in the correspondence between "inner" and "outer" worlds. Even critical readers admired
"the strength of life that accompanies this art in its presentation"; Merck thought
it to be the source of a new poetry that could serve as an example for all novice
writers, and felt that one dared not "present or write about the [slightest] object
if one had not specifically caught sight of its true presence somewhere in nature,
be it internal or external to us" (PM, p. 198). That this would, as Thomas Mann
indicated, lead to "a dangerous art," which "[gave] a poetic form to the
real . . . and the stamp of the real to the invented,"[81] was admitted *nolens volens* by Goethe himself when he added this warning at the beginning of the second
edition: "So, be a man and do not do what I have done." But the dangerous aspect
of this little book—its *fascinosum*—is not adequately explained by its refusal to
point its finger the way the *fabula docet* did.

Of course, the decision to forgo all moral commentary was a bold step on the
part of the young Goethe, since such commentary was in no way reactionary in
the eighteenth century, and in fact served as a weapon in the hands of Enlightenment authors, who used it to establish the autonomy of middle-class morality.
Rousseau's moral tirades and didactic excursuses, which today's reader might find
disruptive, documented for his contemporaries the new, enlightened function of
movere et docere—freeing the moral from its ties to what was narrated, and making literature the seat of moral legislation.[82] On the other hand, this step that was
taken at the intersection of French Enlightenment and German idealism released
the reader, now declared to be mature, from the guardianship of the philosophers
of the Enlightenment. He is expected to arrive at his own moral judgments on the
basis of his aesthetic understanding. In the case of *Werther*, this expectation was
met only by a small group of readers of which Merck, Blankenberg, and Lenz
are representative. The wide majority of readers, who took up the book with edification in mind and who reread it intensively, were misled into identifying literature and life, though generally not into direct emulation.[83] This brought the
spokesmen of the German Enlightenment into action. They turned against the *fascinosum* of the text by writing either critical or satirical responses, and by calling
for a return to reason and the rules of bourgeois existence. Since, for the
minority, *Werther* did indeed espouse a morality, one that the majority did not
recognize, the *fascinosum* of its authenticity—its appellative structure, which
made the fictive and the real indistinguishable—must have a deeper basis. I have
elsewhere tried to explain this *fascinosum* in terms of the particular structure of
the imaginary (see pp. 10–25), which, when employed in successful poetic fiction,
can evoke the perfect as a means of creating greater believability. When Goethe's
Werther for the first time omitted the warnings and made it possible to understand
"how a person might feel when he has decided to throw off the ordinarily agreeable burden of life" (p. 59), and, through its amoral description, unintentionally

transfigured Werther's "sickness unto death," the spontaneous, but indirect effects of the imaginary made themselves felt. The perfection of the representation and its vivifying power unintentionally lead the imagination to an idealization of Werther's sorrows, an idealization that creates the feeling that that which was so perfectly represented must be perfect in itself, and that, consequently — to use Lessing's phrase — "he who has so engaged our sympathy must be good" (PM, p. 160).

As far as *Werther* is concerned, the reader's misunderstanding, which, briefly stated, conflated "poetic beauty" with "moral beauty" (PM, p. 160), was not the only price to be paid for entering the realm of aesthetic autonomy. Along with the discrepancy between intention and effect there emerged a gap between the author and his public, one that Goethe noticed and lamented in his later comments about *Werther* (*SW* 10, p. 648). This new gap, as Martin Fontius and Manfred Naumann have shown, is a historical symptom of the process that began in the German classical period, and in which the institutionalization of art caused the spheres of production and reception to split apart and allowed a third sphere, that of literary circulation and the anonymous literary market, to thrust itself between them, thereby utterly transforming the communicative rapport between author, work, and public. Thus, the realization of aesthetic autonomy, which liberated the author from dependency on patronage, and, along with the independent work of art, produced the independent reader, soon resulted in the now autonomous work of art being caught up in a new economic and ideological dependency that has defined its fate down to our day: "The dissociation of the social and the aesthetic, of the useful and the beautiful, use value and intrinsic value . . . — these and other contradictions . . . can, here, be studied at their source."[84]

"The novel is the common fodder of the reading world, it does not distinguish between stomachs, it recognizes no differences between classes" (GJ, p. 82). This is how a contemporary voice had already come to regard the subversive effects of the new wave of sentimental novels. The difference between classes that seemed to have disappeared from the shared world of reading continued to exist within the horizon of reality that novelistic fiction so naturally continued to construct, so it is surprising in retrospect to see how *La nouvelle Héloïse* was regarded by its contemporaries as a sign of liberation from the fetters of the past (SW *10*, p. 660), and from the *petits lois despotiques des misérables sociétés* (Mercier, in DM, p. 254). Since the actions of both lovers come up against the resistance of external conventions about which they complain, but about which they can do nothing, thus, even with Rousseau, the exemplary power of the new models arose from a return to inner freedom, to the free "voice of conscience," the natural law of "moral sense," and the transparency of empathy — points of reference within the realm of the private that allow one to maintain the hope of a new form of society founded on the gentle law of sentimentality. This goal of Rousseau's was not taken up by *Sturm und Drang* readers. They saw in Saint-Preux a leader in the struggle for the right to self-determination, honor, and equality, and were particularly fond of the words spoken by Lord Bromston, who fought against the prejudices of the narrow-minded landed aristocracy so convincingly and irrefutably in the eyes of the reasonable, and so unacceptably as far as Julie's father was concerned, and whose efforts had such disastrous consequences for her suitor (I, lxii). Even later, the class conflict was pursued not by Saint-Preux, the subaltern tutor with a dubious background, but by the well-bred daughter of the Baron d'Etanges, and, consequently, on the same social plane as before.

That Rousseau allowed the pathos-filled confrontation between the father and daughter to end with Julie's submission and consent to marry the unloved Wolmar inevitably raised the hackles of his emancipated readers. "I have to admit," wrote Albertine von Grün in a letter to Merck, "that never have lovers made me so envious of them as these when they speak the language of their hearts, and never has a girl's behavior been so painful to me as this Julie's. No, I could never have acted so. It would mean one cared more for one's own peace and quiet than for the happiness of one's beloved. . . . My father at my feet, begging? What unspeakable squalor! My father? Well, I would have resisted" (ES, p. 128). Such readers were incensed by what they regarded as an impossible retreat into the conventions of a society based on class, whereas Lessing praised it as the finest scene in a novel he otherwise thought very little of, and this despite his own support for the idea of natural equality: "It belongs to Rousseau. I am myself not sure what degree of outrage is mixed with feelings of pathos when we see a father beg something from his daughter on bended knee." The outrage, which Lessing does not pursue, points back to a dilemma that is merely covered over, not resolved, in Rousseau's novel. Paternal authority thrust Julie out of the sphere of sentimental harmony in which she believed herself to live while in the bosom of her family: "Les soins d'une tendre mère, d'un père, dont vous êtes l'unique espoir; l'amitié d'une cousine . . . une ville entière fière de vous avoir vue naître: tout occupe et partage votre sensibilité" (*OC* II, 73).p. [85] Her first reaction is not free of harsh words about her "perverse and barbarous father," who has sold her "like merchandise, like a slave" (p. 94). And if she finally consents to marry her father's friend, her submission—and here we see Rousseau's real discovery—is preceded by that of the other. The same authoritarian father whose anger leads him to beat his grown daughter mercilessly, so much so that her mother must throw herself between them, confesses his shame about this deed, not in words, but with gestures, by taking his daughter on his knees, caressing her, and mixing his own tears with hers (I, lxiii). "Ici finit le triomphe de la colère et commença celui de la nature"[86]—what begins here is the triumph of sentimentality, which, as Rousseau supposed, can transform all social positions: the father must appeal to the daughter's heart in order to win her accord, the daughter must surrender the prerogatives of her heart in order to reestablish the natural harmony of the family, which will take on a new form—that of a community of beautiful souls—because of these actions. The new community cannot, however, be the old family founded by Baron d'Etanges. It calls for a new father to replace feudal, paternal authority, one who will be able to bring the lovers together in a new family even though they must remain apart. It is Wolmar in whom Julie—this is my interpretation of the latent meaning in this famous scene—seeks a spouse who will at the same time function as the new paternal authority, and to whom the responsibility falls for reconciling virtue and passion, the dictates of reason and the prerogatives of the heart—in that *douce égalité* that is to reign in the autarkic family circle in Clarens and is to restore the *ordre de la nature* (*OC* II, p. 608).

The utopian nature of this solution—through which Rousseau hoped to sublate individual conflicts in the sociability of a new family that is free of domination (the germ of the new bourgeois society)—becomes clear in the contradictions between Wolmar's role, the mode of existence in his autarkic household, and religious legitimation, which can be hidden only with difficulty during the "idyll in Clarens." Wolmar, who risks his exclusive rights as spouse, and who seems to agree to the *ménage à trois* in the belief "qu'il n'y a rien de bien qu'on n'obtînt des belles âmes avec de la confiance et de la franchise" (IV, xii),[87] is in reality an "enlightened despot" who secretly turns from his proclaimed principle of unconditional sincerity to a padagogical strategy meant to bring about the "healing" of the two lovers. He gains knowledge of the letters about their first, secret love behind their backs, and does not hesitate to "profane" things that they hold sacred, such as the grove where they first kissed ("Julie, ne craignez plus cet asile, il vient d'être profané"; *OC* II, p. 496).[88] He also frequently prescribes new tests of their virtue that, according to his homeopathic recipe, are meant to stir up their love in order to distill it into friendship.[89] The "taste for order," the only principle of action to which this "good atheist" admits (p. 490), creates on the level of education what Julie had created in her new garden, that Elysium depicted by the idyll in Clarens: a perfect work of art that awakens an impression of nature's perfection (JS, p. 136). But in the work of education, the price paid for the undertaking is more obvious; it is basically the same as that which is openly admitted to in the *Contrat social*: "Il faut forcer les hommes d'être libres."[90]

The new community that this God-like father of the family[91] establishes in Clarens is founded on a contradiction analogous to that between natural and social existences. As Jean Starobinski and L. Gossmann have shown in their penetrating analyses, Wolmar's reform and its patriarchal tendencies trail far behind contemporary developments related to manufactory labor and the commercial forms of bourgeois economy. In the end, the economic actualization of moral autarky only leads to a "sentimental Robinsonade" (JS, p. 135), one in which the proclamation of a democratic *douce egalité* is no more able to hide the real social and economic inequality between master and servant than the Sunday-like quality of the festival is able to hide the abiding tasks of the workday quota: if, here, one works only in order to enjoy (*OC* II, p. 470), one must nevertheless work—in order to be able to enjoy.

The latent, but fundamental, contradiction in *La nouvelle Héloïse* is also of significance with regard to the claims made regarding the emancipation of religious feelings. However bold the reformist principles that Julie puts to the test in the religious instruction of her children may sound, and however much it may have scandalized the orthodox that in Rousseau's novel only the atheist, Wolmar, fits the ideal of the good and the wise, nonetheless Julie's attempt to follow the "dictates of the heart" alone, and to compensate for the "indiscretion" of her first passionate encounter by being a virtuous wife and mother is, from the very start, caught up in the Christian doctrine of sin, grace, and redemption, the very notions from whose authority her efforts at self-deliverance are supposed to liberate her. That she constantly refers to her first act of self-realization, her free choice in consummating her initial love for Saint-Preux, as *ma faute*—a usage that must irritate the modern reader—shows that she has not overcome her dependency on the dogma of the "sinful person." Interestingly enough, it was Rousseau himself who had disputed the legitimacy of this orthodox Christian concept. The final act of her life, her confession that the outward success of her reform was, as far as her inner life was concerned, actually an extended and arduously maintained illusion, is likewise not a sign of having achieved the autonomy of a self-contained subject. It is, rather, an indication that this possibility has been revoked in favor of a paradoxical salvation of her "virtue," a salvation made possible by submission to the will of an absent third party. The Father on high takes Wolmar's place in the closing triadic community so that in his presence the happiness that has been denied the two lovers on earth because of their virtue can nonetheless be achieved in eternity. The contradictory nature of this otherworldly solution, which of necessity involves abandoning Wolmar and the *Contrat social* established in Clarens (JS, p. 148), irritated even Rousseau's most ardent admirers. G. J. Hamann wrote to J. G. Lindner that "Wolmar's character reveals the comic sublime as only Rousseau knew how to portray it. A calm, wise, honest man without God in his heart . . . Julie, who has become his wife, expresses some very silly ideas on her death bed, ideas that only a Wolmar could find worthy of noting down, and that only an addled brain could be moved by" (November 7, 1761). Rousseau did not have the means to resolve the antinomies between natural and social existence, feeling and reason, self-determination and morality. But neither did the young Goethe, to whose response I will now return.

The formal innovation introduced by Goethe's *Werther* (the one-sidedness produced by moving from the dialogic principle underlying the epistolary novel to a monologue in the form of letters) "to which we can no longer imagine fitting responses" (GM, p. 197), and the abandonment of moral commentary led to more than the postulate that the work and the reader were aesthetically autonomous.

The change in horizon introduced by these events also produced a new understanding and legitimation of the individual: through the return to the self, the *homme sensible* is supposed to rediscover the lost wholeness of the *homme naturel*, and reestablish in his inner world the original form of that outer world on which he has turned his back.[92] This is why Goethe's response to Rousseau immediately lays claim to, and promulgates, aesthetic autonomy in the name of the literary discovery of the autonomous individual. This withdrawal into the interiority of personal feelings may have arisen from Goethe's earlier insight into the narrowness of the possibilities that existed in Germany for accomplishing "meaningful actions" solely "in order to hold out against dragging, spiritless, bourgeois existence" (*SW* 10, p. 637). But this does not mean that Goethe's *Werther* has abandoned Rousseauesque social criticism. The new cult of interiority – as Wolf Lepenies has shown – remains oriented toward an outer and countersocial model. The return to nature creates the distance that allows the isolated individual, despite his melancholy, to engage in a critique of social alienation (WL, p. 74).[93] In this critique, Goethe was a little harder on the institutions of the world around him than was Rousseau. In *Werther*, the conflict between classes is further developed as a conflict with the ideals of bourgeois society itself, with the norms of the bourgeois family and the ethos of bourgeois labor. It confronts Christian orthodoxy with the most consequent form of self-deliverance – suicide; but with its tragic outcome, it also transfers the proposed ideal of self-realization into the aporia of a "sickness unto death."

Werther cannot be thought of as a pioneer in the struggle against class society and absolutism because it is the incipient bourgeois society itself – the class of his own origin – whose "disgraceful . . . conditions" (p. 81) he condemns. This is already evident in the episodic quality of the events that transpire in the aristocratic world, events that bring Werther's efforts at "activity" (p. 81) to a definite halt. The insult Werther suffers at the envoy's table – which he brushes aside by remembering the contrasting harmony that existed between the king and the swineherd in Homer – did not play much of a role in the work's initial reception. It seems to me that this is evidenced by the fact that even as late as 1813, one of the book's most famous readers, Napoleon, in a conversation in Erfurt, criticized "mixing the motive of hurt pride with that of passionate love" (KR, p. 138), and that Heine was the first to find the episode of the insult at an aristocratic gathering "far more significant than the whole business with the pistol shot" (KH, p. 18). It was not the passing protest against snobbery, but the rebellion, undertaken in the name of nature against the ideal of life and the whole alienated reality of the bourgeois world, the rebellion that from beginning to end was embodied in Werther's fate, that was the real provocation for Goethe's contemporaries. Garve's critique culminates in the following: "Nature – solitary, dead, and silent – seems far nobler and grander to him. And so, all the sensitivity of his heart is bent on hating human life as we now live it, and on loving only the existence of nature, with which we seem to unite in death" (PM, p. 152). And if this lonely apostle of nature and enemy of human society nonetheless finds one or two people that he holds worthy of his attention and love, "his imagination leads him to heap on them the combined perfections that he has denied the rest of mankind" (ibid.).

On the other hand, Werther's defenders could turn to no new community of "beautiful souls" such as that which Wolmar, the new father, had created in order to heal the lovers. The frequently invoked middle-class nuclear family, which in this period replaced the "big house" and the *patria potestas* of the feudal family with a life founded on sentimental relations between parents and children, can be found registered in Nicolai's caricature *Friends of the Young Werther*, but not in Werther's *Sorrows*! How distant this family is from him as a moral institution (though marriage between others is inviolable for him, and becomes more and more the external cause of his suffering) was made provocatively clear by Lenz: "A man can nowhere find a more secure gage for his honor than his wife's tenderest feelings about that which is noble and excellent. A Lotte who could prefer and idolize an infant above a Werther deserves never again to be in the company of people like Werther" (PM, p. 223). From the vantage point of Rousseau's work, this is already an indication of the partially recast, in part incomplete configuration of Lotte's family, a family into which Werther enters as a stranger after Albert has been chosen as her fiancé. Most striking is the bracketing of the role of father: the prince's bailiff *no longer* concerns himself with it because, since his wife's death, he finds "life . . . in his bailiff's quarters too painful" (p. 11); Albert, since he is only engaged to be married, is *not yet a father*. He exists on the same level as Lotte and Werther, but without any of the features that predestine Wolmar for paternal authority. The position of mother is equally precarious, since Lotte only stands in for her. Of course Lotte was chosen for this role by her dying mother, who had also already recommended the "worthy Albert" as Lotte's future husband (pp. 74–75). Reinhart Meyer-Kalkus places this scene of investiture at the center of an interpretation that frees Lotte from the old, patriarchal standard of love by means of the mother's last wish—though the daughters of middle-class drama would still have to suffer the consequences of this standard (RM, p. 109). Here it is a question of a "specifically matriarcal 'hominization' within the framework of the patriarchal family," one that also makes it possible to explain the pathological nature of Werther's suffering in terms of the "misfortune of an adolescence in which the 'emancipation' from the family space was unsuccessful" (RM, p. 78). Following this line of thought, the dynamic core of Werther's suffering in the second part of the book is his search for his absent father, and his craving for death can be understood as a "longing for reintegration in the family unit even beyond death" (RM, p. 78). However convincing this interpretation is regarding the second half of the book, it nonetheless seems questionable to me that in the first half Lotte embodies "the mother-imago as such" for Werther. Could not his longing for the absolute family also be explained by the fact that

Lotte, who provides a responsive counterimage to nature, seems to promise a fulfillment denied him by the family as bourgeois institution?

If, at first, Werther still believes that he can find happiness as a "member of this charming family" (p. 55), one must not overlook that Lotte, who is at the center of this ideal image, was, in their earlier encounters, a hybrid figure—both girl and woman, she was a sister who could play the role of mother without having to be one. Was not this the source of the fascination produced by the apparition? Might not the fascination have resided in Werther's illusion of being able to participate in the joys of this charming family without being burdened by its responsibilities, and without having to submit to natural instincts. This was the explanation that Goethe himself gave in retrospect to the aura that surrounded Lotte's "family" in that imaginary space between convention and nature: "Well, although it is a pleasant sight to see parents caring steadfastly for their children, it is still more beautiful to see siblings doing the same for each other. In the first instance we believe we see more instinct and bourgeois convention, in the second, more choice and freedom of spirit" (*SW* 10, p. 594). Werther's ideal soon disappears in part because his position in this very charming family[94] requires that he, like Saint-Preux, relinquish his claim to another man's wife, although her requital of his love seems to offer the only possible salvation for his soul. But the intimate community created by the bourgeois nuclear family could not remain Werther's ideal for another reason as well: he totally rejected the form of life embodied by this type of family—its separation of love and work.

Goethe's critique of the "fateful bourgeois condition" of his era goes furthest beyond Rousseau's critique of civilization, and—in a surprisingly anticipatory manner—beyond his contemporaries' horizon of expectations as well, there where he recognizes the division of labor to be the fundamental principle upon which the bourgeois economy then coming into existence was built. He condemns it as the actual and malevolent source of alienated being in bourgeois society. Rousseauesque suffering, that produced by the separation of man and citizen, natural and social existences, is first experienced as alienation when the results of man's work, that through which he believes he will produce his world, nullifies his determination to be free: "There is a certain monotony about mankind. Most people toil during the greater part of their lives in order to live, and the slender span of free time that remains worries them so much that they try by every means to get rid of it. O Destiny of Man!" (p. 9). This experience, which Goethe names here for the first time, and which he describes in a number of ways in Werther's subsequent letters, is not coincidentally the starting point for the most recent, normative concretization in the reception history of *Werther*—the *New Sorrows of Young W.* by Ulrich Plenzdorf.[95] It is precisely this experience that marks most clearly the shift in horizons that took place between Rousseau and Goethe.

Although Rousseau's social criticism also targeted the bourgeois society then coming into being, taking particular aim at "embryonic capitalism, he [did] so because it destroyed older forms of peasant/petty bourgeois community."[96] But he remained unaffected by the—Calvinistic—bourgeois work ethic. In the patriarchal economy founded in Clarens, man works in order to enjoy—as if the actual, sustained exploitation of the members of the household by its masters simply did not exist! In the idyll in Wahlheim on the other hand, Werther, who is inactive, regards Lotte as the unique embodiment of a life of joyously active, nonalienated labor (*SW* 10, p. 593). In contrast, Albert represents the well-ordered, industrious bourgeois, whose life is divided between the tribulations of business and the freedom of the private sphere, between the day's work and "the hours of relaxation" (p. 15), between "drudging" for others and satisfying one's own needs (p. 49). Apparently, Goethe's contemporaries had not yet realized that Werther's satirical tirades against middle-class competitiveness arose from a newly acquired understanding of the *circulus vitiosus* created by the division of labor and alienation. Whatever indignation was not vented immediately in Nicolai's assertion that one who has "enjoyed the benefits of society" is obligated to it (GJ, p. 97) could be deflected as it was by Garve. Garve took the awareness of the "limits imposed on us" (namely, our limitation to one narrow social set) seriously, but only in order to counter this awareness with the argument that one ought then thank the Creator for "even on occasion giving me leisure time and freedom of spirit sufficient to judge my feelings and other things as well" (PM, pp. 148, 150). This appeal to "freedom of spirit" neither recognizes nor answers the question inherited from Rousseau: given the conditions discerned by Goethe—those of a reality based on the division of labor—how is one to produce whole human beings who can resist the separation of civil and social existence?[97]

Goethe does not yet have an answer in *Werther*. Instead, Werther's fate reveals that the solitary individual's effort to slip behind society's back so to speak, to rediscover his lost wholeness through nature, and to find fulfillment in an autonomy based on self-esteem was doomed to failure. Nonetheless, *Werther* indicates a solution, one developed more fully later, in the *Bildungsroman*. Lotte's "life of joyous activity" points the way, since it already contains what Heinz Schlaffer uncovered in the female role in Goethe's poem "The Bridegroom": "Active only in the narrow confines of the home, not involved in what could be called alienated labor, she seems to lead the kind of aesthetic existence . . . that is denied the male."[98] In contrast, *Wilhelm Meister* can be interpreted as Goethe's attempt to resolve the problem for the male as well—by means of the detour of an aesthetic education meant to make of him a whole human being.

The change in the horizon of life-world experience visible in the connections between *La nouvelle Héloïse* and *The Sorrows of Young Werther* can be even more precisely defined from the dual perspective of nature and religion. If one asks what Goethe might have had in mind when he spoke of "what it had cost [him] . . . to stand on [his] own feet in a truer rapport with nature," one must remember first of all that in the Sulzer review of 1772 he had already assailed Rousseauesque optimism on the grounds that all was not "well in nature's plan." He also objected to the idea of a "loving Mother Nature" by pointing to her all-consuming power, and the "suffering and trouble" that she constantly meted out to her children (*SW* 13, p. 28). The nature scenes from Ossian referred to in the second part of *Werther* and the dynamic pantheism they suggest are a far cry from the sublime mountainscapes and the deism that underlies Rousseau's feelings about nature.[99] The same is true for sentimental psychology. Although it frequently brushes up against the unconscious part of human nature in Rousseau's novel, and although the merciless self-criticism in the *Confessions* first brought the unconscious to light, Goethe's novel was the first to break with the moralism inherent in the idea of "sentimental humanity" by describing Werther's "sickness unto death" as a natural, observable process leading to a final *exitus*. As Paul Mog phrased it, borrowing from Odo Marquard, this marks the completion of "the most radical psychic transformation of the century: the return of nature, which had been displaced by civilization, a nature that exercises its effect in the form of the unconscious—though somewhat ambiguously, as a liberation of the better that had been suppressed, but also as dangerous regression and destruction" (PM 1976, p. 3). In this process, Lotte appears to Werther in a sequence of images that are themselves colored by the ambivalence of a return *to* nature and the return *of* nature: as a presentiment of his beloved conveyed by his oneness with the May landscape (p. 6); as a "counterpart" responding to nature, who, at their first encounter, seems to promise "an expansion of his inner feeling to the whole and to certainty";[100] as a forbidden image of fulfillment in love, a love that, because of Albert's presence, is denied him by the institution of marriage; as the angel of death finally, who hands him the "cold, terrible cup" along with Albert's pistols.[101] But, as the natural powers of passion intensify his impossible love to the point of a "sickness unto death," the displaced authority of the father also reappears in the sacral images that form part of the story of his sorrows. This is the final authority to which he entrusts himself when he decides to take the ultimate step toward self-deliverance. He alone can be the guarantor of a hope that is already familiar to us because of Julie's last letter: "From now on you are mine! mine, Lotte! I go before you. I go to my Father, to your Father. I shall put my sorrow before Him, and He will comfort me until you come; and I shall fly to meet you and clasp you and stay with you before the Infinite Being in an eternal embrace" (p. 157).

Returning to *La nouvelle Héloïse* one final time now, one can readily identify the altered horizon that caused this secular contrafact of Christ's Passion (HF, pp. 165ff.) to scandalize orthodox as well as rationalist critics in Germany. In France, orthodox souls had been outraged primarily by Wolmar's atheistic rationalism and Julie's reliance on herself when reforming her faith, not, however, by the use of sacral figures drawn from the Bible or Christian ritual. Rousseau could use these without fear, since the "language of passion" had – as he himself remarked – always drawn on both the language of piety and that of love poetry (*OC* II, p. 15). For the German reader, able as he was to read *Werther* as the secular contrafact of a Christian devotional booklet, the sacral images, since they were given consistent motivational linkage, called Christ's Passion to mind, and – according to orthodox critics such as J. M. Goetze – placed Werther's utterly profane suffering in the "false light," if not exactly of an *imitatio Christi*, then of a justification for suicide that misused the example of Christ's sacrificial death "to the detriment of our religion" (PM, pp. 119ff.). But the deeper reason for the scandal was not mentioned by orthodox critics. It did not lie in the implicit apologia for suicide, or in the fact that this apologia had been fitted out in trappings from the lexicon of secular Christian texts. It lay, rather, as Herbert Schöffler suggests, in the fact that this, the "first German account of passion to employ a pantheistic notion of God . . . [was] the first tragedy to posit no guilt, no principle of evil" (HS, p. 181).

No matter how one defines secularization in terms of the role it plays in literature, seen from the vantage point of Rousseau's works, Goethe's *Werther*, with its reprise of the parable of the prodigal son, and its worldly contrafact to the Gospel of John, had to strike one as a provocative secularization of the story of Christ's Passion. Provocative especially because the Christian model was usurped in order to present a view of God that denied Christ, the Son of God and Intercessor, and allowed Werther, the prodigal son, to perform the act of his own deliverance while invoking God – a deliverance that he is deluded into believing is a self-punishment for consciously indulging in the "sin" (p. 157) of having embraced and kissed his only beloved this once, without regard for the commandment of the church or the laws of society. If Goethe has thus brought *La nouvelle Héloïse* to its logical conclusion, letting Werther deliver himself, while Julie – in highly novelistic fashion – dies at the "right moment" and is thereby redeemed before her confession of sin can be translated into action, Goethe has also gone beyond Rousseau's example by denying the notion of otherworldly salvation at the end of *Werther*: "The terrible, naturalistic death scene and the impact of an unemotional description of the death rattle deny all metaphysical comfort. Two centuries after the appearance of *Werther* it will seem as if 'that night around eleven' one not only buried 'nature's darling,' but hope for a natural deliverance from history and civilization as well" (PM 1976, p. 138).

Mog's interpretation of the novel's end, which, it seems to me, will be difficult to improve on, leaves only one further question to be asked: why is it that both Rousseau and Goethe begin the fateful tale of the *homme sensible* (the individual who is destined for autonomy, and who must experience the contradiction between nature and civilization as the actuality of his own alienation) with a longed-for return to nature, end with an unintentional return to nature, and, in addition, bring the Christian dogma of sin, justification, and grace into play – much to the detriment of the emancipatory process? If one does not wish to assume at once that this remarkable need for justification is simply a replay of the theological assumption that such "resurgence of repressed belief" reveals the cunning of a theological reason that, even at the moment of apparent triumph over dogma, is able to assert its indestructible substance, then one can turn to Marquard's theory.[102] It maintains that the collapse of the Leibnizian theodicy, and—we can add—that of Rousseau's diagnosis of nascent alienation led, in the second half of the eighteenth century, to man's being obliged to act both as prosecutor and judge, since responsibility for justifying the evil in the world had fallen to him. Faced with this "overadjudication of the reality of human existence" man sought compensation by attempting to flee into a realm free of social and juridical consequence. The newly developed philosophical anthropology and aesthetics, the turn to nature in literature, and the economy of individuality can be interpreted as attempts of this sort. If such flight did not succeed in *La nouvelle Héloïse* and *Werther*, the reason may be that, once incriminated, man's exculpation cannot simply lead to his being released without punishment in a realm free of consequence. Seen in this light, Goethe's second response to Rousseau may well show how much hope had already been invested in aesthetic education in Germany. As the sought-after third way, it was meant to resolve the antinomy between natural and social existence, eliminating both the need to justify oneself and the urge to flee into the inconsequential, thereby reestablishing one's personal liability and responsibility.

5. An overview of *Wilhelm Meister* (the *Emile* of aesthetic education)

Just as *La nouvelle Héloïse* went unmentioned as the covert model for *Werther*, Goethe nowhere refers to the model for *Wilhelm Meister*, despite the fact that the impact of *Emile* is readily felt there. *Emile* crops up in the basic plan of the novel's action, and in the idea of an aesthetic education as soon as one realizes that, in the *Apprenticeship*, Goethe has reinvoked the problem that Rousseau's example of natural education had left unresolved.[103] This realization makes it possible to see that the supposed "theatrical calling," in its function as the new path opened by aesthetic education, leads the German Emile out of the aporia that Rousseau was unable to resolve: "Il faut opter entre faire un homme ou un citoyen."[104] The scene of action for the apprenticeship is not one of rural seclusion but that of the theater. This locale seems to have the same function, that of at first blocking the influence of a "society of coarse people,"[105] but it has the advantage of allowing a natural education to be acquired here while in the company of others. It also releases Wilhelm from the fundamental contradiction that confronts Emile, who must first grow to manhood alone and then, nonetheless, become a citizen. Thus, in *Wilhelm Meister*, the theater becomes the site of aesthetic education, and thereby—as Körner formulates it in his letter—"the bridge out of the real world into the ideal."[106] In the hybrid world of the theater, human nature can unfold in terms of the totality of the individual and, through the beautiful, can be led without constraint to the useful: "only together do the two compose a human being" (p. 592). Wilhelm—who is secretly guided by the Society of the Tower, as Rousseau's governor guides his pupil—after these years of apprenticeship, set free by nature (p. 466), and having freely decided to forgo his passion for the theater, will discover in himself the virtues of citizenship, will find in Felix his son, in Natalia the "Sophie" meant for him, and, as a surgeon-to-be, return to society in order to serve it.

In *Wilhelm Meister*, the basic model provided by *Emile* is above all the source of the contrasting destinies of Wilhelm and Werner, of the two-phased development of Wilhelm's life, and of the role the Society of the Tower plays as fate. "What good were it," writes Wilhelm to Werner, "to manufacture perfect iron while my own breast is full of dross? What would it stead me to put properties of land in order, while I am at variance with myself? To speak it in a word, the cultivation of my individual self, here as I am, has from my youth upwards been constantly though dimly my wish and my purpose" (p. 277). Becoming either a man or a citizen, these are the alternatives, the divide that separates their two ways of life—and the point at which they are reunited at the end of their apprenticeships. Werner, who as the more successful businessman, able to increase and enjoy his capital, pursues the ideal of "the happiness of civic life" (p. 276), is worn out by the time they meet again, a "melancholic drudge" who seems "rather to have retrograded than advanced" (pp. 467–68). Wilhelm, on the other hand, although he has not found his "calling" in the theater, has nonetheless acquired the "cultivation" that he wished for himself, and has, much to the surprise of his brother-in-law, become a "bit of a person" as well as—and now without the irony of the diminutive—that which his middle-class birth had previously denied him because it was the privilege of the aristocracy: a personality (p. 278). The path of aesthetic education that had led Wilhelm to this position thereby reaches the same point Emile had reached when he was removed from the self-centeredness of his natural education into the obligations of social life, and expected henceforth to be ready "to live for the sake of others, and to forget himself in an activity prescribed by duty" (p. 461). The difficulty of this transition, which in *Emile* requires the creed espoused by the Père Savoyard, seems to have solved so little for Rousseau that in a continuation he has Emile tell how his family was doomed to failure because of the entangled state of society, thereby denying the pedagogical myth of natural education.[107] If, in contrast, Wilhelm is to be expected "to lose himself in a larger mass" now, thanks to his aesthetic education, and begin the *Wanderjahre* as the second phase of his education, the experience of the earlier phase must have prepared him for this, as, in fact, the initiation ritual organized by the Society of the Tower makes clear to him.

If the two-part development of Wilhelm's life obviously points back to *Emile*, the ritual of transition in the tower makes it clear that "dutiful activity" in bourgeois society is the telos at which his natural education in aesthetic culture was meant to arrive. The final action, after which nature can release him from his training, is not the receipt of the certificate of apprenticeship, but Wilhelm's question as to whether Felix is his son. The right question, posed at the right time, indicates to the governor — embodied by the Abbé — that the work of his natural education has been a success. "In this sense his apprenticeship was ended: with the feeling of a father, he had acquired all the virtues of a citizen" (p. 471). Having Wilhelm develop from a man into citizen through the role of father as a means of solving the aporia of natural education and social existence runs the risk of giving the whole business the appearance of a *coup de théâtre*. This in no way diminishes Goethe's revision of Rousseau's *Emile*: the "sentiments of a father" will awaken in Wilhelm that which could not be reached by or even imposed through the abstract imperatives of morality. The social is to emerge from the mistakes of the apprentice years in the form of a natural education requiring no further assistance: "O needless strictness of morality! . . . while Nature in her own kindly manner trains us to all that we require to be" (p. 471). This expectation would smack of pure optimism if Goethe had not supported it with a principle of negative education that is formulated novelistically in terms of the secret workings of the Society of the Tower.

The "mysterious watchmen of the tower" (p. 511) who, from a literary-historical point of view, are a relic of the baroque novel, assume the same functions here as did the governor in *Emile*. The latter, by constantly arranging situations that seemed objective and necessary to the pupil, though remaining hidden, makes sure that the learning process maintains a balance between talents and needs. The world-immanent foresight of the Society of the Tower secretly directs the apprentice's experience in the same manner, so that he can also learn through errors while developing his "whole nature" (p. 513). The Abbé, who asserts that "error can never be cured, except by erring" (p. 514), is applying Rousseau's principle of negative education,[108] which dictates that the pupil not be taught about virtue and truth, but instead gain insight and experience from things themselves. To what degree a natural education through error must be aided by a "teacher of men" is ultimately made clear by the correction of his erroneous wish to marry Theresa instead of Natalia. In order to bring the apprentice phase of his life to a close, Wilhelm must have acquired insights that surpass all his individual experiences, and that go furthest beyond anything expected in *Emile*: "None of thy follies wilt thou repent; none wilt thou wish to repeat; no luckier destiny can be allotted to a man" (p. 464). For Goethe, the wholeness achieved by this naturally educated man includes his history — the past that is inscribed in his certificate of apprenticeship and affirmed in toto.

This affirmation is embodied in the close of the ritual, when Wilhelm opens the "Hall of the Past" and his attention turns from his individual fate to that of mankind as a whole: "Everyone who entered felt himself as if exalted above himself; while the co-operating products of art, for the first time, taught him what man is and what he may become" (p. 505). One could, of course, take Goethe's "Hall of the Past," a hall where all styles of all periods are mixed together and where the assembled works have lost their auratic aspect, to be an early manifestation of the "imaginary museum." Such is Hannelore Schlaffer's contention.[109] In this case Goethe bids farewell to the principle of aesthetic education as soon as he makes the transition to the *Wanderjahre*, and, along with it, dismisses the solution the apprentice years offered with regard to the problem of educating a natural man, thereby showing the historical limits of its validity: "His journey takes him from inspiration to economy, and Wilhelm himself thus becomes an allegory of the novel's theme. It describes the journey from art into a modern world that is hostile to art."[110] In this case, Goethe's *Wilhelm Meister* bequeathed a rather ambivalent model to the German *Bildungsroman* of the nineteenth century. The principle of aesthetic education required a "teacher of men" in order to resolve the antinomy between natural and social existence. In the form of the Society of the Tower, this teacher served to "guide one who errs" and gave a hand to nature in its chance unfolding—the secret teleology to which Friedrich Schlegel responded with the dictum that, in *Wilhelm Meister*, "chance itself [turns out] to be an educated man."[111] When the fictive educator was eliminated, and the pupil was left unprotected while gleaning experience from the delusions produced by his mistakes, a question arose that turned out to be fateful for *Grünen Heinrich*:[112] could the principle of aesthetic education still be brought to bear fruit, and if so, how, since it had to stand its own ground at a time when history, a thoroughly "uneducated man," emerged as its antagonist?

Selective Bibliography for Chapter 4

Rousseau (OC), *Oeuvres complètes*, ed. B. Gagnebin and M. Raymond (Paris, 1964).

Goethe (SW), *Sämtliche Werke*, ed. E. Beutler (Zurich, 1977)

Attridge, Anna (AA), "The Reception of *La Nouvelle Héloïse*," in *Studies on Voltaire*, 120 (1974), pp. 227–67.

Bogumil, Sieghild (SB), *Rousseau und die Erziehung des Lesers* (Bern/Frankfurt, 1974).

Buck, Günther (GB), "Über die systematische Stellung des *Emile* im Werk Rousseaus," in *Allegemeine Zeitschrift für Philosophie*, 1 (1980), 1–40.

Galle, Roland (RG), "*Socialpsychologische Überlegungen zu Rousseaus Autobiographie,*" in *Freiburger Literaturpsychologische Gespräche*, ed. J. Cremerius et al. (Frankfurt, 1981), pp. 39–61.

Grossmann, Lionel (LG), "The Worlds of *La Nouvelle Héloïse*," in *Studies on Voltaire*, 41 (1966), pp. 235–76.

Hammer, Carl (CH), *Goethe und Rousseau* (Lexington, Ky., 1973).

Haverkamp, Anselm (AH), "Illusion und Empathie—Die Transferstruktur der teilnehmenden Lektüre in den *Leiden Werthers*," in *Poetica*, 1982.

Hohendahl, Peter Uwe (PH), *Der europäische Roman der Empfindsamkeit* (Wiesbaden, 1977).

Hotz, Karl (KH), *Goethes Werther als Modell für kritisches Lesen* (Stuttgart, 1974).

Jäger, Georg (GJ), *Empfindsamkeit und Roman* (Stuttgart, 1969).

Launay, Michel (ML), *Rousseau et son temps* (Paris, 1969).

Lepenies, W. (WL), *Melancholie und Gesellschaft* (Frankfurt, 1972).

Maag, G. (GM 1981), "Das Ästhetische als echte und als scheinbare Negativität bei Rousseau," in *Romanistische Zeitschrift für Literaturgeschichte*, 4 (1981), pp. 415–42.

Mattenklott, Gert (GM), "Briefroman," in *Deutsche Literatur: Eine Socialgeschichte*, vol. 4, ed. H. Glaser (Hamburg, 1980), pp. 185–203.

Maurer, Karl (KM), "Die verschleierten Konfessionen," in *Festschrift für Friedrich Maurer* (Stuttgart, 1963), pp. 424–37.

Meyer-Kalkus, Reinhard (RM), "Werthers Krankheit zum Tode," in *Urszenen*, ed. A. Kittler and H. Turk (Frankfurt, 1977), pp. 76–138.

Mog, Paul (PM 1976), *Ratio und Gefühlskultur* (Tübingen, 1976).

Mornet, Daniel (DM), *La Nouvelle Héloïse* (Paris, 1925).

Mounier, Jacques (JM), *La fortune des écrits de J.-J. Rousseau dans les pays de langue allemande de 1782, à 1813* (Paris, 1980).

Müller, Peter (PM), *Der junge Goethe im zeitgenösseschen Urteil* (Berlin, 1969).

Oettinger, Klaus (KO), "Eine Krankheit zum Tode: Zum Skandal um Werthers Selbstmord," in *Der Deutschunterricht*, 28 (1976), p. 63.

Rothmann, Kurt (KR), *Erläuterungen und Dokumente* (zu Goethes "Werther") (Stuttgart, 1974).

Sauder, Gerhard (GS 1974), *Empfindsamkeit*, vol. 1 (Stuttgart, 1974).

——, (GS), "Subjektivität und Empfindsamkeit im Roman," in *Sturm und Drang*, ed. W. Hinck (Kronberg, 1978), pp. 163–74.

Schlaffer, Hannelore (HS), *Nachwort zu Goethe: Wilhelm Meisters Lehrjahre* (Stuttgart, 1979), pp. 641–66.

——, (HS 1980), *Wilhelm Meister: Das Ende der Kunst und die Wiederkehr des Mythos* (Stuttgart, 1980).

Schlaffer, Heinz (HS, 1973), *Der Bürger als Held* (Frankfurt, 1973).

Schmidt, Erich (ES), *Richardson, Rousseau und Goethe* (Jena, 1942).

Schöffler, Herbert (HS), "Die Leiden des jungen Werther," in *Deutscher Geist im 18. Jahrundert* (Göttingen, 1967), pp. 115–84.

Spaemann, Robert (RS), "Genetisches zum Naturbegriff des 18. Jahrhunderts," in *Archiv für Begriffsgeschichte*, 11 (1967), pp. 59–74.

Stackelberg, Jürgen v. (JS 1980), "Das Bild der Frau im französischen Roman des 18 Jahrhunderts," in *Studien zum achtzehnten Jahrhunderts*, vol. 2/2, ed. B. Fabian et al. (Munich, 1980).

Starobinski, Jean (JS), *J.-J. Rousseau. La transparence et l'obstacle* (Paris, 1971).

Stierle, Karlheinz (KS), "Theorie und Erfahrung, Das Werk J.-J. Rousseaus und die Dialektik der Aufklärung," in *Europäische Aufklärung*, ed. J. v. Stackelberg (Wiesbaden, 1980).

Taylor, Samuel S.B. (ST), "Rousseau's Contemportary Reputation in France," in *Studies on Voltaire*, 27 (1963), pp. 1545–74.

Tönz, Leo (LT), "Von der 'asiles' der *Nouvelle Héloïse* zu dem 'Lieblingsplätzschen' Werthers," in *Germanisch-romanisch Monatsschrift*, 20 (1970), pp. 412–25.

Voisine, Jacques (JV), "L'influence de *La Nouvelle Héloïse* sur la génération de *Werther*," in *Etudes Germaniques*, 5 (1950), pp. 120–33.

Vosskamp, Wilhelm (WV), "Dialogische Vergegenwörtigung beim Schreiben und Lesen. Zur Poetik des Briefromans im 18. Jahrhundert," in *Deutsche Vierteljahrsschrift*, 45 (1971), pp. 80–116.

Weber, Heinz-Dieter (HDW), "Stella oder die Negativität des Happy End," iin *Rezeptionsgeschichte oder Wirkungsästhetik* (Stuttgart, 1978), pp. 142–67.

Winter, Hans-Gerhard (HW), "Gesellschaft und Kultur . . . " and "Antiklassizismus: Sturm und Drang," in *Geschichte der deutschen Literatur vom 18. Jahrhundert bis zur Gegenwart*, ed. V. Zmegac (Königstein, 1979), pp. 175–256.

E. Horizon Structure and Dialogicity

The revival of literary hermeneutics that began in the 1960s has moved a particualr concept to the forefront of methodological reflection, a concept that the historical and philological disciplines have always taken for granted when interpreting texts, but which they have seldom dealt with in terms of its specifics, and not at all in terms of method. The concept in question is that of the horizon insofar as it—as historical marker and, at the same time, the necessary condition for the possibility of experiential knowledge—constitutes all structures of meaning related to human action and primary modes of comprehending the world.

The effort expended in comprehending the historical distance between the alien horizon of the text and the horizon of the interpreter did not appear problematic as long as the notion of the mind generated by German idealism or the later ideal of exactitude generated by positivism guaranteed direct access to an interpretation. On the other hand, the historicist model recognized that the interpreter was bound to a specific site and, thus, made the qualitative difference between the past and the present a hermeneutic problem. It allowed one to believe the problem of comprehending an alien horizon had been solved if one's own horizon—the interpreter's interests or biases—were bracketed. This cut the work of historical understanding in half so to speak, limiting it to the disinterested reconstruction of past life within the horizon of its historical differentness. A renewed critique of historicism, pioneered by Hans-Georg Gadamer in particular, has fully exposed the—no doubt quite fruitful—objectivist illusion underlying this sort of one-sided hermeneutics. It has also demonstrated that a prior event cannot be understood without looking at its consequences, nor a work of art without investigating its impact. Furthermore, a history of the reception and interpretation of an event or a work from the past really provides the first occasion for understanding it in terms of a multiplicity of meanings that could not have been foreseen by its contemporaries. If the original horizon of life in an earlier time were not always already contained within our own, later, horizon, historical understanding would not be possible. After all, such understanding can have a grasp of things past and their differentness only when and to the degree that the interpreter knows how to differentiate between his own and the alien horizon. The work of historical understanding requires a conscious, fully implemented mediation between the two horizons. Whoever believes that it is possible to arrive at the other horizon, that of some prior time, by simply disregarding one's own inevitably introduces subjective criteria concerning selection, perspective, and evaluation into his supposedly objective reconstruction of the past. Such criteria, without which no context of meaning can come into being, remain inscrutable prejudices as long as one's own preconceptions are not rendered transparent. Understood as anticipatory moves, they must also remain open to the corrections suggested by the answers our questions have elicited from the sources or texts under study.

The renewed interest in historical knowledge—sparked by the triumphant advance and the aporias of the structuralist method during the 1960s—distinguishes itself from classical historicism primarily through a methodological awareness of the historicity of understanding itself. This mode of understanding requires one to take up the task of mediating between present and past horizons, thereby meeting the expectation that one again fully activate the hermeneutic triad constituted by understanding, interpretation, and application. Once this new awareness was established, the concept of the horizon became the fundamental category of philosophical as well as literary and historical hermeneutics. It emerged as the problem confronted when trying to understand something alien despite the alterity of past and present horizons of apprehension, or of one's own and that of a culturally different world, to understand it, that is, as the problem of aesthetic experience that arises during the reconstruction of the horizons of expectation evoked when a literary work is read by its contemporaries and by later readers; as a problem concerning the social function of literature when an effort is made to mediate between the horizons of aesthetic and life-world apprehension; as the problem posed by changes in horizon that come about when teleological or evolutionary notions of tradition are desubstantialized and historical processes, including those in the arts, are enmeshed in the dialectics of appropriation, selection, preservation, and rejuvenation; as the problem generated by a critique of ideology, when it attempts to elucidate the latent horizons within which disguised interests and repressed needs operate, a critique that, today, makes our humanistic confidence in the transparency of communication about art seem rather dubious.

This sketch of the history of the problem ought to be expanded to include other disciplines, but here I can only point out a few recent efforts to examine the hermeneutic assumptions underlying certain theoretical constructs. All these efforts have either explicitly or implicitly brought the concept of the horizon into play: as a thematic field in the theory of relevance developed by the sociology of knowledge (Alfred Schütz); as the frame of reference allowing actions and observations to acquire meaning in the theory of science (Karl Popper); as the presuppositions of speech in the logical analysis of language (according to Gottlob Frege); in generative semantics (Herbert Brekle) and linguistic pragmatics (Dieter Wunderlich); as the isotropic level in structural semantics (Algirdas Greimas); as cultural code in semiotics (Jurij Lotman); as situating context in speech-act theory (Karlheinz Stierle); as the intertext in structural stylistics (Michael Riffaterre); and, finally, but no less significant, as the linguistic play in analytic philosophy that, in Wittgenstein's late work, enables all comprehension of meaning, and, in this sense, does what the logical form of a precise, world-reflecting language was supposed to do.[1]

My own contribution to this historical shift within the disciplines can be found in *Toward an Aesthetic of Reception*, where I first put the analysis of horizons to work in literary hermeneutics. If I return to that text here, it is in order to correct the one-sidedness and fill in the holes that became apparent as this program was put to the test. That as I do so I will leave many of the questions raised by my critics unanswered is clear to me. But I believe I can now serve our common interests better if I do not lay out the theoretical and polemical aspects of the earlier theoretical discussion in full here, and instead provide a résumé of the instances in which my own interpretive work has suggested a variety of new approaches to the problem of mediating between horizons. As of today, no one can claim to have found an adequate solution to this problem, so it seems to me that it would be worthwhile to examine the ways in which the history of the concept and of the problem itself can contribute to understanding our preconceptions concerning the *Horizon*.

1. Understanding and interpreting as acts of mediation between horizons

The etymological meaning of "horizon," derived from the Greek *horizein* (to delimit, to cut off), is the limit of the field of vision. In his interpretation of Nietzsche, Heidegger provides the most striking account of the comprehensive shift in meaning that the term has undergone: "Aim, view, field of vision, mean here both the sight beheld and seeing, in a sense that is determined from out of the Greek, but that has undergone the change of *idea* from *eidos* to *perceptio*."[2] At the beginning, in Plato's simile, the horizon stands for the orbit of the sun, the light of which reveals the suprasensual world to be the world of true being. At the end the horizon no longer sheds its own light, but is, according to Nietzsche, "only the point of view posited in the value-positing of the will to power."[3] Patristic and Scholastic theology understood the horizon to be the divide between *mundus sensibilis* and *mundus intelligibilis*. Man was, therefore, a citizen of two worlds, standing "on the horizon," the frontier between temporal and eternal things; or, as Thomas sees it, man, because he is both spiritual and physical in nature, has within him the frontier between the two worlds. Thus, one can so construe the shift in the meaning of the term within the Greek/occidental tradition that, at the beginning, horizon is the name given to the location of the soul in the cosmic hierarchy but, at the end, means the self-generated, human experience of the world delimited by the horizon. "Man no longer is but instead has a horizon, one that he himself defines through reflection on his own consciousness."[4]

The partiality of human experience is informed by the concept of the horizon to an equal degree in the older and the modern contexts, but by different circumstances. The act of looking at (regarding) something necessarily involves looking away from (disregarding) something else—this is an element in the horizon structure of all experience of the world. If the move toward recognition of the suprasensual world in Platonic understanding at the same time necessitated a turning away from sensorial phenomena, so too, the sense perception allowed in modern understanding is able to perceive something as something only after it has ordered (regarded) that which comes within its field of vision from a certain point of view—thereby disregarding other perspectives. Prior to the beginning of the modern era Guillaume d'Auvergne had already located the epistemological element in the concept of the horizon: the horizon is the circle that divides two hemispheres, of which one is, of necessity, absent from view. The horizon—that which is delimited by our gaze (*finitor visus nostri*)—can, of course, be either fixed and unalterable (that is, the permanently closed frontier between sensorial and intelligible knowledge) or movable and changing (that is, a unique and momentary field of vision that, as experience moves on, opens out onto an endless succession of new horizons). This second definition actually only designates the horizon structure underlying modern experience of the world. However remarkable it may seem, an observation that has no doubt always been available in the praxis of life—that every current horizon gives way to new horizons as one moves along or travels—found no entry into the epistemology of the classical period or the Middle Ages. But the idea of an immovable, world-encompassing horizon survived the Copernican revision in the legendary form: the mythologem of that divide where the heavens meet the earth.

From a hermeneutic point of view, the divide between the closed horizon of expectations of innerworldly knowledge and the open horizon of onmoving experience corresponds to the divide between understanding as the recognition and interpretation of a professed or revealed truth on the one hand, and understanding as the search for or investigation of a possible meaning on the other. In the first instance, the act of comprehension is always unquestioningly taken for granted in the interpretation – conflation of the text's and the interpreter's horizons takes place naively, as if the separation in time could only result in a growing distance, and not in an intervening alienation. Basically speaking, understanding means nothing other than translation in this case, and a grammatical interpretation is sufficient to derive the authentic meaning of an obscure text, or an allegorical interpretation that actualizes the text in terms of contemporary understanding, thereby wiping out the alterity of that which is past, and revivifying the one, undiminished truth of the canonical text. In the second instance, however, the recognition of something that has been previously understood can no longer guarantee correct understanding. As soon as historical consciousness begins to uncover the qualitative difference that exists in the temporal distance between past and present life, the mediation between the text's horizon and that of the interpreter must transpire reflectively. The identity of the truth embodied in the text can then be recovered only when it is sought in the change in the horizon of historical experience – and comprehended as an onmoving, and always only partial, concretization of meaning.

Since the beginning of the modern era the metaphysical horizon has disappeared and the astronomical distinction between the visible and the true horizon has become crucial for any critical assessment of the limits of human knowledge. The modern paradigm, which proposes an understanding that is always only partial, had its beginning in a theory of knowledge dealing with nature, and then spread to experience of history, to aesthetics, and to anthropology. Leibniz, who was the first to give systematic expression to the question of the *Horizon de la doctrine humaine*, had also already explained the difference between rational and historical truth on the basis of the temporal limitation of man's consciousness to the horizon of his current situation. As far as literary hermeneutics is concerned, it is significant that Baumgarten's aesthetics introduced the concept of the horizon in order to distinguish not only between the *horizon logicus* and the *horizon aestheticus*, but also the higher and lower cognitive capacities. He thereby established the basic premise for the independence of aesthetic apprehension from the theory and practice of human action. For Baumgarten, the aesthetic horizon is also the locus on which the claims of the individual emerge and begin to develop their own horizon: "in aestheticis . . . quilibet suum horizontem habet, et potest aliquid esse multorum in horizonte aesthetico, quod tamen non est intra meum" (§149).[5] If this formulation restricts recognition of the particualr horizon of individual apprehension (apparently tying it to nongeneralizable aesthetic judgment), the aesthetic horizon nonetheless has the capacity for openness, and is free to narrow as well as to grow. This marks the beginning of aesthetic education. With regard to Kant's comprehensive conceptual explanation, one needs to mention here only that the logical and aesthetic horizons were supplemented by the practical, thereby creating a triad that is defined and differentiated in terms of the interests espoused by understanding, feeling, and morality. The result is that the "absolute and universal horizon" that defines the limits of human knowledge in the *Critique of Pure Reason* is distinguished from the "particular and limited private horizon," which is "dependent on empirical and special considerations such as age, sex, class, life-style, etc.,"[6] a plurality of particular horizons that anticipate the theory of "subuniverses" propounded by the sociology of knowledge![7]

The next development in the history of the concept of the horizon, one that has shaped the apprehension of history and society right up to our own day, has already been dealt with by Reinhart Koselleck. If it is true for the modern era as a whole that "it was first understood to be a new era after keen anticipation began to distance itself more and more from all that had been experienced previously,"[8] it is equally true that along with the unexpected and radical political changes after 1789, the self-alienation that developed in democratic societies as the industrial revolution progressed, and the constant revision that occurred in technology and the natural sciences, a rupture in continuity occurred that drove the frontiers of experience and the horizon of expectations further apart than ever before. Of course, at the heart of historical knowledge has always been an awareness that experience and expectations do not coincide, and that the future cannot simply be derived from the past. Koselleck defines the temporal structure of historical experience—in which the "presentness of the past is necessarily other than the presentness of the future"—on the basis of a fundamental "asymmetry between experience and expectation" that must be accounted for in anthropological terms (pp. 355ff.). Whereas experience can organize the past into a spatial and perspectival whole, expectation is directed at the open horizon of individual, not yet realized possibilities, and is thus open to the incursion of unexpected events that break through the closed horizon of earlier experience and found new expectations that will themselves be corrected through experience and are themselves able to engender new perspectives.[9] Prior to the onset of the modern era (and even in the rustic world of the eighteenth century), the asymmetry between the closed horizon of the past and the open horizon of future experience was offset by the Christian doctrine of divine order, providence, and the last judgment, which placed unalterable restrictions on the horizon of expectations.[10] The history of the technical innovations that, in the Middle Ages, were either suppressed or could only be put to use much later provides a striking demonstration of the manner in which these premises of the Christian faith could insulate everyday apprehension of the world from new experience by linking everything related to the future to the truth revealed by the past. In contrast, nothing is more characteristic of the change in the apprehension of time and history in the modern era than the newly established rule (validated by the as yet unimpaired faith in progress and the possibility of emancipating humanity) that "previous experience cannot be put forward as a means of objecting to the otherness of the future" (p. 364).

Koselleck, who presents the asymmetry between experience and expectation as a metahistorical mode of apprehending history, does not overlook the fact that it had remained hidden within the closed horizon of Christian expectations about the future, and that, historically, it first became an epistemological problem during the epochal transformation that took place on the threshold of the nineteenth century. It is only since this radical shift took place that history as a whole has been apprehended as unique, that past and future have been looked at as qualitatively different, and that there has been a need for compensatory paradigms with which to come to grips with them. Among these, "conceptual movements" with specific prognosticative horizons (e.g., republicanism, democracy, and communism) are especially important. It follows from Koselleck's thesis that historical hermeneutics has a pressing task on its hands: regrounding the possibility of historical knowledge at a time when the gap opened up between expectation and experience has made learning from history—a history that had proved to be unpredictable and nonrepeatable—untenable, and after the regressive dialectic of enlightenment has made progress, now understood as the cunning of reason, seem illusory.

The result for literary hermeneutics has been that the aesthetics of innovation, with its literary-historical paradigm of an ongoing emergence of new horizons of expectation, no longer stands as the ultimate and real problem underlying aesthetic experience. This model is no less one-sided in its view of the formation of aesthetic experience in modern literature than is its opposite, which, in linking all interpretations to the original horizon of signification of a text or to the authoritative pretensions of the tradition, also fails to do justice to the norm-constituting achievements of older literature. The new as such, that which would do away with all prior experience, is no more available to apprehension than is the "other" as such—an other that, as a manifestation of a far-off past, can no longer be gotten at with anything belonging to the present. If "experience and expectation" are so entwined in one another as a conceptual pair—both in the apprehension of history and in the horizon of aesthetic experience—that "no expectation [can exist] without experience, and no experience without expectation" (p. 352), then, even after the radically jolting events of modern history, and the radical break with tradition in modern art, the onset of the new and the other must be understood from the vantage point of the old and familiar.

Thus, whether in terms of the continuity of tradition formation prior to the advent of the modern era, or in terms of the discontinuity embodied in the contemporary decline of the tradition, the difference between experience and expectation leads us to the problem of the shift of horizons. A discussion of this problem can take as its starting point yet another turn in the history of the concept of the horizon, one negotiated by Husserl in *Experience and Judgment* (1939), further developed by Heidegger and Gadamer, and finally summed up by Günther Buck.[11]

Phenomenological analysis of the horizon structure of all apprehension reveals "all that is already involved in the experience of an object, i.e., in this apparent ultimacy and originality of a primitive grasping."[12] Every experience has its horizon of expectation: all consciousness exists as a consciousness of something, and thus, always also exists within the horizon of already formulated and still forthcoming experiences. This definition indicates that the horizon structure of experience is rooted in the temporality of consciousness; it asserts that the experience of an object is conditioned equally by knowledge and lack of knowledge. Every perception presupposes "the empty horizon of familiar unfamiliarity" (p. 38). Experience is formed in the functional swing from anticipation (preconception) to fulfillment or disappointment of the anticipation. Even the new that is unexpected is "new in the context of a certain knowledge";[13] within the horizon of disappointed expectation, it becomes something that can be experienced, something that opens a new horizon, and thus demonstrates that "every actual horizon . . . [has] within it a system of potential horizons" (p. 57). It is important to note that, in this description of the shift of horizons involved in the process of formulating experience, the anticipation that guides experience is not a purely formal a priori (as it is for Kant), but brings with it an anticipation of possible experience, the content of which remains "vague and general." It is precisely "this undogmatic trait that distinguishes correctly understood anticipation from mere prejudice, which claims for itself the validity of real experience" (pp. 51–52). Under these conditions, a shift in horizons can be understood as a "move from the narrower and more particular to the broader and more general horizon," a move that allows no negative instance of experience to subvert the whole of the signifying structure, "since, in contrast to the hypothesis, which, because of its particularity, can be invalidated as a whole, the horizon as a whole remains untouched, thanks to the vague and general nature of the negative instances that it enables" (p. 55). The history of the process of canon formation and transformation in the arts confirms Buck's thesis insofar as the new work of art—even when, as in the modern era, it provocatively negates all previous art—still presupposes the horizon of the tradition as the instance of understanding that has been negated and, far from simply doing away with the past, realigns the art of the past within the newly opened horizon, reclassifying it in contemporary terms, and often even finding in it previously unrecognized significance.

Although Husserl's explication of the horizon structure of experience is especially serviceable as a means of understanding the process of aesthetic perception and the constitution of meaning in terms of shifts in the horizons of reading,[14] it still is in need of further development when attempting to understand a text whose horizon of signification is no longer immediately available, but instead has become alien due to its distance in time. In this case, the false assumption of immediacy—the supposed timeless presence of all classical art—must be recognized for what it is, and the naive alignment of a historically distant text with contemporary expectations about meaning avoided. In addition, the critical demands of literary hermeneutics must be met by consciously unfolding the tension between the text and the present. "This is why it is part of the hermeneutic approach to project a historical horizon that is different from the horizon of the present."[15] As is well known, Gadamer developed his "principle of effective history" after recovering this fundamental hermeneutic problem. The particular source of this development is the insight that a "positive and productive possibility of understanding" lies in temporal distance itself (p. 264). Distance in time is to be put to use and not—as historicism would have it—overcome, that is, abolished through a one-sided transplanting of the self into the spirit of the past. The horizons of the past and the present must necessarily be contrasted before they are fused if the text in its otherness is to serve as a means of appraising the interpreter's prejudices and, finally, of allowing the interpretation to become an experience that changes the person experiencing it (p. 92). This seems to be—or is my understanding of—the upshot of the chapter entitled "The Principle of Effective History," although other explanations have been suggested,[16] explanations that fault Gadamer because his "fusion of horizons," conceived of as the "unification of two image-fields in a new field of vision," is an anticipatory category in his hermeneutic theory. This "ocular metaphoric" may indicate an ultimately passive notion of understanding, thereby revealing that his primary interest is actually in maintaining the validity and continuity of the classical cultural tradition.[17] If this is the case, the self-understanding proposed in Gadamer's hermeneutics, oriented as it is toward a history of being, and insofar as it would trace all understanding back to "entering into the process of transmitting the tradition," would negate the basic thrust of his theory of the historical and dialogic nature of understanding—the very theory whose task it is to discover the historical difference generated by temporal distance and then, through question and answer, to retrieve the text from this past, bringing it into the living presence of conversation. The contradiction between contrasting horizons and fusing them, between an active and a passive definition of understanding in *Truth and Method*, seems, therefore, to be obvious. To resolve it would entail opting either for a hermeneutics that mediates the tradition, and that attempts to retrospectively demonstrate the validity of the truth claim made by that which has been handed down, or for a hermeneutics of historicity that would take on the task of producing a dialogic exchange of understanding in the fullest sense—a dialogue between the text and the interpreter, between the tradition and the present, that is open to the future.[18]

Regardless of whether Gadamer is correctly assumed to have left this contradiction unresolved in *Truth and Method*, the discussion of hermeneutics in the 1970s was enriched because of it.[19] This is also true of the reception aesthetic I supported. It considered the differentiation of horizons—the mapping of the alien horizon—an indispensable phase in the process of understanding (p. 273), a phase that allowed for the inscription of the past in the current horizon of understanding, tested interpretive procedures as a means of reconstructing the contemporary horizon of expectation, and tried to reestablish the dialogic reciprocity between the text and the present, the interpreted and the interpreter, through the interplay of question and answer. The other direction in which interest has been moving can be found in Buck's recent attempt to construct a theory of action and culture by drawing on Gadamer's earlier work. Buck starts with the premise (one that I share) that "in hermeneutic praxis, while apprehending something about a different existence, being made alien by its historical distance from us, we also apprehend something about ourselves."[20] The gap between an alien horizon and our own is unbridgeable as far as Buck is concerned, since understanding in all its variegated forms has a uniform structure. It "explicates implicit meaning," thus defining hermeneutics as the "making aware of a meaning that was not previously available to consciousness" (p. 30). This definition has the advantage of enabling meaning to be understood even when the active agent is not at all conscious of the meaning that is revealed through the completion of an action. The limits of the definition obviously lie there where the alien meaning of an action *cannot* be rendered transparent merely by making that which is still in the realm of the unconscious conscious. This can be the case when the other's action is not a prereflective "presentation of self" (p. 25) because the unconscious meaning of such an action has been obscured by repressed interests or drives; or when a historical event is the result of the heterogeneity of the various goals of various subjects, and, thus, not "the presentation of an internally dominant meaning" (p. 25); or when the resistance of alien meaning cannot be overcome through recourse to that which is familiar in the alien because the original horizon has been conditioned by a preconception that the interpreter no longer shares with the interpreted. For example, the action of the Homeric hero, who, despite all modern psychology, is motivated by the presence of mutually competitive divine powers, certainly cannot be grasped by making one aware of something of which one was not previously conscious. At best, it can made available to contemporary understanding by alienating one's own preconceptions through a contrastive reconstruction of the alien horizon of meaning, or perhaps through modern allegoresis, that is, through the recovery of alien meaning by transposing it and giving it topical presence.

Thus, in practice, the reconstruction of an alien horizon of meaning cannot normally (as Buck would have it) "take the form of an initial anticipation in which the interpreter's own horizon is assimilated to the horizon of the interpreted" (p. 58). The meaning that a historically distant text can recapture for us does not emerge solely from the folds of the original horizon. It stems to an equal degree from the later horizon of experience belonging to the interpreter. Clearly the ongoing process of constituting meaning cannot be based on the mere negation of expectations revealed by a change in the horizon of experience. And by itself, the disappointment of an anticipation is not sufficient to reveal the folds of a possible meaning that remained unnoticed by the author and his contemporaries in the original horizon of a literary work (p. 57). Since such folds can first be discovered only through the interpreter's later horizon, and can be expounded on only by assimilating them in a new interpretation, this horizon ought not simply be erased by aligning it with the earlier horizon when an anticipatory assumption proves unfounded. Instead, the content of the horizon of one's own experience must be brought into play, and mediated through the alien horizon in order to arrive at the new horizon of another interpretation. This dialectical description of the historicity of understanding intends basically the same thing as does Heidegger's hermeneutic maxim that a correct elucidation must not only draw on the substance of text, but "must also, without presuming, imperceptibly give to the text something out of its own substance." This also means that "while a right elucidation never understands the text better than the author understood it, it does surely understand it differently. Yet this difference must be of such a kind as to touch upon the Same toward which the elucidated text is thinking."[21]

This leads us to the question of whether philosophical hermeneutics has at this point also solved—or merely hidden—the problem that literary hermeneutics finds so pressing today: is self-understanding in a matter and more particularly, the matter of a text, the prototype for all understanding, or only a fundamental possibility that can be arrayed with other equally original possibilities for self-understanding? This question leads us into the discussion that arose in literary criticism at the time of the appearance of Mikhail M. Bakhtin's later, even more widely read, books. His *Aesthetics of Verbal Creation*,[22] which develops the dialogic principle in terms of the notion of truth, the constitution of consciousness, the function of language, the genres of speech, and, in particular, literature, provided the impetus for an interdisciplinary discussion whose results I have reviewed elsewhere from my own perspective.[23] I return to these matters here in order to sketch out both the actuality of the problem of dialogic understanding and its scientific and historical genesis.

2. Dialogic understanding in literary communication

The new interest that aesthetic theory has shown in the question of how art is apprehended (art's communicative function, which surfaced recently as a much discussed problem; its apprehension in other historical worlds, and in other cultures; and the possibility that understanding can make art available to us both in its distance and its alienness) has once again brought to light the circularity of literary communication and, in addition, its dialogic character.

Just as the producer is always a recipient as soon as he begins to write, so too the interpreter must bring himself into play as reader when he wishes to enter into a dialogue with the literary tradition. It is not merely the conversational partners that constitute a dialogue. The willingness to recognize and acknowledge the other in his otherness also plays a role. This is all the more true when the other is represented by a text that no longer speaks directly to us. Literary understanding first becomes dialogic when the alterity of the text is sought out and acknowledged before the horizon of one's own expectations – with the result that instead of attempting a naive fusion of horizons, one's own expectations will be corrected and expanded through the experience of the other.

Recognition and acknowledgment of the dialogicity of literary communication runs up against the problem of alterity in many areas: that between producer and recipient, between the past of a text and the present of the recipient, between different cultures. Hermeneutic reflection and semiotic analysis compete today as methods for coming to grips with the alterity of texts that lie distant from us. Neither can lay claim to any prior guarantee of understanding, however; neither the continuity of meaning in effective history nor the universality of semiotic/logical systems is able to offer such a guarantee. One must remember Schleiermacher's axiom: nonunderstanding is not the exception when dealing with alien discourse. One must expect this condition to obtain wherever an alien discourse comes into contact with one's own. At this moment, literary hermeneutics is faced with a further question. Given a text's alterity, what, if anything, can enable us to bridge this gap and penetrate its alienness and silence? As has already been suggested, the utterly alien would be just as incomprehensible as the utterly new.

When approached in this manner, the problem of alterity cannot simply be dismissed with the assertion that the literary work somehow discloses itself thanks to the effect of literary distance, that is, through pure contemplation on the part of the beholder. Bakhtin's demand that understanding be grounded in the "dialogicity of the word" takes a step beyond contemplative hermeneutics here. If, in a literary dialogue between eras, self-apprehension becomes possible through apprehending the other, then aesthetically mediated alterity must contain something that can be found, something that is recognizable even in that which is alien. The current, very acute interest in developing a historical anthropology can probably also be explained in terms of this question. Although until recently looking for "anthropological constants" was frowned upon, today, unquestionable validity has once again been accorded an anthropology that proposes a theory of human needs that is historical, and an archaeology of knowledge that reconstructs the elementary discriminatory and orienting episteme of earlier life-worlds. The great advantage of literary communication in this case is that through the medium of art, the shared understanding enabled by an object and the responsive self-understanding enabled by the other achieve an ideal transparency. Thus, literary hermeneutics now finds itself in the fortunate position of realizing that its subject matter – human apprehension as it arises from productive and receptive interaction with art – is by its very nature most able to render communicable that which religious ritual concealed from the noninitiate, and what the political or juridical document suppresses or passes over in silence. It is a peculiarity of the aesthetic object that it both preserves and discloses the historically other, since it not only allows subjective experience of the world to be represented, but, in the space opened by art, also renders this experience understandable as an apprehension of the self in an apprehension of the other. This allows us to repose the question as to what dialogic understanding has to offer, and what its limits are when trying to make art and literature in their temporal or spatial, historical or cultural alterity amenable to knowledgeable appropriation—thereby drawing them into the ongoing dialogue generated by aesthetic communication.

Theology—as Walter Magass argued in relation to Franz Rosenzweig and Martin Buber[24]—can offer the theory of speech genres or speech acts practical knowledge that would illuminate aspects of the problem of dialogic understanding that are often ignored. Dialogicity manifests itself as a particular trait of the Christian religion—the verbal rapport of I and Thou between God and man. This I-Thou relationship is constituted as early as Genesis 3:9, where God addresses and summons man: "Adam, where art thou?" The Old Testament exchange between God and man that begins here continues to unfold primarily in the vocative. Man as an individual is awakened from among the dumb things of the world when his name is pronounced. But the vocative can also elevate man to the level of a confederate. This dimension of address and response distinguishes the Christian origins of dialogue from the "idealism of generative concepts," which is at home in a monologic world. In the Bible, God's first monologue ("And God said, Let there be light") is incorporated in the narrative of the creation story, thus allowing one to derive a theological triad of speech acts: *verbal exchange*, the mode of revelation, moves between *narrative*, the mode of creation, and song or *hymn*, the mode of praise, with the result that, at the third stage, *I* and *Thou* are overtaken by the liturgical paradigm of the *We*, and verbal exchange melts into song and the silence of Sabbath stillness. It remains to be seen how this theological triad is represented beyond the Bible in the operations of the various types of speech—whether a relational order like that found in the order of the components in Genesis 1 is suitable for all narrative, whether the dialogue, by its very nature, reaches beyond or breaks through fixed orders, and which other ways of opening and closing a dialogue are antithetical to the dialogue between God and man, which begins in the vocative and ends in complete silence ("the divided must go on talking, the united can be silent; man is silent because all is said and done"—but man can also remain silent as a means of protesting!).

Theological hermeneutics knows both the ideal form of verbal exchange that surmounts itself in fulfilled communication, and forms of decaying dialogicity. Christian dialogue, which uses the act of supping together—taking, giving, sharing—as a means of alluding to the perfecting of the world, can deteriorate into an un-Christian debate about dogma, into a "religious dialogue" ("since the participants were only after meanings"), or can turn from an apologia (which in its baldest form turns the heretical opponent's system of invective back against him) into a crude refusal to converse. The progressive dogmatization of the *ecclesia militans* also manifests itself in subtler instances of refusal to converse: by proscribing inquiry, whether *curiositas* or *novitas*, it anchored itself in catechisms that had fixed answers for all admissible questions, and asserted itself in a (no longer discussable) profession of faith that "[has] a residue of political intolerance and reserve, a residue of incompatibility with the dialectic." Must it be the case (one might now ask the theologian), or is it only explicable historically in terms of the development of Christian apologetics and its concomitant risks, that the profession of faith (strengthened by the first-person form of the text spoken in unison) here becomes monologic even though the speech act of bearing witness in no way necessitates the end of dialogue in the life-world, and actually often initiates or reinitiates such dialogue? Are there also dialogically open forms of religious profession?

From the theological point of view, the magistral discussion, which is generally defined by the superiority of the first voice over the second, the teacher over the student, requires a third voice — an absent presence, the authoritative third party whose participation can be represented by an ancient text or by the binding teachings of Jesus. In its New Testament form, the magistral discussion has four essential phases: the *conversatio*, which frequently links the discussion to conditions of place; the *quaestio*, showing want or helplessness to which the teacher can respond by giving presence to the past or by delivering the questioner from an overpowering past; the *interpretatio*, in which the rabbi must interpret both texts and situation; the *communio*, in which the rabbi-interpreter becomes the giver of gifts, or establishes agreement through a magistral statement. Literary hermeneutics has, up to now, paid little attention to the magistral dialogue. A closer examination would show that it is not simply a repressive technique of canon formation, but a means of formulating experience (e.g., through the learning that takes place in a question-and-answer sequence).

The step from the magistral dialogue of the New Testament sort to the Socratic form is a rather large one. In the first instance the discussion is guided throughout by the teacher, and an authoritatively prescribed meaning is concretized in an interpretation of the current situation; in the second, a free-floating discussion moves in roundabout fashion from question to answer until it finally produces a meaning that is the result of a mutual inquiry, and that emerges out of a knowledge of one's lack of knowledge. This ideal opposition between types would no doubt manifest an interesting degree of relativity in actual practice (to what extent is the Socratic dialogue, too, guided by the primacy of the question and the order in which the "right questions" are posed? what degree of openness can the New Testament dialogue reclaim by allowing the pupil the freedom to ask any question, and by obliging the teacher to interpret the scripture on the basis of the present situation, thereby reinterpreting it?). The effective power of these two competing forms of dialogue is clear, but it seems to me that the history of their reception has hardly been touched upon.

As long as it remained in the grips of an aesthetics of the autonomous work of art, the *philosophy of art* dealt with dialogicity primarily in terms of an elevated dialogue between authors who, ascending to the highest realms of poetry, rose above the traditional foothills of mediocrity into the timeless, opening one's eyes to the genesis of great works, which could be understood in terms of a dialectic of creation and imitation, of the formation and revision of the aesthetic canon. To include the receiver of literature in the dialogue maintained by its producers, to recognize his participation in the constitution of meaning, and to ask how the work of art can be something closed on itelf and, at the same time, open to interpretation requires a retreat from contemplative hermeneutics and its substantialist conception of the work. Gábor Bonyhai recently introduced into discussion a little known, but very informative, document concerning the movement toward our modern aesthetic theory.[25] His work focuses on an unjustly forgotten predecessor of contemporary hermeneutics in art and literature, Leo Popper, and fully demonstrates Popper's importance for the philosophy of art and literature by showing how his theory of "double misunderstanding" paved the way for more recent theoretical insights. One personal and historical reason for his having been forgotten is the success of his contemporary, friend, and opponent, Georg Lukács, whose *Heidelberger Philosophie der Kunst* (written in 1912–14, but first published in 1974) was admittedly a reworking of Popper's ideas, but who parted ways with Popper soon thereafter regarding one very important point.

Their common point of departure had been the desire to move beyond divinatory hermeneutics, the aesthetics of expressivity, and the theory of empathy or identification.[26] Aloys Riegl's notion of a "will to art" that was supposed to enter the work in toto as an expression of the artist's intention, and was to serve as the norm for measuring the adequacy of the observer's understanding, delineates most clearly the position they called into question. As an alternative, Popper proposed a new hermeneutics, one that wished to make inadequate understanding the prerequisite and characteristic feature of all understanding in art. Popper's theory of "double misunderstanding" is an aesthetic of nonidentity. It arises from the insight that the work of art does not function monologically to reveal a transcendent meaning that subsumes both the will of the artist and the understanding of the observer. Between the author's intention and the completed work and its meaning for the observer occurs a double hiatus that makes the constitution of meaning an endless process that operates between the production and reception of a work. In this same period, but without knowing of Popper's work, Paul Valéry championed a fully analogous conception of the "open work": the product of the author's aesthetic activity is never fully completed by him; the completed work is, rather, an illusion of reception, an illusion that is also the point of departure for a necessarily inadequate interpretation of the work ("mes vers ont le sens qu'on leur prête").[27] This interpretation is, in turn, the starting point for an unending process of productive understanding. Given this concurrence, Bonyhai can justifiably assert that Popper's theory marks a beginning of the developments that lead from a monologic aesthetics of the autonomous work to the currency of dialogic understanding, to effective historical hermeneutics, and the aesthetic of reception.

Lukács's movement toward a "synthesis of sociology and aesthetics," which even in its later, materialist mode retained an element of the Platonic in its theory of reflection, is already evident in his initial use of Popper's thesis. Lukács interprets the double misunderstanding as a "duality consisting of the work of art, which rises in solitary splendor above life, and man's wistful, intimate relation to it." He separates creative activity from the merely receptive, and ultimately tries to maintain a separation between the historicity and the timelessness of the work of art. Popper's as yet unpublished "Dialog über Kunst" places both this beginning difference between Lukács and Popper, and the crossroads in aesthetic theory they embody, in an interesting light.

Their dialogue begins with the introduction of the opposition between the open and the closed work. Lukács draws from this distinction two fundamental possibilities for art—the representation of the condition of desire (Rodin's *Paolo et Francesca*) or that of fulfillment (Rodin's *Le Baiser*). The theory of double misunderstanding, which Popper tied to two moments of nonidentity in productive and receptive understanding of a work of art, is thus read as two different types of artistic works. This also relativizes the theory historically, since from the beginning Lukács's distinction (the dichotomy between the ultimate or limited and the penultimate or unlimited) implies a historical/typological opposition between the classical and the romantic conceptions of art. Popper replied that the distinction between closed and open would have to prove its worth in terms of the absoluteness of form, and Lukács countered by turning to the classical principle of the adequacy of form and content (a notion he regularly used later as well), and placed work having an open form in the contemporary avant-garde. Only the most recent art is supposed to have brought this new technique, "this breaking off, this leaving-one-in-the-lurch," into play. Popper's answer reveals the romantic substratum (the unfulfilled as the really perfect) in Lukács's notion of the modern as fragmentary. He counters this notion with the thesis that the perfect is no longer an ontological quality to which the work gives expression. Instead, it arises from man's need for perfection, a perfection that he is obliged to fashion for himself despite the resistance of the material, and, ultimately, that of nature, which offers "only moments of transition, never the closed itself."

At this point, the dialogue diverges into two diametrically opposed definitions of the work of art, Lukács's formulation, "unfinished in its finishedness," and Popper's, "finished in its unfinishedness." Popper dissolves the initial distinction from within: the work of art, is, in its unfinishedness, *finished*, since "art makes the penultimate the ultimate," which is to say that "through art, we take from nature that which it takes from us through the fact of our being alive: eternity." For Popper art is acosmic, it is "the human formulation of things"; the work of art is finished in its *unfinishedness*, since it first achieves closure—be it in itself open or not—at the moment of the receiver's participation: "the ultimate conclusion of any given work of art is the receiver." On the other hand, Lukács maintains his differentiation by giving it a transcendental justification. The work of art is *unfinished* in its finishedness because "it brings the temporal into relation with the timeless," which can also mean that "the question is our absolute," since it presupposes the "great answer" to which man is yoked without knowing it. Thus, the new theory of the open work brings the hermeneutics of art to a crossroads: the work of art, which for Popper opens out to the receiver, points aesthetics in the direction of the dialogicity of aesthetic communication; the work of art that, for Lukács, opens out into the "transcendental," reclaims for aesthetics the Platonic reassurance of a timeless perfection that, in its monologic truth, leaves nothing for the receiver but the role of contemplative understanding.

With regard to *philosophical hermeneutics*, a brief reminder will suffice. Gadamer designated dialogicity as the prerequisite for all understanding, whether of an alien discourse or a distant text. According to Gadamer, the Platonic dialogue provides the hermeneutic model in which understanding is constituted not as a monologic interpretation of, but as a dialogic inquiry into, meaning, and in which the question has the particular capacity to bring experience into the open: "Thus, the dialectic of question and answer always precedes the dialectic of interpretation. It is what determines understanding as an event."[28] To understand something therefore means to understand something as an answer, and, more precisely, to test one's own view against that of the other, through question and answer. This holds good for understanding distant texts as well as for understanding the discourse of the other. One part of the hermeneutic task consists of bringing the text that has become alien because of its distance in time "back out of the alienation in which it finds itself and into the living presence of conversation, whose fundamental procedure is always question and answer" (p. 331). I should add that the expression "begin a conversation with the text" remains necessarily metephorical, since the interpreter must himself first stage the role of the other so that the text can speak, respond to a question, and be understood in the end as a "question posed to me." As certain as it is that a text from the tradition can only become a question for an inquiring person, it is equally certain that a "conversation with the past" must take the form of an appropriating understanding that mediates between the other's horizon and one's own (something that the ocular metaphor of a "fusion of horizons" often causes to be misunderstood) in order to avoid falling into the one-sidedness of traditionalism or the topicality of present-day concerns.

The other part of the hermeneutic task consists of illuminating the dialogicity of the understanding that arises from a conversation or discussion in which an alien discourse enters into a direct relation with one's own. Gadamer defines this understanding that arises during a conversation as shared understanding enabled by an object, and thereby asserts a commonality between understanding a text and reaching an understanding in a conversation (p. 341). But this pushes another, equally original concern of conversation–understanding the other in his otherness–into the background. Of course the shared understanding enabled by an object that is the goal of the conversation can also bring with it an understanding of the alterity of the conversational partner.

But this is not necessarily the case, and there is obviously also a second manner of understanding the other through conversation, one in which agreement about an object plays no role at all. Gadamer's critique of the hermeneutics of identification that he thinks is implicit in Schleiermacher's psychological mode of interpretation, justifiable though it may be, has the effect of immediately reducing Schleiermacher's desire to understand alien discourse to a mere fascination with the "obscure you."[29] Still, Schleiermacher's shift from understanding texts to understanding speech in general leads to a a need for a hermeneutics of dialogicity, one that is unavailable even today, a hermeneutics that would place responsive self-understanding enabled by the other on an equal footing with shared understanding enabled by an object as a matter of epistemological interest. Literary hermeneutics, which has genuine access to understanding through aesthetic experience of a work of art (in the how, not the what, of the said), and not through a search for some initial agreement about an object, might find new stimulus for asking how poetic language can serve to reveal the otherness of the other by turning to the aesthetic and literary works of Mikhail Bakhtin.

In its premises and implications–to which I have limited myself here–Bakhtin's aesthetic theory can be understood in terms of the same theoretical shift that was decisive for Popper and Lukács–a turning away from the aesthetics of expressivity and the theory of identification that held sway after 1900.[30] Bakhtin's point of departure is Wilhelm Worringer's *Abstraktion und Einfühlung* (1908). There, Theodor Lipps's theory of *Einfühlung* (identification) is used as a means of approaching aesthetic activity as an act of self-relinquishment in which the "I" loses itself in the external world in order to bring forth the work of art as the objectification of that which has thus been experienced: "Aesthetic pleasure is objectified pleasure of the self. To experience aesthetic pleasure is to have pleasure in oneself in a sense object, distinct [from] oneself, it is to be in empathy with it."[31] Bakhtin adopted the act of self-alienation from this model, but then broke it down into two contrary movements: empathy as an outward movement, a seeing and recognizing of the self in the other must be followed by a return to the self, so that the identification that has taken place can become a productive and once again receptive aesthetic experience by distancing the self from or "finding oneself outside" (*vnenakhodimost'*) it.[32] Identification is a necessary intermediary step, not the goal of aesthetic experience. A prior identification with the other is necessary to achieve a return to the self in the state of aesthetic eccentricity (Plessner's concept should come close to Bakhtin's *vnenakhodimost'*), which makes it possible to experience the other in his difference, and the self through his otherness. The mutuality of experiencing the alien and experiencing the self is the decisive revision that Bakhtin introduces in his new formulation of the theory of identification. It is not simply that this new formulation insists that human consciousness is by its very nature dialogic: "His consciousness of self is constantly perceived against the background of the other's consciousness of him."[33] It is also that aesthetic experience is distinguished by the way in which experiencing the self is facilitated, if not in fact generated, by experience of the other:

> I cannot perceive myself in my external aspect, feel that it encompasses me and gives me expression. . . . In this sense, one can speak of the absolute aesthetic need of man for the other, for the other's activity of seeing, holding, putting together and unifying, which alone can bring into being the externally finished personality; if someone else does not do it, this personality will have no existence.[34]

Although only recently published, this bold theory about the dialogic nature of consciousness sketched by the young Bakhtin (and to the undefined hermeneutic implications of which I will return) is the premise for his later *Aesthetics of Verbal Creation*. Its primary theses are these: dialogue is the initial form of human utterance; language is a social event entailing verbal interaction; a fundamental opposition between voice (hearing) and writing (reading), the dialogic principle of openness and the monologic principle of completed truth; the three categories of word—the direct, the represented, and that tuned in to alien discourse; the historical origin of the polyphonic word in the Socratic dialogue, and its subversive continuation in the Menippean satire and in the polyphonic novel—in opposition to which official monologism has always managed to have the unanimity of discourse prevail; prose as the site of the polyphonic (alien and misunderstood) word, the lyric as the medium of the (unwitnessed) word about the self and the world. If Bakhtin's *Aesthetics of Verbal Creation*, with its antithesis between dialogic and monologic principles, offers a framework of categories that is particularly useful for redefining the communicative roles of speech and literature as genres, it must also be added that Bakhtin ultimately expanded his dialogic model to incorporate three voices.

For Bakhtin, the dialogue, which must seek its truth in an understanding of the spoken exchange, and is, therefore (as is the history of interpretations as it develops out of a constantly renewable dialogue with the art of the past), basically endless, ultimately assumes the existence of a higher authority, a third party or *superaddressee*, "whose absolutely just responsive understanding is presumed, either in some metaphysical distance or in distant historical time. . . . In various ages and with various understandings of the world, this superaddressee and his ideally true responsive understanding assume various ideological expressions

(God, absolute truth, the court of dispassionate human conscience, the people, the court of history, science, and so forth)."[35] We have already met this third party in theological hermeneutics. However, it appears here not as an ultimate, judgmental authority, but as an ultimate superreceiver whose understanding is "absolutely appropriate," and who—as an always present (or absent) third party assumed to intervene in the dialogue between the text and the interpreter (between the alien voice and one's own)—apparently serves as guarantor of the possibility that understanding will take place at all. A problematic aspect of *The Aesthetics of Verbal Creation* comes to light in this charming and remarkable secularization. Bakhtin, who at first developed his aesthetic theory of alterity only in terms of an aesthetics of production involving the contrary movements of self-alienation and self-perception, and who only began in his later writings to expand his theory in terms of reception aesthetics,[36] leaves open the hermeneutic question as to what enables the reader to understand the text in its alterity in the first place, and what he, as the second party, must himself contribute to this dialogue in order to engage his understanding in a dialogue with the text and its earlier interpretations. Bakhtin's aesthetic of alterity, which so effectively contributed to the reinvigorating of the ideological principle behind the poetic word, needs hermeneutic support with regard to the historical continuity of dialogic understanding.

Anyone who shares Bakhtin's position (one at which I arrived, too, but through its correlate in an aesthetics of reception, and without knowledge of his work)[37]—that to experience art is an excellent way in which to experience the alien "you" in its otherness, and, thereby, in turn to have an enriched experience of one's own "I"—cannot assume that the responsive self-understanding enabled by the other engendered by aesthetic communication requires nothing more than the reciprocal movements of empathy and its return as self-reflection (*vnenak-hodimost*). Even if the work of art is able to represent and disclose the alien "I" as subject, and even if, according to Bakhtin's lengthy interpretation of Dostoyevsky, the polyphonic word found in the novel is especially able to represent and disclose alien speech through speech, the receiver cannot simply leap over the hermeneutic difference and arrive at the alterity of the text or the "alien utterance in its discourse" on the basis of his own aesthetically mediated self-reflection. If the process of understanding literary texts is not to give way to a free-floating production of differences (a danger that Julia Kristeva's abbreviated version of Bakhtin's dialogic—the theory of "intertextuality" now fashionable in France—has not escaped),[38] responsive self-understanding enabled by the other of the text and the life-world self-understanding arising from the statements and counterstatements of the other must be anchored in a prior understanding of the already said, misunderstood, and previously valid. Furthermore, Bakhtin's dialogic, however much it exposes the difference in polyvalence between grammatical persons and speaking voices, nonetheless—it seems to me—assumes the transparency of the poetic word and is unable to elicit the hermeneutic difference between the author's intention, the meaning of the text, and the significance for a given reader. The hermeneutic difference between textual and received meaning sets in as soon as the listener or reader does not think the same per se as the speaker or author concerning a word; it grows with historical distance, and achieves the secondary alterity of a temporal gap. But it can also have already sharpened into the problem of the deceptiveness of dissimulating utterances if it is consciously used for ideological ends or if it unconsciously plays a role in a poetic text. Bakhtin's dialogic principle can open up these aspects of the alterity of a text only when expanded through the use of other instruments of understanding, and when access to responsive self-understanding enabled by the other is made possible by constructing hermeneutic bridges in those places where such access had at first given the appearance of being immediate.

The first hermeneutic bridge is already implicit in Bakhtin's thesis about the nature of the word as an answer, at least insofar as the word first becomes an answer by responding dialogically to a question. And since, as Karlheinz Stierle has shown with regard to the narrative form, the answer in a literary text "always overflows the question for which it can serve as an answer," it is "not only a source of information or the monolithic answer to a question that has been asked, but, for the individual to whom it is directed, it is also an appeal to coax out of the narrative the questions to which that narrative has provided the answer."[39] In this case, the dialectic of question and answer becomes a genuine hermeneutic instrument, one with which the reader can go beyond his own horizon in order to examine the horizon of the other, and reengage in the dialogue with the text, a text that can answer only when it has been asked again. But not every poetic text has as its answer the hermeneutic structure found in the word, as is clearly demonstrated by the lyric, which Bakhtin defines as a medium for the word that offers no evidence about itself or the world. In that case, the relationship to the world that is opened up by the lyric voice can itself become the hermeneutic bridge to a responsive self-understanding enabled by the other, because this opening up of discourse to subjective experience of the world, as Paul Ricoeur has shown,[40] reveals the nature of the text as a work that has achieved scriptive form. The poetic word distinguishes itself from merely informative or goal-oriented utterance to the degree that it can free itself from the intention of its producer, and, at the same time, from the pragmatic limits of the specific speech context. This grants a semantic autonomy that enables even a much later receiver to look beyond the occasional nature of the lyric situation to the fullness of meaning found in a world seen differently.

One may wonder whether the so-defined semantic autonomy of the poetic word does not still presuppose an understanding of the notion "world" that is at home first and foremost in Greek/occidental culture, and, thus, insufficient as a means of bridging over the alienness of other cultures. But the understanding of alien discourse can always be aided by an anthropologically sustained prior understanding that draws on the immemorial existence of myth, and allows one to construct a bridge of understanding via the forms and configurations of the imaginary. If, as Hans Blumenberg suggests, mythic experience of the world has always already gone beyond the supposed alterity of a "primal situation," and has immediately concretized itself in "work on myth,"[41] aesthetic understanding can begin at the point where the imaginary surrounds the forms and configurations of the mythic with the aura of completion, thereby satisfying an initial aesthetic need. If my thesis is correct, and the (or a powerful) *fascinosum* of the imaginary is to be found in the complete or perfect,[42] then that "anticipation of perfection" that Gadamer sees as an outstanding source of understanding would be worth looking at.[43] It might from the outset condition that responsive self-understanding enabled by the other, even when—as part of the progressive emancipation of the subject—the other is recognized, idealized literarily precisely in terms of his incompletion and contingency—his individuality—and made the real problem of dialogic understanding.

3. Looking back and ahead

It was no accident that the study of a literature quite distant from us was the source of my initial desire to do further research concerning the reader's horizon of expectations, that for which the literary text was originally written. This work soon demonstrated the error in that which traditional philological interpretation believed it could understand about a text that had become alien: that such understanding could take place directly or "aesthetically"—"through the text alone"—despite the distance in time, or else that it was available through "historical" mediation—by a return to the text's sources and to additional factual information about the era. The vernacular literature of the Middle Ages, or, more precisely, the rather curious poetry about animals that blossomed in the twelfth century, was what first led me to focus on the alien horizon of expectations as the crux of the problem of understanding. Because of the break in continuity introduced by the Renaissance, the literature of the Middle Ages had achieved a certain degree of alterity. In contrast, the literature of the classical era has, until recently, maintained its canonical validity throughout the history of occidental culture, and thus provides hermeneutic reflection with other, though perhaps not smaller, problems. That the literature of the Middle Ages could serve as an exemplary model for contemporary study remained hidden during the 1950s because traditional interpretive practice involved doing "source studies," and more particularly because of the unexpected and monumental legitimation it had received due to the paradigmatic status of E. R. Curtius's *European Literature and the Latin Middle Ages* (1948). Thereafter, any philologically exact and aesthetically blind positivist, while impoverishing the humanist motto, *ad fontes*, by retreating from sources to the sources of sources, could rely on the belief that even the smallest discovery made by a source study contributed to the overall demonstration of an unbroken, though latent, continuity in the "indispensable" heritage of the classical era. The Middle Ages thus became a link in the "golden chain of the literary tradition" and lost almost all of its historical integrity. Leo Spitzer's now famous Villon interpretation had been published in 1938 under the provocative title "Etude ahistorique d'un texte," but the aesthetic approach he championed against the objectivism of the source study failed to carry the day. The ideal for serious research remained a work like Italo Siciliano's *François Villon et les thèmes poétiques du moyen âge*, which pushed the search for sources so far that every element in Villon's revolutionizing lyric poems proved to have an antecedent in the universal repertoire of poetry that had preceded it.

Heinrich Lausberg converted the implicit assumption underlying such source research into the fundamental principle of a type of research on the tradition that was meant to further develop Curtius's program for a historical topics based on rhetoric, and in which rhetoric, though previously held in little esteem, was equated with literature.[44] This principle embodied the substantialist postulate that every new literary work, rather than potentially arising from the *summa* of the entire literary heritage, ultimately only adapted the archetypal substance of the tradition, despite the appearance of historical innovation. Such a theory and metaphysics of the tradition arises from the (supposedly) humanistic conviction that "in the book, the poem is really present."[45] This makes of the philologist the true reader for whom the text is written, one who, as a "superreader," can better understand the author's use of sources than the author himself did. It is only the philologist, who, within the later horizon of a more complete, if not actually universal, knowledge, is able to recognize the sources upon which an author has drawn, whether consciously or unconsciously. From the hermeneutic point of view, research in the tradition understood in this manner maintains its absolute virginity. For the superreader-philologist, who naively assumes the existence of his later horizon of knowledge within the earlier horizon of a work's inception, temporal distance—and with it the limitation of the historical horizon—fades into the timeless presence of great literature. Even minor literature remains steadfastly within the "unbreakable chain, the tradition of mediocrity."[46]

At about this same time, doubt-free philological research and its hermeneutic innocence were challenged in France by Robert Guiette and Arthur Nisin, and in Germany by Walther Bulst, who used almost identical, paradoxically formulated arguments: no text has ever been written so that philologists could read and interpret it philologically, or so that historians could do so historically.[47] This laid the foundations for a new literary hermeneutics, one that insisted on eliminating the fallacious notion that the text is as immediate to the philologist as (according to Ranke) every epoch is to God. The meaning of the text was to be gotten at through the reader who was its actual addressee. This hermeneutic task brings with it a double problem. On the one hand, the author's reconstructed intention can no longer constitute the final level of understanding, although it must be retained as a point of reference. On the other hand, the readerly experience of the earlier reader can be recovered only by means of the actual reading done by the later reader, so the difference between the past and the present horizon of reading must be worked out within the interpretation itself.

The above-mentioned critics were unable to find a methodological solution for this double problem. Bulst was inclined toward differentiating between the subjective experience of reading and objective research into the genesis of the text. He also doubted whether the experience of the earlier reader could be reconstructed unless it were testified to by that reader.[48] Guiette tried to rehabilitate an unmediated enjoyment of medieval texts by interpreting the Arthurian novel in terms of the charm of the obscure, the unresolved (as *symbolisme sans signification*), and the lyric poetry of the troubadours in terms of the charm of a *poésie formelle*, with each offering the conscious pleasure of endless variation.[49] In so doing, he discovered the specific aesthetic attitude implicit in these and other literary genres, but without reflecting about the degree to which these discoveries were made possible by a modern set of presuppositions derived from the antiromantic poetics that arose after Verlaine and Mallarmé. Nisin is to be credited with revealing the latent Platonism of academic philology—its belief in the timeless existence of the classical work and the neutral position of the observer. In his unjustly forgotten work, *La littérature et le lecteur* (1959),[50] he also paved the way for a hermeneutics of reading in which the literary work is to be understood as a "score" that can be actualized only through readings, but always with new and different results. Genuine understanding of an aesthetic text also requires that the philologist make sure his interpretation and critically evaluative reflections refer back to his initial experience as reader. This expectation is exactly the opposite of an empowering of the merely subjective in reading: in opposition to the reader's arbitrariness, the *sens vécu* of his first reading, the text offers the resistance of its *sens vérifiable*. The work as "score" becomes a site of understanding to the degree that the reader, as part of a second reading, or by giving renewed presence to what has been read through a knowledge of the whole, verifies in the text itself that which appeared to him to be its possible meaning during his initial, aesthetic perception of the work. The shortcoming of this theory lay in the fact that Nisin assumed the spontaneity of the initial reading—the initial contact that seemed to transport the reader directly into the unknown of another world of imagination—was absolute. The limit of his theory becomes evident as soon as the *sens vécu* of an earlier text is no longer available to us without the mediation or translation supplied by a philologist, in other words, when we lack historical understanding. Gaëtan Picon has already shown that, since one cannot understand a work of art without providing it with some kind of past, and since the aesthetic value of a literary work can be measured only when it is regarded as an unknown within the horizon of known works, there is no such thing as virginity as far as aesthetic experience is concerned.[51] But how can one escape the fallacy of a pure, spontaneous/emotional ingestion of literature without sacrificing the reflexive link between the interpretation and the initial readerly experience? How is one then to elucidate the preconceptions that guided this spontaneous reading of the text, and what is to be done in order to have access to other experiences that the (historically) first addressee might have had during his reading?

These are the questions with which I became entangled in my *Untersuchungen zur mittelalterlichen Tierdichtung* (1959). *Reineke Fuchs*, the medieval tale that Goethe revised, disconcerts today's reader primarily because of the so-called anthropomorphism of its animal figures, that is, because of fictive conduct that can be understood neither mimetically — as the observable life of animals in nature — nor allegorically — in terms of the spiritual significance of their "natures." Beginning with Jacob Grimm, and throughout the later history of its interpretation, the remarkable mixture of human attributes and animal forms in the *Roman de Renart* has been dealt with in terms of either one of these aspects or the other. Thus, the romantic distinction between the poetry of nature and the poetry of artifice remained in effect as a latent paradigm even in historicopositivist interpretations. If one looked at the figures in these loosely connected comic tales in terms of the naive — the natural poetry arising from an early harmony between man and animal — then one could postulate the existence of a pure form of original *animal fable* behind the anthropomorphic features, which themselves could be dismissed as later accretions. If, on the other hand, one looked at the animal characters as historically understandable disguises for epic heroes, then the feud between Renart and Ysengrim could be interpreted as a satiric art form, an *animal epic*, which, as a parody of the knightly epos, and a mirror of feudal society, merely employed the animal figures as a superficial cover, or means of maintaining decorum. The one-sidedness of these contrasting interpretive paradigms leads them both to overlook the obvious question as to what the addressee for whom this episodic work was begun in 1176 might have made of the analogy between animal and human nature played out in the *Roman de Renart*.[52] Should we not consult the answer to this question in order to discover the basis for the pleasure that the medieval reader gleaned from the novelty of such comic animal tales, and might it not also explain why the work of Pierre de Saint-Cloud brought so many imitators onto the field? Why was aesthetic interest so inexhaustible that the fable of the "real origin of the enmity between the fox and the wolf" could be constantly resumed, and its conclusion, the trial that takes place when the lion's court assembles, regularly revised? Why was the oldest animal epos in vernacular French spun out into the never-ending adventures of a rogue in a feudal animal kingdom, and why was it able to survive the fall of medieval literature along with *Tristan* and the *Roman de la Rose*?

One solution to these questions arose from the happy coincidence that, in his prologue, Pierre de Saint-Cloud, the author of the oldest parts of the *Roman de Renart* (II-Va), took the standard "I bring you something entirely new" quite literally. He names the previous types of literature that his new work is supposed to put in the shade, listing individual works and literary genres that had found particular favor with his public: *Troy* and *Tristan* as well as the classical and courtly novels, the *fabliau* and the *chanson de geste*. Drawing on this canon, on other already known material, and last, but not least, on the (up to then unknown) context surrounding the continuation of the work of a predecessor unmentioned in the prologue, the Latin *Ysengrimus* by Maître Nivardus, I was able to derive the horizon of expectations that Pierre de Saint-Cloud called upon in order to emphasize the newness of his work. The resulting textual analysis showed that in the course of the narrative the author had indeed fulfilled the promise made in the prologue. With reference to the first of the expectations he evokes, he either satisfies or disappoints them, usually implicitly, but sometimes explicitly and critically as well, by parodying the *chanson de geste*, or by travestying the casuistry of the courtly love poem. Thus, it becomes possible for the later interpreter to reconstruct the preconceptions of the original addressee, even after the passage of a period of time. In addition, by establishing the difference between retrospective expectations and the prospective, new experience that arises during the reading process itself, it is also possible to trace the shift in horizons that this text might have signaled to the public of the *chanson de geste* and courtly poetry in 1176. Pleasure in the new genre—the comic tale of the fox—sets in when and to the degree that the reader takes its "anthropomorphism" as an indication that he is expected to see aspects of human nature in the animal figures. Then the promised "incredible struggle between the two barons" can be read as a contrafact to heroic poetry, one that for the first time calls the elevated ethos of the chivalric world into question by using a jovial satire to point out the unideal, creaturely nature of man in comparison with his projected literary perfection.

Although my effort to interpret this medieval text from the vantage point of its contemporary public's horizon of expectations may have provided modern understanding with a new point of entry, as I look back, I cannot fail to see that this reconstruction of the alterity of an aesthetic experience that had become alien to us depended on the hermeneutic anticipation of a modern anthropological theory. Lipps's phenomenological analysis of *The Nature of Man* had opened my eyes to what the animal, for whom it is typical to have "the nature of its species written in its face" and an "unbroken connection to its nature," can reveal about a natural substratum of spiritual being that is an aspect of human character.[53] Of course even this theoretical leap could not recover the spontaneous readerly experience of the first readers, but it could elicit from the text the implicit point of view that was a condition for understanding the text in the first place. The spontaneous readerly experience of a historically distant reader is of no hermeneutic value, and to want to reconstruct it as such is an illusion, since spontaneity can never be fully elicited through reflection. Such an effort would also fail to appreciate that aesthetic experience, by its very nature, involves mediated, thus heightened, perceptions, and, consequently, can never be totally equated with emotional spontaneity. But theoretical anticipation can at least disclose those connections that make aesthetic experience communicable in the first place. It can do so systematically, in terms of the point of view implicit in the text, and historically, in terms of the preconceptions that come into play along with a shift in the horizon of expectation and experience. They thus become available for use in an interpretation, especially when, as in this case, the theoretical leap brings into play generalities that have been anticipated by phenomenological anthropology in some vague, general way, but that are in need of closer definition.

The new interpretation of the *Roman de Renart* that was engendered by these efforts had, of course, arisen from a modern concern: the historical and literary genesis of individuation. But this does not mean that it projected a contemporary concern into the past. Rather, because of its conscious evocation of a horizon, the theoretical leap became historically more concrete, and the interpretation revealed a manner of experiencing human character and nature that was new to the life-world of the twelfth century. On the one hand, the work of Pierre de Saint-Cloud brings to light a whole world of character types that are set apart from the movement of history; but on the other hand, it already manages to provide Renart—the negative hero who brings out the unideal, all-too-human side of all the others as he outsmarts them—with the rogue's wit that marks the initial appearance of individuality. Even if this innovation was not noticed or seen as such by the majority of its contemporary addressees, there nonetheless exists extraliterary proof that it could be so understood then. The threshold of individuation, which, from the point of view of later interpreters, manifests itself literarily in the *Roman de Renart*, is likewise attested to historically for the first time in this period: after Otto von Freising, *persona* could denote not only the exchangeable (mask, role), but also the unexchangeable *individualitas* of the secular person.[54]

In historical hermeneutics, the threshold metaphor is used to indicate the transition from the old to the new does not necessarily take place all at once, and that not all of its contemporaries need participate in it. Moving beyond the realm of experience embodied in the medieval life-world—a realm that, because of its closed horizon of future events, seemed unalterable in a Christian understanding of the world—enabled new experiences to be unleashed, experiences that were not constrained by a distrust of *curiositas*. Apparently, the license to break the spell of the ideal embodied in the norms of chivalric and courtly life, the license to present human nature beyond good and evil, in all its imperfection and ordinariness, was easier to acquire if one turned to fiction dealing with the animal kingdom. This being the case, literary hermeneutics can make its own contribution to the process of historical discovery by revealing the implications of that which the contemporaries of a bygone life-world experienced only as a latent need, wish, or presentiment regarding the future. Literary hermeneutics can accomplish this by examining such experience within the context of a change in the horizon of aesthetic experience, thereby making its initially indefinable significance available to conscious understanding as part of the history of its interpretation.

Although my work as a medievalist had emphasized the hermeneutic problem of contrasting horizons, and led me to a critique of the traditionalism of positivistic philology, my first attempt to translate such ideas into a project for an aesthetic of literary reception (*Literaturegeschichte als Provocation*, 1967)[55] arose from different motives. I tried to imagine a new literary history, one that opened the closed circuit of author and work in the direction of the receiver, and was meant to make of this receiver, whether a reader or the public, the intermediary between the past and the present, the work and its effects. Such a history would have to stand up against the ideal of objectivity espoused by the old, discredited literary history, and also the demands for exactness laid down by those sociologists and structuralists who scoffed at historical understanding. At the center of my project stood the shift in horizons, a paradigm I had developed as part of my investigation of modern literature. In ideal cases, such as those found in works like *Don Quixote* and *Jacques le fataliste*, it was possible to develop this paradigm rigorously, since such works "evoke the reader's horizon of expectations, formed by a convention of genre, style, or form, only in order to destroy it step by step — which by no means serves a critical purpose only, but can itself once again produce poetic effects."[56] This shift from a preconceived horizon of expectations to a sketch of new experience struck me as the embodiment of the principle of aesthetic mediation that, in the literary-historical process, permits a contemporary reorganization of the canon that also renews the way in which all works from the past are seen. Understanding the shift in horizons in this way also permits one to grasp the artistic character of a work in proportion to the aesthetic distance it implies, that is, the distance between expectation and experience, tradition and innovation, and to separate a work's constitutive negativity from the affirmative aspect of that which in consumer literature merely satisfies a norm.

Of course, although I was not fully aware of it while formulating this paradigm, the Russian formalist perception that aesthetic innovation is the agent of literary evolution, and Adorno's aesthetics of negativity, according to which the autonomous work acquires a social function only and precisely through its specific negation of the extant, were the forces behind my work. The flagrant modernism of this earliest paradigm for a reception aesthetic was due to the one-sidedness of the situation defined by my inaugural lecture at Constance. The response to the lecture and the lively polemic it unleashed were quite unexpected,[57] but the obligation to respond gave me the chance to expand my initial plan for an aesthetic of reception step by step, testing it in practice as part of the debate with my critics. I first introduced the concept of the horizon of expectations as an instrument for analyzing readerly experience:

> The analysis of the literary experience of the reader avoids the threatening pitfalls of psychology if it describes the reception and the influence of a work within the objectifiable system of expectations that arise for each work in the historical moment of its appearance, from a preunderstanding of the genre, from the form and themes of already familiar works, and from the opposition between poetic and practical language.[58]

This thesis was directed at those who were of the opinion that an analysis of the reader's experience would inevitably end in the subjectivism of individual reaction ("as many interpretations as there are readers"), or in the collectivism of a sociology of taste. It established the possibility that literary experience could be apprehended in the objective difference between normative expectation and norm-creating experience, but intraliterarily. What remained unanswered was the question as to what part of such a shift in horizons could be attributed to the effect of the text, and what to its appropriation by its initial as well as later addressees. So, the task of distinguishing between the two sides in the text-reader relationship, that is, between the *effect*, which is conditioned by the text, and the *reception*, the concretization of meaning, which is dependent on the reader, was left to the literary-historiographic process itself. Contrary to appearances, the formation of a tradition does not come about so to speak of its own accord as a passive synthesis, a "fusion of horizons." The "event" produced by the literary work turned out to be a moment in the process of mediation between two horizons, between the horizon of experience evoked, confirmed, or surpassed by the work, and the horizon of experience that accompanies the receiver—an active synthesis involving understanding and then understanding differently.

The active role played by the reader in the ongoing historical process of concretizing meaning—the possibility of a "productive reception" (Sartre)—was also left unexplored when I called for a literary history that, instead of being written as an autonomous history, would reveal its "partiality," by having its particular conditions linked to those of the general historical situation, thereby exposing its social functions and its history-making energy: "The social function of literature manifests itself in its genuine possibility only where the literary experience of the reader enters into the horizon of expectations of his lived praxis, preforms his understanding of the world, and thereby also has an effect on his social behavior."[59] This last portion of my Constance theses was aimed at the theory of reflection, which, having recently been reinvigorated by Lukács, remained within the closure of an aesthetics of production and representation. Although it had intended to give priority to the norm-building rather than to the representative function of literature, this thesis left unexplained how the horizon of experience of lived praxis, if not the product of mute economic conditions, could otherwise be ascertained from the primary attitudes of those concerned, from their latent interests, needs, and wishes. It also failed to describe the relationship between this horizon and the horizon of aesthetic experience. The nature of this relationship had to be settled; otherwise the rather bold assertion in which my essay "Literary History as a Challenge to Literary Theory" culminated—that today literature is once again in a position to revise our fixed perceptions of things, and to subvert the taboos of the dominant morality—would have remained not a lovely but an empty wish. The problem was how to locate reception aesthetics, here conceived of as intraliterary, within the horizon conditioned by social praxis, and to ask whether and how the historical concretization of a literary work found in its reader's passive or productive reception is a response to a social situation—how it takes up the contradictions inherent in that situation, and attempts to project solutions for them. And, not least, one had to take seriously the ideologico-critical suspicion that literary transmission may not unfold in absolute freedom, that it may be pseudocommunicatively constrained. In this case, the transparency of literary communication between individuals and ages can no longer simply be seen as a given; it may first have to be retrieved from the cunning of the tradition, that which enables it to incorporate whatever is heteronomous within the harmonic canon of the classical.

If the theses in my inaugural lecture at the University of Constance were not sociological enough for the majority of my critics,[60] there were some who reproached me for the opposite. They thought the lecture was too sociological: my proposal for a new aesthetic of reception had not moved beyond hermeneutic and functionalist sociology, and would prevent one from seeing which aspect of the reader's experience was actually aesthetic. Furthermore, Sreten Petrović correctly observed that my quite necessary critique of the then dominant ontology of art and its surrogates, those operative in classical aesthetics' concept of the work, and in the concept of reflection found in orthodox Marxist aesthetics, had led me to the opposite extreme, to a literary theory that sacrificed aesthetic value along with the work, making it a predefined aspect of reception, and thereby reducing aesthetic experience to the level of changes in the social norms of taste. Taste, he suggested, is in fact merely the condition that makes literary communication possible; it does not forge the content and certainly not the results of such communication. The latter becomes aesthetic experience, and aesthetic experience is rendered understandable in terms of its difference from pragmatic experience only when its formation through the "materialization of the aesthetic object" (both on the level of the prereflective absorption of aesthetic meaning [aistheton] and on the reflective level of aesthetic judgment) is investigated, and more closely defined as the specific aesthetic activity of the producing and receiving subject.[61] I found it a quite surprising and equally happy coincidence of critical labors that Petrović had, as part of the critique he presented at the 1976 Belgrade symposium, postulated de facto the further development of the first paradigm of my reception aesthetic. He also outlined the desiderata of a theory of aesthetic experience, a theory that was overdue and that I had in the meantime already outlined in my second Constance lecture, "A Brief Apologia for Aesthetic Experience" (1972), and then consolidated in my "Theory and History of Aesthetic Experience," published in 1977.[62] Since it has already been published, here I need only to provide a brief summary of this step in my work.

I tried to define the particular nature, and the life-world function of aesthetic experience historically (as the process of its liberation from the authoritative heritage of Platonic aesthetics) and systematically (in terms of the three fundamental modes in which aesthetic activity is experienced, the productive, the receptive, and the communicative). I reexamined these modes of experience from the point of view of conceptual history as the triad poiesis, aesthesis, and catharsis, and traced them back to a common source in aesthetic pleasure. By starting here, it was possible not only to view aesthetic experience as it manifests itself in autonomous modern art—art that refuses to have a use value—but also to see that it was already at work in the earlier, practical (i.e., religious) and social functions of older art. Thus, the gulf created by the then dominant aesthetics of negativity, the gap between preautonomous and autonomous, "affirmative," and "emancipatory" art could be bridged. Revision of the modernist one-sidedness of my first sketch began, therefore, with a critique of Adorno's aesthetic theory. In opposition to Adorno, I began the task of rehabilitating pleasurable understanding—as the causal condition for aesthetic reflection—and aesthetic judgment that demands a consensus—as the specific result of aesthetic communication, although in the age of mass media and the culture industry its effects have been submerged.

   In this book,[63] my contribution to the problems researched by literary hermeneutics is represented by the essays discussed below, the introductions to some of which also document parts of the theoretical debate that took place in the seventies. "Racine's and Goethe's *Iphigenia*" (1973),[64] which arose out of my confrontation with Marxist literary theory, elucidates two fundamental concepts in literary hermeneutics: the partial nature of the historical horizon of understanding, and the dialogicity of production and reception in processes of literary communication. In order to reconstruct the original challenge laid down by Goethe's "devilishly humane act of daring," which masked the shift in horizons from historical to aesthetic classicism by incorporating it in concrete representations of the neohumanist ideal of culture, the first concretization (revealed by Hegel) had to be set off both from the proximate horizon of French classicism and the distant horizon of Greek tragedy. This made it possible to interpret the new *Iphigenia* as Goethe's response to Racine, and as a reprise of the classical myth, a reprise in which Iphigenia's "incredible deed" brings about the liberation of mankind from its mythic entanglement in nature. Since this mastering of mythic heteronomy in Goethe's play ultimately comes at the price of a new myth—that of an all-redeeming, pure femininity—the resolution offered in the final scene with Thoas appears spurious to our contemporary understanding. This in turn introduces the question of the possibilities for and the limits to an actualization of the classical, an actualization with which literary hermeneutics, after reconstructing the temporally distant horizon, and, after working up normative interpretations ("concretizations"), which are handed on to contemporary understanding as part of a history of reception, arrives at the question of application, and thus manages to complete the three-part movement from understanding, to interpretation and application in its own way.

I took up this problem again in "The Classical—Modern Once Again?" (1975), where I dealt with a tendency in contemporary theater that first manifested itself in avant-garde experiments, but later had a much wider impact on literary production and staging practices. How can a classical work be decanonized; how can a new understanding bring it within the horizon of contemporary understanding despite its seemingly timeless validity; how can it be rejuvenated on the contemporary stage so that the links between past and present understanding are not broken—as is inevitably the case with a naive actualization or a rigorous historicization? Rejuvenating reception demands something other than an unquestioning belief in historical fusion such as that operative in the neoclassical period, for example. Any fusion must be consciously created through a dialectical mediation of past and present horizons, and emerge as a new concretization of meaning. Hildesheimer's new *Mary Stuart* and Plenzdorf's *New Sorrows of Young W.* announce a literary-historical change insofar as they manage to break through the taboo that makes textual wording untouchable, and the form of a classical work unchangeable, thereby managing to give new life to a classic that had been declared dead. Their method was one of applied literary hermeneutics: the spectator is provided with a specific representation of the historical distance separating the text and the present, while the familiar horizon of the classical is only quoted, so that, to start with, it is possible to recognize how distant the bygone world actually is. Then, after revealing the existence of another meaning for this prior experience, this meaning must be reconstructed by means of an ongoing confrontation between that which is one's own and that which is other, so that by taking up and reactivating the play of a past no longer with us, a new experiential horizon is opened for present-day understanding.

My attempt to solve the hermeneutic problem of how shifts in the horizons of expectation and experience proper to literature are related to the external horizon of the life-world involved three steps. In *La douceur du foyer* (1974),[65] I borrowed a theory about the manner in which social reality is constituted from the sociology of knowledge. I applied this theory to the *foyer* [here understood to mean "hearth" and "home"], a term that embodied the hopes of the bourgeois family of the Second Empire, and used this epochal paradigm to elucidate the communicative role played by lyric poetry in mediating, internalizing, legitimating, and changing social norms. Thus, the sociology of knowledge elaborated by Alfred Schütz and Thomas Luckmann contributed an element that history, even after its revision in the direction of social history, had not yet worked out: a theory about the perspectival structure of everyday reality that could be applied historically — a theory that dealt with the prestructuring of one's experience of the surrounding world (the here/there situation), of one's fellow beings (the vis-à-vis situation), and of the movement of time (the now as delimiter of time), as well as with the horizon structures of specific, limited, realms of meaning ("subuniverses") of human action. By itself, a transcendental schema delineating the structure of the social world would not have been sufficient as a means of apprehending a prior horizon in great part constituted by latent attitudes and norms; but as a means of theoretical anticipation it allowed me to look for the latent horizon of expectations of the historical life-world of 1857 in the lyric poetry of the era. This led to the possibility of describing such poetry as a system of literary communication that gave transparency to things that had been accepted as a natural part of the routine and the constraints of everyday praxis and thus had remained latent. The sociology of knowledge had not investigated the status of aesthetic experience in social praxis. Its relative importance remained hidden because aesthetic experience had been isolated as one "subuniverse" among others, and because no one had realized that the specific social contribution of this "subuniverse" begins at the moment aesthetic experience, operating within the horizon of fiction, renders the fixed horizons and ideological legitimations of other (e.g., religious, political, professional) subuniverses transparent — when it makes possible once more communication with the closed world in which the other lives, and, thus, contributes its share to opening the seemingly immutable horizon of a social order to new experiences.

This definition of the way in which aesthetic experience abuts and impinges on the other realms of human activity justifies the hermeneutic priority granted to the reception-aesthetic approach. If one first begins the reconstruction of the social situation using only knowledge borrowed from historical and economic sources, one readily arrives at the point where whatever one had already ascertained historically is confirmed by the mirror of literary testimony. However, the role of literature as a response or answer first becomes visible when one discovers its mediations. They in turn become transparent only through the medium of literary experience, and understandable when the horizon has been delineated. Goethe responded to Rousseau's *Julie* with his *Werther* even though he made no reference whatsoever to the provocative model supplied by his much admired predecessor. But this becomes clear, as does the nature of the social situation to which first the French and then the German *catechism of sentimentality* responded, only when one reconstructs the horizon of expectations conveyed in the literature of the era, a horizon that the enthusiastic German as well as French reception of *La nouvelle Héloïse* bequeathed to *The Sorrows of Young Werther*. My analysis of this horizon ("Rousseau's *Nouvelle Héloïse* and Goethe's *Werther*") initially proposed the thesis that the uncommonly widespread success of the two works was constitutive not only of literary but of social norms as well, primarily because the contemporary reader felt that the *homme sensible* represented by Rousseau's couple, and by the "German Saint-Preux" in Goethe's *Werther*, seemed to eliminate the self-alienation engendered by bourgeois existence that Rousseau had diagnosed in the first and second *Discours*. The dissatisfaction Goethe must have felt with Rousseau's solution can be objectified in terms of Goethe's response to the contradictions Rousseau had laboriously masked with his portrayal of the "ménage à trois" in the utopia set up in Clarens. In his own fictive extension of Rousseau's work, Goethe resolves these contradictions in such a way that the autonomy of self-esteem proclaimed in Rousseau's text emerges as a topic for discussion, a discussion precipitated by the outcome of Werther's "sickness unto death." This shift in horizons also allows one to grasp how different the social substrata of those bourgeois institutions, the family, religion, and work, were and how differently they were regarded on either side of the line separating the French Enlightenment from German idealism, a division that itself becomes comprehensible in a new way at this point.

The final essay, "The Poetic Text within the Change of Horizons of Reading" (1980),[66] used lyric poetry as a means of testing the viability of Gadamer's demand that the triadic unity of the hermeneutic procedure once again be fully realized in practice. If the horizon that structures aesthetic experience is the privileged hermeneutic medium that allows a text from the past to be understood in its alterity, and which allows one to mediate between this text and the horizon of one's own experience, it must also be possible to determine through hermeneutic reflection on reading itself what aspect of the aesthetic experience is actually aesthetic, and, thus, what it is that makes historical understanding possible in the first place. My interpretation of Baudelaire's *Spleen II* represents an attempt to separate methodically the acts of aesthetic perception and interpretive understanding that, in a reading, are always intertwined. This is accomplished by contrasting the open horizon of a first reading with the retrospective horizon of a second reading. Thus, in the first phase of an analysis, one can trace the formation of aesthetic perception *in actu*. It can be described in terms of poetic structure and still-undefined expectations about the meaning of the text. In the second phase of the analysis, when one circles back from the end of the poem and the whole that has been established to the beginning, the aesthetic experience of the first reading can become the horizon of interpretive understanding, an understanding that elaborates a context of meaning from the conjecture and unanswered questions that were part of that experience. Since this interpretation leaves unclear which of its elements have been engendered by the text and which have been imposed by the interpreter, the third phase of the analysis must delineate the earlier horizon in order to bring into play the temporal distance that was at first ignored. In addition, the meaning intended by the author must be reconstructed as a historical countervoice, and the interpreter's own understanding must be elucidated on the basis of the reception history that defines his horizon of interpretation. After this, one's own interpretation must be justified both by asking if it allows the text to be understood in a new and different manner, and by asking if it grants the work of one's predecessors its rights too. It is only after satisfying this final requirement that literary hermeneutics can fulfill its particular purpose, which, according to Marquard, resides in the possibility of carrying out the interpretive struggle in such a way that it does not deteriorate into a life-and-death political battle. After all, within the horizon of aesthetic experience, it is fitting that even different interpretations do not necessarily have to contradict each other. Literary communication opens a dialogue in which true and false are measured only in terms of whether another's interpretation contributes to the further unfolding of the inexhaustible meaning found in the work of art.

Notes

Notes

A. The Communicative Role of the Fictive

1. Iser, English translation (1979), pp. 53ff.; Stierle (1975a), pp. 378ff.; on the research in France, see D. Poirion, *Le merveilleux dans la littérature fr. du MA* (Paris, 1982). In what follows I draw in part on essays appearing in *Poetik und Hermeneutik X* (Munich, 1983).

1. On the origins of the differentiation between fiction and reality

2. Manfred Fuhrmann, "Wunder und Wirklichkeit," in *Poetik und Hermeneutik*; Wolfhart Pannenberg, "Das Irreale des Glaubens," in *Poetik und Hermeneutik X*. Soon afterward a study by W. Rössler, "Die Entdeckung der Fiktionalität in der Antike," *Poetica*, 12 (1980), pp. 283–319, suggested that the Greeks' discovery of fictionality was ultimately a result of the advent of writing.

3. Here I follow the thesis developed by Odo Marquard in his essay "Kunst als Antifiktion," in *Poetik und Hermeneutik X*.

4. Blumenberg, *Paradigmen zu einer Metaphorologie* (Bonn, 1960), p. 89. See also p. 88: "The metaphor no doubt has its roots in the ambivalence of antique rhetoric: the orator can allow the true to 'appear' in its legitimate splendor, but he can also allow the untrue to 'look like' the true."

5. [In the German original, the wordplay is slightly different. Jauss repeats Blumenberg's distinction by juxtaposing *Hervorscheinen* to *blossen Schein.* – Trans. (Hereafter all notes by the translator will be set off in brackets).]

6. Cf. Blumenberg, *Paradigmen*, p. 92, to Laktanz, and on Augustine's supposed restoration of the "Platonic residue," p. 93.

7. See "Catharsis: The Communicative Efficacy of Aesthetic Experience (*movere et conciliare*)," in Jauss, (1982), pp. 92–111.

8. Garlandia distinguishes between three *species narrationis* in this context: *res gesta* (or *historia*), *res ficta* (or *fabula*), and *res ficta quae tamen fieri potuit* (or *argumentum*). See Jauss (1977), p. 346, on the divorce of fiction from reality in the twelfth century. See as well Marc Bloch, *La société*

féodale, 2 (Paris, 1949), especially p. 168: "expressions of an age that was now refined enough to separate pure literary diversion from the description of the real."

9. H. Fuhrmann, "Die Fälschung im Mittelalter: Überlegungen zum mittelalterlichen Wahrheits-begriff," in *Historische Zeitschrift*, 197 (1963), p. 537. In the trove of documents related to Charlemagne, close to 100 of the 262 official missives are forged.

10. Ibid., p. 543.

11. Virgil, *Aenead*, "Cadit et Ripheus, justissimus unus, / Qui fuit in Teucris et servantissimus aequi" (II, 426).

12. *Liber de Confessione, PL* CCVII, 1088.

13. See the *Roman de Rou*, ed. H. Andresen, ll. 6395ff.

14. In Gautier d'Arras, *Ille et Galeron*, ll. 1934–36, cited in Dietmar Rieger's introduction to Marie de France, *Die Lais* (Munich, 1980). Other references of the same sort can be found in this text.

15. Cited by Rieger, ibid., p. 21.

16. What follows is drawn from Douglas Kelly, *Medieval Imagination: Rhetoric and the Poetry of Courtly Love* (Madison, Wis., 1978), especially pp. 26–56.

17. ["O painting with your new wonders! What can have no real existence comes into being and painting, aping reality and diverting itself with a stange art, turns the shadows of things and changes every lie to truth." Translated in Kelly, *Courtly Love*, p. 29.]

18. This formulation comes from Stierle (1975a), p. 378.

19. I have interpreted Rousseau's foreword to his *Nouvelle Héloïse* as a further major demonstra-tion of the provocative intercourse between fiction and antifiction. See "Rousseau's *Nouvelle Héloïse* and Goethe's *Werther*," in this volume, pp. 148–96.

2. The perfect as the fascinosum of the imaginary

20. "Zur Problemlage gegewärtigen Literaturtheorie: Das Imaginäre und die epochalen Schlüssel-begriffe," in *Auf den Weg gebracht: Idee und Wirklichkeit der Gründung der Universität Konstanz*, ed. H. Sund and M. Timmerman (Constance, 1979), pp. 335–74; "Akte des Fingierens oder: Was ist das Fiktiv im fiktionalen Text?" in *Poetik und Hermeneutik X*. Supplementary material can be found in the first two chapters of Jauss (1982), pp. 142–51 (divine predicates) and pp. 167–77, 181–88 (admiring identification).

21. [As used by Jauss, *fascinosum* designates an object of fascination with which the observer has a productive rather than a purely contemplative rapport. I have retained the term because it draws attention to this interplay—the participation and appropriation that involves the subject with its object.]

22. Jakob Burckhardt, *Griechische Kulturgeschichte*, III/2, in *Gesammelte Werke*, 6 (Darmstadt, 1956), pp. 97–98.

23. Blumenberg (1979), pp. 251ff.

24. Ibid., p. 36. Furthermore, "the epoch's mistaken belief that this could be the conceptual/sys-tematic version of the biblical God is almost incomprehensible since self-sufficiency is exactly the op-posite of that which makes the expenditure of this God in salvation both understandable and be-lievable."

25. *The Works of Francis Bacon*, 3, ed. J. Spedding et al. (Stuttgart, 1963), p. 343.

26. *Le temps retrouvé*, 2, in *A la recherche du temps perdu*, 15 (Paris, 1949), p. 23.

27. *Götzen-Dämmerung*, 2, in *Werke*, ed. K. Schlechta (Munich, 1966), p. 995. [This English translation is a slightly revised version of the lines found in *The Twilight of the Idols, The Complete Works of Friedrich Nietzsche*, 16, ed. Oscar Levy (London and New York, 1911), p. 67.]

28. With the founding of aesthetics as a science, perfection changes from being the completion of the ontological predicate into a determinant of material knowledge. See Baumgarten, *Aesthetica*, section 14: "The goal of aesthetics is the perfection (completion) of material knowledge as such. How-

ever, what is meant in this instance is beauty. Correspondingly, the imperfection of material knowledge as such, meaning the ugly, is to be avoided."

29. See section 1 of this chapter.

30. In this regard, see Lotman (1977), pp. 327ff.

31. Jolles (1956), p. 200.

32. Blumenberg (1979), p. 86.

33. *Confessions*, in *Oeuvres complètes*, 1 (Paris, 1964), pp. 18, 43. On this subject see Jean Starobinski, "Le remède dans le mal," in *Rousseau secondo Jean-Jacques* (Rome, 1979), pp. 19–40, where the first misstep is interpreted as birth, the "première des malheurs."

34. C. Lugowski, *Wirklichkeit und Dichtung: Untersuchungen zur Wirklichkeitsauffassung Heinrich von Kleists* (Frankfurt, 1936).

35. For a detailed discussion, see the author's *Zeit und Erinnerung in Marcel Prousts 'A la recherche du temps perdu,'* 2nd ed. (Heidelberg, 1970), pp. 143ff., and Gerard Genette, *Mimologiques: Voyage en Cratylie* (Paris, 1976), pp. 315ff., which, however, fails to note the significance of the *Age des choses* with regard to the transformative function of memory.

36. ["Verweile doch, du bist so schön" Faust I, l. 1700.]

37. ["Blessed be the day, the month, and the year." Canzoniere 61.]

38. "Immer wieder, ob wir der Liebe Landschaft auch Kennen."

39. "Schwarze Milch der Frühe wir trinken sie abends" [from Celan's "Todestage"].

40. ["One flash . . . then darkness!—Radiant fugitive / Whose glance that instant resurrected me, / Shall I no more behold you while I live? // Elsewhere, far off, too late, *never* maybe! / Your goals unknown to me, and mine to you— / You, whom I could have loved, who knew it too!" *The Flowers of Evil and All Other Poems*, trans. P. Higson and E. Ashe (Chester, 1975), p. 99].

41. See Pannenberg, "Das Irreale des Glaubens," in *Poetik und Hermeneutik X.*

42 See Kelly, *Medieval Imagination*, p. 37. The formulation *laetus horror* derives from Statius's *Epistolae duorum amantium* (24 and 108).

43. ["It is an absolute perfection and virtually divine to know how to enjoy our being rightfully." *The Complete Works of Montaigne*, trans. D. Frame (Stanford, 1957), p. 857. Hereafter cited as *Montaigne*.]

44. ["And on the loftiest throne in the world, we are still sitting on our own rump." *Essais* (Paris, 1950), p. 1257; *Montaigne*, p. 857.] On Socrates, see *Essais*, p. 1156. "Ces humeurs transcendentes m'effrayent, comme les lieux hautaines et inaccessibles; et rien ne m'est à digerer facheux en la vie de Socrate que ses ecstases et ses demoneries, rien si humain en Platon que ce pourquoy ils disent qu'on l'appelle divin." ["These transcendental humors frighten me, like lofty and inaccessible places; and nothing is so hard for me to stomach in the life of Socrates as his ecstasies and possessions by his deamon, nothing is so human in Plato as the qualities for which they say he is called divine" (*Montaigne*, p. 856).]

45. Les reveries du premeneur solitaire," V, Edition de la Pléiade, vol. 1, p. 1047. ["What do we enjoy in such a situation? Nothing external to ourselves, nothing if not ourselves and our own existence. As long as this state lasts, we are sufficient unto ourselves." *The Reveries of the Solitary Walker*, trans. C. E. Butterworth (New York, 1979), p. 69.]

46. "Aus Ottiliens Tagebuche," in *Die Wahlverwandtschaften*, part 2, chapter 9 [(Berlin, 1965), p. 214.]

47. *Arbeit am Mythos*, part 4, especially pp. 167ff.

48. See E. Köhler, "Narcisse, la fontaine d'amour et Guillaume de Lorris, in *Journal des savants* (1963), pp. 86–103, reprinted in *Esprit und arkadische Freiheit* (Frankfurt and Bonn, 1966), pp. 123ff. See also J. Rychner, "Le mythe de la fontaine de Narcisse dans le roman de la Rose," in *Le lieu et la formule: Hommage à Marc Eigeldinger* (Paris, 1979), pp. 33ff.

49. ["Because it was he, because it was I." *Montaigne*, p. 139.]

50. Herder, *Sämtliche Werke*, vol. 32, ed. B. Suphan, p. 79. See also H.-D. Weber, *Friedrich Schlegels "Transzendentalpoesie"* (Munich, 1973), p. 94.

51. *Gesammelte Schriften*, 4/1 (Frankfurt, 1980), p. 92. [The English version is taken, in slightly amended form, from Walter Benjamin, *One-Way Street and Other Writings*, trans. Edmond Jephcott and Kingsley Shorter (London, 1978), p. 52.]

52. The following draws on Manfred Fuhrmann, "Die Rezeption der aristotelischen Tragödienpoetik in Deutschland," in *Handbuch des deutschen Dramas*, 1, ed. W. Hinck (Dusseldorf, 1980), pp. 93-105.

53. Ibid., p. 94.

54. From a letter to Eschenburg, October 26 1774, in *Sämtliche Schriften*, 18, ed. Karl Lachmann (Leipzig, 1907), pp. 115-16.

55. Marquis de Sade, *Idée sur les romans*, in *Oeuvres complètes*, 4 (Paris, 1961), p. 67.

56. Cited in Klaus Oettinger, "Eine Krankheit zum Tode: Zum Skandal um Werthers Selbstmord," in *Der Deutschunterricht*, 28 (1976), p. 63.

57. See Oettinger, ibid.

58. Jean-Paul Sartre, in *L'imaginaire* (Paris, 1940), p. 225, writes: "Just as King Midas transformed everything he touched into gold, consciousness is determined to transform everything it grasps into the imaginary: from this derives the fatal nature of the dream."

59. R. M. Lenz, "Briefe über die Moralität der Leiden des jungen Werthers," in P. Müller, *Der junge Goethe im zeitgenössischen Urteil* (Berlin, 1969), p. 225.

60. [Instead of chasing after the chimera of perfection, let's look for the best possible as it accords with the nature of man and the constitution of society.] "Lettre à d'Alembert," cited in P. Robert, *Dictionnaire alphabétique et analogique de la langue française* (Paris, 1962), under the word "Perfection."

61. [An age that questions everything, that lives to test everything, to look at everything as if it is open to being improved on and, therefore, provisional . . . cannot be a time of repose for the Arts and Letters. The quest for improvement precludes a search for perfection. To improve on is not the same as to perfect.] Paul Valéry, *Oeuvres*, Edition de la Pléiade, 1 (Paris, 1957), p. 719.

62. For the precise references to these ideas, which are drawn from *Léonard et les Philosophes* and *Eupalinos*, see my chapter on poiesis in *Aesthetic Experience and Literary Hermeneutics*, pp. 55-57, and Hans Blumenberg (1964), pp. 285-323.

63. See H.-G. Gadamer, "Vom Zirkel des Verstehens," in *Kleine Schriften*, 4 (Tübingen, 1977), pp. 58-59: "The contentual significance of the circle created by the whole and the part, which is the basis for all understanding, must, however . . . be expanded by the inclusion of another modifier, one which I would like to call the 'anticipation of perfection.' This formulation describes a presupposition that precedes all understanding. It suggests that only that which really represents a perfect unity of meaning is understandable."

3. The use of fiction in the perception and representation of history

64. See Koselleck (1979), p. 283.

65. See *Französische Geschichte*, ed. O. Vossler (Stuttgart, 1954). Hereafter, all references cited in the text will be to the first volume of this edition.

66. From the program of the conference on "Forms of Historical Writing" (1979) organized by the "Theory and History" study group of the Werner Reimer Foundation, at which I presented this work. The results of this conference were published in *Formen der Geschichtschreibung*, ed. R. Koselleck and J. Rüsen (Munich, 1982). The second quotation is from Stierle (1979), p. 899.

67. Koselleck (1979), pp. 281ff. See above, section 1, regarding the history of the *verisimile*.

68. Koselleck (1979), p. 187.

69. Ibid., pp. 280-82.

70. *Historik: Vorlesungen über Enzyklopädie und Methodologie der Geschichte*, ed. R. Hübner (Munich, 1967), p. 322. Hereafter, page numbers or paragraphs from Droysen's *Grundriss der Historik* will be cited in the text.

71. *Historik*, pp. 144, 149. See as well the entries indexed under the heading "Fantasy," pp. 155, 228, 339, 418, 423. Interestingly enough, the terms "illusion" and "fiction" are not listed in the index.

72. See "Geschichte der Kunst und Historie," in *Poetik und Hermeneutik V*, pp. 175–209.

73. I will leave to the professional historian the task of comparing the results of my revised analysis with that arising from the work others have done on Ranke (e.g., B. K. H. Metz, *Grundformen historiographischen Denkens* [Munich, 1979]), or to that produced by historical hermeneutics and historiographic research.

74. From the program of the conference "Forms of Historical Writing." See note 66, this chapter.

75. Koselleck (1979), p. 280.

76. For an examination of the genuine religious framework (*theatrum mundi*) found in Ranke's notion of historical occurrences see A. Borst's article in *Poetik und Hermeneutik V*, pp. 536ff.

77. A. Thierry, *Sur les trois grandes méthodes historiques en usage depuis le seizième siècle* (1820); de Barente, *Préface de l'histoire des Ducs de Bourgogne* (1824); and the anonymous article, "De la nouvelle école historique" (1828), as cited in K. Massmann, *Die Rezeption des historischen Romans von Sir Walter Scott in Frankreich von 1816 bis 1832* (Heidelberg, 1972), especially p. 89.

78. That there is a "parallelism in goals" here, "which justifies the claim that the idea of the historical novel as it was shaped by Scott was better able to fulfill the program of the Scottish school of history than was this school itself," has also been demonstrated by W. Wolff in "Zwei Versionen des historischen Romans: Scotts *Waverley* und Thackerays *Henry Esmond*," in *Lebende Antike*, Symposium for Rudolf Sühnel, ed. H. Meller and H.-J. Zimmermann (Berlin, 1967), pp. 348–69, especially p. 357.

79. According to Kurt Badt, the beginnings of a particular style often "do not emerge in tentative or incomplete fashion, but, rather—like Athena from Zeus's forehead—the new style appears before us in its entirety, a little awkwardly perhaps, but complete and fully developed in its characteristics." *Eine Wissenschaftslehre der Kunstgeschichte* (Cologne, 1971), p. 102.

80. "It is understandable that this prince awakened in Dante, the greatest poet of the epoch, . . . an antipathy that broke out in vociferous reproach" (p. 80); "In order to understand even a little bit about her [the Maid of Orléans], one must remember" (p. 89).

81. "What a *pernicious* blow Edward dealt the nobles when he came of age and decided to exercise his rights" (p. 82); "finally the *most wonderful* apparition emerged from the lower class, from the tillers of the soil: the Maid of Orléans" (p. 90); "It was a grand gesture Charles VII made when, after he had once again become master of the city, he took no vengeance on his old adversaries" (p. 90).

82. "Fiktion in konversationellen Erzählungen," in *Poetik und Hermeneutik X*.

83. This is also confirmed by the hermeneutics of behavioral science. As Theodor Luckmann shows, "The meaning of an experience is produced . . . when the I of the prior event . . . turns toward itself and places the event in a context that goes beyond the superficial features of the experience. In other words, meaning is constituted through an awareness of a relation between an experience and something else; thus, strictly speaking, it is constituted in retrospect, with reference to the experience. This other can be an earlier experience, one that, for example, is seen as similar ('this flower again'), or as a schema of experience ('this is a snow carnation'), or a maxim of behavior ('snow carnations are a protected species'), etc." See "Zum hermeneutischen Problem der Handlungswissenschaften," in *Poetik und Hermeneutik IX* (1981), p. 517.

84. Algirdes Greimas and Joseph Courthès, *Sémiotique: Dictionnaire raisonnée de la théorie du langage* (Paris, 1979), pp. 250–51: "La narrativité généralisée—libérée de son sens restrictif qui la liait aux formes figuratives des récits est considérée comme le principe organisateur de tout discours."

85. See Jauss (1977a), pp. 34–47.

86. "Geschichte und Norm: Wahrheitskriterien der historischen Erkenntnis," in *Normen und Geschichte*, ed. W. Oelmüller (Paderborn, 1979), p. 110.

87. Stierle (1979), p. 93.

88. Arno Borst, "Vlamy 1792: Ein historisches Ereignis?" in *Der Deutschunterricht*, 26 (1974). The contributions to this volume by Heinz-Dieter Weber, Borst, and Ferdinand Fellman continue the debate over the concept of the event that was begun at the conference "Poetik und Hermeneutik V" (see especially in Part II B of the published proceedings of this conference).

89. Fellmann, "Ereignis und geschichtliche Erfahrung," in *Der Deutschunterricht*, 26 (1974), p. 115.

90. See Borst, "Vlamy 1792: Ein historisches Ereignis?" pp. 101ff.

91. It is at this point that I must disagree with Fellmann, with whom I am otherwise in full accord. It may well be that the power of the historically developed concept of the event lies in its individualizing function, unlike the report of an actual experience cited by Borst (ibid., pp. 89ff.), which could well have come from participants in other campaigns. But the singularity of an event, reconstructed by the historian from all available sources, does not per se establish its comprehensibility as the meaning of historical experience. Such meaning always also takes for granted the limited generalizability of historical truth or—as Fellmann says—"the relation of the factual to the possible."

92. From a paper on the history of forms in Christian hagiography presented at a colloquium in Bochum (1979) that served as the basis for the volume on historiography in the *Grundriss der romanischen Literaturen des Mittelalters*, vol. 11, ed. H. U. Gumbrecht (Heidelberg, 1987).

93. "System und Diachronie: Untersuchungen zur theoretischen Grundlegung geschichtsschreibender Praxis im Mittelalter," in *Historisches Jahrbuch der Görresgesellschaft*, 95 (1975), p. 309.

94. "Was heisst: 'Das kann man nur historisch erklären'?" in *Poetik und Hermeneutik V*, pp. 542–53.

95. In an essay entitled "Geschichtsschreibung als Theorieproblem der Geschichtswissenschaft." See note 66, this chapter.

96. J. P. Hebel, *Erzählungen und Betrachtungen des Rheinischen Hausfreundes*, 2, ed. Wilhelm Altwegg (Freiburg, n.d.), pp. 369ff.

97. Jolles (1956), pp. 165–80. Here the reference is to p. 173.

98. Klaus Oettinger has provided a broad demonstration of this movement in Hebel's historical descriptions. See "Ein Beispiel, bei dem man Gedanken haben kann," in *Der Deutschunterricht*, 26 (1974), pp. 37–53. The lines cited here are on p. 43. He concludes that "[J. P. Hebel] presents world politics as if he is conversing with ordinary people. He tries to present the great issues of the larger world from the perspective of his provincial readers by using their language and their conceptual categories." This conclusion is supported by my analysis of the process of "rigorously imposing a perspective" (ibid., p. 42), and equally by the manner in which the appeal embodied in the oppositive detail is structured.

99. Jolles (1956), p. 167.

100. Ibid., p. 40.

B. A Questioning Adam: On the History of the Functions of Question and Answer

1. Adam, where art thou?

1. This idea comes from Bastian (1970), p. 15, who drew together a rich assemblage of materials from all the relevant disciplines for his theological dialectic, and thereby prepared the way for my own study. I want to thank Jürgen Mittelstrass and the members of the seminar that we held together in the winter semester 1980–81 for their crucial suggestions.

2. A literary demonstration of this point can be found in the lines "We want only answers from you! We have never conversed with your sort" in Hildesheimer's *Mary Stuart* and the comparable scene in Schiller's *Maria Stuart*. (See "Hildesheimers Reprise von Schillers *Maria Stuart*" in the German edition of the present volume.)

3. Blumenberg (1979), p. 142.

4. See "Three Case Studies in Aesthetic Application" in this volume.

5. See Pannenberg in *Poetik und Hermeneutik X*, p. 414.

6. See Gadamer (1975), Chapter 2, 3c, "The Hermeneutic Priority of the Question."

7. Pannenberg, pp. 420-21.

8. See E. Straus (1953), p. 149.

9. O. Marquard, "Frage nach der Frage, auf die Hermeneutik die Antwort ist," in (1981), pp. 117-46; this citation, p. 130. The thesis here is that the civil wars between Catholics and Protestants were experienced as hermeneutic wars about the absolute text, and that this was the historical situation to which hermeneutics responded by moving from singularizing to pluralizing interpretation and to the empowering of the literary (i.e., the nonabsolute) reader.

2. Thou shalt never ask me!

10. See Hans Blumenberg (1979), p. 299.

11. [The first of these is to be found in *Toward an Aesthetic of Reception*, pp. 110-38; the other, on *Amphitryon*, has not yet been translated and can be found in the German edition of the present book.]

12. See Jolles (1929), pp. 80, 86. The example is taken from Pindar's first Pythian Epinician.

13. See Berger and Luckmann (1970), pp. 74, 118 (mythology as the most archaic form of conceptual support and legitimation of sensual worlds).

14. On Hermann Lübbe's statement see *Poetik und Hermeneutik V*, pp. 542-54.

15. Jolles (1929), p. 80.

16. See Fellmann (1976), p. 28.

17. See "Befragung des Mythos und Behauptung der Identität in der Geschichte des 'Amphitryon,' " pp. 534-84 in the German edition of this book.

18. See Bakhtin (1979), pp. 168ff.

19. Blumenberg seems inclined toward the second hypothesis. See, for example, p. 681: "To bring a myth to its end was once supposed to be the task of the logos. This self-consciousness in philosophy – or rather, that of the historians of philosophy – is contradicted by the fact that the mythic work on the conclusion of a myth is itself always consummated in a metaphor about myth. To make the principle of insufficient reason embodied in the *acte gratuit* the central idea of aesthetics amounts to mythifying aesthetics in the same manner as did, for example, the idea of 'genius.' "

20. Freud, *Standard Edition*, 17, p. 249.

21. Ibid., p. 245.

22. Ibid., p. 241.

23. See Fuhrmann (1973), p. 85.

24. Especially in "The Creative Writer and Day-Dreaming," *Standard Edition*, 9, pp. 143-53.

25. See *Aesthetic Experience and Literary Hermeneutics*, pp. 22-36.

26. See Starobinski (1970), p. 179.

27. See "Die literarische Angst," in *Aspekte der Angst*, ed. H. v. Dithfurth (Munich, 1977), pp. 38-52. See as well pp. 53 and 152 of Jürgen Habermas's essay in the same volume.

28. From F. Panzer's critical edition one gathers that it was not in the original collection of *Grimm's Fairy Tales*.

29. See M.-L. Tenèse, "Du conte merveilleux comme genre," in *Arts et traditions populaires*, 18 (1970), p. 11.

30. "The Uncanny," p. 246.

3. Inquiry as the source of understanding

31. See W. Brugger, "Der Mensch, das fragende Wesen," in *Epimeleia*, ed. F. Wiedmann (Munich, 1964), p. 26.

32. See Gadamer (1959), p. 34, and (1975), p. 325.

33. Gadamer (1975), p. 330.

34. Koselleck (1979), pp. 205–6, 282–83. See also H. Marrou, *De la connaissance historique* (Paris, 1954), pp. 60–61: "Logically speaking, the process of elaborating history is unleashed not by the existence of documents, but by an original gesture, the question posed, that is inscribed in the choice, the delimitation, and the conception of the subject."

35. W. Kamlah asserts the priority of reception over action in his *Philosophische Anthropologie* (Mannheim, 1973); the way in which it is experienced also defines the dialogue, where – in a manner analogous to a tennis match – "each receives the answer of the other . . . each is in turn 'active' and 'passive' " (p. 37).

36. See Gadamer (1975), p. 341, where the main similarity between textual understanding and the understanding that occurs in a conversation consists above all in the fact that "both [the understanding of a text and the understanding that occurs in conversation] are concerned with an object that is placed before them." The prerequisite for the self-understanding enabled by this object is, on the other hand, the "anticipation of perfection that guides all our understanding" (1959, p. 30), which, it would seem, Gadamer assumes also makes possible an understanding of the alien "you." It seems to me, however, that this anticipation is not necessary for a specific understanding of the other. In fact, it needs to be gotten rid of if it proposes the otherness of the imperfect other as the very model of perfection (as is frequently the case in the first, so-called platonic experience of love).

37. As I show in my interpretation of Baudelaire's "Spleen II" in "The Poetic Text within the Change of Horizons of Reading: The Example of Baudelaire's 'Spleen II' " [in *Toward an Aesthetic of Reception*, pp. 139–85].

38. Bultmann (1961), p. 217.

39. E. Fuchs, *Hermeneutik*, 2nd ed. (Tübingen, 1958), p. 133; G. Ebeling, "Wort Gottes und Hermeneutik," in *Wort und Glaube*, 3rd ed. (Tübingen, 1967), p. 343.

40. Pannenberg (1971), p. 139.

41. Ibid., p. 111.

42. Gadamer (1975), p. 258, and the afterword to the third German edition (Tübingen, 1973), pp. 539, 540.

43. See Bultmann (1961), where he gives an example of the reception of a religious work of art.

4. First, ultimate, and impudent questions

44. See Blumenberg (1973), and my essay, "The Ambiguity and the Refractoriness of the Beautiful – a Backward Glance at a Platonic Legacy," in *Aesthetic Experience and Literary Hermeneutics*, pp. 36–45.

45. Bloch (1970), p. 5.

46. "Humanistic Studies: Their Object, Methods, and Meaning," in *Daedalus*, Spring 1970, p. 250.

47. See, for example, Wittgenstein's *Tractatus Logico-philosophicus*: "When the answer cannot be put into words, neither can the question be put into words. *The riddle* does not exist. If a question can be framed at all, it is also *possible* to answer it" [trans. D. Pears and B. McGuinness (London, 1972)], 6.5.

48. Lewis (1964), p. 221. The example that follows is drawn from Bede, *Hist. eccl. genetis Anglorum*, II13., translated as *Bede's Ecclesiastical History of the English People* (Oxford, 1969), p. 185.

49. Kuhn (1962); see also J. Mittelstrass, "Towards a Normative Conception of the Growth of Knowledge," in *Nature and System*, 2 (1970), pp. 231-44.

50. Kuhn (1962), p. 37.

51. James D. Watson, *The Double Helix*. A new critical edition, ed. Gunther Stent (London, 1981), p. 34.

52. See Blumenberg, "Kosmos und System" (1957a), "Epochenschwelle und Rezeption" (1958), "Kritik und Rezeption antiker Philosophie in der Patristik" (1959), and "Die Legitimität der Neuzeit" (1966).

53. Blumenberg (1959), p. 486. Specifically, "[Christianity] had to make some connection and, at the same time, disguise the fact that this was both a problem and a necessity. The aim of reception is to mask its own background."

54. Ibid. The reference here is to Paul's speech on the Areopagus.

55. Blumenberg (1958), p. 105.

56. On this subject, see Blumenberg's "Die Vorbereitung der Neuzeit," in *Philosophische Rundschau*, 9 (1962), pp. 81-133.

57. Bakhtin (1984), pp. 115-16: "Typical for the menippea is syncrisis (that is, juxtaposition) of precisely such stripped-down 'ultimate situations in the world.' Take, for example, the carnivalistic representation of the *Vitarum auctio*, in, for example, the final life situations in Lucian, the fantastic trips over ideological seas in Varro (*Sesculixes*), travels through all the philosophical schools (apparently already in Bion), and so forth."

58. See on this subject "Brunetto Latini als allegorischer Dichter" and "Allegorese, Remythisierung und neuer Mythus," in Jauss, *Aesthetische Erfahrung und literarische Hermeneutik*, vol.1 (Munich, 1977), pp. 239ff., 285ff.

59. Jolles (1929), pp. 160-61; a catalogue of questions belonging to courtly casuistics can also be found there.

60. See "The dialogic and the dialectic *Neveu de Rameau*" in this volume, pp. 118-47, and R. Warning's "Opposition und Kasus," in Warning (1975), pp. 467-93.

61. This becomes clear in his dispute with the priest, who quotes ever more subtle interpretations, only to reject them in the end because they are mere opinions concerning the unchangeable and therefore unknowable meaning of the scripture. "The scriptures are unalterable and the comments often enough merely expressions of the commentator's despair." *The Trial*, trans. W. and E. Muir (New York, 1964), p. 217.

62. Gadamer (1975), p. 326.

63. "Tragedy consists precisely in choosing questions without an outcome, so as to nourish in a sure way the appetite for failure." Roland Barthes, *On Racine*, trans. R. Howard (New York, 1977), p. 132.

64. Jolles (1929), p. 200.

5. Didactic questions, catechisms, and their consequences

65. See G. Bardy, "La littérature patristique des 'Quaestiones et Responsiones' sur l'Ecriture Sainte," in *Revue biblique*, 41 (1932), pp. 210-36; Heinrich Dörrie, "Erotapokriseis," in *Reallexikon für Antike und Christentum*, 6 (1966), esp. pp. 366-69; P. L. Schmidt, "Frühchristlicher lateinischer Dialog," in *Entretiens sur l'antiquité classique*, ed. O. Reverdin, 23 (Geneva, 1977), pp. 101-80.

66. "To justify his questions and doubt, Abelard turned expressly to the 'seeking' mentioned in Matthew 7:7 and to Jesus' questions in the temple." Bastian (1970), p. 293.

67. See M. Grabmann, *Die Geschichte der scholastischen Methode*, 2 (1961) pp. 426-27.

68. "Scholastische Aesthetik und höfische Dichtung," in Köhler (1962), pp. 21-28, and "Zur Entstehung des altprovenzalischen Streitgedichts," ibid., pp. 153-92.

69. Köhler (1962), p. 173.

70. Ibid., p. 178.

71. See Sebastian Neumeister, *Das Spiel mit der höfischen Liebe* (Munich, 1969).

72. Ibid., p. 122.

73. Ibid., p. 193.

74. It is especially striking that Dante makes no reference to Augustine in his canon of the blessed.

75. Auerbach (1953), p. 193.

76. This first appeared in *Dante als Dichter der irdischen Welt* (Berlin and Leipzig, 1929).

77. ["And I fell, as a dead body falls." Dante, *The Divine Comedy*, trans. H. R. Huse (New York, 1954).]

78. ["Here pity lives when it is completely dead."]

79. For example, *Inferno*, XXVIII, 126: "Com' esser può, quei sa che sì governa" ["How this can be He knows who ordains"]; see also Jauss (1982), pp. 42–43, 142ff.

80. See Bastian (1970), p. 294. I employ his argument in what follows as well.

81. A. H. Franke, cited in Bastian (1970), p. 297.

82. For example, the *lettres de conseil*, which answered readers' inquiries—a literary form that survives today in our magazines. On this see S. Yahalom in *Poétique*, 44 (1980), p. 418.

83. "Je renonce à des questions oiseuses, qui peuvent inquiéter mon amour-propre, mais qui sont inutiles à ma conduite et supérieures à ma raison." *Du Contrat social* (Paris, 1960), p. 426. [I can do without those otiose questions that may trouble my self-esteem, but that are unprofitable in terms of my conduct and beyond my understanding.]

84. See F. Nies, 'Zeitzeichnen—Gattungsbildung in der Revolutionsperiode . . . ," in *Francia*, 8 (1981), p. 48.

85. See Gumbrecht (1980), pp. 276–77.

86. Ibid., p. 282.

87. [*Amphitryon*, trans. M. Sonnenfeld (New York, 1962), p. 49.]

88. See "Befragung des Mythos und Behauptung der Identität in der geschichte des *Amphitryon*," in Jauss (1982) , pp. 534–84.

89. *Die Erziehung des Menschengeschlechts*, § 70–75.

90. On this topic, see Conze (1972), p. 202.

91. *Mélanges philosophiques* (Paris, 1785).

92. See *Aesthetic Experience and Literary Hermeneutics*, pp. 269–84.

93. Lobsien, *Der Alltag des Ulysses* (Stuttgart, 1978), especially pp. 128–30.

94. James Joyce, *Ulysses* (New York, 1961), pp. 723–24.

95. "An old man, widower, unkempt hair, in bed, with head covered, sighing: an infirm dog, Athos: aconite, resorted to by increasing doses of grains and scruples as a palliative of recrudescent neuralgia: the face in death of a septuagenarian suicide by poison" (p. 724).

96. Stierle (1979), p. 110.

97. Molly's monologue contains no syntagma of a questioning or of an answering sort except in its closing lines.

6. *Mais où sont les neiges d'antan?*

98. In the *Handbuch der literarischen Rhetorik* (Munich, 1960), which is representative of the work then being done, and in *Elemente der literarischen Rhetorik* (Munich, 1963), §445, by Heinrich Lausberg, the rhetorical question remains quite marginal within the classification of the *quaestiones*, and, as far as I know, what little research has been done on it remains limited to the study of its classical sources: Aristotle's *Rhetoric* III.18; Quintilian IX.2; Cicero, *De oratore* II.68, III.53; *Rhetorica ad Herennium* IV.22; *Peri Hypsous* XVIII. The most telling demonstration of the absence of any historical examination of the function of the rhetorical question seems to me to be found in the remarks made by Hugo Friedrich (1964), pp. 449–50.

99. De Man (1979), pp. 9ff. See as well J. D. Black's review "Rhetorical Questions and Critical Riddles," in *Poetics Today*, 1 (1980), pp. 189–201. De Man's examples are television's Archie Bunker and a line from Yeats ("How can we know the dancer from the dance?"), which I have supplemented with two classic academic examples.

100. De Man (1979), p. 10.

101. ["How much longer will you abuse our patience, Cataline?"]

102. "The deconstruction states the fallacy of reference in a necessarily referential mode" (ibid., p. 125).

103. Ibid., p. 10.

104. Here I draw on Friedrich (1964), p. 449.

105. It reaches its high point in this well-known sequence of questions: "Qu'est-ce que le tiers état? Tout. —Qu'a-t-il été jusqu' à présent dans l'ordre politique? Rien. —Que demande-t-il? A y devenir quelque chose. [What is the third estate? Everything. —What has it been in the political order up to now? Nothing. —What does it want? To have a meaningful place in that order."]

106. This example is take from Goebbels's famous Sports Palace speech of November 18, 1943. See Bastian (1970), pp. 211–12, "Simulated questions are even worse than authoritarian answers," and p. 16 concerning totalitarian statements about "the Jewish question, the race question, and the population question."

107. See Bastian (1970), pp. 338ff.

108. Friedrich (1964), p. 449.

109. [The English version of this poem is taken from the G. Cuttino translation (New York, 1955), p. 3.]

110. ["Where are they who came before us in the world?"]

111. See L. Spitzer, "Etude a-historique d'un texte: Ballade des dames du temps jadis," in Spitzer (1959), pp. 113–29, especially p. 117.

112. Ibid., pp. 117, 119–21.

113. ["O Prince, seek not to know this week / Where they may be, or yet this year // While this refrain returns to speak: // Where are the snows of yesteryear?"]

114. Spitzer (1959), p. 116. ["The refrain must 'remain,' the cortege has to disappear without a trace, only the refrain is destined for immortality."]

115. Ricoeur (1978), p. 79.

116. [*Poems By Eduard Mörike*, trans. N. Cruickshank and G. Cunningham (London, 1959), pp. 41–42.]

117. ["Wer sleht den lewen? Wer sleht den risen? / wer überwindet jenen und diesen? / Daz tuot einer, der sich selbst twinget . . . " (Walter von der Vogelweide).]

118. ["Halt an, wo laufst du hin? Der Himmel ist in dir . . . "]

119. ["Why do they search the heavens, all these blind men?"]

120. ["Emma, sage mir die Wahrheit: / Ward ich närrisch durch die Liebe? / Oder ist die Liebe selber / Nur die Folge meiner Narrheit? // Ach! mich quälet, teure Emma, / Ausser meiner tollen Liebe, / Ausser meiner Liebestollheit, / Obendrein noch dies Dilemma." The English version is drawn from *New Poems* in *the Works of Heinrich Heine*, 18, trans. C. G. Leland (New York, n.d.), pp. 70–71.]

121. ["Are you sleeping, my love? / Is your dream sweeter than my kiss? / Listen, a little bird / Is singing in the linden outside our window."]

122. In the Middle High German original the first two lines are, "Slâfst du, friedel ziere? / man weckt uns leider schiere" (*MF* 39, 18).

123. [H. M. Enzenberger, *poems for people who don't read poems*, trans. M. Hamberger (New York, 1986), p. 21.]

124. [A slightly different, but full, translation of this poem can be found in *Paul Celan's Poems*, trans. M. Hamberger (New York, 1980), p. 157.]

125. ["Warum gabst du uns die tiefen Blicke . . . warum gabst uns Schicksal, die Gefühle . . . "]

126. ["Prometheus," in *The Poems of Goethe*, 2nd ed., trans. E. A. Bowring (London, 1874), p. 182. "Wer half mir / Wider der Titanen Übermut / Wer rettete vom Tode mich, / Vor Sklaverei? Hast due nicht alles selbst vollendet, / Heilig glühend Herz?"]

127. "These are all questions that have always been covered over again by more questions or that (at best) showed more transparent under the influence of other self-illuminating questions—; they are the great question-dynasties—who then has ever answered?" Letter to L. H., November 8, 1915, in *Wartime Letters of Rainer Maria Rilke*, trans. M. D. H. Norton (New York, 1940), p. 51. "Try to cherish the questions themselves, like closed rooms and like books written in a very strange tongue." From a letter to F. X. Kappus, July 16, 1903, in *Letters to a Young Poet*, trans. Reginald Snell (London, 1945), p. 21. I am indebted to August Stahl for these references.

128. ["Und fast end Mädchen wars und ging hervor / aus diesem Glück von Sang und Leier / und glänzte klar durch ihre Frühlingsschleier / und machte sich ein Bett in meinem Ohr. // Und schlief in mir. Und alles war ihr Schlaf. / Die Bäume, die ich je bewundert, diese / fühlbare Ferne, die gefühlte Wiese / und jedes Staunen, was mich selbst betraf. // Sie schlief die Welt. Singender Gott, wie hast / du sie vollendet, dass sie nicht begehrte, / erst wach zu sein? Sieh, sie erstand und schlief. // Wo ist ihr Tod? O, wirst du dies Motiv / erfinden noch, eh sich dein Lied verzehrte?– / Wo sinkt sie hin aus mir? . . . Ein Mädchen fast . . . " The English version is from R. M. Rilke, *Sonnets to Orpheus*, trans. David Young (Middletown, Conn., 1987), p. 5.]

129. ["Wir Gewaltsamen, wir währen länger. / Aber *wann*, in welchem aller Leben, / sind wir endlich offen und Empfänger?"]

C. Three Case Studies in Aesthetic Application

1. The myth of the Fall (Genesis 3), interpreted literarily

1. ["Where art thou?"]

2. ["Who told thee that thou wast naked?"]

3. ["Behold, the man is become as one of us . . . "]

4. ["And when the woman saw that the tree was good for food, and that it was a delight to the eyes, and that the tree was to be desired to make one wise . . . "]

5. ["The woman whom thou gavest to be with me . . . "]

6. ["And the eyes of them both were opened . . . "]

7. ["And the eyes of them both were opened, and they knew that they were naked."]

8. ["Who told thee that thou wast naked?"]

9. ["Hast thou eaten of the tree . . . "]

10. ["Be fruitful and multiply."]

11. ["Because thou hast harkened unto the voice of thy wife."]

12. ["Cursed is the ground for thy sake."]

13. ["Behold, the man is become as one of us . . . "]

14. Ernst Bloch, "Betrachtungen der Schlange," in *Atheismus im Christentum*, reprinted in *Die Sache mit dem Apfel*, ed. J. Illies (Freiburg, 1972), p. 146.

15. "Die Taktik der Verführung," in *Die Sache mit dam Apfel*, pp. 80-89.

16. Hegel, *Werke*, ed. H. Glockner, IX, p. 413; on this see Bloch, "Betrachtungen der Schlange," p. 149.

17. ["verdant paradise of childhood loves."]

18. ["The real paradises are those one has lost."]

19. See the sections "Poiesis" and "Aesthesis" in *Aesthetic Experience and Literary Hermeneutics*, pp. 46-92.

20. See Grimm (1977).

21. ["It is not good that the man should be alone; I will make him a helpmeet for him."] On this topic, see H. Spaemann, "Die angebissene Frucht," in *Die Sache mit dem Apfel*, p. 94.

22. At that very important moment of self-recognition when Adam and Eve first meet, Milton uses the metaphor of the mirror as a means of thematizing the intersubjective relationship *inter pares*, thus contrasting it with the nonreflective relation that arises from being made in the image of God. Eve, awakening into life, first discovers her reflection in the water of a lake. A voice explains that this is her "self," and then leads her to Adam, her other self in persona. She shrinks from him, just as she had from her own reflection, but then realizes that she is "his flesh," "his bone," and the "other half" of his soul (IV, ll. 460ff.)

23. See IV, ll. 288ff.: Two of far nobler shape erect and tall, / Godlike erect, with native Honour clad / In naked Majestie seemd Lords of all, / . . . ; though both / Not equal, as thir sex not equal seemd; / For contemplation hee and valour formd, / For softness shee and sweet attractive Grace, / Hee for God only, shee for God in him . . .

2. Job's questions and answers from afar (Goethe, Nietzsche, Heidegger)

24. This essay, which was written in memory of Erich Köhler, was first published in *Poetika*, 13 (1981), pp. 1-15.

25. See 9:34ff.; 13:3, 22; 19:7; 23:5; 30:20; 31:35; 42:4. In the rest of the essay, I also draw on the literature mentioned in Bastian (1970), pp. 272ff., and the article entitled "Hiobbuch," in *Religion in der Geschichte der Gegenwart*, ed. K. Gallling, 3rd ed. (Tübingen, 1957). [The citations in the original essay are taken from the "Zurich Bible" (1970), this translation uses the revised King James version.]

26. *Poetik und Hermeneutik III*, p. 536.

27. Ibid., p. 545.

28. Ibid., p. 547.

29. I have demonstrated elsewhere that the heroic/gallant novel can be seen as a theodicy in the Leibnizian sense. See "The perfect as the *fascinosum* of the imaginary" in this volume, particularly p. 16.

30. See *Poetic and Hermeneutik III*, p. 545.

31. The Hebrew word means "avenger" ("blood avenger"), and, later, "advocate," not "redeemer."

32. *Theologie des alten Testaments*, 1 (Munich, 1962-65), p. 428. See also Ernst Bloch's critique in *Atheismus im Christentum* (Frankfurt, 1977), p. 127.

33. ["No one is against God except God himself"], *Dichtung und Wahrheit*, epigraph to Part 4. Although Blumenberg's arguments in *Arbeit am Mythos* (1979), Part 4, Chapter 4, have convinced me that we can ascribe this saying to Goethe himself, the fact in no way interferes with my interpretation. Indeed, thanks to the parallels with the Book of Job it suggests, it further exposes the *monstrosity* of such a cleft in the idea of God, and actually deepens my interpretation.

34. Bloch, *Atheismus im Christentum*, p. 123.

35. Ibid.

36. Ibid., p. 124.

37. Bastian (1970), p. 274.

38. Ibid., p. 275.

39. *Atheismus im Christentum*, p. 133.

40. ["Let God cease to exist!"]

41. See Marquard (1973), especially pp. 61-62.

42. It is from this perspective that I address these two works in "Goethe's and Valéry's *Faust*: On the Hermeneutics of Question and Answer" [*Toward an Aesthetic of Reception*, pp. 110-38].

43. [This and all further quotations from *Faust* are taken from the Norton critical edition, trans. W. Arndt (New York, 1976).]

44. "The Word of Nietzsche: 'God is Dead,' " in Martin Heidegger (1971), pp. 53–112.

45. Ibid., p. 58.

46. [Friedrich Nietzsche, *The Gay Science*, trans. W. Kaufmann (New York, 1974), pp. 181–82.]

47. On this variant, see Heidegger, ibid., pp. 60–61.

3. The dialogic and the dialectic Neveu de Rameau; or, The reciprocity between Diderot and Socrates, Hegel and Diderot

48. Galle, "Diderot–oder die Dialogisierung der Aufklärung," in *Neues Handbuch der Literaturwissenschaft*, 13, ed. J. v. Stackelberg (Wiesbaden, 1980), pp. 209–48.

49. See Jürgen Mittelstras, "Aufklärung," in the *Enzyklopädie: Philosophie und Wissenschaftstheorie*, which he edited (Mannheim, 1980), vol. 1, p. 213.

50. Bakhtin (1984), especially p. 109.

51. J. Seznec, *Essais sur Diderot et l'antiquité* (Oxford, 1975), p. 2.

52. This is a summary of Bakhtin, pp. 114–22.

53. See Chapter 1, "Le Socrate imaginaire."

54. "Das Verhältnis zwischen Diderots *Satire I* und *Satire II*," in Dieckmann, *Diderot und die Aufklärung*, (Stuttgart, 1982), p. 155.

55. Bakhtin (1984), p. 115.

56. *Jacques le fataliste*, in *Oeuvres romanesques* (Paris, 1962), p. 493. ["How had they met? By chance, like everyone else. What were their names? What does it matter to you? Whence had they come? From the nearest possible spot. Where were they going? Do we ever know where we are going? What were they saying? The master said nothing and Jacques said that his captain said that everything that happens to us down here, good or bad, was written up yonder." *Jacques the Fatalist and His Master*, trans. J. Loy (New York, 1959), p. 3.]

57. Jolles (1929), p. 158.

58. An analysis of the "Reader as Casuist" in Diderot's novels can be found in Warning (1975), pp. 467–93.

59. ["Is he good? Is he bad?"]

60. Diderot, *Oeuvres romanesques*, ed. H. Bénac (Paris, 1951), p. 812. ["Now, put your hand on your heart and tell me, Mr apologist for deceivers and the unfaithful, whether you would be willing to have the doctor from Toulouse as a friend? . . . You hesitate? That says it all."]

61. Of special relevance for my analysis are D. Mornet, "La véritable signification du N. de R.," *Revue des deux mondes* (1927), pp. 881–908; Lionel Trilling, "The Legacy of Sigmund Freud," *Kenyon Review* (1940), pp. 153ff.; J. Fabre, introduction to the critical edition, *Le neveu de Rameau* (Geneva, 1950); P. Meyer, "The Unity and Structure of Diderot's *N. de R.*," *Criticism* (1960); James Doolittle, *Rameau's Nephew* (Geneva, 1960); Roger Laufer, "Structure et signification du Neveu de Rameau," *Revue des sciences humaines* (1960), pp. 399–423; Lester G. Crocker, "Le neveu de Rameau, une expérience morale," *Cahiers de l'Ass. Int. des Etudes Fr.* (1961), pp. 133–55; Gita May, "L'angoisse de l'échec et la genèse du N. de R.," *Studies on Voltaire*, 25 (1963), pp. 493–507; H. Josephs, *Diderot and the Dialogue of Gesture and Language* (Princeton, N.J., 1963); C. Sherman, "Diderot and the Art of Dialogue," *Histoire des idées et critique littéraire*, vol. 156 (Geneva, 1976); Michele Duchet and Michel Launay, *Entretiens sur le N. de R.* (Paris, 1967).

62. Doolittle, *Rameau's Nephew*, pp. 121–26.

63. Starobinski, "Le dîner de Bertin," in *Poetik und Hermeneutik VII*, pp. 191–204.

64. ["What have you done?"]

65. ["The good conscience of the dialoging philosopher is undermined by the Nephew's disrupted consciousness, which is then surpassed by the superior consciousness of the philosopher-writer."]

66. Laufer, "Structure et signification du N. de R.," p. 400 (see note 61, this chapter).

67. [The citations in the German version of this essay are taken either from J. Fabre's critical edition of *Le neveu de Rameau* (Paris, 1950) or from Goethe's translation, which Jauss draws upon because of its relevance in the reception history of Diderot's work. Unless otherwise noted, all the English quotations in this translation are from *Rameau's Nephew and Other Works* (Indianapolis and New York, 1964).]

68. ["He brought philosophy back to earth from the regions near the sun where it had gone astray."]

69. ["His philosophy was not an example of ostentatious parading but of courage and practice."]

70. ["The stunning use of irony . . . which effortlessly reveals the ridiculous aspect of opinions; and of induction, which, moving from one group of unrelated questions to another, leads you imperceptibly toward acceptance of precisely that which had been rejected."]

71. ["Socrates readily understood that the truth is like a thread, one end of which emerges from darkness, while the other loses itself in darkness; and that, in regard to every question, light increases by degrees up to a certain point along the length of this thread, beyond this point, the light dims little by little and finally goes out. The philosopher is that person who knows just when to stop; the sophist, being imprudent, goes on, and leads himself and others astray: the whole of his dialectic terminates in uncertainties."]

72. Page 12: "But I don't know any history because I don't know anything at all"; p. 18: "You know that I am an ignoramus, a fool, a lunatic, a lazy, impudent, greedy"; p. 29: "And you were entirely ignorant of both? *He*: Not really. That's why the others were worse than I, namely those who thought they knew something."

73. [The term "maieutic" is in fact derived from the Greek word *maieuomai*, to act as a midwife.]

74. H. Josephs, *Diderot and the Dialogue of Gesture and Language* (see note 16, pp. 127f.) wants to place *Moi* in the role of the midwife, and interprets the same lines (p. 78) ["voilà ce que c'est que de trouver un accoucheur qui sait irriter"] as if they referred to *Moi*. But in context, "accoucheur" refers to the previous pantomime in which *Lui* himself portrays the "birth of an idea," beginning with blows to his forehead.

75. Quoted from the transcript of the colloquium on June 13, 1969, pp. 29f. (later published in *Diderot und die Aufklärung, Wolfenbütteler Forschungen*, 10 [Munich, 1980], where the citation is found on p. 182).

76. ["The disarray of the conversation."]

77. D. O'Gorman points this out in *Diderot the Satirist* (Toronto, 1971), p. 93.

78. I have borrowed this interpretation from Jean Starobinski, "Le dîner de Bertin," pp. 197ff.

79. *Phenomenology of Spirit*, trans. A. V. Miller (1977), p. 315. All further references to this edition will be made in the text with page numbers only.

80. [This line has been slightly altered in order to more accurately convey the sense of the original German.]

81. *Genèse et structure de la phénoménologie de l'esprit de Hegel* (Paris, 1946; reprinted 1967), Part V, Chapters 3-4, especially pp. 375, 398-401, 415, 420.

82. Benjamin, "Eduard Fuchs: Collector and Historian," in *The Essential Frankfurt School Reader* (New York, 1982), p. 227.

83. ["A sorry type."]

84. [In this instance Goethe's German translation is at variance with the original French, but has been cited because it serves nicely to make a point about the selectivity of Hegel's references (to culture and education in this case) in his reception of the work—which, it must be remembered, was based on Goethe's text. The French runs as follows: "A great scoundrel is a great scoundrel, he isn't a 'type.' Before the molecule could recapture him [i.e., the nephew's son] and reproduce the state of perfect abjection which I have reached, it would take endless time. He would waste his best years."]

85. [Jauss cites the Fabre edition of Diderot's text here, p. 24.]

86. I would particularly like to object to the interpretation Lionel Trilling imposes on Hegel's

Diderot reception in the second chapter of *Sincerity and Authenticity* (Cambridge, Mass., 1971), when he suggests that sincerity, as it is represented by Diderot's philosopher, is misunderstood by Hegel to be a virtue of a bygone era. As far as I can see, exactly the opposite arises out of the nephew's *franchise*: a new form of authenticity, characterized by its negativity—that of the "disrupted consciousness" (i.e., the "speech of this mind which is fully aware of its confused state").

87. On this subject, see J. Fabre's commentary in his edition of *Le neveu*, p. 222: "If this 'trinity' so dear to Diderot is something other than mere scholastic verbiage rejuvenated by a parody of doubtful taste, then it must signify that man arrives at morality and truth via the intermediary of the beautiful, which is the 'Holy Ghost.' This primacy which in practice was granted to the beautiful may well be the final word in Diderot's philosophy."

D. Rousseau's *Nouvelle Héloïse* and Goethe's *Werther* within the Shift of Horizons from the French Enlightenment to German Idealism

1. A selected bibliography appears at the end of this essay. All quotations are drawn from these works, which will be cited in the text by their initials along with the page number.

2. See R. Engelsing, *Der Bürger als Leser* (Stuttgart, 1974), especially Chapter 12 (intensive reading always presupposes constant rereading, an absorption in the already known, and, consequently, spiritual edification through the text).

3. "Werther is a more ardent, somber, and *überspannt* [extravagant] Saint-Preux" (Julie von Bondeli, quoted in JV, p. 132).

1. The gap between expectation and experience in Rousseau's Nouvelle Héloïse

4. "Il n'en est pas ainsi, ma Julie, entre deux amants de même âge, tous deux épris du même feu, qu'un mutuel attachement unit, qu'aucun lien particulier ne gêne, qui jouissent tous les doux de leur première liberté, et dont aucun droit ne proscrit l'engagement réciproque" (*OC* II, p. 86). ["It is different, Julie, with two lovers of the same age, both seized with the same passion, united by a mutual attachment, not bound by any special ties, both enjoying their original liberty, and forbidden by no law to pledge themselves to each other."] Rousseau does not realize that this same claim "nihil umquam, Deus scit, in te nisi te cupivi [God knows that in you I never longed for anything but you"] was also made in the original exchange of letters between Abelard and Héloïse. See *Aesthetic Experience and Literary Hermeneutics*, pp. 24, 140–41.

5. On Voltaire's pamphlet see AA, pp. 234ff., and the mocking lines, "Ma Julie, avec moi perdant son pucelage, / Accouche d'un foetus, et n'en est que plus sage" (ibid., p. 236). ["My Julie, who, losing her virginity with me / bears a fetus, and is nothing if not wiser for it."]

6. As Rousseau's partner in conversation in the *Seconde Préface* expressly indicates (*OC* II, pp. 18, 21).

7. ["The world didn't know her while it had her: / I knew her, I who remain here to weep."]

8. Benjamin defines aura as a "unique phenomenon of distance however close it may be." Walter Benjamin (1969), p. 243.

9. This is Rousseau's translation of *E'l cantar che nell'anima si sente* [The singing that is heard by the soul]. *Canzoniere* 178.

10. [A "little world different from our own."]

11. The specific places where these authors appear are noted in the index of *OC* II. I have not included Plato in this group because the manner in which he is used (III, xxi; VI, xi) problematizes his authority.

12. ["Grand passions are smothered, seldom are they purified."]

13. ["His melancholy book will never suit the tastes of decent people."]

14. Julie replaces these fables with little narrative examples, most of which are taken from the Bible. The Bible itself is, in general, only marginally present, in the footnotes. Postclassical literature is also ignored or included only in documentary fashion—for example, Béat de Muralt, Madame Riccoboni, or *Le voyage de l'amiral Anson*. See the index to *OC* II.

15. In separating herself from Saint-Preux, Julie uses arguments against the *inquiétude* of love's passions that read like quotations from *Le Princesse de Clèves* (III, p. xx; see the analogue in VI, viii). But here they must serve to justify her forthcoming marriage to Wolmar, whom she does not love. This said, the highly complex, critical reception given *Le Princesse de Clèves* in *La nouvelle Héloïse* has been broached only in question form, and still stands in need of a thorough interpretation.

16. ["Big cities have to have plays and corrupt novels. I have observed the morals of my era, and published these letters. Would that I had lived during a century in which I could have thrown them in the fire!"]

17. Cited in WV, p. 111. Diderot presents the same argument in his "Eloge de Richardson," which was published after *La nouvelle Héloïse*.

18. Reinhart Koselleck, *Kritik und Krise* (1959); Jürgen Habermas, *Strukturwandel der Öffentlichkeit* (1962); Wilhelm Vosskamp.

19. ["Reasoning like a Platonist about love, and practicing it like an Epicurean."] J. B. Suard, "Parallèle entre la Clarisse de Richardson et la Nouvelle Héloïse de M. de Rousseau," in *Variétés littéraires* (Paris, 1804; reprint Geneva, 1969).

20. ["To whom are you praising unsullied purity? Well, let's hear about a purity that can be recovered."]

21. *OC* II, p. 754. In the footnote to letter III, p. xviii, Richardson is mentioned expressly in order to reprimand him for his failure to understand "love at first sight."

22. ["I find him all the more immoral because it all has the air of being upright."]

23. ["Oh! That I had been born in a century when I could have thrown this collection in the fire!"]

24. ["The style will put off people of taste; the content will alarm those who are severe; all the sentiments will seem unnatural to those who don't believe in virtue."]

25. ["Who will it please then? Perhaps only me."]

26. Habermas (1962), p. 69.

27. On this question see H. Weinrich, "Muss es Romanlektüre geben?" in *Leser und Lesen im 18. Jahrhundert*, ed. R. Grünter (Heidelberg, 1977) with reference to L. Nelson and R. J. Ellrich. The fundamental idea here is that of a "pact of generosity" between author and reader such as Sartre first described and understood it (1965, p. 49).

28. Symptomatic of the original negativity of Rousseau's novel is the judgment made by Formey in the *Annales typographiques*: "Tout est problème à ses yeux, et il voudrait tout rendre problématique à ses Lecteurs. Ses ouvrages deviennet par-là beaucoup plus dangereux que ceux des Ecrivains déclarés pour l'irréligion." ["Everything is problematic for him, and he wants to problematize everything for his readers. Thus, his works become much more dangerous than those of writers who have openly declared themselves supporters of irreligiosity"] (cited in AA, p. 246).

29. For a more extended discussion of this topic, see "On the origins of the differentiation between fiction and reality," pp. 4–10 in this volume.

30. ["Did I make it all up; is the entire correspondence a fiction? You in high society, what concern is it of yours? For you it is without doubt a fiction."]

31. ["Nature made them; your institutions spoiled them."]

2. *A reconstruction of the question to which* La nouvelle Héloïse *and* The Sorrows of Young Werther *were the answer*

32. J. Jubert gives contemporary testimony to this effect in F. Baldensperger, *La critique et l'histoire littéraires en France* (New York, 1945), p. 22.

33. See Arnold Hauser, *The Social History of Art*, 2 (New York, 1952), p. 571: "The depth and the extent of Rousseau's influence are without precedent. He is one of those minds which, like Marx and Freud in more recent times, change the thinking of millions within a single generation, and of many who do not even know them by name."

34. See Georg Jäger (GJ, pp. 79ff.). With regard to the history of sentimentality, I have relied on the comprehensive presentation by Gerhard Sauder (GS 1974) and P. U. Hohendahl's summary (PH), which is valuable as a comparative study.

35. This critical distinction was introduced by J. H. Campe in 1779, in a brief text entitled "*Über Empfindsamkeit und Empfindelei*." See GJ, p. 21.

36. See Jürgen v. Stackelberg (1980), p. 140.

37. Cited from PH, p. 15 and JS (1980), p. 150.

38. "Il y a une sensibilité physique organique, qui, purement passive, paraît n'avoir pour fin que la conservation de notre corps et celle de notre espèce par les directions du plaisir et de la douleur. Il y a une autre sensibilité que j'appelle active et morale qui n'est autre chose que la faculté d'attacher nos affections à des êtres qui nous sont étrangers" (*OC* I, p. 805). ["There is a physical and organic sensibility that, being purely passive, has no other purpose but to preserve our body and that of our species through indications of pleasure and pain. There is another sensibility, one that I deem active and moral, that is nothing but the ability to attach our affections to beings who are strangers to us."] On this see GS (1974), p. 91, who expands considerably on my view of this historical question.

39. ["We must be happy, dear Emile; it is the end of every feeling creature; it is the first desire taught us by nature, and the only one which never leaves us." *Emile*, trans. B. Foxley (New York, 1966), p. 407. All further citations in English will be from this translation.]

40. Letter of October 12/14, 1767. ["The more refined their mores, the more depraved men become."]

41. On this subject see Krauss (1963), pp. 437ff.

42. ["We have physicists, geometricians, chemists, astronomers, poets, musicians, painters; we no longer have any citizens."]

43. On the ambivalence of the concept of nature in the eighteenth century, and its retrospective genesis in Rousseau's writing, see RS, pp. 66ff., especially p. 73: "Nature in this full sense of the term is a late product. Bourgeois society is the first to liberate it as subjectivity." See also J. Starobinski, "Das Rettende in der Gefahr," in *Neue Rundschau*, 92, (1981), pp. 42ff., where light is shed on the aporia that while on the one hand Rousseau sees natural existence as irrevocably lost, on the other he constantly tries, homeopathically as it were, to extract a principle of recovery and health from the ills of civilization themselves.

44. "Celui qui chantoit ou dansoit le mieux, le plus beau, le plus fort, le plus adroit, ou le plus éloquent, devint le plus considéré; set ce fut là le premier pas vers l'inégalité, et vers le vice en même temps [Whoever sang or danced best, the best looking, the strongest, the most adroit, or the most eloquent, became the most esteemed; that was the first step toward inequality, and toward vice as well]" (*OC* III, p. 169). Günther Buck has uncovered the practical principle underlying Rousseau's general critique of that "comparative exisence, in which the subject tries to become itself by making itself dependent on others," and shown the value of this principle for modern and contemporary ethics (GB, 10).

45. *Naive and Sentimental Poetry*, trans. J. Elias (New York, 1966), pp. 101 and 128-29, where Schiller interprets *Julie* as an idyll in order to enable his critique of this backward-looking genre: "Unhappily, [such works] place that purpose *behind* us, *toward* which they should, however, lead us, and hence they imbue us only with sad feeling of a loss, not with joyous feelings of hope" (p. 149). The translation has been slightly altered to better render the meaning of the German.]

46. These comments were made by Paul Mog (1976) in reference to *Emile* and the *Rêveries*, p. 79.

47. ["Forced to combat either nature or society, you must make your choice between the man or the citizen; you cannot train both"; p. 7.]

48. Adorno (1972), p. 153. The classic lines in the introduction to Emile run as follows: "L'homme naturel est tout pour lui; il est l'unité numérique, l'entier absolu, qui n'a de rapport qu'à lui-même ou à son semblable. L'homme civil n'est qu'une unité fractionnaire qui tient au dénominateur, et dont la valeur est dans son rapport avec l'entier, qui est le corps social" (*OC* IV, p. 249). ["The natural man lives for himself; he is the unit, the whole, dependent only on himself and on his like. The citizen is but the numerator of a fraction, whose value depends on its denominator; his value depends upon the whole, that is, on the community"; p. 7.]

49. ["But how will a man live with others if he is educated for himself alone?"]

50. Herbert Marcuse, *One-Dimensional Man* (Boston, 1964), p. 41. He adds: "But despite all its truth this argument cannot answer a time-honored question: who educates the educators and what proves that they are in possession of the good?"

51. ["Before having acquired the uniform prejudices of the world we have uniform ways of feeling and hearing."]

52. ["We are both young, it's true; we are in love for the first and only time in our lives, and have no experience of passion: but can the honor that guides us lead us astray?"]

53. ["Never do or say anything that you do not want everyone to see and hear."]

54. ["Kiss your sister and friend, treat her as such always; the more familiar you are with her the better I will think of you"] (*OC* II, p. 423). He then adds, "Mais vivez dans le tête-à-tête, comme si j'étais présent, ou devant moi comme si je n'étais pas; voilà tout ce que je vous demande" [But live this intimacy as if I were there, or, in front of me, as if I weren't; that's all I ask of you]."

55. ["A sentimental heart is heaven's fatal gift."]

56. ["I was forced to drain the bitter-sweet cup of sentimentality to the lees."]

57. ["The virtue which separated us on earth will reunite us in eternity."]

58. On this question, I would direct the reader's attention to the—already classic—essay by Eric Weil, "J. J. Rousseau et sa politique," in *Politique*, the second volume of *Essais et conférences* (Paris, 1971), pp. 115–48, especially 123ff.

59. *Ideen zu einer allgemeinen Geschichte in weltbürgerlicher Absicht*, in *Werke in zwölf Bänden*, ed. W. Weischedel (Frankfurt, 1964), vol. 11, p. 44. The thesis concerning the genesis of aesthetic education, which will be dealt with in what follows, was developed in a seminar on "Self-alienation: The History of the Problem of Rousseauism from German Idealism to the Present" given in the summer semester of 1980 in cooperation with J. Mittelstrass, to whose interpretation of Kant I am especially indebted.

60. On these two well-known lines, see *Sämtliche Werke*, 15/2 (Berlin, 1923), pp. 887, 896, and 636. Then see H. Blumenberg, *Wirklichkeiten, in denen wir leben* (Stuttgart, 1981), p. 51.

61. See *Mutmasslicher Anfang der Menschheitsgeschichte*, ed. Weischedel, ibid., vol. 11, pp. 89–90.

62. See Buck, "Identität und Bildung," in Buck (1981), pp. 123ff.

3. Goethe's Werther *within the horizon of expectation defining the German reception of Rousseau*

63. [All citations from *Werther* are drawn from the English translation by E. Mayer and L. Bogan (New York, 1971). Here, p. 2.]

64. E. A. A. Göchhausen, *Das Wertherfieber* (1777), p. 102. The basic emphatic model that is the source of the illusory effect was recently examined by A. Haverkamp in a work that complements my own interpretation. It shows how Goethe's *Werther* manages the transition from the theoretical mode of communication in reading for the exemplary to the aesthetic mode of communication in emphatic reading. See AH.

65. ["I can hardly imagine what sort of goodness a book could have if it doesn't lead its readers to the good."]

66. In passing the name of another authority in sentimentality is mentioned when Werther disparages the wife of the new pastor, "who shrugs her shoulders at the excessive enthusiasm of Lavater" (p. 108).

67. *SW* 10, p. 536. In what follows, I base my analysis on H.-G. Winter's presentation of the *Sturm und Drang* epoch and his chapter "Subjektivität und Empfindsamkeit im Roman," in HW, p. 175.

68. Lenz as cited in HW, p. 204.

69. M. Mendelssohn, *Briefe, die neuste Literatur betreffend* (1761), letters 166–70: "What is this so-called St. Preux . . . As far as I can see he is the silliest person in the world. He makes general proclamations that extol reason and wisdom to the heavens, but has not the slightest spark of them. . . . Wolmar is a splendid character, and is an honor to Mr. Rousseau. The invention of a situation in which the impetuous passions of two lovers are soothed by their association with a calm, somewhat cold, but exceptionally virtuous man – this invention, I say, belongs entirely to Mr. Rousseau, and is worthy of him."

70. Chapters 33, 34, and see *SW* 4, p. 497.

71. ["Everyone is on the most familiar of terms; everyone is equal, and no one forgets himself."]

72. ["Then, the whole group was offered a drink: each drank to the health of the victor, and went to bed, happy with a day passed in labor, gaity, innocence, a day that we would not have been sorry to begin again the next day, the day after, and for the rest of our lives."]

73. Bloom (1973).

74. KM, pp. 424–37.

75. See Reinhold Grimm as cited in the following note.

76. See Wolfgang Preisendanz, "Glückslandschaften als Gegenwalt," in *Interpretationen zu H. Heine*, ed. L. Zagari and P. Chiarini (Stuttgart, 1981), pp. 112–23, and R. R. Grimm, "Der bukolische Roman der Neuzeit," in *Bukolik*, ed. B. Effe et al. (Munich, 1982).

77. This is the veiled manner in which Goethe, when looking back at his Frankfurt liaison with Gretchen, refers to Rousseau: "She saw in him the creator of her spiritual being, and he saw in her a creature that owed its perfection not to nature, accident, or a one-sided desire, but to mutual will; and this interaction is so sweet that we ought not be surprised if, in the period since the old and new Abelard, powerful passions and as much happiness as unhappiness have arisen from such cooperation between two beings" (*SW* 10, p. 207).

4. The Sorrows of Young Werther *as Goethe's initial response to Rousseau*

78. As, for example, in *OC* II, p. 506: "Chaque homme apporte en naissant un caractère, un génie et des talents qui lui sont propres. Ceux qui sont destinés à vivre dans la simplicité champêtre n'ont pas besoin, pour être heureux, du développement de leurs facultés . . . Mais dans l'état civil . . . il importe d'apprendre à tirer des hommes tout ce que la nature leur à donné [Every man has at birth a certain character, genius, and talents that are his alone. Those who are destined to live a simple country life have no need to develop their faculties in order to be happy . . . But in the civil state it is important to learn how to draw from men everything that nature has given them]."

79. Among such items would be: Lotte's readerly canon (examined earlier), which corresponds to Julie's literary acid test; Werther's favorite locales, which replace the lovers' sanctuaries in the *La nouvelle Héloïse* (Leo Tönz has dealt in detail with the transposition of this prototype, see LT, pp. 412ff.); the tragic love story of the peasant lad, and its function as a parallel to Werther's own, and which has as its sentimental counterpart the story of Claude Anet, etc.

80. ["The sentiment is there; it is communicated to the heart bit by bit."]

81. *Lotte in Weimar*, Chapter 3 (the line is given to Dr. Riemer).

82. See S. Yagolom, "Du non-littéraire au littéraire," in *Poetique*, 44 (1980), pp. 406–12, here, p. 415.

83. But here is at least one instance, from a letter to Lavater from D. Hartmann: "I read Werther's

'Sorrows' with her. I've devoured it ten times. The book will remain my friend, and, Lavater, think of the similarities between my fate and Werther's . . . I have taken Werther's walks, roamed through the night in a sleigh that I drove myself. Now I'd even be willing to die for Goethe" (PM, p. 196).

84. Martin Fontius, "Produktivkraftentfaltung und Autonomie der Kunst," in *Literatur im Epochenumbruch*, ed. G. Klotz, et al. (Berlin/Weimar, 1977), pp. 409-521; M. Naumann, "Das Dilemma der 'Rezeptionsästhetik,' " in *Teorijska istrazivanja*, 1 (Belgrade, 1980), pp. 16ff.

85. ["The tender care of a mother, of a father, all of whose hopes reside in you; the friendship of a cousin . . . an entire village proud to have witnessed your birth: everyone is part of and shares your feelings."]

86. ["At this point, the triumph of anger ended and that of nature began."]

87. [" . . . that there is nothing good which one cannot obtain from sensitive souls through confidence and sincerity."]

88. ["Julie, fear that refuge no longer, it has just been profaned."]

89. "Qu'ils brûlent plus ardemment que jamais l'un pour l'autre, et qu'il ne règne plus entre eux qu'un honnête attachement; qu'ils soient toujours amants et ne soient plus qu'amis" (p. 508). ["Let them burn more ardently than ever for each other, but feel only the reign of an honest attachment between them; let them be lovers always, but nothing more than friends."]

90. "People must be forced to be free."

91. "Un père de famille qui se plaît dans sa maison a pour prix des soins continuels qu'il s'y donne la continuelle jouïssance des plus doux sentiments de la nature. Seul entre tous les mortels, il est maître de sa propre félicité, parce qu'il est hereux comme Dieu même, sans rien désirer de plus que ce dont il jouït" (*OC* II, p. 466). ["A family father who is content at home is compensated for the continual efforts he expends there by constantly enjoying the sweetest sentiments of nature. Among all mortals, he is the only one who is master of his own happiness, because he is happy as God himself is, having nothing to desire except that which he already enjoys."] Concerning this highest status ever granted to the bourgeois family father J. Starobinski remarks, "L'athée Wolmar ne refuse de croire en un Dieu personnel que pour s'en faire son successeur dur la terre" (JS, p. 139). ["The atheist, Wolmar, only refuses to believe in a personal God in order to become His earthly successor."]

92. I refer here to a letter from Goethe to Jacobi dated 1777: "Just look my dear man at what the beginning and end of all writing is (!) the reproduction of the world around me through an inner world that takes hold of everything, unites, recreates, kneads, and restores to its original form and style" (HW, p. 239).

93. WL, p. 74; One might raise this point when criticizing Meyer-Kalkus, who denies Werther's "narcissism" its sociohistorical significance when he asserts that "the necessary correlate of Werther's narcissism is that reality becomes a phantom instead of functioning as the far-off lodestar for the creation of work and passion" (RM, p. 97).

94. Significantly enough, this position remains unclear in the wording of the original lines themselves: "To be a member of this charming family, to be loved by the father like a son, by the children like a father, and by Lotte! —And then . . . the worthy Albert . . . who meets me with warm friendship" (p. 55). The dash after "Lotte" must stand for that which cannot be said, that which would immediately destroy the ideal: "to be loved by Lotte in the same way she loves her husband."

95. See "Plenzdorfs *Neue Leiden des jungen W.*," Jauss, *Äesthetische Erfahrung und literarische Hermeneutik I*, pp. 806-12.

96. Ihring Fetscher, *Rousseaus politische Philosophie* (Frankfurt, 1975), pp. 15, 19.

97. Heinz Schlaffer (HS, 1973, p. 45) sees this as the dilemma—traceable to Rousseau—that Jean Paul's *Bildungsroman* attempts to solve by "countering bourgeois economic structures with the ideal of aristocratic existence."

98. HS (1973), p. 66.

99. Cf. Schöffler, who believes that "Ossian is the great bible for a pantheism of Rousseauesque coloring" (HS, 164).

100. I have borrowed this formulation from Paul Mog, who interprets the heightening of self that Werther experiences with Lotte in terms of Goethe's comments about sympathetic coexistence in *Winckelmann und seine Jahrhundert* (*SW* 13, pp. 415f.); see PM (1976), p. 125.

101. This is taken from Reinhart Meyer-Kalkus, who adds that an ecstatic death at the hands of one's beloved was a literary novelty in Goethe's era (RM, p. 134).

102. Marquard (1981), "Der angeklagte und der entlastete Mensch," pp. 49ff.

5. *An overview of* Wilhelm Meister *(the* Emile *of aesthetic education)*

103. How far Rousseau actually was from aesthetic education as a solution was recently demonstrated by G. Maag in "Das ästhetische als echte und als scheinbare Negativgrosse bei Rousseau" (GM 1981).

104. ["One must choose between creating a man or a citizen."]

105. [*Wilhelm Meister's Apprenticeship*, trans. T. Carlyle (New York, 1959), p. 472. All further references in the text will be to this edition.]

106. In *Schillers Werke*, Nationalausgabe, 36 (Weimar, 1972), p. 372.

107. On Rousseau's fragment "Emile et Sophie ou les solitaires," see Stierle (KS, pp. 179ff.).

108. The following lines point back even more clearly to Rousseau: "To guard from error is not the instructor's duty, but to lead the erring pupil; nay, to let him quaff his error in deep, satiating draughts, this is the instructor's wisdom" (*Apprenticeship*, pp. 463-64).

109. HS (1979), p. 662.

110. Ibid., p. 664.

111. "Characteristik des *Wilhelm Meister*" (1797/98), in *Meisterwerke deutscher Literaturkritik*, ed. H. Mayer (Berlin, 1956), vol. 1, p. 598.

112. [The reference is to Gottfried Keller's mid-nineteenth-century novel *Green Henry*.]

E. Horizon Structure and Dialogicity

1. See the bibliography in the article "Horizont" by M. Scherner in the *Historisches Wörterbuch der Philosophie*, ed. J Ritter (Basel and Stuttgart, 1971), p. 1204. Hereafter *HWPh*. In addition, see K. Stierle, "Sprechsituation, Kontext, und Sprachhandlung," in *Handlungentheorien— interdisziplinär*, ed. H. Lenk (Munich, 1980), vol. 1, pp. 439-83, and Michael Riffaterre, "Interpretation and Undecidability," in *New Literary History*, 12 (1981), pp. 227-39.

1. *Understanding and interpreting as acts of mediation between horizons*

2. *Questions Concerning Technology and Other Essays* (1977), p. 211.

3. Ibid., p. 241.

4. M. Scherner, *HWPh*, p. 1191.

5. ["In aesthetics . . . any and everything can reside within one's own horizon, and others can have within their horizons things which are, nonetheless, not in mine."]

6. See Scherner, *HWPh*, p. 1198

7. [For the sake of consistency the term "subuniverse" has been taken over from Michael Shaw's translation of *Aesthetic Experience and Literary Hermeneutics*. More accurate renderings of *Subsinnwelt* might be "subordinate structures of meaning" or "subordinate discourses."]

8. Koselleck (1979), p. 369.

9. I have laid out Koselleck's dichotomy between the closed realm of apprehension and open horizon of expectations somewhat dialectically here. Here, new expectations, which can no longer be der-

ived from sedimented experience, can be triggered both by "the push of events" and through free antic-ipation (in the form of prognostications, utopias, or poetic imaginings).

10. Koselleck, p. 361: "Of course, as long as Christian eschatology placed unalterable restrictions on the horizon of expectation — roughly speaking, up until the middle of the seventeenth century — the future remained tied to the past."

11. What follows draws on Buck (1981), especially Chapter 3.

12. Husserl (1973), §8, p. 37.

13. Buck (1981), p. 50.

14. I use it as the basis for my interpretation of Baudelaire's *Spleen II*. See *Toward an Aesthetic of Reception*, pp. 139-85.

15. Gadamer (1975), p. 273.

16. The assumption that the "horizon of the present cannot be formed without the past" does not exclude altogether the possibility of understanding the alterity of the past as reconstructed within a historical horizon seen from today's perspective. This despite the implications of the following asser-tion: "Understanding . . . is always the fusion of these horizons which we imagine to exist by them-selves" (p. 273). Is the "closed horizon that is supposed to enclose a culture" really only "an abstrac-tion" (p. 271)? The contrary is suggested by the results of the treatise by Koselleck that I have already discussed (1979). Gadamer has failed to perceive that his description of the horizon as "something into which we move and that moves with us" holds good for the open horizon of a present time, but not the closed horizon of an absent past, which, construed as an *epoch*, is a thoroughly genuine cate-gory of historical apprehension.

17. Dietrich Böhler, "Philosophische Hermeneutik und hermeneutische Methode," in *Poetik und Hermeneutik IX*, p. 500ff.

18. Ibid., p. 510.

19. On this topic, one should above all turn to Apel (ed.), *Hermeneutik und Ideologiekritik* (1971), to which P. Ricoeur wrote an outstanding epilogue. See *Political and Social Essays*, ed. D. Stuart and J. Bein (Athens, 1974), pp. 243-70.

20. Buck (1981), p. 19.

21. Heidegger, *The Question Concerning Technology and Other Essays*, p. 58; and later, Gadamer would write that "one understands differently, if one understands at all" (1975, p. 280).

22. *Estetika slovensnogo tvorchestva* (Moscow, 1979).

23. *Dialogizität in Prozessen literarischer Kommunikation*, Constance Colloquium, 1980, ed. Renata Lachmann (Munich, 1982).

2. Dialogic understanding in literary communication

24. In his articles "Der religionsphilosophische Aspekt des Dialogischen," "Der grosse Sabbat — oder vom Ende des Dialogs," "Episkopales und Pastorales zum Dialog/zur Dialektik" (see note 23 this chapter).

25. In his article, "Leo Popper (1886-1911) und die moderne Hermeneutik" (see note 23), which annotates the accompanying, then unpublished "Dialog über Kunst" in which Popper used "A" and "B" to represent the positions held by himself and Lukács (I have reinserted their names in what follows).

26. ["Identification" will be used throughout the remainder of this translation except in citations that specifically employ the German word *Empathie*.]

27. ["My verses have the meaning one lends them."]

28. Gadamer (1975), p. 429.

29. Concerning the most recent research on Schleiermacher, and for a critique of the primacy of that self-understanding enabled by an object that results in "the being of the other qua other is left

by the wayside," see Manfred Frank, *Das individuelle Allgemeine: Textstrukturierung und - interpretation nach Schleiermacher* (Frankfurt, 1977), pp. 20-34, here, p. 33.

30. In this part of my discussion I rely on Bakhtin, *Problems of Dostoevsky's Poetics* (1984), *Estetika slovensnogo tvorchestva* (Moscow, 1979), and, in addition, T. Todorov, "Bakhtine et l'alterité," in *Poétique*, 40 (1979), pp. 502-23 [reprinted in Todorov, *Mikhail Bakhtin: The Dialogical Principle* (Minneapolis, 1984), pp. 94-112].

31. W. Worringer, *Abstraktion und Einfühlung* (Munich, 1918), p. 4. [This English translation is taken from Todorov, *Mikhail Bakhtin*, p. 98.]

32. "The first moment of aesthetic activity is identification: I must experience, i.e., see and know, what he experiences, put myself in his place, in a way coincide with him. . . . But is this plenitude of internal fusion the ultimate end of aesthetic activity? . . . Not at all: properly speaking, aesthetic activity has not even begun. . . . Aesthetic activity begins properly only when one returns within oneself at one's place, outside of the [other], and when one gives form and completion to the material of identification" ("Avtor i geroj vesteticheskoj dejatel'nosti" [Author and Character in Aesthetic Activity], written between 1922 and 1924, published in Bakhtin, *Estetika slovesnogo tvorchestva*, pp. 24-26. [Cited from Todorov (1984), p. 99.]

33. Bakhtin (1984), p. 207.

34. "Avtor i geroj v esteticheskoj dejatel'nosti," pp. 33-34. [Cited from Todorov, p. 95.]

35. Bakhtin, "The Problem of the Text in Linguistics, Philology, and the Human Sciences: An Experiment in Philosophical Analysis," in *Speech Genres and Other Late Essays* (Austin, 1986), p. 126.

36. See Todorov, p. 107.

37. My definition of aesthetic pleasure ("self-enjoyment in the enjoyment of something other," or perhaps, "experiencing oneself in a possibly being other" – see *Aesthetic Experience and Literary Hermeneutics*, p. 32) was formulated as part of a critique that I along with others leveled at M. Geiger, though not W. Worringer. It corresponds very closely to Bakhtin's model of *vnenakhodimost'*, especially given the fact that they offer similar, implicit critiques and extensions of the above cited formulation by Worringer – someone I had not thought of, but certainly could have.

38. The theory of intertextuality alters the notion of voice in such a way that polygraphy takes the place of polyphony while at the same time the other as subject disappears from the "dialogue the texts have among themselves." On this, see R. Lachmann's contribution to *Poetik und Hermeneutik XI*, "Bachtins Dialogizität und die akmeistische Mythopoetik als Paradigma dialogisierter Lyrik."

39. Stierle (1979), pp. 110-17.

40. Ricoeur (1978), p. 79.

41. Blumenberg (1979).

42. See "The Perfect as the *fascinosum* of the imaginary," pp. 25-50 in this volume.

43. Gadamer (1959).

3. Looking back and ahead

44. Lausberg, *Handbuch der literarischen Rhetorik* (Munich, 1960). In addition, see the programmatic text written by his student, W. Babilas, *Tradition und Interpretation* (Munich, 1961). [Concerning Curtius's plan for a historical topics, see his *European Literature and the Latin Middle Ages* (1953), Chapter 5/2.]

45. Curtius (1953), p. 14.

46. Curtius (1953), p. 400.]

47. Further discussion of this matter can be found in Jauss (1970), p. 168.

48. "Bedenken eines Philologen" (1954), in *Medium Aevum Vivum, Festschrift für W. Bulst*, ed. H. R. Jauss and D. Schaller (Heidelberg, 1960), pp. 7-10.

49. In Guitte, *Questions de la littérature* (1960/1972). See also Jauss (1977a), pp. 411-27.

50. See my review in *Archiv für das Studium der neueren Sprachen*, 197 (1960), pp. 223ff.

51. See my review in *Philologische Rundschau*, 4 (1956), pp. 113ff.

52. I do not include here Olschki, Vossler, and Spitzer, whose controversy I tried to resolve in my own interpretation. See Jauss (1977a), pp. 106ff.

53. Lipps (1941), pp. 19, 25; and on this see Jauss (1977a), pp. 201ff.

54. See Arno Borst, *Poetik und Hermeneutik VIII*, p. 638.

55. [Translated in part in *Toward an Aesthetic of Reception* (Jauss 1982b).]

56. Jauss (1982b), p. 24.

57. On this, see "Die Partialität der rezeptionsästhetischen Methode" (1973, reprinted in *Ästhetische Erfahrung und literarische Hermeneutik* [1982], pp. 735–52); *Rezeptionsästhetik: Zwischenbilanz*, a special issue of *Poetika*, 7 (1975); the reader entitled *Rezeptionsästhetik: Theorie und Praxis*, ed. R. Warning (Munich, 1975), whose critical introduction discusses the theoretical formulations up to 1975; and especially the criticism offered by Manfred Naumann (1973), pp. 131–44, Beate Pinkerneil (1975), pp. 60–68, and Streten Petrović in *Teorijska Istrazivanja*, ed. Z. Konstantinović (1980), pp. 63–74.

58. Jauss (1982b), p. 22.

59. Ibid., p. 39.

60. See Pinkerneil (1975), p. 67.

61. Petrović (1980), pp. 63ff.

62. [Found in English in Jauss (1982a), pp. 3–151.]

63. [The reference is to the 1982 edition of *Ästhetische Erfahrung und literarische Hermeneutik*, which includes a number of essays in addition to those found in the 1977 volume of the same title.]

64. [The date is that of the essay's initial publication. It was later included in *Ästhetische Erfahrung*, but has not yet been translated into English.]

65. [Translated in Jauss (1982a).]

66. [Translated in Jauss (1982b).]

Bibliography

Bibliography

Adler, Alfred, *Epische Spekulanten: Versuch einer synchronen Geschichte des altfranzösischen Epos* (Munich, 1975).

Adorno, Theodor W., and Max Horkheimer, *Dialectic of Enlightenment*, trans. J. Cummings (New York, 1972).

——, *Ästhetische Theorie, Gesammelte Schriften*, vol. 7 (Frankfurt, 1971).

Apel, Karl-Otto, ed., *Hermeneutik und Ideologiekritik* (Frankfurt, 1971).

Auerbach, Erich, *Mimesis: The Representation of Reality in Western Literature*, trans. Willard Trask (Princeton, N.J., 1953).

Bakhtin, Mikhail, *Rabelais and His World*, trans. Helene Iswolsky (Cambridge, Mass., 1968).

——, *Die Ästhetik des Wortes* (Frankfurt, 1979).

——, *Problems of Dostoevsky's Poetics*, trans. Caryl Emerson (Minneapolis, 1984).

——, *Speech Genres and Other Late Essays*, trans. Vern McGee (Austin, Texas, 1986).

Bastian, Hans Dieter, *Theologie der Frage*, 2nd ed. (Munich, 1970).

Baudelaire, Charles, *Oeuvres Complètes*, Edition de la Plèiade (Paris, 1951).

Benjamin, Walter, *Gesammelten Schriften* (Werkausgabe) (Frankfurt, 1980).

——, *Illuminations*, trans. Harry Zohn (New York, 1969).

Berger, Peter, and Thomas Luckmann, *Die Gesellschaftliche Konstruktion der Wirklichkeit* (Frankfurt, 1970; 2nd ed. 1971).

——, *The Social Construction of Reality* (New York, 1967).

Binder, Wolfgang, " 'Genuss' in Dichtung und Philosophie des 17. und 18. Jahrhunderts," in *Archiv für Begriffsgeschichte*, 17 (1973), pp. 66–92.

Bloch, Ernst, *Das Prinzip Hoffnung* (Frankfurt, 1959).

——, *Tübinger Einleitung in die Philosophie* (Frankfurt, 1964). Translated as *A Philosophy of the Future*, trans. J. Cumming (New York, 1970).

Bloom, Harold, *The Anxiety of Influence* (New York, 1973).

Blumenberg, Hans, "Nachahmung der Natur: Zur Vorgeschichte des schöpferischen Menschen," in *Studium Generale*, 10 (1957), pp. 61–80.

——, "Kosmos und System. Aus der Genesis der kopernikanischen Welt", in *Studium Generale*, 10 (1957a), pp. 266–83.

——, "Epochenschwelle und Rezeption," in *Philosophischer Rundschau*, 6 (1958), pp. 94–120.

——, *Paradigmen zu einer Metaphorologie* (Bonn, 1960).

——, "Sokrates und das 'objet ambigu': Paul Valérys Auseinandersetzung mit der Tradition der Ontologie des ästhetischen Gegenstandes," in *Epimeleia, Helmut Kuhn zum 65. Geburtstag*, ed. F. Wiedmann (Munich, 1964), pp. 285–323.

——. *Die Legitimität der Neuzeit* (Frankfurt, 1973).

——. *Paradigmen zu einer Metaphorologie* (Bonn, 1960).

——. *Der Prozess der theoretischen Neugierde* (Frankfurt, 1973).

——, *Arbeit am Mythos* (Frankfurt, 1979).

Borinski, Karl, *Die Antike in Poetik und Kunsttheorie*, vol 1. (Leipzig, 1914), vol. 2 (Leipzig, 1924).

Borst, Arno, *Lebensformen im Mittlealter* (Frankfurt/Berlin, 1973).

Buck, Günther, "Kants Lehre vom Beispiel," in *Archiv für Begriffsgeschichte*, 11 (1967), pp. 148–83.

——, *Hermeneutik und Bildung* (Munich, 1981).

Bultmann, Rudolf, "Das Problem der Hermeneutik," in *Glauben und Verstehen*, vol. 2 (Tübingen, 1961), pp. 211–35.

Callois, Roger, *Vocabulaire esthétique* (Paris, 1947).

Conze, Werner, "Arbeit," in *Geschichtliche Grundbegriffe: Historisches Lexikon zur politisch-sozialen Sprache in Deutschland*, ed. O. Brunner, W. Conze, R. Koselleck (Stuttgart, 1972), vol. 1, pp. 154–215.

Curtius, Ernst Robert, *European Literature and the Latin Middle Ages*, trans. W. R. Trask (New York, 1953).

Dehn, Wilhelm, ed., *Ästhetische Erfahrung und literarisches Lernen* (Frankfurt, 1974).

de Man, Paul, *Blindness and Insight*: Essays in the Rhetoric of *Contemporary Criticism* (New York, 1971).

——, *Allegories of Reading*: Figural Language in Rousseau, Nietzsche, *Rilke, and Proust* (New Haven and London, 1979).

Dockhorn, Klaus, review of H.-G. Gadamer, *Wahrheit und Methode*, in *Göttingische Gelehrte Anzeigen*, 218 (1966), pp. 169–206.

Dufrenne, Mikel, *Phénoménologie de l'expérience esthétique* (Paris, 1967).

Engelsing, R., *Der Bürger als Leser* (Stuttgart, 1974).

Fellmann, Ferdinand, *Das Vico-Axiom. Der Mensch macht die Geschichte* (Freiburg/Munich, 1976).

Freud, Sigmund, *The Standard Edition of the Complete Psychological Works* (London, 1956–1962).

Friedrich, Hugo, *Die Struktur der modernen Lyrik*, 2nd ed. (Hamburg, 1966).

——, *Epochen der italienischen Lyrik* (Frankfurt, 1964).

Frye, Northrop, *Anatomy of Criticism* (Princeton, N.J., 1957).

Fuhrmann, Manfred, *Einführung in die antike Dichtungslehre* (Darmstadt, 1973).

Gadamer, Hans-Georg, "Vom Zirkel des Verstehens," in G. Neske, ed., *Festschrift: Martin Heidegger zum siebzigsten Geburtstag* (Pfullingen, 1959), pp. 24–34.

——, *Truth and Method*, ed. G. Barden and J. Cumming (New York, 1975).

Galling, K., ed., *Die Religion in Geschichte und Gegenwart* (Tübingen, 1957).

Geiger, Moritz, "Beiträge zur Phänomenologie des ästhetischen Genusses," in *Jahrbuch für Philosophie und phänomenologische Forschung*, vol. 1, no. 2 (1913), pp. 567–684.

Grimm, Reinhold, *Paridisus coelestis – paradisus terrestris: Zur Auslegungsgeschichte des Paradieses im Abendland bis um 1200* (Munich, 1977).

Guiette, Robert, *Questions de la littérature*, vol 1. (Ghent, 1960), vol. 2 (Ghent, 1972).

Gumbrecht, Hans Ulrich, "Soziologie und Rezeptionsästhetik," in *Neue Ansichten einer künftigen Germanistik*, ed. H. Kolbe (Munich, 1973), pp. 48–74.

——, "Skizze einer Literaturgeschichte der französichen Revolution," in *Neues Handbuch der Literaturwissenschaft*, vol. 13, ed. J. von Stackelberg (Wiesbaden, 1980), pp. 269–328.

Habermas, Jürgen, *Strukturwandel der öffentlichkeit* (Neuwied, 1962).

——, *Technique und Wissenschaft als "Ideolgie"* (Frankfurt, 1968).

——, *Kultur und Kritik: Verstreute Aufsätze* (Frankfurt, 1973).

Harth, Dietrich, *Philologie und praktische Philosophie*, Humanistische Bibliothek I, 1 (Munich, 1970).

——, "Romane und ihre Leser," in *Germanisch-romanische Monatsschrift*, 20 (1970), pp. 159–79.

Hartman, Geoffrey, *The Fate of Reading and Other Essays* (Chicago, 1975).

Hegel, G. W. F., *Phenomenology of Spirit*, trans. A. V. Miller (Oxford, 1977).

——, *Werke*, vol. 9, ed. H. Glockner (Stuttgart, 1929).

Heidegger, Martin, "The Word of Nietzsche: 'God is Dead,' " in *The Question Concerning Technology and Other Essays*, trans. W. Lovitt (New York, 1977), pp. 53–112.

Henrich, Dieter, "Kunst und Kunstphilosophie der Gegenwart (überlegungen mit Rücksicht auf Hegel)," in *Poetik und Hermeneutik II* (1966), pp. 11–32.

——, *Hegel im Kontext* (Frankfurt, 1971).

Hervieux, Marcel, *Les écrivains français jugés par leurs contemporains*, vol 1: *Le XVIe et le XVIIe siècle* (Paris, 1911).

Historisches Wörterbuch der Philosophie, ed. J. Ritter (Basel and Stuttgart, 1971).

Hohendahl, Peter Uwe, ed., *Sozialgeschichte und Wirkungsästhetik* (Frankfurt, 1974).

Husserl, Edmund, *Experience and Judgment: Investigations in a Genealogy of Logic*, trans. J. Churchill and K. Ameriks (Evanston, Ill., 1973).

Iser, Wolfgang, *The Implied Reader: Patterns of Communication in Prose Fiction from Bunyan to Beckett* (Baltimore, Md., 1974).

——, *The Act of Reading: A Theory of Aesthetic Response* (Baltimore, Md., 1979).

Jauss, Hans Robert, *Untersuchungen zur mittelalterlichen Tierdichtung* (Tübingen, 1959).

——, "Diderots Paradox über das Schauspiel," in *Germanisch-romanische Monatsschrift*, 11 (1961), pp. 380–413.

——, *Ästhetische Normen und geschichtliche Reflexion in der "Querelle des Anciens et des Moderns"* (Munich, 1964).

——, *Zeit und Erinnerung in Marcel Prousts "A la recherche du temps perdu*, 2nd ed. (Heidelberg, 1970).

——, *Kleine Apologie der ästhetischen Erfahrung* (Constanz, 1972).

——, *Alterität und Modernität in mittelalterlichen Literatur: Gesammelte Aufstze 1956–1976* (Munich, 1977a).

——, *Ästhetische Erfahrung und literarische Hermeneutik*, vol. 1: *Versuche im Feld der ästhetischen Erfahrung* (Munich, 1977b).

——, *Ästhetische Erfahrung und literarische Hermeneutik* (Frankfurt, 1982).

——, *Aesthetic Experience and Literary Hermeneutics*, trans. Michael Shaw (Minneapolis, 1982a).

——, *Toward an Aesthetic of Reception*, trans. Timothy Bahti (Minneapolis, 1982b).

Jolles, A., *Einfache Formen* (Halle, 1929; 2nd ed. 1956).

——, "Die literarischen Travestien Ritter/Hirt/Schelm," in *Blätter für deutsche Philosophie*, 6 (1932–33).

Kalivoda, Robert, *Der Marxismus und die moderne geistige Wirklichkeit* (Frankfurt, 1970).

Kamlah, Wilhelm, *Philosophische Anthropologie* (Mannheim, 1973).

Kelly, Douglas, *Medieval Imagination: Rhetoric and the Poetry of Courtly Love* (Madison, Wis., 1978).

Köhler, Erich, *Trobadorlyrik und höfischer Roman* (Berlin, 1962).

——, *Esprit und arkadische Freiheit* (Frankfurt/Bonn, 1966).

Koselleck, Reinhart, *Vergangene Zukunft: Zur Semantik geschichtlicher Zeiten* (Frankfurt, 1979).

Kosík, Karel, *Die Dialektik des Konkreten* (Frankfurt, 1967).

Krauss, Werner, *Gesammelte Aufsätze zur Literatur und Sprachwissenschaft* (Frankfurt, 1949).

——, *Studien zur deutschen und französichen Aufklärung* (Berlin, 1963).

Kuhn, Helmut, *Vom Wesen und Wirken des Kunstwerks* (Munich, 1960).

Kuhn, Thomas, *The Structure of Scientific Revolutions* (Chicago, 1962).

Lesser, Simon, *Fiction and the Unconscious* (New York, 1962).

Lewis, C. S., *The Discarded Image* (Cambridge, 1964).

Lipps, Hans, *Die menschliche Natur* (Frankfurt, 1941).

Löwith, Karl, *Das Individuum in der Rolle des Mitmenschen* (1928; 2nd ed. Darmstadt, 1962).

Lotman, Jurij, *The Structure of the Artistic Text*, trans. Ronald Vroon (Ann Arbor, Mich., 1977).

Malraux, André, *Les voix du silence* (Paris, 1951). Translated as *The Voices of Silence*, trans. Stuart Gilbert (New York, 1953).

Mandelkow, Karl Robert, "Rezeptionsästhetik und marxistische Literaturtheorie," in *Historizität in Sprach- und Literaturwissenschaft*, ed. W. Müller-Seidel (Muncih, 1974), pp. 379–88.

Marcuse, Herbert, "On the Affirmative Character of Culture," in *Negations: Essays in Critical Theory*, trans. J. J. Shapiro (Boston, 1968).

——, *Counterrevolution and Revolt* (Boston, 1972).

Marquard, Odo, *Schwierigkeiten mit der Geschichtsphilosophie* (Frankfurt, 1973).

——, *Abschied vom Prinzipiellen: Philosophische Studien* (Stuttgart, 1981).

Mead, George, *Mind, Self, and Society* (Chicago, 1934).

Mittelstrass, Jürgen, *Neuzeit und Aufklärung: Studien zur Entstehung der neuzeitlichen Wissenschaft und Philosophie* (Berlin/New York, 1970).

Müller, P., *Der junge Goethe im zeitgenössischen Urteil* (Berlin, 1969).

Mukarovsky, Jan, *Aesthetic Function, Norm, and Value as Social Facts*, trans. Mark Suino (Ann Arbor, Mich., 1970).

——, *Structure, Sign and Function*, trans. and ed. John Burbank and Peter Steiner (New Haven, Conn., 1978).

Naumann, Manfred, ed., *Gesellschaft—Literatur—Lesen. Literaturrezeption in theoretischer Sicht* (Berlin/Weimar, 1973).

Neuschäfer, Hans-Jörg, *Populärromane im 19. Jahrhundert* (Munich, 1976).

Nietzsche, Friedrich, *The Twilight of the Gods*, ed. Oscar Levy. Vol. 16 of *The Complete Works of Friedrich Nietzsche* (London and New York, 1911).

Nisin, Arthur, *La Littérature et le lecteur* (Paris, 1959).

——, *Les oeuvres et les siècles* (Paris, 1960).

Pannenberg, Wolfhart, "Hermeneutik und Universalgeschichte," in *Grundfragen systematischer Theologie* (Göttingen, 1971), pp. 91–122.

Panofsky, Erwin, *Idea: Ein Beitrag zur Begriffsgeschichte der älteren Kunsttheorie* (Berlin, 1960).

Petrović, Streten, "L'esthétique de réception: Est-elle possible?" in *Teorijska istrazivanja* (Belgrade, 1980), pp. 63–74.

Pinkerneil, Beate, "Literaturwissenschaft seit 1967," in *Methodische Praxis der Literaturwissenschaft*, ed. D. Kimpel and R. Pinkerneil (Kronberg, 1975), pp. 1–84.

Plessner, Helmuth, "Soziale Rolle und menschliche Natur" (1960), in *Diesseits der Utopie* (Cologne, 1966).

——, *Laughing and Crying: A Study of the Limits of Human Behavior*, trans. J. S. Churchill and Marjorie Grene (Evanston, Ill., 1970).

——, *Die Frage nach der Conditio Humana. Aufsätze zur philosophischen Anthropologie* (Frankfurt, 1976).

Poetik und Hermeneutik: Arbeitsergebnisse einer Forschungsgruppe
    I. Nachahmung und Illusion (1964), ed. H. R. Jauss.
    II. Immanente Ästhetik: Ästhetische Reflexion (1966), ed. W. Iser.

III. *Die nicht mehr schönen Künste* (1968), ed. H. R. Jauss.

IV. *Terror und Spiel* (1971), ed. M. Fuhrmann.

V. *Geschichte: Ereignis und Erzählung* (1973), ed. R. Koselleck and W. D. Stempel.

VI. *Positionen der Negativität* (1975), ed. H. Weinrich.

VII. *Das Komische* (1976), ed. W. Preisendanz and R. Warning.

IX. *Text und Applikation* (1981), ed. M. Fuhrman, H. R. Jauss, and W. Pannenberg.

X. *Funktionen des Fiktiven* (1983), ed. D. Henrich and W. Iser.

Poirion, Daniel, "Chanson de geste ou épopée?" in *Travaux de linguistique et de littérature*, vol. 10, no. 2 (Strasbourg, 1972), pp. 7–20.

Preisendanz, Wolfgang, *Humor als dicterische Einbildungskraft* (Munich, 1963).

Ricoeur, Paul, *Le conflit des interprétations: Essais d'herméneutique* (Paris, 1969). Translated as *The Conflict of Interpretations: Essays on Hermeneutics* (Evanston, Ill., 1974).

——, *Freud and Philosophy: An Essay on Interpretation*, trans. Denis Savage (New Haven, Conn., 1970).

——, "Die Schrift als Problem der Literaturkritik und der philosophischen Hermeneutik," in *Sprache und Welterfahrung*, ed. J. Zimmerman (Munich, 1978), pp. 67–88.

Riffaterre, Michael, *Essais de stylistique structurale* (Paris, 1971).

Ritter, Joachim, "Ästhetik," in *Historisches Wörterbuch der Philosophie*, vol. 1 (Basel and Stuttgart, 1971), pp. 555–80.

——, *Subjektivität* (Frankfurt, 1974). This volume contains "über das Lachen" (1940) and "Landschaft: Zur Funktion des Ästhetischen in der modernen Gesellschaft" (1963).

Rüfner, Vinzenz, "Homo secundus Deus: Eine geistesgeschichtliche Studie zum menschlichen Schöpfertum," in *Philosophisches Jahrbuch*, 63 (1955), pp. 248–91.

Sartre, Jean-Paul, *What Is Literature*, trans. Bernard Frechtman (New York, 1965).

——, *The Psychology of the Imagination*, trans. Bernard Frechtman (London, 1972).

Schlaffer, Heinz, ed., *Erweiterung der materialistischen Literaturtheorie durch Bestimmung ihrer Grenzen* (Stuttgart, 1974).

Schmidt, Siegfried J., *Ästhetizität: Philosophische Beiträge zu einer Theorie des Ästhetischen* (Munich, 1971).

Seznec, J., *Essais sur Diderot et l'antiquité* (Oxford, 1975).

Schütz, Alfred, and Thomas Luckmann, *Strukturen der Lebenswelt* (Neuwied/Darmstadt, 1975).

Spitzer, Leo, *Romanische Literaturstudien* (Tübingen, 1959).

Stackelberg, Jürgen von, *Literarische Rezeptionsformen* (Frankfurt, 1972).

Starobinski, Jean, *L'Oeil vivant*, vol. 1 (Paris, 1961); vol. 2: *La Relation critique* (Paris, 1970).

——, *Jean-Jacques Rousseau: La transparance et l'obstacle* (Paris, 1971).

——, "Le reméde dans le mal," in *Rousseau secondo Jean-Jacques* (Rome, 1979), pp. 19–40.

Stempel, Wolf-Dieter, ed., *Texte der russischen Formalisten*, vol. 2: *Texte zur Theorie des Versus und der poetischen Sprache* (Munich, 1972).

Stierle, Karlheinz, *Text als Handlung: Perspektiven einer systematischen Literaturwissenschaft* (Munich, 1975).

——, "Was heisst Rezeption bei fiktionalen Texten?" in *Poetika*, 7 (1975a), pp. 345–87.

——, "Erfahrung und narrative Form," in *Theorie und Erzählung in der Geschichte*, ed. J. Kocka and T. Nipperdey (Munich, 1979), pp. 85–118.

Straus, Erwin, "Der Mensch als ein fragendes Wesen," in *Jahrbuch für Psychologie und Psychotherapie*, 1 (1953), pp. 139–53.

Striedter, Jurij, ed., *Texte der russischen Formalisten*, vol. 1: *Texte zur allgemeinen Literaturtheorie und zur Theorie der Prosa* (Munich, 1969).

Todorov, Tzvetan, *Mikhail Bakhtin: The Dialogic Principle*, trans. Wlad Godzich (Minneapolis, 1984).

Vodička, Felix, *Die Struktur der literarischen Entwicklung* (Munich, 1976). With an introductory essay by Jurij Striedter.

Warning, Rainer, *Funktion und Struktur: Die Ambivalenzen des geistlichen Spiels* (Munich, 1974).

——, introductory essay in *Rezeptionsästhetik: Theorie und Praxis* (Munich, 1975).

Weinrich, H., "Muss es Romanlektüre geben?" In *Leser und Lesen im 18. Jahrhundert*, ed. R. Grünter (Heidelberg, 1977).

Werckmeister, Otto, *Ende der Ästhetik* (Frankfurt, 1971).

Wygotski, Lew, "Kunst als Katharsis" (1965), in *Ästhetische Erfahrung und literarisches Lernen*, ed. W. Dehn (Frankfurt, 1974), pp. 81–89.

Zimmerman, Hans Dieter, *Vom Nutzen der Literatur* (Frankfurt, 1977).

Zumthor, Paul, *Essai de poétique médiévale* (Paris, 1972).

Index

Index

Compiled by Hassan Melehy

Theory and History of Literature

Hans Robert Jauss is professor of literary criticism and romance philology at the University of Konstanz, West Germany, and is founder and co-editor of *Poetik and Hermeneutik*. He has taught at Columbia, Yale, and the Sorbonne. His writings include studies of medieval and modern French literature as well as theoretical works. The University of Minnesota Press has published two volumes of his work: *Toward an Aesthetic of Reception* and *Aesthetic Experience and Literary Hermeneutics*.

Michael Hays is professor of dramatic literature and criticism at Cornell University. He is author of *The Public and Performance: Essays on the History of French and German Theatre, 1870–1900*; he has also published numerous essays on nineteenth- and twentieth-century European literature and criticism. Hays edited and translated *Theory of the Modern Drama* by Peter Szondi (Minneapolis, 1987).